# HITCH-22

## Also by Christopher Hitchens

### Books

*Hostage to History: Cyprus from the Ottomans to Kissinger*
*Blood, Class, and Empire: The Enduring Anglo-American Relationship*
*Imperial Spoils: The Curious Case of the Elgin Marbles*
*Why Orwell Matters*
*No One Left to Lie To: The Triangulations of William Jefferson Clinton*
*Letters to a Young Contrarian*
*The Trial of Henry Kissinger*
*Thomas Jefferson: Author of America*
*Thomas Paine's "Rights of Man": A Biography*
*god Is Not Great: How Religion Poisons Everything*

### Pamphlets

*Karl Marx and the Paris Commune*
*The Monarchy: A Critique of Britain's Favorite Fetish*
*The Missionary Position: Mother Teresa in Theory and Practice*
*A Long Short War: The Postponed Liberation of Iraq*

### Collected Essays

*Prepared for the Worst: Selected Essays and Minority Reports*
*For the Sake of Argument: Essays and Minority Reports*
*Unacknowledged Legislation: Writers in the Public Sphere*
*Love, Poverty, and War: Journeys and Essays*

### Collaborations

*Vanity Fair's Hollywood* (with Graydon Carter and David Friend)
*James Callaghan: The Road to Number Ten* (with Peter Kellner)
*Blaming the Victims* (edited with Edward Said)
*When the Borders Bleed: The Struggle of the Kurds* (photographs by Ed Kashi)
*International Territory: The United Nations* (photographs by Adam Bartos)
*The Portable Atheist: Essential Readings for the Nonbeliever* (edited)

# HITCH-22

## A Memoir

Christopher Hitchens

ATLANTIC BOOKS

LONDON

First published in 2010 in the United States of America by Twelve, an imprint of
Grand Central Publishing, 18 West 18th Street, New York, 10011.

First published in Great Britain in 2010 by Atlantic Books, an imprint of Grove Atlantic Ltd.

1 2 3 4 5 6 7 8 9

A CIP catalogue record for this book is available from the British Library.

Hardback ISBN: 978 184354 921 5
Export and Airside Trade Paperback ISBN: 978 184887 175 5

Printed in Great Britain by the MPG Books Group

Atlantic Books
An imprint of Grove Atlantic Ltd
Ormond House
26–27 Boswell Street
London
WC1N 3JZ

www.atlantic-books.co.uk

For James Fenton

# Caute

I can claim copyright only in myself, and occasionally in those who are either dead or have written about the same events, or who have a decent expectation of anonymity, or who are such appalling public shits that they have forfeited their right to bitch.

For those I have loved, or who have been so lenient and gracious as to have loved me, I have not words enough here, and I remember with gratitude how they have made me speechless in return.

# Contents

# CONTENTS

# HITCH-22

The desires of the heart are as crooked as corkscrews
Not to be born is the best for man
The second best is a formal order
The dance's pattern, dance while you can.
Dance, dance, for the figure is easy
The tune is catching and will not stop
Dance till the stars come down with the rafters
Dance, dance, dance till you drop.

W.H. Auden, "Death's Echo"


We are going to die, and that makes us the lucky ones. Most people
are never going to die because they are never going to be born. The
potential people who could have been here in my place but who will
in fact never see the light of day outnumber the sand grains of the
Sahara. Certainly those unborn ghosts include greater poets than
Keats, scientists greater than Newton. We know this because the set
of possible people allowed by our DNA so massively outnumbers
the set of actual people. In the teeth of these stupefying odds it is
you and I, in our ordinariness, that are here.

Richard Dawkins, *Unweaving the Rainbow*


Ah, words are poor receipts for what time hath stole away...

John Clare, "Remembrances"

# Prologue with Premonitions

What can the England of 1940 have in common with the England of 1840? But then, what have you in common with the child of five whose photograph your mother keeps on the mantelpiece? Nothing, except that you happen to be the same person.

—George Orwell: "England Your England: Socialism and the English Genius" [1941]

Read your own obituary notice; they say you live longer. Gives you second wind. New lease of life.

—Leopold Bloom in *Ulysses*

B EFORE ME IS a handsome edition of *Face to Face*, the smart magazine that goes out to the supporters of London's National Portrait Gallery. It contains the usual notices of future events and exhibitions. The page that has caught and held my eye is the one which calls attention to a show that starts on 10 January 2009, titled "Martin Amis and Friends." The event is to feature the work of a gifted photographer named Angela Gorgas, who was Martin's lover between 1977 and 1979. On the page is a photograph taken in Paris in 1979. It shows, from left to right, myself and James Fenton and Martin, ranged along a balustrade that overlooks the city of Paris. I remember the occasion well: it was after a decent lunch some-where in Montmartre and we would have been looking over Angela's shapely shoulders at the horrible wedding-cake architecture of Sacre Coeur. (Per-haps this explains the faintly dyspeptic expression on my features.) In the

accompanying prose, apparently written by Angela, is the following sentence
about the time she first met the bewitching young Amis:

> Martin was literary editor of the *New Statesman*, working with *the
> late Christopher Hitchens* and Julian Barnes, who was married to Pat
> Kavanagh, Martin's then literary agent.

So there it is in cold print, the plain unadorned phrase that will one day
become unarguably true. It is not given to everyone to read of his own
death, let alone when announced in passing in such a matter-of-fact way.
As I write, in the dying months of the year 2008, having just received this
reminder-note from the future, that future still contains the opening of the
exhibition and the publication of this memoir. But the exhibition, and its
catalogue references, also exemplify still-vital elements of my past. And now,
rather abruptly:

> Between the idea
> And the reality
> Between the motion
> And the act
> *Falls the Shadow.*

T.S. Eliot's "Hollow Men" do not constitute my cohort, or so I hope, even
though one might sometimes wish to be among the stoics "who have crossed,
with direct eyes, to death's other Kingdom." The fact is that all attempts to
imagine one's own extinction are futile by definition. One can only picture
the banal aspects of this event: not in my case the mourners at the funeral
(again excluded by the very rules of the game itself) but the steady *thunk* of
emails into my inbox on the day of my demise, and the way in which my ter-
restrial mailbox will also become congested, until somebody does something
to arrest the robotic electronic stupidity, or until failure to pay up leads to
an abrupt cancellation of the bills and checks and solicitations, none of them
ever in my lifetime arriving in the right proportions on the right day. (May
it be that I gain a lifetime subscription to *Face to Face*, and that this goes on
forever, or do I mean to say for all eternity?)

The director of the National Portrait Gallery, the excellent Sandy Nairne, has written me an anguished letter in which he not only apologizes for having me killed off but tries to offer both explanation and restitution. "The display," he writes, "also includes a photograph of Pat Kavanagh with Kingsley Amis. A last minute change was made to the text, and instead of it reading 'the late Pat Kavanagh' it refers to yourself."

This kindly meant missive makes things more poignant and more eerie rather than less. I have just opened a letter from Pat Kavanagh's husband, Julian Barnes, in which he thanks me for my note of condolence on her sudden death from cancer of the brain. I had also congratulated him on the vast critical success of his recent meditation on death, sardonically titled *Nothing to Be Frightened Of,* which constituted an extended reflection on that "undiscover'd country." In my letter to Julian, I praised his balance of contrast between Lucretius, who said that since you won't know you are dead you need not fear the condition of death, and Philip Larkin, who observes in his imperishable "Aubade" that this is *exactly* the thing about the postmortem condition that actually does, and must, make one afraid (emphasis mine):

> The sure extinction that we travel to
> And shall be lost in always. Not to be here,
> Not to be anywhere,
> And soon; nothing more terrible, nothing more true...
> And specious stuff that says *no rational being*
> *Can fear a thing it will not feel,* not seeing
> That this is what we fear...

So it is at once a small thing and a big thing that I should have earned those transposed words "the late," which had belonged editorially to Julian's adored wife and then became accidentally adhered to myself. When I first formed the idea of writing some memoirs, I had the customary reservations about the whole conception being perhaps "too soon." Nothing dissolves this fusion of false modesty and natural reticence more swiftly than the blunt realization that the project could become, at any moment, ruled out of the question as having been undertaken too "late."

But we are all "dead men on leave," as Eugene Levine said at his trial in Munich for being a revolutionary after the counter-revolution of 1919.

There are still those, often in India for some reason, who make a living claiming land-rents from the deceased. From Gogol to Google; if one now looks up the sodality of those who have lived to read of their own demise, one strikes across the relatively good cheer of Mark Twain, who famously declared the report to be an exaggeration, to Ernest Hemingway, whose biographer tells us that he read the obituaries every morning with a glass of champagne (eventually wearing out the cheery novelty of this and unshipping his shotgun), to the black nationalist Marcus Garvey who, according to some reports, was felled by a stroke while reading his own death-notice. Robert Graves lived robustly for almost seven decades after being declared dead on the Somme. Bob Hope was twice pronounced deceased by the news media: on the second occasion I was called by some network to confirm or deny the report and now wish I had not so jauntily said, having just glimpsed him at the British embassy in Washington, that the last time I saw him he had certainly seemed dead enough. Paul McCartney, Pope John Paul, Harold Pinter, Gabriel García Márquez . . . the roll of honor and embarrassment persists but there is one striking instance that is more than whimsical. Alfred Nobel, celebrated manufacturer of explosives, is alleged to have been so upset by the "merchant of death" emphasis that followed mistaken reports of his own extinction that he decided to overcompensate and to endow an award for peace and for services to humanity (that, I would add, has been a huge bore and fraud ever since). "Until you have done something for humanity," said the great American educator Horace Mann, "you should be *ashamed* to die." Well, how is one to stand that test?

In some ways, the photograph of me with Martin and James *is* of "the late Christopher Hitchens." At any rate, it is of someone else, or someone who doesn't really exist in the same corporeal form. The cells and molecules of my body and brain have replaced themselves and diminished (respectively). The relatively slender young man with an eye to the future has metamorphosed into a rather stout person who is ruefully but resignedly aware that every day represents more and more subtracted from less and less. As I write these words, I am exactly twice the age of the boy in the frame. The occasional pleasure of advancing years — that of looking back and reflecting upon how far one has come — is swiftly modified by the immediately succeeding thought of how relatively little time there is left to run. I always knew I was born into a losing struggle but I now "know" this in a more objective *and* more subjective way than I did then. When that shutter clicked in Paris I was working and hoping for the overthrow of capitalism. As I sat down to set this down, having done somewhat better out of capitalism than I had ever expected to do, the financial markets had just crashed on almost the precise day on which I became fifty-nine and one-half years of age, and thus eligible to make use of my Wall Street–managed "retirement fund." My old Marxism came back to me as I contemplated the "dead labor" that had been hoarded in that account, saw it being squandered in a victory for finance capital over industrial capital, noticed the ancient dichotomy between use value and exchange value, and saw again the victory of those monopolists who "make" money over those who only have the power to earn it. It was decidedly interesting to have become actuarially extinct in the last quarter of the very same year that saw me "written off" in the more aesthetic and literary sense as well.

I now possess another photograph from that same visit to Paris, and it proves to be even more of a Proustian prompter. Taken by Martin Amis, it shows me standing with the *ravissant* Angela, outside a patisserie that seems to be quite close to the Rue Mouffetard, praise for which appears on the first page of *A Moveable Feast*. (Or could it be that that box of confections in my hand contains a madeleine?) Again, the person shown is no longer myself. And until a short while ago I would not have been able to notice this, but I now see very clearly what my wife discerns as soon as I show it to her. "You look," she exclaims, "just like your daughter." And so I do, or rather, to be fair, so now does she look like me, at least as I was then. The very next observation is again more evident to the observer than it is to me. "What you really look," she says, after a pause, "is Jewish." And so in some ways I am—even though the concept of a Jewish "look" makes me bridle a bit—as I shall be explaining. (I shall also be explaining why it was that the boy in the frame did not know of his Jewish provenance.) All this, too, is an intimation of mortality, because nothing reminds one of impending extinction more than the growth of one's children, for whom room must be made, and who are in fact one's only hint of even a tincture of a hope of immortality.

And yet here I still am, and resolved to trudge on. Of the many once handsome and beautiful visages in the catalogue a distressing number belong to former friends (the marvelous illustrator and cartoonist Mark Boxer, the charming but fragile Amschel Rothschild, the lovable socialite and wastrel—and half-brother to Princess Diana—Adam Shand-Kydd) who died well before they attained my present age. Of some other departures, the news had not yet reached me. "I had not thought death had undone so many." In my career, I have managed to undertake almost every task that the hack journalist can be asked to perform, from being an amateur foreign correspondent to acting as stand-in cinema critic, to knocking out pieces of polemical editorial against the clock. Yet perhaps I have misused the word "undertake" above, because two jobs only I could not manage: covering a sporting event and writing an obituary of a still-living person. The former failing is because I neither know nor care anything about sports, and the second is because—in spite of my firm conviction that I am not superstitious—I cannot, not even for ready money, write about the demise of a friend or colleague until Minerva's owl has taken wing, and I know that the darkness has actually come. I dare say that somebody, somewhere, has already written my provisional death-notice. (Stephen Spender was staying with W.H. Auden when the latter received an invitation from the *Times* asking him to write Spender's obituary. He told him as much at the breakfast table, asking roguishly, "Should you like anything said?" Spender judged that this would not be the moment to tell Auden that he had already written *his* obituary for the same editor at the same paper.) Various death-watch desk managers at various times entreated me to do the same for Edward Said and Norman Mailer and Gore Vidal—to drop some names that will recur if you stay with me—and I always had to decline. Yet now you find me, trying to build my own bridge from, if not the middle of the river, at least some distance from the far side.

Today's newspaper brings news of the death of Edwin Shneidman, who spent all his life in the study and prevention of suicide. He referred to himself as a "thanatologist." The obituary, which is replete with the pseudo-irony so beloved by the near-moribund profession of daily print journalism, closes by saying: "'Dying is the one thing—perhaps the only thing—in life that you don't have to do,' Shneidman once wrote. 'Stick around for long enough and it will be done for you.'" A more polished obituarist might have noticed the connection to a celebrated piece of doggerel by Kingsley Amis:

> Death has this much to be said for it:
> You don't have to get out of bed for it.
> Wherever you happen to be
> They bring it to you—*free*.

And yet I can't quite applaud this admirable fatalism. I personally want to "do" death in the active and not the passive, and to be there to look it in the eye and be doing something when it comes for me.

Surveying the list of all his friends as they were snatched up in turn by the reaper, the great Scottish bard William Dunbar wrote his "Lament for the Makers" in the early sixteenth century, and ended each stave of bereavement with the words *Timor Mortis conturbat me*. It's a near-liturgical refrain—"the fear of death distresses me"—and I would not trust anyone who had not felt something like it. Yet imagine how nauseating life would become, and how swiftly at that, if we were told that there would be no end to it... For one thing, I should have no incentive to write down these remembrances. They will include some account of the several times that I could already have been dead, and very nearly was.

Mention of some of the earlier names above makes me wonder if, without having known it at the time, I have now become retrospectively part of a literary or intellectual "set." The answer seems to be yes, and so I promise to give some account of how it is that "sets" are neither deliberately formed nor made but, as Oscar Wilde said about the arrangement of screens, "simply *occur*."

Janus was the name given by the Romans to the tutelary deity who guarded the doorway and who thus had to face both ways. The doors of his temples were kept open in time of war, the time in which the ideas of contradiction and conflict are most naturally regnant. The most intense wars are civil wars, just as the most vivid and rending personal conflicts are internal ones, and what I hope to do now is give some idea of what it is like to fight on two fronts at once, to try and keep opposing ideas alive in the same mind, even occasionally to show two faces at the same time.

# Yvonne

There is always a moment in childhood when the door opens and lets the future in...

—Graham Greene: *The Power and the Glory*

Something I owe to the soil that grew—
More to the life that fed—
But most to *Allah* who gave me two
Separate sides to my head.

—Rudyard Kipling: *Kim*

——◄○►——

I OF COURSE do not believe that it is "Allah" who determines these things. (Salman Rushdie, commenting on my book *god Is Not Great*, remarked rather mordantly that the chief problem with its title was a lack of economy: that it was in other words exactly one word too long.)

But whatever one's ontology may be, it will always seem tempting to believe that everything must have a first cause or, if nothing quite as grand as that, at the very least a definite beginning. And on that point I have no vagueness or indecision. I do know a little of how I came to be in two minds. And *this* is how it begins with me:

I am standing on a ferry-boat that is crossing a lovely harbor. I have since learned many versions and variations of the word "blue," but let's say that a brilliant if slightly harsh sunshine illuminates a cerulean sky-vault and an azure sea and also limns the way in which these two textures collide and reflect. The resulting tinge of green is in lambent contrast with the darker vegetation on the hillsides and makes an almost blinding combination when, allied with those discrepant yet melding blues, it hits the white buildings that reach down to the edge of the water. As a flash of drama and beauty and sea-scape and landscape, it's as good an inaugural memory as one could wish.

Since this little voyage is occurring in about 1952 and I have been born in 1949, I have no means of appreciating that this is the Grand Harbor at Valletta, the capital of the tiny island-state of Malta and one of the finest Baroque and Renaissance cities of Europe. A jewel set in the sea between Sicily and Libya, it has been for centuries a place of the two-edged sword between the Christian and Muslim worlds. Its population is so overwhelm-ingly Roman Catholic that there are, within the walled city, a great plethora of ornate churches, the cathedral being decorated by the murals of Caravag-gio himself, that seductive votary of the higher wickedness. The island with-stood one of the longest Turkish sieges in the history of "Christendom." But the Maltese tongue is a dialect version of the Arabic spoken in the Maghreb and is the only Semitic language to be written in a Latin script. If you hap-pen to attend a Maltese Catholic church during Mass, you will see the priest raising the Communion Host and calling on "Allah," because this after all is the local word for "god." My first memory, in other words, is of a ragged and jagged, but nonetheless permeable and charming, frontier between two cultures and civilizations.

I am, at this stage, far too secure and confident to register anything of the kind. (If I speak a few phrases of Maltese, it is not with a view to becoming bilingual or multicultural but in order to address my priest-ridden nannies and the kitchen maids with their huge broods of children. This was the place where I first learned to see the picture of Catholicism as one of plump shep-herds and lean sheep.)* Malta is effectively a British colony—its most heroic recent chapter the withstanding of a hysterical aerial bombardment by Hitler and Mussolini—and it has remained a solid possession of the Royal Navy, in which my father proudly serves, ever since the Napoleonic Wars. Much more to the immediate point, I am standing on the deck of this vessel in company with my mother, who holds my hand when I desire it and also lets me scamper off to explore if I insist.

---

* Everything about Christianity is contained in the pathetic image of "the flock."

So, all things being considered, not too shaky a start. I am well-dressed and well-fed, with a full head of hair and a slender waist, and operating in a context of startling architectural and natural beauty, and full of *brio* and self-confidence, and on a boat in the company of a beautiful woman who loves me.

I didn't call her by this name at the time, but "Yvonne" is the echo with which I most piercingly and yearningly recall her memory to me. After all, it *was* her name, and it was what her friends called her, and my shell-like ear detected quite early on a difference between this and the various comfortable Nancys and Joans and Ethels and Marjories who—sterling types all—tended to be the spouses and helpmeets of my father's brother-officers. *Yvonne.* A bit of class there: a bit of style. A touch or dash of garlic and olive and rosemary to sweeten the good old plain English loaf from which, the fact must be faced, I was also sliced. But more of this when I come to Commander Hitchens. I mustn't pretend to remember more than I really do, but I am very aware that it makes a great difference to have had, in early life, a passionate lady in one's own corner.

For example, noticing that I had skipped the baby-talk stage and gone straight to speaking in complete sentences (even if sometimes derivative ones such as, according to family legend, "Let's all go and have a drink at the club"), she sat me down one day and produced an elementary phonetic reading-book, or what used to be known to the humble as "a speller." This concerned the tedious adventures of a woodland elf or goblin called Lob-a-gob (his name helpfully subdivided in this way) but, by the time I was done with it, I was committed for life to having some sort of reading matter within reach at all times, and was always to be ahead of my class in reading-age.

By this period, however, our family had left Malta and been posted to the much more austere surroundings of Rosyth, another naval base on the east coast of Scotland. I think Malta may have been a sort of high point for Yvonne: all British people were a cut above the rest in a semicolony and there was that club for cocktails and even the chance of some local "help." Not that she longed to wallow in idleness but, having endured a girlhood of scarcity, slump, and then war, she couldn't have minded a bit of color and Mediterranean dash and may well have felt she'd earned it. (On our way back from Malta we stopped for a few hours at Nice: her and my first taste of the

Riviera. I remember how happy she looked.) The grayness and drabness of "married quarters" in drizzle-flogged Fifeshire must have hit her quite hard.

But she and my father had first been thrown together precisely because of drizzle and austerity, and the grim, grinding war against the Nazis. He, a career Navy man, had been based at Scapa Flow, the huge, cold-water sound in the Orkney Islands which helped establish and maintain British control over the North Sea. She was a volunteer in the Women's Royal Naval Service or, in the parlance of the day, a "Wren." (My most cherished photograph of her shows her in uniform.) After a short wartime courtship they had been married in early April 1945, not long before Adolf Hitler had shoved a gun into his own (apparently halitosis-reeking) mouth. One young and eager girl from a broken Jewish home in Liverpool, wed to one man twelve years her senior from a sternly united if somewhat repressed Baptist family in Portsmouth. Wartime was certainly full of such improvised unions, in which probably both at first counted themselves fortunate, but I know for a fact that while my father never stopped considering himself lucky, my mother soon ceased to do so. She also decided, for a reason that I believe I can guess, to engage in the not-so-small deception of not mentioning to anyone in the Hitchens family that she was of Jewish descent.

She herself had wanted to "pass" as English after noticing some slight unpleasantness being visited on my grandmother, who in the 1930s toiled in the millinery business. And Yvonne could pass, too, as a light brunette with hazel-ish eyes and (always to my fancy and imagination) a "French" aspect. But more to the point, I now feel sure, she did not want either me or my brother to be taxed with *die Judenfrage*—the Jewish question. What I do not know is quite what this concealment or reticence cost her. What I can tell you something about is what it meant for me.

The paradox was this: in postwar Britain as in Britain at all other times, there was only one tried and tested form of social mobility. The firstborn son (at least) had to be educated at a private school, with an eventual view to attending a decent university. But school fees were high, and the shoals of class and accent and social position somewhat difficult for first-timers to navigate. Neither of my parents had been to college. One of my earliest coherent memories is of sitting in my pajamas at the top of the stairs, eavesdropping on a domestic argument. It was an easy enough one to follow. Yvonne wanted me to go to a fee-paying school. My father — "The Commander" as we some-times ironically and affectionately called him — made the heavy but obvious objection that it was well beyond our means. Yvonne was having none of this. "If there is going to be an upper class in this country," she stated with decision, "then Christopher is going to be in it." I may not have the words exactly right — could she have said "ruling class" or "Establishment," terms that would then have been opaque to me? — but the purport was very clear. And, from my hidden seat in the gallery, I silently applauded. Thus a further paradox discloses itself: my mother was much less British than my father but wanted above all for me to be an English gentleman. (You, dear reader, be the judge of how well *that* worked out.) And, though she wanted to keep me near, she needed to argue hotly for my sake that I be sent away.

I registered this contradiction very acutely as, alternating between the beams and smiles of maternal encouragement and the hot tears of separa-tion, she escorted me to my boarding school at the age of eight. I shall always be slightly sorry that I didn't make more of an effort to pretend that I was desolated, too. I knew I would miss Yvonne but I suppose by then I'd had the essential experience of being loved without ever being spoiled. I was eager to get on with it. And at the school, which I had already visited as a prospective boarder, there could be found a library with shelves that seemed inexhaustible. There was nothing like that at our house, and Yvonne had taught me to love books. The cruelest thing I ever did, at the end of my first term away from home, was to come home for Christmas and address her as "Mrs. Hitchens." I shan't forget her shocked face. It was the enforced etiquette to address all females at the school, from masters' wives to staff, in this way. But I still sus-pect myself of having committed a mean little attention-getting subterfuge.

This perhaps helps explain the gradual diminution of my store of mem-ory of Yvonne: from the ages of eight to eighteen I was to be away from home for most of the year and the crucial rites of passage, from the pains of sexual maturity to the acquisition of friends, enemies, and an education, took place outside the bonds of family. Nonetheless, I always somehow knew how she was, and could generally guess what I didn't know, or what was to be inferred from between the lines of her weekly letters.

My father was a very good man and a worthy and honest and hard-working one, but he bored her, as did much of the remainder of her life. "The one unforgivable sin," she used to say, "is to be boring." What she wanted was the metropolis, with cocktail parties and theater trips and smart friends and witty conversation, such as she had once had as a young thing in prewar Liverpool, where she'd lived near Penny Lane and briefly known people like the madly gay Frank Hauser, later director of the Oxford Playhouse, and been introduced by a boyfriend to the work of the handsome Ulster poet Louis MacNeice, contemporary of Auden and author of *Autumn Journal* and (her favorite) *The Earth Compels*. What she got instead was provincial life in a succession of small English towns and villages, first as a Navy wife and then as the wife of a man who, "let go" by the Navy after a lifetime of service, worked for the rest of his days in bit-part jobs as an accountant or "bursar." It is a terrible thing to feel sorry for one's mother or indeed father. And it's an additionally awful thing to feel this and to know the impotence of the adolescent to do anything at all about it. Worse still, perhaps, is the selfish consolation that it isn't really one's job to rear one's parents. Anyway, I knew that Yvonne felt that life was passing her by, and I knew that the money that could have given her the occasional glamorous holiday or trip to town was instead being spent (at her own insistence) on school fees for me and my brother, Peter (who had arrived during our time in Malta), so I resolved at least to work extremely hard and be worthy of the sacrifice.

She didn't just sit there while I was away. She tried instead to become a force in the world of fashion. Perhaps answering the call of her milliner forebears, but at any rate determined not to succumb to the prevalent dowdiness of postwar Britain, she was forever involved in schemes for brightening the apparel of her friends and neighbors. "One thing I *do* have," she used to say with a slightly defensive tone, as if she lacked some other qualities, "is a bit of good taste." I personally thought she had the other qualities too: on those official holidays when parents would visit my boarding school and many boys almost expired in advance from the sheer dread of embarrassment, Yvonne never did, or wore, anything that I could later be teased about (and this was in the days when women still wore hats). She was invariably the prettiest and brightest of the mothers, and I could always kiss her gladly, right in front of everyone else, without any fear of mushiness, lipstick-stains, or other disasters. In those moments I would have dared anyone to tease me about her, and I was small for my age.

However, the dress-shop business didn't go well. If it wasn't for bad luck,

in fact, Yvonne would have had no luck at all. With various friends and partners she tried to float a store called Pandora's Box, I remember, and another
called Susannah Munday, named for an ancestress of ours on the paternal
Hampshire side. These enterprises just didn't fly, and I couldn't think why
not except that the local housewives were just too drab and myopic and
penny-pinching. I used to love the idea of dropping by as I went shopping,
so that she could show me off to her friends and have a general shriek and
gossip over some coffee, but I could always tell that business wasn't good.
With what a jolt of recognition did I read, years later, V.S. Naipaul's uncanny
diagnosis of the situation in *The Enigma of Arrival*. He was writing about
Salisbury, which was close enough to Portsmouth:

> A shop might be just two or three minutes' walk from the market
> square, but could be off the main shopping track. Many little busi-
> nesses failed—quickly, visibly. Especially pathetic were the shops
> that—not understanding that people with important shopping to
> do usually did it in London—aimed at style. How dismal those
> boutiques and women's dress shops quickly became, the hysteria of
> their owners showing in their windows!

I might want to quarrel with the choice of the word "hysteria," but if you
substituted "quiet desperation," you might not be far off. Even years later,
when the term "struggle" had become for me almost synonymous with the
words "liberation" or "working class," I never forgot that the petit bourgeois
knew about struggling, too.

I am speaking of the time of my adolescence. As the fact of this development became inescapably evident (in the early fall of 1964, according to my
best memory) and as it came time to go back to school again, my mother took
me for a memorable drive along Portsmouth Harbor. I think I had an idea of
what was coming when I scrambled into the seat alongside her. There had been
a few fatuous and bungled attempts at "facts of life" chats from my repressed
and awkward schoolmasters (and some hair-raising speculations from some
of my more advanced schoolmates: I myself being what was euphemistically
called "a late developer"), and I somehow knew that my father would very
emphatically *not* want to undertake any gruff moment of manly heart-to-heart
with his firstborn—as indeed my mother confirmed by way of explanation for

what she was herself about to say. In the next few moments, guiding the Hill-man smoothly along the road, she managed with near-magical deftness and lightness to convey the idea that, if you felt strongly enough about somebody and learned to take their desires, too, into account, the resulting mutuality and reciprocity would be much more than merely worthwhile. I don't know quite how she managed this, and I still marvel at the way that she both recognized and transcended my innocence, but the outcome was a deep peace and satis-faction that I can yet feel (and, on some especially good subsequent occasions, have been able to call clearly to my mind).

She never liked any of my girlfriends, ever, but her criticisms were some-times quite pointed ("Honestly darling, she's madly sweet and everything but she does look a bit like a pit-pony.") yet she never made me think that she was one of those mothers who can't surrender their sons to another female. She was so little of a Jewish mother, indeed, that she didn't even allow me to know about her ancestry: something that I do very slightly hold against her. She wasn't overprotective, she let me roam and hitchhike about the place from quite a young age, she yearned only for me to improve my education (aha!), she had two books of finely bound poetry apart from the MacNeice (Rupert Brooke, and Palgrave's *Golden Treasury*), which I will die to save even if my house burns down; she drove me all the way to Stratford for the Shakespeare anniversary in 1966 and on the wintry day later that year that I was accepted by Balliol College, Oxford, I absolutely *knew* that she felt at least some of the sacrifice and tedium and weariness of the years had been worthwhile. In fact, that night at a fairly rare slap-up dinner "out" is almost the only family celebration of unalloyed joy that (perhaps because it was mainly if not indeed exclusively about me) I can ever recall.

It pains me to say that last thing, but the truth is that I can remember many nice country walks and even one epic game of golf with my father, and many good times with my brother, Peter, as well, and more moments with Yvonne than I can possibly tell about here. But like many families we didn't always succeed in managing as a "unit." It was better if there were guests, or other relatives, or at least a pet animal to which we could all address our-selves. I'll close this reflection with a memory that I cannot omit.

We had been for a family holiday—I think it may have been the last one we all had together—on the Devonshire coast at the John Betjeman–style resort of Budleigh Salterton. I hadn't thought it had been too tense by Hitchens standards, but on the last day my father announced that the men of the family would be going home by train. Yvonne, it seemed, wanted a bit of time to herself and was going to take the car and get home by easy and leisurely stages. I found I approved of this idea: I could see her cruising agreeably along in the roadster, smoking the odd cigarette in that careless and carefree way she had, stopping as and when it pleased her, falling into casual and witty conversation at some of the better hostelries along the roads. Why on earth not? She was way overdue for a bit of sophistication and refinement and a few days of damn-the-expense indulgence.

She was home the next day, with her neck in a brace, having been painfully rear-ended by some idiot before she had even properly embarked on the treat that was rightfully hers. My father silently and efficiently took charge of all the boring insurance and repair details, while Yvonne looked, for the first time I had ever seen her, deflated and defeated. I have never before or since felt so utterly sorry for anybody, or so powerless to assist, or so uneasy about the future, or so unable to say *why* I was so uneasy. To this day, I can't easily stand to hear the Danny Williams version of her favorite "Moon River," because it captures the sort of pining note that is the more painful for being inchoate. While shifting scenery at the Oxford Playhouse not long afterward (for one of the first wage-packets I ever earned) I saw a production of *The Cherry Orchard* from the wings—a good point of vantage for a Chekhov play, incidentally—and felt a pang of vicarious identification with the women who would never quite make it to the bright lights of the big city, and who couldn't even count on the survival of their provincial idyll, either. Oh Yvonne, if there was any justice you should have had the opportunity to enjoy at least one of these, if not both.

She soon afterward gave me a black-tie dinner jacket as a present to take to Oxford, being sure that I'd need formal wear for all the Union debates and other high-toned events at which I would doubtless be starring. I did actually don this garment a few times, but by the middle of 1968 Yvonne had become mainly used to reading about my getting arrested while wearing jeans and donkey jacket and carrying some insurgent flag. I have to say that she didn't complain as much as she might have done ("though I do rather hate it, darling, when my friends ring up and pretend that they are *so sorry* to see you on TV in that way"). Her politics had always been liberal and humanitarian, and she had a great abhorrence of any sort of cruelty or bullying: she fondly thought that my commitments were mainly to the underdog. For my father's flinty and adamant Toryism she had little sympathy. (I do remember her once asking me why it was that so many professional revolutionaries were childless: a question which seemed beside the point at the time but has recurred to me occasionally since.) Unless the police actually came to the house with a warrant—which they did, once, after I had been arrested again while still on bail for a previous offense—she barely uttered a moan. And I, well, I was impatient to outgrow my family and fly the nest, and in the vacations from Oxford as well as after I graduated and moved impatiently and ambitiously to London, I didn't go home any more than I had to.

Even after all these years I find I can hardly bear to criticize Yvonne, but there was something about which I could and did tease her. She had a slight—actually a definite—weakness for "New Age" and faddish and cultish attractions. When I was a boy it was Gayelord Hauser's "Look Younger, Live Longer" regimen: a smirking charmer's catch-penny diet-book that enthralled about half the lower-middle-class women we knew. As time progressed, it was the bogus refulgences of Kahlil Gibran and the sickly tautologies of *The Prophet*. As I say, she could take some raillery about this from me, at least when it was about unwanted poundage or unreadable verses. But (and this is very often the awful fate of the one who teases) I did not realize how much unhappiness was involved, and I did not remotely appreciate how much damage had been done, until it was far too late. Allow me to relate this to you as it unfolded itself to me.

Going back to Oxford one day, and after I had moved to London and had begun working at the *New Statesman*, I was striding down the High Street and ran straight into Yvonne just outside The Queen's College. We embraced at once. As I unclasped her, I noticed a man standing shyly to one side, and evidently carrying her shopping-parcels. We were introduced. I proposed stepping into the Queen's Lane coffee house. I don't remember how it went: I was in Oxford to keep some pressing political and sexual engagements that seemed important at the time. The man seemed nice enough, if a bit wispy, and had an engaging grin. He was called Timothy Bryan, which I also remember thinking was a wispy name. I felt no premonition.

But next time I saw her, my mother was very anxious to know what I thought of him. I said, becoming dimly but eventually alert, that he seemed fine. Did I really, *really* think so? I suddenly understood that I was being asked to *approve* of something. And it all came out in a rush: Yvonne had met him on a little holiday she'd managed to take in Athens, he seemed to understand her perfectly, he was a poet and a dreamer, she had already decided to break it all to my father "The Commander" and was going to live with Mr. Bryan. The main thing I remember thinking, as the sun angled across our old second-floor family apartment, was "Please don't tell me that you waited until Peter and I were old enough." She added, at that moment, with perfect sincerity, that she'd waited until my brother and I were old enough. It was also at about that time—throwing all caution, as they say, to the winds— that she told me she had had an abortion, both *before* my own birth, and after it. The one *after* I could bring myself to think of with equanimity, or at least some measure of equanimity, whereas the one before felt a bit too much like a close shave or a near-miss, in respect of *moi*.

This was the laid-back early 1970s and I had neither the wish nor the ability to be "judgmental." Yvonne was the only member of my family with whom I could discuss sex and love in any case. I was then informed that she and Timothy had another thing in common. He had once been an ordained minister of the Church of England (at the famous church of St.-Martin-in-the-Fields, off Trafalgar Square, as I later discovered) but had seen through organized religion. Both he and she were now devotees of the Maharishi Mahesh Yogi: the sinister windbag who had brought enlightenment to the Beatles in the summer of love. I had to boggle a bit at this capitulation to such a palpable fraud—"Have you given The Perfect Master any money? Has he given you a secret mantra to intone?"—but when the answer to the second question turned out to be a sincere and shy "yes," I forgave her in a burst of laughter in which she (with a slight reserve, I thought) nonetheless joined.

It was arranged that Yvonne and the ex-Rev would come to dine with me in London. Feeling more loyal to my mother than disloyal to my father, I took the happy couple to my favorite Bengali restaurant, The Ganges in Gerrard Street. This was the heart of my culinary leftist Soho, and I knew that the management would be warmly hospitable to any guests of mine. All went well enough, and I could also affect to be cutting a bit of a figure in my novice years as a scribbler in the capital. A hint of Bloomsbury and Fitzrovia and Soho was, I knew, just the sort of spice that Yvonne would appreciate. I dropped an author's name or two...ordered that second carafe with a lazy flick of the hand, paid the bill carelessly and wondered how I would conceal it on my expense account the next day. The former priest Mr. Bryan was not a bad conversationalist, with a fondness for poetry and the quotation of same. Outside in the street, importuned by gypsy taxi drivers, I used the word "fuck" for the first time in my mother's presence, and felt her both bridling a bit and shrugging amusedly at the inevitability of it. At any rate, I could tell that she was happy to be in the metropolis, and happy, too, that I liked her new man well enough. And I still have a rather sharp pang whenever I come to that corner of Shaftesbury Avenue where I kissed her goodbye, because she had been absolutely everything to me in her way and because I was never ever going to see her again.

I think that I must have *talked* to her after that, though, because the curry supper had been in the early fall of 1973 and she telephoned me in London (and this is certainly the last time that I was to hear her voice) at around the time of what some people call the Yom Kippur War and some the Ramadan War, which was in October of that year. This call was for the purpose of advising me that she intended to move to Israel. I completely misinterpreted this as another quasi-spiritual impulse ("Oh, Mummy, honestly": I did still sometimes call her "Mummy") and my impatience earned me a short lecture about how the Jews had made the desert bloom and were exerting themselves in a heroic manner. We were perhaps both at fault: I ought to have been less mocking and dismissive and she might have decided that now if ever was the moment to tell me what she'd been holding back about our ancestral ties. Anyway, I counseled her against removing herself to a war zone, let alone taking someone else's bleeding holy land, on top of her other troubles, and though I didn't know it, we bid farewell. I would give a very great deal to be able to start that conversation over again.

For my father to call was almost unheard-of: his taciturnity was renowned and the telephone was considered an expense in those days. But call he did, and not that many days later, and came to the point with his customary dispatch. "Do you happen to know where your mother is?" I said "no" with complete honesty, and then felt that slightly sickened feeling that comes when you realize that you are simply but politely not believed. (Perhaps this emotion was the late residue of my own recent complicity with Yvonne and Timothy, but my father did sound distinctly skeptical of my truthful answer.) "Well," he went on evenly enough, "I haven't seen or heard from her in days, and her passport isn't where it usually is." I forget quite how we left it, but I shall never forget how we resumed that conversation.

What it is to be twenty-four, and fairly new to London, and cutting your first little swath through town. I'd had a few Fleet Street and television jobs and gigs, and had just been hired by one of the best-known literary-political weeklies in the English-speaking world, and was lying in bed one morning with a wonderful new girlfriend when the telephone rang to disclose, as I lifted the receiver, the voice of an old girlfriend. Bizarrely, or so it seemed to my pampered and disordered senses, she asked me the very same question that my father had recently asked. Did I know where my mother was? I have never quite known how to ask forgiveness, but now I wish I had been able to repress the irritable thought that I was getting just a bit too grown-up for this line of inquiry.

Melissa in any case was as brisk and tender as I would have wanted to be if our situations had been reversed. Had I listened to that morning's BBC news? No. Well, there was a short report about a woman with my surname having been found murdered in Athens. I felt everything in me somehow flying out between my toes. *What?* Perhaps no need to panic, said Melissa sweetly. Had I seen that morning's London *Times*? No. Well, there was another brief print report about the same event. But listen, would there have been a man involved? Would this woman called Hitchens (not that common a name, I dully thought) have been traveling with anybody? Yes, I said, and gave the probable or presumable name. "Oh dear, then I'm very sorry but it probably is your mum."

So the rather diffident and wispy ex-Reverend Bryan, so recently my guest at dinner, had bloodily murdered my mother and then taken his own life. Beneath that scanty exterior had lain a raving psycho. That was what all the reports agreed in saying. In some hotel in Athens, the couple had been found dead separately but together, in adjoining rooms. For my father, who was the next person to ring me, this was especially and particularly devastating.

He was not far short of his sixty-fifth birthday. He had also had to reconcile himself to the loss of his adored wife's affection, in a day when divorce was still considered scandalous, and had reluctantly agreed that she would spend much of her private time at the house of another man. But at the respectable boys' prep school where he kept the books, and in the surrounding society of North Oxford, the two of them had had a pact. If invited to a sherry party or a dinner, they would still show up together as if nothing had happened. Now, and on the front pages at that, everything was made known at once, and to everybody. I do not know how he bore the shock, but there was no question of his coming to Athens, and I myself, in any case, was already on my way there and honestly preferred to face it alone.

This lacerating, howling moment in my life was not the first time that the private and the political had intersected, but it was by some distance the most vivid. For many people in my generation, the seizure of power in Greece by militaristic fascists in April 1967 had been one of the definitive moments in what we were retrospectively to call "the Sixties." That a Western European country—the stock phrase "cradle of democracy" was seldom omitted—could have been hijacked by a dictatorship of dark glasses and torturers and steel helmets and yet remain within NATO: the whole idea made a vulgar satire of the Cold War propaganda about any "free world." I had spoken at the Oxford Union alongside Helen Vlachos, the heroic publisher of the Athens daily paper *Kathimerini*, which had closed and padlocked its doors rather than submit to censorship. I had taken part in protests outside the Greek embassy, and passed out numberless leaflets echoing Byron's line "that Greece might yet be free." And then, almost as my mother lay dying, the Athens junta had in fact been overthrown—but only from the extreme right, so that its replacement was even more vicious than its predecessor. Thus it was that when I first saw the city of Pericles and Phidias and Sophocles, its main square was congested with dirty-gray American-supplied tanks, and its wine-dark sea at Phaleron Bay and Sounion full of the sleek shapes of the U.S. Sixth Fleet.

The atmosphere of that week at the end of November 1973 is instantly accessible to me, and in an almost minute-by-minute way. I can remember seeing the students yelling defiance from behind the wrecked gates of the rebellious Athens Polytechnic, after the broad-daylight and undisguised massacre of the unarmed anti-junta protestors. I can remember meeting friends with bullet wounds that they dared not take to the hospital. I recall, too, a party in a poor student's crummy upstairs apartment, where those present made the odd gesture of singing "The Internationale" almost under their breath, lest they attract the attention of the ever-prowling secret police. My old notebook still contains the testimony of torture victims, with their phone numbers written backward in my clumsy attempt to protect them if my notes were seized. It was one of my first forays into the world of the death squad and the underground and the republics of fear.

With Yvonne lying cold? You are quite right to ask. But it turns out, as I have found in other ways and in other places, that the separation between personal and public is not so neat. On arrival in Athens, I had of course gone directly to meet the coroner in my mother's case. His name was Dimitrios Kapsaskis. It rang a distinct bell. This was the man who had, without wishing to do so, taken a starring part in that greatest of all Sixties movies, _Z_. In this filmic-political masterpiece by Constantine Costa-Gavras, Kapsaskis testified that the hero Gregory Lambrakis had broken his skull accidentally in a fall, rather than having had it smashed by a secret-police operative. Sitting opposite this shabby official villain and trying to talk objectively about my mother while knowing what was happening to my friends outside on the street was an education of a kind.

It was the same when I had to go to the local police station for other formalities. Captain Nicholas Balaskas faced me across a desk in a forbidding office on Lekkas Street which displayed the blazing phoenix: the compulsory logo and insignia of the dictatorship. At the British embassy, which was then run by a genial old diplomat whose son had been with me at Balliol, I had to sit through a lunch where a reactionary creep of a Labour MP named Francis Noel-Baker gave a lecture about the virtues of the junta and (the first but not the last time I was ever to hear these two arguments in combination) both _denied_ that it tortured its prisoners while asserting that it would be quite justified if it _did_ do so!

I then had a strange moment of shared mourning, which helped remind me of what I obviously already "knew": namely that my own bereavement was nothing unique. In a run-down restaurant near Syntagma Square I endured a melancholy lunch with Chester Kallman. This once-golden boy, who W.H. Auden had feared might be "the wrong blond" when they first met in 1939, had since been the life-partner and verse-collaborator of the great poet, the source of much of his misery as well as much of his bliss, and the dedicatee of some especially fervent and consecrated poems. He was fifty-two and looked seventy, with an almost grannyish trembling and protruding lower lip and a quivering hand that spilled his *avgolemono* soup down his already well-encrusted shirtfront. Difficult to picture him as the boy who had once so insouciantly compared himself to Carole Lombard. I had only a few weeks previously gone to Christ Church Cathedral in Oxford to attend Auden's memorial. My dear friend James Fenton, who had been a protégé of Auden's and a sometime guest at the Auden-Kallman home in Kirchstetten, had just won the Eric Gregory Award for poetry and decided to invest the prize money in an intrepid voyage to Vietnam that was to yield its own poetic harvest, so I had gone back to Oxford in part to represent him in his absence, as well as to witness a gathering of poets and writers and literary figures, from Stephen Spender to Charles Monteith (discoverer of *Lord of the Flies*), who were unlikely ever to gather in one place again. Kallman, who had about two years left to live, was not especially desirous of hearing about any of this. "I do not wish," he said slurringly, "to be thought of as Wystan's *relict*." Uncharitably perhaps, and even though I knew he had done some original work of his own, I wondered if he seriously expected to be much or long remembered in any other way.

Even this minor moment of pathos was inflected with politics. Kallman had done his level best over the years to seduce the entire rank-and-file of the Hellenic armed forces and had once been threatened with arrest and deportation by a certain Brigadier Tsoumbas. ("*Soom*-bass": I can still hear his knell-like pronunciation of the dreaded name.) The recent swerve from the extreme right to the even more extreme fascist right was threatening to bring the vile Tsoumbas into high office, and Chester was apprehensive and querulous, with his own safety naturally enough uppermost in mind.

I was going through all of these motions while I awaited a bureaucratic verdict of which I was already fairly sure. My mother had not been murdered. She had, with her lover, contracted a pact of suicide. She took an overdose of sleeping pills, perhaps washed down with a mouthful or two of alcohol, while he—whose need to die must have been very great—took an overdose with booze also and, to make assurance doubly sure, slashed himself in a hot bath. I shall never be sure what depth of misery had made this outcome seem to her the sole recourse: on the hotel's switchboard record were several attempted calls to my number in London which the operator had failed to connect. Who knows what might have changed if Yvonne could have heard my voice even in her extremity? I might have said something to cheer or even tease her: something to set against her despair and perhaps give her a momentary purchase against the death wish.

A second-to-last piece of wretchedness almost completes this episode. Whenever I hear the dull word "closure," I am made to realize that I, at least, will never achieve it. This is because the Athens police made me look at a photograph of Yvonne as she had been discovered. I will tell you nothing about this except that the scene was decent and peaceful but that she was off the bed and on the floor, and that the bedside telephone had been dislodged from its cradle. It's impossible to "read" this bit of forensics with certainty, but I shall always have to wonder if she had briefly regained consciousness, or perhaps even belatedly regretted her choice, and tried at the very last to stay alive.

At all events, this is how it ends. I am eventually escorted to the hotel suite where it had all happened. The two bodies had had to be removed, and their coffins sealed, before I could get there. This was for the dismally sordid reason that the dead couple had taken a while to be discovered. The pain of this is so piercing and exquisite, and the scenery of the two rooms so nasty and so tawdry, that I hide my tears and my nausea by pretending to seek some air at the window. And there, for the first time, I receive a shattering, full-on view of the Acropolis. For a moment, and like the Berlin Wall and other celebrated vistas when glimpsed for the first time, it almost resembles some remembered postcard of itself. But then it becomes utterly authentic and unique. That temple really must be the Parthenon, and almost near enough to stretch out and touch. The room behind me is full of death and darkness and depression, but suddenly here again and fully present is the flash and dazzle and brilliance of the green, blue, and white of the life-giving Mediterranean air and light that lent me my first hope and confidence. I only wish I could have been clutching my mother's hand for this, too.

Yvonne, then, was the exotic and the sunlit when I could easily have had a boyhood of stern and dutiful English gray. She was the cream in the coffee, the gin in the Campari, the offer of wine or champagne instead of beer, the laugh in the face of bores and purse-mouths and skinflints, the insurance against bigots and prudes. Her defeat and despair were also mine for a long time, but I have reason to know that she wanted me to withstand the woe, and when I once heard myself telling someone that she had allowed me "a second identity" I quickly checked myself and thought, no, perhaps with luck she had represented my first and truest one.

# A *Coda* on the Question of Self-slaughter

I have intermittently sunk myself, over the course of the past four decades or so, into dismal attempts to imagine or think or "feel" myself into my mother's state of mind as she decided that the remainder of her life would simply not be worth living. There is a considerable literature on the subject, which I have made an effort to scrutinize, but all of it has seemed to me too portentous and general and sociological to be of much help. Suicide-writing in our time, moreover, has mainly been produced long after the act itself ceased to be regarded as ipso facto immoral or as deserving an extra round of postmortem pain and punishment in the afterlife. I was myself rather astounded, when dealing with the Anglican chaplain at the Protestant cemetery in Athens (which was the only resting place consistent with her wishes), to find that this epoch had not quite ended. The sheep-faced Reverend didn't really want to perform his office at all. He muttered a bit about the difficulty of suicides being interred in consecrated ground, and he may have had something to say about my mother having been taken in adultery...At any rate I shoved some money in his direction and he became sulkily compliant as the priesthood generally does. It was fortunate for him, though, that I couldn't feel any more dislike and contempt for him and for his sickly religion than I already did. If I had been a red-blooded Protestant of any conviction, he would soon enough have found out what a boot felt like when it was planted in his withered backside. (On my way out, through the surrounding Greek Orthodox precincts, I paused to place some red carnations on the huge pile of tribute that surmounted the grave of the great George Seferis, national poet of the Greeks and foe of all superstitions, whose 1971 funeral had been the occasion for a silent mass demonstration against the junta.)

To an extraordinary degree, modern suicide-writing takes its point of departure from the death of Sylvia Plath. When I myself first read *The Bell Jar*, the phrase of hers that most arrested me was the one with which she described her father's hometown. Otto Plath had originated in Grabow, a dull spot in what used to be called "the Polish corridor." His angst-infected daughter had described this place as "some manic-depressive hamlet in the black heart of Prussia." Her poem "Daddy" must be the strictest verdict passed by a daughter on a male parent since the last reunion of the House of Atreus, with its especially unsettling opinion that, as a result of paternal ill-use: "Every woman loves a fascist... the boot in the face."*

My mother's ancestors did in fact come from a small and ultimately rather distraught small town in German-Polish Prussia, and her father had given her mother a truly ghastly time before dematerializing in the fog of war, but Yvonne was not one of those who, having had ill done to her, did "ill in return." She hoped, rather, that it would fall to her to shield others from such pain. I myself don't think, striking though the image may be, that an entire "hamlet" can be manic-depressive. However, I can forgive *la* Plath her possibly subconscious metaphor because most of what I know about manic depression I first learned from *Hamlet*.

"I have, of late," the Prince of Denmark tells us, "but *wherefore I know not*—lost all my mirth." Everyone living has occasionally experienced that feeling, but the lines that accompany it are the best definition of the blues that was ever set down. ("Tired of living, scared of dying" is the next-best

---

* The feminist school has often looked in a manner of marked disapproval at her husband, Ted Hughes. I find it difficult to imagine him actually maltreating Sylvia physically, but there's no doubt that he could be quite stupendously wanting in sensitivity. I once went for some drinks with him at the apartment of my friend and editor Ben Sonnenberg, who was by then almost completely immobilized by multiple sclerosis. Hughes droned on for an agonizingly long time about the powers of a faith-healer in the (perhaps somewhat manic-depressive) Devonshire hamlet where he lived. This shaman, it seemed, was beyond praise for his ability with crippled people. On and on went the encomium. I could not meet Ben's eye but from his wheelchair he eventually asked with commendable lightness: "How is he with sufferers from MS?" "Oh, not bad at all," replied Hughes, before blithely resuming with an account of how this quack could cure disabled farm-animals as well.

encapsulation, offered in "Old Man River.") Who would carry on with the unending tedium and potential misery if they did not think that extinction would be even less desirable or—as it is phrased in another of Hamlet's mood-swing soliloquies—if "the ever-lasting" had "not set his canon 'gainst self-slaughter"?

There are fourteen suicides in eight works of Shakespeare, according to Giles Romilly Fedden's study of the question, and these include the deliberate and ostensibly noble ones of Romeo and Juliet and of Othello. It's of interest that only Hamlet's darling Ophelia, whose death at her own hands is not strictly intentional, is the object of condemnation by the clergy. My own indifference to religion and refusal to credit any babble about an afterlife has, alas, denied me the hearty satisfaction experienced by Ophelia's brother Laertes, who whirls on the moralizing cleric to say:

> I tell thee, churlish priest,
> A ministering angel shall my sister be,
> When thou liest howling.

Memorable to be sure, but too dependent on the evil and stupidity of the heaven/hell dualism, and of scant use to me in deciding how it was that a thoughtful, loving, cheerful person like Yvonne, who was in reasonable health, would want to simply give up. I thought it might have something to do with what the specialists call "anhedonia," or the sudden inability to derive pleasure from anything, most especially from the pleasurable. Al Alvarez, in his very testing and demanding study of the subject, *The Savage God*, returns often to the suicide of Cesare Pavese, who took his own life at the apparent height of his powers. "In the year before he died he turned out two of his best novels...One month before the end he received the Strega Prize, the supreme accolade for an Italian writer. 'I have never been so much alive as now,' he wrote, 'never so young.' A few days later he was dead. Perhaps the sweetness itself of his creative powers made his innate depression all the harder to bear."

This is almost exactly what William Styron once told me in a greasy diner in Hartford, Connecticut, about a golden moment in Paris when he had been waiting to be given a large cash prize, an emblazoned ribbon and medal of literary achievement and a handsome dinner to which all his friends had been bidden. "I looked longingly across the lobby at the street. And I mean *longingly*. I thought, if I could just hurl myself through those heavy revolving doors I might get myself under the wheels of that merciful bus. And then the agony could stop."*

But my poor Yvonne had never suffered from an excess of reward and recognition, of the kind that sometimes does make honest people feel ashamed or even unworthy. However, what she had done was to fall in love, as she had pined so long to do, and then find out that it was fractionally too late for that. In theory she had everything she might have desired—a charming man who adored her; an interval in which her boys were grown and she need not guard a nest; a prospect of leisure and a non-vengeful husband. Many English married women of her class and time would have considered themselves fortunate. But in practice she was on the verge of menopause, had exchanged a dutiful and thrifty and devoted husband for an improvident and volatile man, and then discovered that what "volatile" really meant was… manic depression. She may not have needed or wanted to die, but she needed and wanted someone who did need and did want to die. This is beyond anhedonia.

Examples like hers are also outside the scope of Emile Durkheim's sweeping account of the place of self-slaughter in alienated and deracinated and impersonal societies. I have always admired Durkheim for pointing out that the Jewish people invented their own religion (as opposed to the preposterous and totalitarian view that it was the other way about) but his categorization of suicide doesn't include the Yvonne-sized niche that I have so long been trying to identify and locate. He classified the act under the three headings of the egoistic, the altruistic, and the anomic.

---

* At this diner we were served by a pimply and stringy-haired youth of appallingly dank demeanor. Bringing back Bill's credit card he remarked that it bore a name that was almost the same as that of a famous writer. Bill said nothing. Tonelessly, the youth went on: "He's called William Stryon." I left this up to Bill, who again held off until the kid matter-of-factly said, "Anyway, that guy's book saved my life." At this point Styron invited him to sit down, and he was eventually persuaded that he was at the same table as the author of *Darkness Visible*. It was like a transformation scene: he told us brokenly of how he'd sought and found the needful help. "Does this happen to you a lot?" I later asked Styron. "Oh, *all* the time. I even get the police calling up to ask if I'll come on the line and talk to the man who's threatening to jump."

The "egoistic" is misleadingly titled, because it really refers to suicide as a reaction to social fragmentation or atomization: to periods when old certainties or solidarities are decomposing and people feel panic and insecurity and loneliness. (Thus, a corollary to it is the observable fact that suicide rates decline during wartime, when people rally round a flag and also see their own small miseries in better proportion.) The "altruistic" also has a wartime connotation, in that it signifies the willingness to lay down one's life for the good of the larger collective, or conceivably even the smaller collective such as the family or—Captain Oates on Scott's doomed expedition—the group. Of this phenomenon, Albert Camus provided a nice précis by saying: "What is called a reason for living is also an excellent reason for dying." Alvarez extends Durkheim's tropes to include religious and tribal fanaticism, such as the kamikaze pilots or those Hindus who were ecstatically willing to hurl themselves under the wheels of the divinely powered Juggernaut. The "anomic" suicide, finally, is the outcome of a sudden and jarring change in the person's social position. "A searing divorce or a death in the family" are among the examples Alvarez gives as typical.

It's of interest that this taxonomy appears to say nothing about the so-called suicidal "type." From experience I should say that there is, perhaps, such a type, and that it can be dangerously frivolous to say that attempted suicides are only crying for "help." I have known several who, after some apparently half-hearted "bid," or even bids, made a decisive end of themselves. But Yvonne was by no imaginable measure the "type." She abhorred self-pity and suspected anything that was too ostentatious or demonstrative. However, she had fallen in with someone who very probably was bipolar or in other ways the "type," and she had certainly undergone the wrenching and jarring and abrupt loss of social position and security (and respectability) that had always been of such importance to her. Couple this with the gnawing fear that she was losing her looks...anyway, for me a searing marital separation had indirectly led to "a death in the family."

Durkheim's categories seem almost too grandiose to take account of her suicide (how we all would like our deaths to possess a touch of meaning). The egoistic doesn't really cover it at all; nor did the altruistic when I first read about it; and "anomie" to my Marxist ear used to be what mere individuals had instead of what, with a better understanding of their class position, they would have recognized as alienation. Yvonne's was "anomic," then, but with a hint of the altruistic also. Of the two notes that she left, one (which, pardon me, I do not mean to quote) was to me. The other was to whoever had to shoulder the responsibility of finding her, or rather them. I was quite undone by the latter note as well: it essentially apologized for the mess and inconvenience. Oh Mummy, so like you. In her private communication she gave the impression of believing that this was best for all concerned, and that it was in some way a small sacrifice from which those who adored her would benefit in the long run. She was wrong there.

For the anomic, Cesare Pavese almost certainly provided the best text by observing drily enough that "no one ever lacks a good reason for suicide." And Alvarez furnishes self-slaughterers with the kindest epitaph by writing that, in making death into a conscious choice: "Some kind of minimal freedom — the freedom to die in one's own way and in one's own time — has been salvaged from the wreck of all those unwanted necessities."

I once spoke at a memorial meeting for an altruistic suicide: the Czech student Jan Palach, who set himself on fire in Wenceslas Square in Prague to defy the Russian invaders of his country. But since then I have had every chance to become sickened by the very idea of "martyrdom." The same monotheistic religions that condemn suicide by individuals have a tendency to exalt and overpraise self-destruction by those who kill themselves (and others) with a hymn or a prayer on their lips. Alvarez, like almost every other author, gets "Masada" wrong: he says that "hundreds of Jews put themselves to death" there "rather than submit to the Roman legions." In fact, religious fanatics who had been expelled even by other Jewish communities first murdered their own families and then drew lots for the exalted duty of murdering one another. Only the very last ones had to settle for killing themselves.

So, divided in mind once more, I often want to agree with Saul Bellow's Augie March who, when rebuked by his elders and enjoined to conform and to "accept the data of experience," replies: "it can never be right to offer to die, and if that's what the data of experience tell you, then you must get along without them." Yet my next subject is a man who for a long time braved death for a living and would have been perfectly willing to offer to die in a cause that he considered to be (and that was) larger than himself.

# The Commander

He loved me tenderly and shyly from a distance, and later on took a naïve pride in seeing my name in print.
—Arthur Koestler: *Arrow in the Blue*

I heard the news today, Oh Boy.
The English army had just won the war.
—The Beatles: *Sergeant Pepper*: "A Day in the Life"

AN ANCIENT PIECE of Judaic commentary holds that the liver is the organ that best represents the relationship between parents and child: it is the heaviest of all the viscera and accordingly the most appropriate bit of one's guts. Only two of the six hundred and thirteen Jewish commandments, or prohibitions, offer any reward for compliance and both are parental: the first is in the original Decalogue when those who "honor thy father and thy mother" are assured that this will increase their days in the promised or stolen Canaanite land that is about to be given them, and the second involves some convoluted piece of quasi-reasoning whereby a bird's egg can be taken by a hungry Jew as long as the poor mother bird isn't there to witness the depredation. How to discern whether it's a mother or father bird is not confided by the sages.

Commander Eric Ernest Hitchens of the Royal Navy (my middle name is Eric and I have sometimes idly wondered how things might have been different if either of us had been called Ernest) was a man of relatively few words, would have had little patience for Talmudic convolutions, and was not one of those whom nature had designed to be a nest-builder. But his liver—to borrow a phrase from Gore Vidal—was "that of a hero," and I must have inherited from him my fondness, if not my tolerance, for strong waters. I can remember perhaps three or four things of the rather laconic and diffident sort that he said to me. One—also biblically derived—was that my early socialist conviction was "founded on sand." Another was that while one ought to beware of women with thin lips (this was the nearest we ever approached to a male-on-male conversation), those with widely spaced eyes were to be sought out and appreciated: excellent advice both times and no doubt dearly bought. Out of nowhere in particular, but on some unusually bleak West Country day he pronounced: "I sometimes think that the Gulf Stream is beginning to weaken," thereby anticipating either the warming or else the cooling that seemingly awaits us all. When my firstborn child, his first grandson, arrived, I got a one-line card: "glad it's a boy." Perhaps you are by now getting an impression. But the remark that most summed him up was the flat statement that the war of 1939 to 1945 had been "the only time when I really felt I knew what I was doing."

This, as I was made to appreciate while growing up myself, had actually been the testament of a British generation. Born in the early years of the century, afflicted by slump and Depression after the First World War in which their fathers had fought, then flung back into combat against German imperialism in their maturity, starting to get married and to have children in the bleak austerity that succeeded victory in 1945, they all wondered quite where the years of their youth and strength had gone, and saw only more decades of struggle and hardship still to come before the exigencies of retirement. As Bertie Wooster once phrased it, they experienced some difficulty in detecting the bluebird.

It could have been worse. My father's father, the stern Alfred Ernest Hitchens, was a mirthless Calvinist patriarch who took a dim view of everything from music to television. The old man's forebears hailed from the backlands of Thomas Hardy's Wessex and perhaps even farther west—Hitchens being in its origin a Cornish name—and my brother possesses ancestral birth and marriage certificates that are "signed" with an "X" by the peasants who were most probably recruited into Portsmouth to help build the historic dockyards.

Portsmouth. The true home port of the Royal Navy, and nicknamed

"Pompey" (as is its soccer team) by those locals for whom no other town will do. It is one of the world's most astonishing natural harbors, rivaling even Valletta in the way that it commands the Channel approaches to the Atlantic and the North Sea, and it looms over the French coast while sheltering in the lee of the Isle of Wight, which the conquering Romans once named Vectis. The last place that Horatio Nelson set foot on dry land, and to this moment the home of his flagship the *Victory*. The birthplace of Charles Dickens and the home of Rudyard Kipling and Arthur Conan Doyle. Here I drew my first squalling breath on 13 April 1949, and here my male ancestors embarked time and again to slip down the Channel and do the King's enemies a bit of no good. My grandfather had been a ranker in the army in India, and was to the end of his days only softened in his general puritan harshness by his warm affection for that country, expressed in a collection of Benares brasses that competed for space in his home with the biographies of forgotten missionaries.

I still have an oil painting, almost my only family heirloom, which depicts a blue-eyed, rosy-cheeked ten-year-old boy in a white collar and blue bow-tied suit. This promising lad is looking into the distance and arguably being instructed to think of his country's destiny. In my own youth, I was made to stand next to this frame while older relatives remarked on the distinct resemblance I bore to "Great-Uncle Harry." The boy in the frame was indeed my great-uncle, acting as the model for an exhibition called "Young England" in 1900. Fifteen years later his cruiser was shattered and sunk at the Battle of Jutland ("There seems to be something wrong with our bloody ships today," as Admiral Beatty commented on seeing yet another vessel burst its boilers and go sky-high) yet he survived in the bitter North Sea waters and is said to have saved the shivering Maltese mess-steward while quietly letting the bar-bills sink unpaid to the bottom.

I don't quite remember how old I was before I met anybody who wasn't concerned with the Navy, or at least with some branch of the armed forces of which ours was always "The Senior Service." I was christened on a submarine, urinating freely as the reverend made me the first Hitchens to eschew baptism and Judaism and become a member of the more middle-class Church of England. I came to understand the difference between a destroyer and a cruiser and a corvette, and could tell someone's rank by the number of gold rings worn on the sleeve. When we moved to Malta, it was for the Navy.

When we migrated to Scotland, it was to the base at Rosyth, quite near the Dunfermline birthplace of Admiral Cochrane, liberator of Chile and model for Patrick O'Brian's Jack Aubrey. When we were tranferred again to Plymouth, I went to a boys' boarding school in the Devonshire town of Tavistock, birthplace of Sir Francis Drake. Every dormitory at the school was named for an admiral who had vanquished England's (and later Great Britain's) enemies at sea.

I have mentioned the disagreement between my mother and father as to whether they could afford that school, and I should now give another instance of the ways in which they did not think alike. We were living in the Dartmoor village of Crapstone, a name for which I didn't much care because it could get me roughed up at school. ("*Where* did you say you lived, Hitchens?") In due time we moved away, but to a village in Sussex called Funtington, which somehow was still not quite the improvement for which I had been quietly hoping.

At all events, at the age of about nine I was listening to a bit of gossip about one of our next-door neighbors, a Marine officer of lugubrious aspect and mien, and his all-enduring wife. "Daphne was telling me," said my mother to my father about this man, "that his temper is so foul that she's taken to diluting his gin bottle with water when he's not looking." There was a significant pause. "If the woman is watering Nigel's bloody gin," said the Commander, "then I'm not surprised that he's always in a filthy temper." From this exchange I learned quite a lot about the different manner in which men and women, or at any rate married couples, can reason. I also added to my store of knowledge about the Commander's attitude to gin, which was a relatively devout one. Alcohol for me has been an aspect of my optimism: the mood caught by Charles Ryder in *Brideshead Revisited* when he discourses on aspects of the Bacchic and the Dionysian and claims that he at least chooses to drink "in the love of the moment, and the wish to prolong and enhance it." I dare say some people have seen me the worse for wear in less charming ways, but I know I have been true to the original as well. The Commander was not a happy drinker. He didn't actually drink all that much, but he imbibed regularly and determinedly, and it was a reinforcement to his pessimism and disappointment, both personal and political.

As I was beginning to say, my entire boyhood was overshadowed by two great subjects, one of them majestic and the other rather less so. The first was the recent (and terribly costly) victory of Britain over the forces of Nazism. The second was the ongoing (and consequent) evacuation by British forces of bases and colonies that we could no longer afford to maintain. This epic and its closure were inscribed in the very scenery around me: Portsmouth and Plymouth had both been savagely blitzed and the scars were still palpable. The term "bomb-site" was a familiar one, used to describe a blackened gap in a street or the empty place where an office or pub used to stand. More than this, though, the drama was inscribed in the circumambient culture. Until I was about thirteen, I thought that all films and all television programs were about the Second World War, with a strong emphasis on the role played in that war by the Royal Navy. I saw Jack Hawkins with his binoculars on the icy bridge in *The Cruel Sea*: the movie version of a heart-stopping novel about the Battle of the Atlantic by Nicholas Monsarrat that by then I knew almost by heart. The Commander, who had seen action on his ship HMS *Jamaica* in almost every maritime theater from the Mediterranean to the Pacific, had had an especially arduous and bitter time, escorting convoys to Russia "over the hump" of Scandinavia to Murmansk and Archangel at a time when the Nazis controlled much of the coast and the air, and on the day after Christmas 1943 ("Boxing Day" as the English call it) proudly participating as the *Jamaica* pressed home for the kill and fired torpedoes through the hull of one of Hitler's most dangerous warships, the *Scharnhorst*. Sending a Nazi convoy raider to the bottom is a better day's work than any I have ever done, and every year on the anniversary the Commander would allow himself one extra tot of Christmas cheer, or possibly two, which nobody begrudged him. (To this day, I observe the occasion myself.)

But he would then become glum, because he had most decidedly not taken the King's Commission in order to end up running guns to Joseph Stalin (he had loathed the glum, graceless reception he got when his ship docked under the gaze of the Red Navy) and because almost everything since that great Boxing Day had been headed downhill. The Empire and the Navy were being wound up fast, the colors were being struck from Malaya in the East to Cyprus and Malta nearer home, the Senior Service itself was being cut to the bone. When I was born in Portsmouth, my father was on board a ship called the *Warrior*, anchored in a harbor that had once seen scores of aircraft carriers and great gray battleships pass in review. In Malta there had still been a shimmer or scintilla of greatness to the Navy, but by the time I was old enough to take notice the Commander was putting on his uniform only to go to a "stone frigate": a non-seagoing dockside office in Plymouth where they calculated things in ledgers. Every morning on the BBC until I was six I would hear the newscaster utter the name "Sir Winston Churchill," who was then prime minister. There came the day when this stopped, and my childish ears received the strange name "Sir Anthony Eden," who had finally succeeded the old lion. Within a year or so, Eden had tried to emulate Churchill by invading Egypt at Suez, and pretending that Britain could simultaneously do without the UN and the United States. International and American revenge was swift, and from then on the atmosphere can't even be described as a "long, withdrawing roar," since the tide of empire and dominion merely and sadly ebbed.

"We won the war—or *did* we?" This remark, often accompanied by a meaning and shooting glance and an air of significance, was a staple of conversation between my father and his rather few friends as the decanter went round. Later in life, I am very sorry to say, it helped me to understand the "stab in the back" mentality that had infected so much of German opinion after 1918. You might call it the politics of resentment. These men had borne the heat and burden of the day, but now the only chatter in the press was of cheap and flashy success in commerce; now the colonies and bases were being mortgaged to the Americans (who, as we were invariably told, had come almost lethargically late to the struggle against the Axis); now there were ridiculous, posturing, self-inflated leaders like Kenyatta and Makarios and Nkrumah where only very recently the Union Jack had guaranteed prosperity under law. This grievance was very deeply felt but was also, except in the company of fellow sufferers, rather repressed. The worst thing the Navy did to the Commander was to retire him against his will sometime after Suez, and then and only then to raise the promised pay and pension of those officers who would later join up. This betrayal by the Admiralty was a never-ending source of upset and rancor: the more wartime service and action you had seen, the less of a pension you received. The Commander would write letters to Navy ministers and members of Parliament, and he even joined an association of "on the beach" ex-officers like himself. But one day when, tiring of his plaintiveness, I told him that nothing would change until he and his comrades marched in

a phalanx to Buckingham Palace and handed back their uniforms and swords
and scabbards and medals, he was quite shocked. "Oh," he responded. "We
couldn't think of doing *that*." Thus did I begin to see, or thought I began to
see, how the British Conservatives kept the fierce, irrational loyalty of those
whom they exploited. "He's a Tory," I was much later to hear of some dogged
loyalist, "but he's got nothing to be Tory about." My thoughts immediately
flew to my father, whose own devoted and brave loyalism had been estimated
so cheaply by what I was by then calling the ruling class.

When I say that we didn't hold much converse, I suppose that I should
blame myself as well as him. But in some ways I don't blame myself that much:
at the age of ten or so I turned from the newspaper to ask him why the paratroopers from Algeria were threatening to occupy Paris and proclaim a military
coup d'etat in mainland France. His typical two-word response—"Gallic tem-
perament"—rather dried up my interest in pursuing the subject any further.
But I disappointed him, too, I know. He would have liked me to be good at
games and sports, as he was. I couldn't even pretend to care about cricket or
rugby or any of that. Convinced that I might want to earn my colors instead
as some kind of Scout, he went to a huge amount of trouble to send me, at my
prep school, miniature versions of complicated knots executed in string and
pipe-cleaner and neatly diagrammed. Had I bothered to master these, I could
have perhaps later made better headway with the nautico-literary descriptions
of the vessels and ropes of Hornblower and Aubrey, and their halliards and
bowlines and mainbraces (the most alarming of the latter being the "cunt-
splice," demanded by Captain Aubrey from his boatswain in a heated moment,
about which I could certainly never have asked Commander Hitchens).

He was quite a small man and, when he took off his uniform (or had
it taken away from him) and went to work as a bookkeeper, looked very
slightly shrunken. For as long as he could, he took jobs that kept him near
the sea, especially near the Hampshire-Sussex coast. He would work for a
boatbuilder here, a speedboat-manufacturer there. We finally drifted inland,
nearer to the center of my mother's beloved Oxford, where there was a boys'
prep school that needed an accountant, and he seized the chance to acquire
a dog. I hadn't realized until then quite how much he preferred the predict-
ability and loyalty of animals to the vagaries and frailties of human beings.
Late in life the landlords of the apartment building where he lived were to tell

him that he couldn't keep his red-setter/retriever mix, a lovely animal named Becket. The now-beached Commander couldn't afford to move house again, so instead of protesting, he meekly gave the dog away. But not before mooting with me a plan to establish Becket somewhere else, "so that I could go and visit him from time to time." Again I had the experience of a moment of piercing pity, of the sort I could only now imagine feeling for a child of mine whom it was beyond my power to help.

I do have a heroic memory of him from my boyhood, and it happens to concern water. We were at a swimming-pool party, held at the local golf and country club that was almost but not quite out of our social orbit, when I heard a splash and saw the Commander fully clothed in the shallow end, pipe still clamped in his mouth. I remember hoping that he had not fallen in, in front of all these people, because of the gin. Then I saw that he was holding a little girl in his arms. She had been drowning, quietly, just outside her depth, until someone had squealed an alarm and my father had been the speediest man to act. I remember two things about the aftermath. The first was the Commander's "no fuss; anyone would have done it" attitude to those who slapped him on the back in admiration. That was absolutely in character, and to be expected. But the second was the glare of undisguised rage and hatred from the little girl's father, who should have been paying attention and who had instead been quaffing and laughing with his pals. That hateful look taught me a lot about human nature in a short time.

Otherwise I am rather barren of paternal recollections, and shall have to settle for the memory of a few walks, and for the strange cult of golf. Seafarer though he was, my father loved the downlands of Hampshire and Sussex and later Oxfordshire and could stride along with his trusty stick, pointing out here a steading and there a ridgeway. He was a Saxon in his own way, and still had the attitude, now almost extinct, that there had been such a thing as "the Norman yoke" imposed upon this ancient landscape and people. A favorite joke on his side of the family concerned the Hampshire yeoman in dispute with his squire. "I suppose you know," observes the squire loftily, "that my ancestors came over with William the Conqueror." "Yes," responds the yeoman. "We were waiting for you." (In an alternative version once offered by the rogue Marxist Welshman Raymond Williams, the yeoman tries to be witty and says: "Oh yes, and how are you liking it over here?") I mention this because a certain kind of British conservatism is quite closely connected with this folk memory of populism and ethnicity, and because it became important for me to comprehend this later on.

The golf game must have taken place when I was about thirteen. I had taken up the sport, and even got myself a few clubs, with the idea that I ought to have something in common with my reticent old man, who loved golf and treasured a pewter mug he had once won in a Navy tournament held on the deck of an aircraft carrier. My effort paid off, if only once. We had a round of nine holes that somehow went well for both of us, and then he treated me to a heavy "tea" in the clubhouse where, if nothing much got said, there was no tension or awkwardness, either. It was the closest I ever came, or felt, to him. There was a very soft and beautiful dusk, I remember, as we drove slowly and quietly home through the purple-and-yellow gorse of the moors.

Once I had left home for university and then for London, and once my mother had been taken from us, and once he had had to hear, and from his son at that, that Yvonne had not been murdered but had slain herself while distraught about another man, a very slight but definite coolness replaced the respectful distance that had developed between me and the Commander. More than anything, this chill consisted of a subject (the prior existence of his wife and my mother) that he simply would not and could not discuss with me. Over time, all the same, there was the occasional thaw. He disliked coming to London on principle and had enraged me when I was younger by refusing to take a job as the secretary of Brooks's Club. (I could have been living in London—in Mayfair, for heaven's sake—and when I was a teenager!) But I did once lure him to the detested city to see a musical (about Fats Waller, an uncharacteristic favorite of his, called *Your Feet's Too Big*) and he once astonished me by asking, in the late 1970s, if I'd care to come with him to the reunion of his old shipmates. Turning up at some down-at-heel Navy veterans' club on the appointed night, I was quick to realize that this late muster was almost certainly going to be the last one for the fine company that had once crewed the good ship *Jamaica*. But how brave and modest and honest and unassuming they were, these men who had bucketed through icy storms and every kind of peril in order to sweep Hitler from the seas. An oddly touching detail stays with me: instead of referring to my father as Eric or the Commander they all called him "Hitch," which was what my close friends were beginning to call me.

At around this time I was starting to turn my thoughts and ambitions toward America, which the grizzled veteran showed no interest in visiting. In uniform at any rate, he had been everywhere from China to Chile to Cyprus to Ceylon, but the New World held no charms for him and at our infrequent meetings he never evinced any curiosity about the place. If he asked a question on another topic, it would be of the rhetorical kind: "Don't you think Northern Ireland could do with a good stiff dose of martial law?"—almost as if force had never yet been tried in the black record of British rule in Ireland—and if he made a statement, there might very well be a rhetorical element there, too. ("If they build this bloody Channel Tunnel and join us to France," he once said in what I'd call the classical statement of his worldview, "I shall never vote Conservative again.") I sometimes used to wonder if he was saying these things for effect, or even because of the gin, but if challenged he would re-state things even more decidedly: a tendency I have since come to notice and sometimes to deplore in myself.

He must have known that he had some kind of a Red for a son, but he seemed to manage to talk to me as if I still had elementary Saxon common sense, and I was very affected when I discovered that, by stealth, to his small circle of friends, he was giving Christmas gift subscriptions to my pinko magazine, the *New Statesman.* "Rather interesting piece by my son in that last issue...don't know if you noticed it." Did this make up for my failures as a sportsman? I doubt it, but then I had to ask myself if I had chosen the field of journalism to compensate for other shortcomings on the field of valor. On this point, too, he administered more of a shock to me than he can have intended. After I had returned from a visit to Lebanon in the mid-1970s, and a trip to the war zone in the south of that country that I had later written up for the magazine, I was sitting at my desk one afternoon when the telephone rang and it was the Commander. This occurrence was rare enough in itself to make me worry that something might be amiss. But he was calling to say that he had admired my article and, while I was still searching for the words in which to respond, he in effect doubled the stakes by saying that he thought it had been "rather brave" of me to go there. And then, as I grappled with *that* rather vertiginous development, he said goodbye and replaced the receiver. A man of few words, as I believe I have said.

At the time, I couldn't make any definite connection between my own visits to the places where he'd been stationed, from the South Atlantic to the Eastern Mediterranean to the Indian Ocean, and the Commander's earlier presence there. I myself could not picture how these one-time colonies must have looked when viewed through a massive ship's gunsight, or from the deck of a superbly engineered war-machine. In truth, when in Cyprus or in Palestine or southern Africa or elsewhere, I generally felt myself so much in sympathy with those who had resisted British rule that I thought it better for the Commander and myself to avoid the subject. If you had asked me then about the likelihood of the Union Jack flying again over Basra or the Khyber Pass, I would have both mocked and scorned the idea. Yet when the Argentine fascist junta invaded the Falkland Islands in the early days of 1982, just after I had immigrated to New York, I felt a sudden stab of partisanship for the Royal Navy as it sailed out to reverse the outcome. I even wrote to the Commander in fairly gung-ho terms, hoping for a hint of common ground. His response surprised and even slightly depressed me. "I don't know if it frightens the enemy," he wrote about Britain's last war-footing fleet as it found its inexorable way to the South Atlantic, "but it certainly frightens me." This slightly hackneyed borrowing, from what the Duke of Wellington had said of his "infamous army" of drunken and homicidal riffraff on the eve of Waterloo, left me feeling flat. ("Waterlooville" was the name of a suburb of Portsmouth, and there was a celebrated pub called "The Heroes of Waterlooville" whose inn sign showed the redcoats smashing Bonaparte's "Old Guard," so he had to know that I would find his historical allusion slightly trite.)

On reflection, though, I am able to see what I did learn from my father. I had once thought that he'd helped me understand the Tory mentality, all the better to combat and repudiate it. And in that respect he was greatly if accidentally instructive. But over the longer stretch, I have come to realize that he taught me—without ever intending to—what it is to feel disappointed and betrayed by your "own" side. He had a certain idea of England, insular to a degree, and conservative for sure but not always, or not necessarily, reactionary. In this England, patient merit would take precedence over the insolence of office, and people who earned their money would be accorded more respect than people who merely had it or "made" it. The antiquity and tranquility of the landscape and the coastline would likewise have earned their share of deference: those who wanted to uproot or to "develop" an area would have to make a case for change rather than be permitted the glib and clever assumption that change was a good thing in itself.

And yet the postwar Conservative Party had become the agent of hectic and greedy modernistic metamorphosis: tearing up the old railway lines and cutting great new swaths of motorway through hill and forest and dale; licensing the commercial principle in everything from television to elections; contemptuous of tradition; handing the skylines and harbors of our grand and blitzed old seaports to builders and speculators who swiftly made them unrecognizable to the veterans who had made those place names honored and famous. And this was just in the time of Harold Macmillan. If the Commander had lived to see the full impact of Thatcherism, he would have felt that there was almost nothing left worth fighting for, or rather having fought for.

I have so few vivid memories of him that one may do duty for many: we had gone as a family into Portsmouth for the opening night of *The Longest Day*. This epic film about the D-Day landings would, I knew from experience, be almost certain to annoy or disappoint the Commander in at least one of two ways. The movie would either understate the role of Britain in the historic storming of the beaches of occupied Europe (reversing an ancient verdict by having us invade Normandy) or it would underplay the part of the Royal Navy in this hinge event. In the event, it was grudgingly agreed in the car on the way home that fairness had at least been attempted. There were a few laughs at the expense of "the Yanks and their gadgets," and a few reminiscences of the Dieppe raid that had raised the curtain on Normandy: a hellish fiasco in which the Commander had helped land the doomed Canadian forces on bullet-swept beaches, with Lord Mountbatten (an especially vain member of the British Royal Family) as part of his ship's company. But this effort at good cheer was all aimed at erasing what had occurred before the cinema's curtains had parted. My father had come back from the box office with the news that only the most absurdly expensive or the most abjectly cheap seats were now available. He looked quite put out at this: Didn't the throng for this film understand that he'd practically *been* there? Yvonne attempted mollification. "Who's snapped up the tickets then? 'The affluent society,' I suppose?" "You have that right," said the Commander with bitterness. He'd done so much for the empire and it had done so little for him in return. If I had had my way, he would have been respectfully escorted to a front-row seat, or perhaps a box.

But I also admired him for his lack of guile and his dislike for anything that was surreptitious or underhand. While in the Royal Navy, he had indignantly refused any advances from the Freemasons, even though this mafia of the mediocre might, had he but joined them, have swung the difference between being promoted and otherwise. One loyalty was enough for him. His candor and modesty once almost caused me to weep. He told of a senior officer who had asked him if he'd come and help out at a cocktail party on the base. It was explained to him in confidence by his superior that the event was meant to soak up all the bores who hadn't been invited to anything yet. "Thank you, sir," he had replied. "But I believe I have already received my invitation." Yvonne's face, when he told this story in company, was a frozen study that I never forgot.

The Commander lost his last proper job in a similarly naïve way, feeling himself obliged to tell the boys' school in Oxford—the place which had furnished his last and only economic security—that he had reached the statutory retirement age. "Honestly, Eric," the somewhat shambolic headmaster later informed me he had told him, "you didn't have to do that. Nobody was going to make anything of it. Nobody had ever even thought of asking. But now that you *have* bloody well told us, the Board of Governors has no legal option but to give you a gold watch or something and let you go." And so he went, quietly and uncomplainingly as ever.* In his last years, in enforced semi-retirement, he did some very small-time bookkeeping work for a medical man of sorts, in the out-of-the-way Oxfordshire village of Sutton Courtenay, where George Orwell is buried and where, when I once visited, the vicar led me to the spot and then said: "Oh, sorry: wrong grave. This one says 'Eric Blair.'"

---

* Strangely, though, the matter of his age was also the only thing in which I ever caught him out in a petty dishonesty. He used to tell us that he had been born in 1912. My brother, Peter, and I were both amateur numismatists in boyhood, and these were the days when hoop-sized pennies from the Victorian and Edwardian era could still turn up in your small change. If we found a 1912 coin, we would show him, and then proudly hoard and sometimes even mount and display it. It was somehow deflating to discover—as he must have known we would— that he had been born in 1909. I still cannot be sure why he practiced this uncharacteristic deception: conceivably to attenuate the difference in years between himself and Yvonne. But she could not possibly have been fooled, as his sons pointlessly were.

Eric Ernest Hitchens's own grave is on Portsdown Hill, overlooking what Arthur Conan Doyle used to call "The Narrow Sea." This historic stretch of water was decidedly and historically "ours." ("I do not say," Lord St. Vincent is supposed to have told Parliament in the Napoleonic epoch, "that our enemies cannot come. I only say that they cannot come by sea.") Here is the chapel where General Eisenhower said a prayer for fine weather and victory the night before the D-Day landings in Normandy: a stained-glass window commemorates the modest warrior who later became president of the United States. Commander Hitchens had once assured me, after a visit to my long-bedridden grandfather, that he would not make a protracted business of dying, and he was as good as his word. He died in 1987, aged 78. Having never spent a day in bed in his life, he went very speedily from diagnosis of an inoperable cancer in his esophagus to a hammer-blow heart attack that gave his hostess, his sister Ena, barely time to rush to his side. (My Aunt Ena had also landed on the beaches of Normandy as a nurse in the second wave — another excellent day's work — and got all the way to Germany before they told her to stop.)

The Commander's funeral took place on a day of bitter and extreme cold. I dismounted from the train at what had once been my home-bound station for the school holidays. By a macabre coincidence, as I walked through the freezing station yard I saw workmen painting out the faint storefront sign "Susannah Munday" on what had once been my mother's sad attempt at a dress shop. I was able to see my father in his last repose before the screwing-on of the lid, and later to do for him what he had once done for me, and carry him on my shoulders. We laid the coffin in the chancel of the D-Day chapel: my brother had made all the liturgical and musical arrangements with a clear eye to tradition and dignity. I rather pity those Anglo-American families to whom the "Navy Hymn" is not a part of the emotional furniture: its words and music are impossibly stirring even to one who finds the opening words "Eternal Father" doubly problematic. The tune is actually called "Melita," after the old name of the island of Malta where St. Paul was shipwrecked, and was written for someone who was about to take ship across the Atlantic for the United States. My own text was from that same Paul of Tarsus, and from his Epistle to the Philippians, which I selected for its non-religious yet high moral character:

Finally, brethren, whatsoever things are true, whatsoever things are honest, whatsoever things are just, whatsoever things are pure, whatsoever things are lovely, whatsoever things are of good report; if there be any virtue, and if there be any praise, think on these things.

Try looking that up in a "modern" version of the New Testament (Philippians 4:8) and see what a ration of bland doggerel you get. I shall never understand how the keepers and trustees of the King James Version threw away such a treasure. But that very thought, if you like, is partly taken from my father's legacy of suspicion of change and of resistance to the rude shock of the new.

The Commander had no surviving friends to speak of and in the misty churchyard there were only a few gaunt Hampshire faces with that Hitchens look: the look of the tough south English peasant that one can sometimes also see in Georgia and the Carolinas. These distant kinsmen gave a hasty clasp of the hand and faded back into the chalky landscape. It was all stark enough to have pleased my father at his most downbeat. An absence of fuss could be noted. I suddenly remembered the most contemptuous word I had ever heard the old man utter. Discovering me lying in the bath with a cigarette, a book, and a perilously perched glass (I must have been attempting some adolescent version of the aesthetic), he almost barked: "What is this? Luxury?" That this was another word for sin, drawn from the repertory of antique Calvinism, I immediately understood.

That my mother would have approved—though perhaps languidly preferring a *chaise longue* to a bath—I also knew. So, here you have my two much-opposed and sharply discrepant ancestral stems: two stray branches that only war and chance could ever have caused to become entwined. I ought not to overstate the contradictions: one of the two apparently stern and flinty and martial and continent and pessimistic; the other exotic and beseeching and hopeful and tentative, yet the first one very much less sturdy than it should by rights have been. Even though it has left me with a strong sense of "fight-or-flight" on family occasions, and a real dread of clan occasions such as birthdays and Christmas and other moments of mandatory gaiety, I am grateful enough for the blessed anxiety and unease that it has bequeathed to me.

# Fragments from an Education

Orwell, Connolly, Waugh, Betjeman, to name only a few, have pungently described the disenchantments of schooldays...I do not wish to appear less competent than my contemporaries in making creep the flesh of the epicure of sado-masochistic school reminiscence.

—Anthony Powell: *Infants of the Spring*

...that stoic redskin interlude which our schools intrude between the fast-flowing tears of the child and the man.

—Evelyn Waugh: *Brideshead Revisited*

———◄o►———

I NOW CLAIM STANFORD, California, as a part of my own turf but I was extremely apprehensive and feeling very junior when I first glimpsed the campus in 1987. The impression of first-day-at-school in its grand quads was only enhanced by the effort of my old friend Edward Said, with whom I was visiting the campus for a conference, to encourage me to feel more at home. "Come on," he said, "we'll go and take a cocktail from Ian Watt." I was made additionally nervous by the thought of introduction to this dry, wry, and donnish figure, the world's expert on Joseph Conrad and the author of *The Rise of the Novel*. On greeting, he caused me to feel even more uneasy by drawing attention to the unusual number of Japanese students who could be seen from his windows. "I know it's silly to say so, but it still makes me feel odd sometimes."

Nobody could have been less chauvinistic than Ian Watt but then, he was one of the few survivors of The Bridge On The River Kwai, The Burma Rail-road, Changi Jail in Singapore, and other Hirohito horrors that I still capital-ize in my mind. He admitted later that, detecting other people's reserve after returning home from these wartime nightmares, he had developed a manner of discussing them apotropaically, as it were, so as to defuse them a bit. And he told me the following tale, which I set down with the hope that it captures his memorably laconic tone of voice:

> Well, we were in a cell that was probably built for six but was hold-ing about sixteen of us. There wasn't much food and we hadn't been given any water for quite a while. The heat was absolutely ferocious. Dysentery had begun to take its toll, which was distinctly disagree-able at such close quarters...
>
> Added to this unpleasantness, we could hear one of our number being rather badly beaten by the Japanese guards, with rifle-butts it seemed, in their guardroom down the corridor. At this rather trying moment one of my young subalterns, who'd managed to fall asleep, started screaming and flailing and yelling. He was shouting: "No, no—please don't... Not any more, not again, Oh God please." Hid-eous noises like that. I had to take a snap decision to prevent panic, so I ordered the sergeant to slap him and wake him up. When he came to, he apologized for being a bore but brokenly confessed that he'd dreamed he was back at Tonbridge.

My laughter at this, for all its brilliant timing and understatement, was very slightly awkward. Watt went on to recall an interview with that other old Asia hand E.M. Forster, in which he'd been asked, as an "old boy" of Tonbridge School, whether he would ever agree to write an article for the school magazine. "Only," said the author of *A Passage to India*, "if it could be against compulsory games." The very phrase "compulsory games" had automatic resonance for me, bringing back not merely the memory of freez-ing soccer and rugby pitches, and of the gloating sadists who infested the changing-rooms that were the aftermath of these pointless contests, but also W.H. Auden's suggestive line in one of his greatest poems ["1 September 1939"]:

And helpless governors wake / To resume their compulsory game...

It was indeed Auden—who had been a master at such a school as well as having been a pupil at one—who had said that the experience had given him an instinctive understanding of what it would be like to live under fascism. (He had also said, when told by the headmaster that only "the cream" attended the school: "yes I know what you mean—thick and rich.")

But this is where I must very slightly disappoint you. The three great subjects of Beating, Bullying, and Buggery (the junior or cadet equivalent of Winston Churchill's naval tryptych of "Rum, Sodomy, and the Lash") are familiar enough to me in their way, and I have often been closely questioned—usually by girls—about their influence on my formation. I was subjected to a certain amount and to a certain extent to the first two of the Big Bs but *not* (my italics) to the third. I should perhaps add that I was never big or strong or desperate enough to inflict any of the above procedures on anyone else. In fact, in the annals of British boarding-school trauma, I scarcely count even as walking wounded. This is because, at the very last moment, I was saved from having to go to Tonbridge.

Have you ever walked away from a car smash without a scathe, or had that other experience so well evoked by Winston Churchill: the sheer perfect relief of being shot at by someone who has missed you? I have in fact had both these experiences, but neither approximates to my sense of deliverance from the Tonbridgean. It was once again a matter of my mother versus my father. Neither of them knowing anything about the upper reaches of the education system, it had been decided when I was born to "put my name down" for the only school with which we had contact, run by someone who had once been on the same warship as the Commander. This seemed an efficient rather than a random way of doing things. However, and just before I was due to take the entrance exam at the age of thirteen, my mother bethought herself that it might be worth taking a look at the place where I was due to be conscripted for the next five formative years.

You would not, gentle reader, be scanning these pages had it been otherwise. Tonbridge was a synonym for those Spartan schools where the empire, the church, the cricket field, the war memorial, and the monarchy were, well, sovereign. The blue-eyed boy, small for his age and with rather feminine eyelashes, who is indifferent to sports and happiest in the library is...buggered. Not to say beaten and bullied. All this Yvonne saw, or I suppose I should say she somehow intuited, at a glance.

My poor parents. During my infancy in Scotland I had had to be taken away from one school, with the forbidding name of Inchkeith, when it had been noticed at home that I cowered and flung up a protective arm every time an adult male came near me. Investigation showed the place to be a minor hell of flagellation and "abuse" (such a pathetic euphemism for the real thing) so I was taken away and put in a nearer establishment named Camdean. On my first day there I was hit between the eyes with a piece of slate during an exchange of views with the Catholic school across the road, with whom our hardened Protestant gangs were at odds. Innocent of any interest in this quarrel, I nonetheless bear the faint scar of it, above the bridge of my nose, to this day.

For the next five years, by now removed southward to Devon, where my Fifeshire accent was duly knocked out of me, I underwent an experience that was once commonplace but has now become as remote and obscure in its way as travel by steam train. Indeed, I often have difficulty convincing my graduate students that I really did go off to prep school at the age of eight, from station platforms begrimed with coal dust and echoing to the mounting "whomp, *whomp*, woof, *woof*" of the pistons beginning to turn, as my own "trunk" and "tuck box" were loaded into a "luggage car." Not only that, but that I wore corduroy shorts in all weathers, blazers with a school crest on Sundays, slept in a dormitory with open windows, began every day with a cold bath (followed by the declension of Latin irregular verbs), wolfed lumpy porridge for breakfast, attended compulsory divine service every morning and evening, and kept a diary in which—in a special code—I recorded the number of times when I was left alone with a grown-up man, who was perhaps four times my weight and five times my age, and bent over to be thrashed with a cane.

The strange thing, or so I now think, was the way in which it didn't feel all that strange. The fictions and cartoons of Nigel Molesworth, of Paul Pennyfeather in Waugh's *Decline and Fall*, and numberless other chapters of English literary folklore have somehow made all this mania and ritual appear "normal," even praiseworthy. Did we suspect our schoolmasters—not to mention their weirdly etiolated female companions or "wives," when they had any—of being in any way "odd," not to say queer? We had scarcely the equipment with which to express the idea, and anyway what would this awful thought make of our parents, who were paying—as we were so often reminded—a princely sum for our privileged existences? The word "privilege" was indeed employed without stint. Yes, I think that must have been it. If we had not been certain that we were better off than the oafs and jerks who lived on housing estates and went to state-run day schools, we might have asked more questions about being robbed of all privacy, encouraged to inform on one another, taught how to fawn upon authority and turn upon the vulnerable outsider, and subjected at all times to rules which it was not always possible to understand, let alone to obey.

I think it was that last point which impressed itself upon me most, and which made me shudder with recognition when I read Auden's otherwise overwrought comparison of the English boarding school to a totalitarian regime. The conventional word that is employed to describe tyranny is "systematic." The true essence of a dictatorship is in fact not its regularity but its unpredictability and *caprice*; those who live under it must never be able to relax, must never be quite sure if they have followed the rules correctly or not. (The only rule of thumb was: whatever is not compulsory is forbidden.) Thus, the ruled can always be found to be in the wrong. The ability to run such a "system" is among the greatest pleasures of arbitrary authority, and I count myself lucky, if that's the word, to have worked this out by the time I was ten. Later in life I came up with the term "micro-megalomaniac" to describe those who are content to maintain absolute domination of a small sphere. I know what the germ of the idea was, all right. "Hitchens, take that look off your face!" Near-instant panic. I hadn't realized I was wearing a "look." (Face-crime!) "Hitchens, report yourself at once to the study!" "Report myself for what, sir?" "Don't make it worse for yourself, Hitchens, you know perfectly well." But I didn't. And then: "Hitchens, it's not just that you have let the whole school down. You have let *yourself* down." To myself I was frantically muttering: Now what? It turned out to be some dormitory sex-game from which — though the fools in charge didn't know it — I had in fact been excluded. But a protestation of my innocence would have been, as in any inquisition, an additional proof of guilt.

There were other manifestations, too. There was nowhere to hide. The lavatory doors sometimes had no bolts. One was always subject to invigilation, waking and sleeping. Collective punishment was something I learned about swiftly: "Until the offender confesses in public," a giant voice would intone, "all your 'privileges' will be withdrawn." There were curfews, where we were kept at our desks or in our dormitories under a cloud of threats while officialdom prowled the corridors in search of unspecified crimes and criminals. Again I stress the matter of sheer scale: the teachers were enormous compared to us and this lent a Brobdingnagian aspect to the scene. In seeming contrast, but in fact as reinforcement, there would be long and "jolly" periods where masters and boys would join in scenes of compulsory enthusiasm—usually over the achievements of a sports team—and would celebrate great moments of victory over lesser and smaller schools. I remember years later reading about Stalin that the intimates of his inner circle were always at their most nervous when he was in a "good" mood, and understanding instantly what was meant by that.

And yet it still wasn't fascism, and the men and women who ran this bizarre microcosm were dedicated in their own weird way. The school was on the edge of Dartmoor—the site of the famously grim prison in Waugh's *Decline and Fall*—and haggard, despairing escaped convicts were more than once recaptured after hiding in the sheds on our cricket grounds. Yet the natural beauty of the region was astonishing, and our teachers were on hand all day and at weekends, many of them conveying their enthusiasm for birds and animals and trees. We were all of us compelled to sit through lessons in the sinister fairy tales of Christianity as well, and nature was sometimes enlisted as illustrating god's design, but I can't pretend that I hated singing the hymns or learning the psalms, and I enjoyed being in the choir and was honored when asked to read from the lectern on Sundays. In fact, as you have perhaps guessed, I was getting an early training in the idea that life meant keeping two separate and distinct sets of books. If my parents knew what really went on at the school, I used to think (not being the first little boy to imagine that my main job was that of protecting parental innocence), they would faint from the shock. So I would be staunch and defend them from the knowledge. Meanwhile, and speaking of books, the school possessed its very own library, and several of the masters had private collections of their own, to which one might be admitted (not always without risk to these men's immortal souls) as a great treat.

This often feels as if it happened to somebody else yet I can be sure it did not because I can recall the element of sadomasochism so well. Awareness of this is no doubt innate in all of us, and I suppose a case could be made for teaching it to children as part of "sex education" or the facts of life, but I had to sit in a freezing classroom at first light, at a tender age, and hear my silver-haired Latin teacher Mr. Witherington approach the verge of tears as he digressed from the study of Caesar and Tacitus and told us with an awful catch in his voice of the way in which he had been flogged at Eastbourne School. And that same brutish academy, we thought as we squirmed our tiny rears on the wooden benches, was one of those to which we were supposed to aspire. I think I wish I had not been introduced so early to the connection between obscure sexual excitement and the infliction—or the reception—of pain.

Again come the two sets of books: I would escape to the library and lose myself in the adventure stories of John Buchan and "Sapper" and G.A. Henty and Percy Westerman, and acquaint myself with imperial and military values just as, unknown to me in the England of the late 1950s that lay outside the school's boundary, these were going straight out of style. Meanwhile and on the other side of the ledger, I would tell myself that I wasn't really part of the hierarchy of cruelty, either as bully or victim. I wasn't any use at sports, I didn't have the kind of "keenness" that made one even a junior prefect, but on the other hand I did need to protect myself from being a mere weed and weakling and kick-bag. Sometimes there was a fatso or freak toward whom I could divert the attention of the mob, but I can honestly claim to have become ashamed of this tactic. There came a day when, without exactly realizing it in a fully conscious manner, I understood that words could function as weapons. I don't remember all the offenses and hurts that had been inflicted on me, but I do recollect exactly what I said as I whirled on my playground tormentor, an especially vile boy named Welchman who was a snitch and a stoolpigeon as well as the embodiment of the (not invariably reliable) maxim that all bullies are cowards at heart. "You," I said in fairly level but loud tones through my split lips, "are a liar, a bully, a coward, and a thief." It was amazing to see the way in which this lummox fell back, his face filling with alarm. It was also quite something to see the tide of playground public opinion turn so suddenly against him.

Looking back, it is the masochistic element that impresses me more than the sadistic one. It's relatively easy to see why people want to exert power over others, but what fascinated me was the way in which the victims colluded in the business. Bullies would acquire a personal squad of toadies with impressive speed and ease. The more tyrannical the schoolmaster, the more those who lived in fear of him would rush to placate him and to anticipate his moods. Small boys who were ill-favored, or "out of favor" with authority, would swiftly attract the derision and contempt of the majority as well. I still writhe when I think how little I did to oppose this. My tongue sharpened itself mainly in my own defense.

The Commander by now not being a huge figure in my universe, the substitute father figures of school authority took up correspondingly more space. Years later Alexander Waugh, inspired biographer of his own father and grandfather, showed me Franz Kafka's "Letter to My Father." I didn't find this fascinating document—which old man Kafka never read—reminding me at all of my domestic pater, but I know exactly what came to me when I read Kafka's recollection of

> the many occasions on which I had, according to your clearly expressed opinion, deserved a beating but was let off at the last moment by your grace, I again accumulated only a huge sense of guilt. On every side I was to blame, I was in your debt.

My memory of how *that* felt was as vivid as possible. Gratitude for having been spared, vague guilt at an offense I had not known about or guessed at (thought crime!), strong fear of a repeat offense that I could not predict or avoid, the emotion of relief colliding with the feeling of unworthiness. And fear of the all-powerful boss, too, combined with an awareness of all the blessings and forgiveness which it was in his Almighty power to bestow. One of the most awful reproaches in the school's arsenal of psychological torture—Orwell catches it very well in his essay "Such, Such Were the Joys"—was the one about one's sickly ingratitude: the selfish refusal to shape up after all that had been done on one's behalf. Of course I now recognize this as the working model, drawn from monotheistic religion, where love is compulsory and must be offered to a higher being whom one must necessarily also fear. This moral blackmail is based on a quintessential servility. The fact that the headmaster held the prayerbook and the Bible during the services also drove home to me the obvious fact that religion is an excellent reinforcement of shaky temporal authority.

Hugh Wortham, my huge and dominating headmaster and introducer to the dark arts of corporal punishment, was a lifelong bachelor, but some of the local mothers found him handsome, and Yvonne gaily said that he put her in mind of Rex Harrison. His huge, brawny, furry arms and his immense horseshoes of teeth made him seem almost gorilla-like to me and a bold contrast to the rather slight figure of the Commander. His rages would shake the windows and make small boys turn white: his "good moods" were a hell to endure and a challenge to manipulate. Heaven knows what he'd been through sexually: he himself didn't stoop to "fiddling" with any of us but if you were occasionally favored, as I occasionally was, you would be given a copy of *David Blaize* or one of the *Jeremy* novels and asked if you'd care to read it "in your free time." Though I didn't have the vocabulary for this in those days, I now know quite a lot about E.F. Benson and Hugh Walpole and I sensed even then that this was the world of the smoldering and yearning and repressed adult homosexual, fixated on his own schooldays and probably most attracted to those who are themselves blithely unaware of the intensity of the attention.

There were also some masters, twitchy and sad and at the end of their tethers and the close of their careers, who by the same herd instinct we knew to be fair game. Poor old Mr. Robertson—"Rubberguts," with his decrepit Austin car and his equally decrepit wife Lydia—could not keep order and made the fatal mistake of trying to curry favor with the boys by little acts of kindness and bribery with sweets. He was childless and pathetic and he taught the unmanly subject of geography, and we somehow knew that the real authorities in the school didn't respect him either, so we felt free to make his life a misery. There was more satisfaction to be had in teasing and torturing a feeble member of the Establishment than there was in cornering some hapless and pustular bedwetter of our own cohort. Rubberguts eventually left the school and for all I know died in poverty in some seaside boardinghouse, but before we broke him the poor childless chap swooped on me one day in the changing rooms, caught me under the armpits, held me up and gave me, or to be exact my forehead, the most chaste possible kiss. Then he put me down and silently, sadly mooched away. At first I thought I had a good tale to share with my fellow gloating little beasts, but then I found myself admitting that there had been nothing so creepy about it, merely something melancholy, and I never said a word to a soul. It is strange how the boundary between the knowing and the innocent is subconsciously patrolled: one may be apparently quite "wised up" while being in reality quite naïve, or entirely unaware of the grosser aspects of existence while yet possessing some intuition of what lies on the other side of the adult veil. I couldn't make this encounter seem dirty while there were boys more advanced than myself who could make even the word "clean" sound suggestive. I suspected that they sometimes pretended to know more than they really did.

I was also pretending. But I was bluffing in a different way, about my aptitude in English literature and history. Backward in hormonal development, I could show precocity when it came to longer words and harder books. The best plan here is to bite off more than you can chew. At the age of twelve I had summoned the nerve to borrow from the headmaster, and to read, *War and Peace*. Emboldened by the sheer bulk of the thing, I swerved into Prescott's *History of the Conquest of Mexico*. Of these, I retained for a long time (apart from the fascinating family trees of the Rostovs and the Bolkonskis) the memory of the Battle of Borodino and of the military alliance between the people of Tlascala and the Spaniards against the Aztecs. In other words, I was inhaling these classics essentially as adventure stories. But when I later had to take an examination on *Henry V*, I was able to make a comparison between King Henry the night before Agincourt and Pierre Bezukhov before Borodino, which made me feel that I hadn't just been showing off to myself, or indeed to others. Nonetheless, I was probably insufferable until one very observant master—a man named Eyre who was later sacked after a horrific lapse into pederasty—instilled in me a sense of proportion. "You might try this," he said diffidently, slipping into my hand the first novel of Evelyn Waugh. The headmaster followed up with some P.G. Wodehouse. How can I forget the moment when, in the company of Paul Pennyfeather and Mr. Mulliner, I learned that to be amusing was not to be frivolous and that language—always the language—was the magic key as much to prose as to poetry?

Perhaps two or three times a year I receive a questionnaire from some writers' organization or some writerly magazine, asking me to name my formative books. The temptation to inflate the currency of the past is always present. "It was when perusing the immortal Gustave Flaubert at the tender age of X that my eyes were opened to..." In fact, I suspect that it doesn't very much matter what one reads in the early years, once one has acquired the essential ability to read for pleasure alone. My parents were less quick than my teachers to "get" this point. I had an erratic godmother who on one of her visits decided to make up for all her previous lapses, and actually to provide me with a present. I was accordingly taken by the whole family to a fine bookshop in Plymouth and told to pick any six books that I liked. It didn't take long: I wanted a garish series of the adventures of Billy Bunter. I was sternly told by my seniors that this wouldn't do at all, and provided instead with a very handsome set of Arthur Ransome's uplifting stories about enterprising English children in the great outdoors. In revenge, these remained moldering on my top shelf, never even opened, until I contrived to leave them behind in one of our many family moves. Thus, all unknowing, I passed up the chance of introduction to an author who, as *Manchester Guardian* correspondent in Moscow in 1918, had exposed the "secret treaties" that were behind the First World War, and had had a fling with Trotsky's secretary into the bargain. (It shocked me to discover this later on, as it would most certainly have shocked the relatives who pressed Ransome on me.) My mother was out of sorts for a whole day: "Silly boy," she said. "Aunt Pam was in such a good mood that you could easily have had a nice wrist-watch if you had asked for it."

But I didn't want a bloody wrist-watch. I wanted to be left alone with a pile of books of my own choice. And very gradually, and as it does, omnivorous reading began to become a little more discriminating. I spent a long time wallowing in the pleasures of the "good-bad book," as G.K. Chesterton (later plagiarized by George Orwell) was to term this tempting genre. John Buchan's Richard Hannay romances and colonial yarns, and then Nevil Shute's stories about Australia, Malaya, engineering, and—with his masterpiece *On the Beach*—the foretaste of nuclear anxiety. Dennis Wheatley's melodramas of Satanism and the occult, spiced with a very heavy dash of reactionary politics, gave me a brief interest in numerology and then helped to inoculate me against superstition in general. C.S. Forester's Hornblower stories had a perhaps unintended effect, in that they showed me that a British naval hero could simultaneously be a martyr to doubt and introspection (as well as be aware of the slave trade, which up until then I thought the Royal Navy had aided only in putting down).

On a seemingly parallel track, I was still being educated for an order of things that, without my fully realizing it, was very rapidly passing away. Hearing something about fighting in far-off British-run Malaya I would ask

a boy whose father served there what the Malays were like. "Jolly loyal," was
his reply: even at the time this struck me as cryptically unsatisfactory. The
situation in the Central African Federation sometimes seeped into the news:
when I inquired about Southern Rhodesia, one of the masters instantly said
that the native inhabitants were "only just down from the trees"—the first
but not at all the last time that I was to hear that loathsome expression.
The only mentionable problem with the existing Conservative government
of Harold Macmillan was that it was too liberal and had given in to the wogs
and "Gyppos" (Egyptians) over the Suez Canal. On Guy Fawkes night, that
wondrous evening of roast chestnuts and fireworks and mellow fruitfulness,
the ceremonial pyre was often surmounted by a symbolically unpopular figure of a later vintage than 1605: one year the headmaster decreed that the
immolated carcass be that of Sir David Eccles, then a blamelessly mediocre
minister of education. He had allowed himself to make some remarks that
were critical of the public or rather "private" schools: the essential rampart of
English educational hierarchy. "Hitchens," said the terrifying Mr. Wortham,
"you have a sense of history or so it seems. If our great public schools were
to be swept away, it would be worse even than *the dissolution of the monas-
teries.*" Having at that stage only cropped and grazed on the lower slopes
of Wordsworthian verse, I could not quite visualize the proportions of this
world-historical calamity, but I seemed to see an epoch passing, and the roofs
of great palaces suddenly open to the pitiless sky.

It was, to a lesser degree, a version of the same crisis that I saw my parents
facing. In the grander houses in the villages where we lived, you could still
see signs saying "Tradesmen's Entrance," directing the vulgar to a side door.
We could not aspire to that sort of standing, but it was considered essential by
my mother in particular that the Hitchenses never sink one inch back down
the social incline that we had so arduously ascended. That way led to public
or "council" housing, to the "rough boys" who would hang around outside
cinemas and railway stations, to people who went on strike and thus "held the
country to ransom," and to people who dropped the "H" at the beginnings of
words and used the word "toilet" when they meant to refer to the lavatory.

In Fifeshire we had briefly had a babysitter called Jeannie: a large, ruddy,
motherly proletarian whose husband was a crane-driver in the Navy dock-
yard. She once took my brother to her "council" house for "tea," by which

she meant "dinner" or at least "early supper": a meat-and-potato *fest* rammed home with a mug of hot and sweet brown nectar. Peter was fascinated above all by the way her husband ate with his knife. Ate *off* his knife, that is to say. I swear that my mother went chalk-white when she heard of this. All I ever had to do, if I wished to tease her, was to wield my knife as if it were a fork, or to hold it as if it were a pen, or to mouth the word "toilet." Lesser prohibitions and anxieties—"notepaper" for writing-paper, "mirror" for looking-glass—were not as absolute. "Phone" for telephone was, however, considered distinctly vulgar. My first introduction to the Mitford sisters and their impossible glamour and charm was by way of Nancy's guide to the pitfalls of class and the fashion in which all English people are branded on the tongue, either by their accent or by their vernacular.*

In this unending social battle, in which private education was a necessary but not sufficient condition for victory, the Hitchens chin was barely above the ever-rising floodwaters. At any moment my father might lose his latest job, and we had no capital of any kind on which to fall back. He himself had relatives who—I find I have to confess this—bought a china plaque with the word "toilet" and helpfully screwed it to the outside of their lavatory door. (To the door of the actual room with a bath and washbasin in it, they also affixed a plaque saying "bathroom." Their house was a five-room bungalow where it was hard to get lost. Thank heaven for the Englishman who invented the saving term "loo.") My mother's exquisite pain at this sort of thing was further accented by deep reticence about her own family background. And all this strain was being undergone so that I, the firstborn, could become an English gentleman at precisely the time when the market for such a finished product was undergoing a steep decline.

---

* The durability of this "Upstairs, Downstairs" ethos is remarkable in point of both time and place. I was to become very close to Jessica Mitford, who was almost a sorceress in her ability to use her upper-class skills for American leftist purposes. Told once by a white Southerner at a cocktail party that "it don't seem possible" that school integration could work, she icily replied: "To me it do!" and turned on her heel leaving him wilted like a salted snail. During the McCarthy period, when her fellow Communists became very timorous, she discovered that the Oakland branch was advising its black members, when turning up for a meeting at the home of a well-to-do comrade, to avoid FBI attention by pretending to be house-servants and using the back door. "Well, I mean to say, I sailed right round and told them I thought that was an absolute *stinker*."

Thus I have to be honest and say that the single book that most altered my life was *How Green Was My Valley*. One day I took up a tattered paperback copy of Richard Llewellyn's classic (it was a Pan or Penguin edition, proclaiming it "the best-seller of the war years," which meant that it seemed kosher to me) and then sat as if snared by an enchantment until I had finished it. Then I read it again. In the next few years I inhaled and imbibed it dozens of times and could at any moment have sat for an examination on its major and minor themes. The world and experience of its boy narrator, Huw Morgan, became more real to me than my own. It was an earthquake, a climacteric, a revelation.

I was one of those rural and suburban boys who, like Ruskin when taking the railway across North London, would feel the impulse to pull down the blinds as my train went through scenes of ugliness and misery and desolation in places called Hackney Downs and London Fields. Once, after staying with a school friend on the Mumbles peninsula of South Wales, I had been as distressed as William Blake by my brief glimpse of the hell-mouth scenes of the steelworks and coal-pits around Port Talbot. But now I realized that, just on the other side of the bright Bristol Channel from the lovely moors and uplands of my upbringing, there was a world as remote from my own as the moon, or as Joseph Conrad's Congo.

Several aspects of this hitherto-occluded other Britain lodged in the mind. First of all, its inhabitants worked mostly *under the ground*, like the Morlocks in H.G. Wells. Second, they spoke a non-English language at home and at church, and considered themselves conquered and dispossessed as a nation as well as suppressed as a class. Third, they thought of going on strike as an act of unselfish solidarity and emancipation rather than as "holding the country to ransom." Fourth — though I do not know why I am placing this last on my list — they conceived of education and learning as the avenues to a better life, for their fellows as well as themselves, and not as an expensively bought means of declaring themselves superior to others less fortunate.

This was a jolt to my system and no mistake: indeed it was a severe and seismic shock to all the other systems that had undergirded my own little position. In the annals of "good-bad," then, I would put *How Green Was My Valley* in the same class as *Uncle Tom's Cabin*: a work that leaves an ineradicable "scratch on the mind," to borrow Harold Isaacs's useful phrase. There was another element as well. At a certain point, on some springy-turfed Welsh hillside far above the scenes of alienation and exploitation that lay below, young Huw contrived to part with his irksome virginity. Richard Llewellyn handled this transition with very slightly too much quasi-poetic euphemism, his crucial error being (to my fevered imagining) the idea that the inflamed heat of young manhood could be assuaged only by the relative "coolness" of a feminine interior. One had had a vague hope that the ardency would be appeased by an even greater heat, rather than sizzled like a red-hot horseshoe dipped in water, but at this stage I would have been willing to settle for anything that offered incandescence in either direction.

It interested me very much, later on, to discover that Huw's creator Richard Llewellyn was not at all the fire-eating partisan of the coal miners' struggles that I had taken him to be, but rather a conservative and old-fashioned type who had been setting down a world he had lost. It only goes to show. If you spend a certain amount of every day memorizing the following incantations, the effects may not always be the ones that are intended:

> Teach us, good Lord, to serve thee as thou deservest:
> To give, and not to count the cost,
> To fight, and not to heed the wounds,
> To toil, and not to seek for rest,
> To labor, and to ask for no reward,
> Save that of knowing that we do thy will.

That is from Ignatius Loyola. Or this, from Sir Francis Drake himself:

> O Lord God, when thou hast given thy servants to endeavour any great matter, grant us also to know that it is not the beginning but the continuing of the same, until it be thoroughly finished, which yieldeth the true glory; through Him that for the finishing of thy work laid down his life...

Even when you have learned later about Loyola's fanaticism or Drake's piracy, verses like these have the faculty of recurring to one at apt or critical moments. Years later I read Lionel Trilling on George Orwell's attachment to "traditional" and "martial" values. Trilling guessed that Orwell esteemed these supposedly conservative virtues because he thought they might come in handy later on, as revolutionary ones.

And this is partly why I can't entirely second or echo his own great memoir of prep-school misery. For me, the experience of being sent away at a tender age was, at any cost, finally an emancipating one. I knew I hadn't been dispatched to boarding school to get me out of the way (an assurance that I don't think the young Orwell shared). I knew it was my only eventual meal ticket for a decent university: that undiscovered country to which no Hitchens had yet traveled. I knew that I owed my parents the repayment of a debt. True, I did get pushed around and unfairly punished and introduced too soon to some distressing facts of existence, but I would not have preferred to stay at home or to have been sheltered from these experiences, and it was probably good for me to be deprived of my adoring mother and taught—I can still remember the phrase—that I wasn't by any means "the only pebble on the beach." Why, I once inquired, was the school boxing tournament into which I had been entered against my will called "The Ninety Percent"? "Because, Hitchens, the fight involves only ten percent skill and ninety percent *guts*." This seemed even then like a parody of a Tom Brown story, and I had the socks knocked off me in the ring, but why do I remember it after half a century? The school motto was *Ut Prosim* ("That I May Be Useful"), and when one has joined in the singing of "I Vow to Thee My Country"—especially on 11 November by the war memorial—or "The Day Thou Gavest, Lord, Is Ended" ("To sing is to pray twice," as St. Augustine put it) then one may in fact be very slightly better equipped to face that Japanese jail or Iraqi checkpoint.

I have just looked up the gleaming new website of Mount House, and realized that if I have set all this down in my turn, it is because I was among the last generation to go through the "old school" version of Englishness. The site speaks enthusiastically of the number of girls being educated at the establishment (good grief!), of the availability of vegetarian diets and caterings for other "special needs," and of its sensitivity to various sorts of "learning disability." Now I cannot say I am completely sorry to think that there will be no more "eat that mutton, Hitchens" or "bend over that chair, Hitchens," or "shall we call him Christine, boys, he's so feeble?" but something in me hopes that it hasn't all become positive reinforcement, with high marks constantly awarded for mere self-esteem.

# Cambridge

————◇————

M Y MOTHER HAVING DECIDED that Tonbridge was
out of the question for her sensitive Christopher, some swift work
had to be done to reposition me in the struggle—the whole aim and object
of the five years at Mount House—to make me into a proper public-school
boy. Mr. Wortham proved adept at the string-pulling of the system. It was
quite rapidly decided that I should instead apply to go to The Leys School, in
Cambridge. The atmosphere there was more intellectual and the headmaster,
Alan Barker, was a friend of Mr. Wortham's. Since I was being taken as a
"late" applicant, I would still sit the same exam—the "Common Entrance"
that has been the fate of the English prep-school boy since records were
kept—but would have to achieve a scholarship mark at it. This I was able to
do without much of a strain. For many years I kept the telegram (ah, those
days of the telegram) which was received by my proud parents: "PASSED
FOR LEYS CONGRATULATIONS WORTHAM." This also enabled me
to "score" a bit over my thirteen-year-old playmates. English public schools
have names like Radley and Repton and Charterhouse and Sherborne and
Stowe (not to mention the Eton and Harrow to which we knew we could not
aspire), and it was quite the done thing to debate the relative merits of these
status-conscious destinations. "Hah, Pugh is going to Sedbergh—moldy
old prison." "Oh yes, well *you're* going to Sherborne, which is full of snobs."
When my turn came, I would portentously say: "I'm going to Cambridge."

That shut them up. Cambridge these little bastards had heard of. They just didn't have anything sarcastic to say about it.

I was bluffing, of course, but I still liked the look of things. My new school was in town, and in the ancient town of Cambridge at that, instead of out on some blasted heath where long and muddy cross-country "runs" could be inflicted on you and even the nearest manic-depressive hamlet was many furlongs or versts or miles away. Most English public schools are affiliated with the national absurdity of the Anglican or "Church of England" confession (as if there could be a version of Christianity specifically linked to a group of northerly islands), whereas The Leys was Methodist, which put it in the Dissenting or Nonconformist tradition, founded by that admitted maniac and demagogue John Wesley but still better than the alliance between a state church, the monarchy, the armed forces, and the Tory Party. Many of the teachers and masters were part-time dons at the university. I was, by the age of thirteen, manumitted from provincial and rural life and enforced infancy, and put at last into long trousers, and allowed in sight of the great libraries and quadrangles that had nurtured Chaucer and Milton and Newton (and Cromwell).

For many people, the Oxford-Cambridge dichotomy is an either/or proposition, like Jack Sprat and his wife, or Harvard versus Yale, or Army versus Navy. In days gone by, plebeian Londoners who had been to neither university would get into loud public disputes every year about which "eight" they favored in the annual Oxford-Cambridge Boat Race from Putney to Mortlake: one of the great "who cares?" events of any epoch. For me, the similarities outdistance the distinctions. Both towns show the unoriginality of the English when it comes to names: there used to be a ford for oxen by the Thames and there was once a place where it was possible to bridge the Cam. Both have colleges rather than a university. Both took a long time to recognize the existence of the railway, so that the station is too far from the center. Some say that Cambridge is more austere and Oxford more louche and luxurious, but could even All Souls be more exotic and languid and exclusive than the Apostles' Club or the courts of Kings and Trinity, nursery of such ripe and gorgeous plants as E.M. Forster and John Maynard Keynes, to say nothing of the coterie of Stalinist traitors from Kim Philby to Sir Anthony

Blunt? ("At least Oxford spies for us," as one portly academic once put it to me, "while Cambridge seems to prefer to spy for the other side.")

They used to say that Cambridge was better at "science"; the deceptive word "scientist" as opposed to the superior term "natural philosopher" not having been coined until the 1830s. Very well, it was at least true that Isaac Newton had operated here (his frantic experiments in bogus alchemy more than once igniting his own rooms) and that Charles Darwin had occupied the very same chambers as William Paley, author of *Natural Theology* and supreme bard of the quixotic argument "from design." More intriguing to me and my young contemporaries, restlessly modern as we aspired to be in the early 1960s, was the chance to walk past the Cavendish Laboratories and see where the atom had first been split, or to pass by the Rose and Crown pub, into which Crick and Watson had strolled with exaggerated nonchalance one lunchtime to announce that with the double helix they had uncovered "the secret of existence."

My encounter with all this liberating knowledge and inquisitive atmosphere was very nearly over before it had begun. In my very first term, in October 1962, President Kennedy went to the brink, as the saying invariably goes, over Cuba. I shall never forget where I was standing and what I was doing on the day he nearly killed me. (It was on the touchline, being forced to watch a rugby game, that I overheard some older boys discussing the likelihood of our annihilation.) At the close of the BBC's programming that night, Richard Dimbleby enjoined all parents to please act normally and send their children to school in the morning. This didn't apply to those of us boarders who were already at school. We were left to wonder how the adult world could be ready to gamble itself, and the life of all the subsequent and for that matter preceding generations, on a sordid squabble over a banana republic. I wouldn't have phrased it like that then, but I do remember feeling furious disgust at the idea of being sacrificed in an American quarrel that seemed largely to be of Kennedy's making in the first place.

I have changed my mind on a number of things since, including almost everything having to do with Cuba, but the idea that we should be grateful for having been spared, and should shower our gratitude upon the supposed Galahad of Camelot for his gracious lenience in opting not to commit genocide and suicide, seemed a bit creepy. When Kennedy was shot the following year, I knew myself somewhat apart from this supposedly generational trauma in that I felt no particular sense of loss at the passing of such a high-risk narcissist. If I registered any distinct emotion, it was that of mild relief.

If politics could force its way into my life in such a vicious and chilling manner, I felt, then I had better find out a bit more about it. At Mount House I had enjoyed the "current affairs" class and taken part in a few school debates, forcing myself to speak in public because for a short while I had developed a stutter. Who knows where this originated in my psyche (my mother later told me that I'd also stuttered a bit when my baby brother was born, no doubt in another cynical bid for attention), but it was certainly made worse by teasing and I once made the huge mistake of trying to say the name of my railway destination at term's end—Chichester—in front of a large group. The driveling Chi-Chi-Chi-Chi-*Chichester* noise that resulted was to follow me around for a bit. Anyway, the main position I can remember taking was in opposition to the Tory attempt to ban "colored" immigration from the West Indies.*

Two aspects of The Leys combined to change not just what I thought, but—always much more important—how I thought. The first pressure was negatively charged, so to speak, and the second more positively so. To begin with the negative: I was highly conscious of being very fortunate to be at the school, and of having parents who were willing to sacrifice to get me there and keep me there. It offended me, in an almost aesthetic way, to find that the bulk of my contemporaries took this immense good fortune as no more than their due. Methodism is a trade like any other, and the majority of the boys were the sons of solid Lancashire and Yorkshire businessmen, who thought it entirely natural that they need not attend the sort of school where they might have to consort with the children of their employees. I found myself immensely disliking this mentality, and the accents in which it was expressed.

On the positive side, The Leys was in Cambridge, and if your father

---

* I was to get over my speech impediment and now find that I can speak perfectly contentedly, often or preferably without interruption, for hours at a time. Let this be an inspiration to all those who contend with childhood disabilities.

was a don at the university you could be a "home boarder": in other words come to the school daily and go home at night. This meant that there was a certain leaven in the lump, and many lifelines to the outside world. There were boys with names like Huxley and Keynes, who really were from those distinguished families, and there was the son of a Jewish Nobel Prize winner named Perutz. As the general election of 1964 approached, a number of Labour bumper stickers were to be seen on our teachers' cars. Then there was one of Methodism's many paradoxes, which was its historic identification with the working class. This has been overstated and often distorted — the historian Élie Halévy had a memorable debate with Eric Hobsbawm over whether it was Methodism that had defused revolution among the lower orders in the nineteenth century — but it meant in practice that some of the visiting preachers on Sunday were unpolished ministers from tough working-class parishes, who gave us some idea of how the other half (actually very much more than half) lived. Donald Soper, the best-known Methodist in the country, was an announced socialist with a column in *Tribune*, George Orwell's old weekly. His visit to address us in assembly was a sensation. The country's other leftist weekly, the *New Statesman*, was kept in the library, along with a specially displayed copy of the Fabian Society pamphlet that called for the abolition of the public school system. The great J.G. Ballard, who had had the reverse of the Ian Watt experience in that he'd been interned by the Japanese (*Empire of the Sun*) as a small boy, *before* being sent to the same house in the same boarding school as me, once did jokingly say that the food at The Leys was inferior to the Lunghua camp in Shanghai, but was later to admit that he'd been agreeably surprised by how comparatively little torture there had been.

This duality in the life and mind of The Leys was beautifully captured for me by an incident in my first year. I was cornered in some chilly recreation room by a would-be bully named E.A.M. Smith, a brainless and cruel lad a year or so my senior. This tough and tasty dunce excelled at games and was a member of a highly exclusive Christian crackpot sect named the Glanton Brethren, which in its own disordered mind constituted an elect of god's anointed. "Hitchens is being gassy," he said, using the school's argot for people like me who talked too much. "The cure for being gassy is a bit of a beating." I wasn't completely sure that he couldn't deliver on this threat, and the uncertainty must have shown on my features because suddenly a voice cut in: "Oh, please, don't give a damn about Smith." The moron's grin began to fade and the few who would probably have sided with him lost interest at once.* My rescuer was a tall, thin boy with a certain presence to him. Who was this chap, who could make a muscular thug shrivel? His name, it turned out, was Michael Prest. He was in the next "house" to me but was a home boarder because his father was an economics don at Jesus College. I recognized him without knowing his name because every morning in chapel, when the rest of us bent forward at the call to pray, he remained sitting up and unbowed. There was nothing the prefects and teachers could do about this: the law said we had to be in chapel every day but they couldn't force us to pray on top of that, or even compel us to pretend to do so. I admired this stand without emulating it. Within a few days I had made a new and fast friend and then one morning, as everyone else but Michael crashed lazily forward in their pews, I took a deep breath and held myself upright. It felt very lonely for a moment but soon there was nothing to it. I started bringing books to read during the sermons and the prayers, in order to improve the shining hour. R.H. Tawney on *Religion and the Rise of Capitalism* was, I remember, an early choice.

The lexicographer Wilfred Funk was once invited to say what he thought was the most beautiful word in the English language and nominated "mange." If asked, I would without hesitation give the word "library." The Leys not only had a fine library of its own, but my house—"North B" (the other houses, since shamed by the magnificence of Hogwarts, being unimaginatively named "North A," "East," "West," and "School")—also had its own mini-version. From this hoard I one evening borrowed a life-changing book called *Hanged by the Neck*, a Penguin paperback issued as part of the growing national debate over the death penalty. It had two authors: one was Arthur

---

* In an excellent instance of the "revenge is sour" rule, I was to meet Smith again many years later. It was on the London underground one morning. He was an abject tramp, carrying two heavy bags of rotting old newspapers and declaiming aloud to the unheeding world around him. He chose to sit down just next to me. I pondered for a moment and couldn't resist: "E.A.M. Smith!" I said into his ear. He jumped like a pea on a hot shovel. "How do you know my name?" Cruelly I replied: "We've had our eye on you for some time." His face betrayed the animal fear of the hopeless paranoid, and so I couldn't bear to continue. "It's all right. I just remember you from school. It's Hitchens here." He said dully: "I remember you. You were a sinner. I used to pray for you." That seemed about right.

Koestler and the other C.H. Rolph. The latter was the crime correspondent for the *New Statesman*: the name concealed the identity of Inspector Bill Hewitt of the City of London police, whom I was later to meet. Between them, these two simply demolished the case for capital punishment and gave some hair-raising examples of cold, hideous miscarriages of justice. This had two effects on me: it drew me further into the then-raging argument over the historic British institution of the gallows, which eventually culminated in its abolition in 1967, and it decided me that I would read anything by Arthur Koestler. Before long I was re-reading *Darkness at Noon* for what felt like (and quite possibly was) the third time in a month.

Things were quickening with me, in other words. I was in a sophisticated city with a treasure-house of culture. (One evening I found myself sitting in King's College chapel, listening as Yehudi Menuhin played, just in front of the newly acquired Rubens, *Adoration of the Magi*. I recall thinking that this was almost too rich a mixture for a Navy brat.) The Leys if anything favored sciences over the arts—its old boys tended to be "quietly eminent," as one newspaper article rather devastatingly phrased it—but we could boast of having produced James Hilton ("Mr. Chips" having been based upon a veteran master of the school named W.H. Balgarnie\*) as well as Malcolm Lowry and J.G. Ballard. I became too omnivorous in my reading, trying too hard to master new words and concepts, and to let them fall in conversation or argument, with sometimes alarming results. I gained a reputation among the sporting types (and perhaps, to be fair, not only among them) as a pseudo-intellectual. I recall two diagnoses from this period. The first, from some school counselor with a psychologist's bent, awarded me an "Aladdin's Cave complex." This was flattering in a way, since it suggested that I had an *embarras de choix*. But it also suggested that I was too brittle to decide among so many possible treats. The second, blunter verdict came from my fairly genial if unillusioned housemaster. He informed me, in the course of one of

---

\* This book, like the several movies that bear its name, has become a synonym for old-school-tie values and general mushy sentiment about the dear old days. In fact, Mr. Chipping's lovely wife, Kathie, is a socialist and a feminist who wins all hearts; she forces him to be honest about homosexual play among the boys; he ends up sympathizing with railway strikers, opposing the British Empire in the Boer War and insisting on decent respect for Germans after 1914.

several harangues about my character, that I was in some danger of "ending
up as a pamphleteer." It was one of those moments that one knows instantly
will always be retained in the memory. At last I had a word for it! And a word
that had been applied to Defoe, at that.

By the time that I was fifteen or so, then, I had acquired some preco-
cious knowledge of the Cambridge-related worlds of Bloomsbury and the
Fabians, symbolized by the figure of Bertrand Russell, whose books I was
also smuggling into the chapel. I knew enough to know that my next stop
ought to be Oxford, which furnished the other half of this socio-intellectual
equation. I even had a clear notion that the ideal Oxford college would be
Balliol, and the desired course of study Philosophy, Politics and Economics,
or the famous "PPE." I was doing well enough at "The Lit": the Literary and
Debating Society run by one of the more urbane classics masters. My stutter
almost banished, I even did a little acting and made a small success of the
part of Taplow in Terence Rattigan's classic *The Browning Version*. And I was
beginning to try some writing.

I had "known" for years that this was what I really wanted to do. Indeed,
in my grander moments I would want to claim that I had always "understood" that it was what I had to do. But I had no real concept of writing as a
"living," let alone as a life. At prep school and in the holidays, I had filled little exercise books with chiefly historical efforts, including a soon-abandoned
grand narrative of the Napoleonic Wars. At The Leys there was an annual
thing called the Thomas Essay Prize, with a book-token at the end of it and
a handshake from the headmaster on the school's open "speech day" every
summer, for the doting parents to witness. I entered myself for this prize in
my first year and was runner-up, and I won it in one form or another every
subsequent year. The only set topic that I can now remember (because there
was always a set topic and it was always a worthy and elevated one) was Martin Buber's homely maxim that "True Living Lies in Meeting." (How was I to
know that this pious old hypocrite, the author of *I and Thou*, had after 1948
moved into the Jerusalem house from which the family of my one-day-to-be
friend Edward Said had been evicted?) *Cacoethia scribendi*, says Paul Cavafy
somewhere: "the itch to scribble." If I could be moved to write by the banali-
ties of Buber, I was plainly a bit more than just itchy. The eclectic urge struck
me in every department of scribbling, and I flung myself into verse parodies,

short stories (for some reason very often about animals) and, in one especially regrettable episode which involved brooding, meaning-of-life, moody walks along the river that led from Cambridge to Grantchester, a project for a "libretto" to be co-written with a musically inclined boy named Spratling.

This could all have ended very badly indeed, with wilting affectation and high self-indulgence. But then I discovered something that I have struggled ever since to convey to my own students. In writing and reading, there *is* a gold standard. How will you be able to detect it? You will know it all right. I got full marks for an essay on Chaucer's wonderful "Prologue" to the *Canterbury Tales* (and how fortunate I was to have Colin Wilcockson, one of the world's experts on Langland, as my instructor). I couldn't sleep for two nights after first reading *Crime and Punishment*. Yet never did I breathe the pure serene, as I might fetchingly have tried to say in those days, until my little craft crashed on the reefs of, first, Wilfred Owen and then George Orwell.

It can be good to start with a shipwreck. Your ideal authors ought to pull you from the foundering of your previous existence, not smilingly guide you into a friendly and peaceable harbor. Just as Llewellyn's tale of Huw Morgan had upended my sense of the social scale, so the words of Owen's "Dulce et Decorum Est" went off like a landmine under my concept of history and empire. The moment came in class. It was the turn of a very handsome boy named Sean Watson to read. As he stumbled his bored and boring way through the lines, I was consumed first by a sense of outrage, as if seeing somebody taking an axe to a grand piano. How could anybody be so brutish and insensitive? I wanted to wrench the book from his hands and *declaim* the poem. But then I found that this would not in fact be possible, because my eyes were blinded with stinging tears. To this day, I have difficulty reciting the poem out loud without a catch in my throat.

I became consumed with the subject and got hold of a revisionist history of the First World War, *In Flanders Fields*, by Leon Wolff, as well as *All Quiet on the Western Front* and an anti-war British novel of the trenches called *Covenant with Death*, by John Harris, the neglect of which I would still define as a huge injustice. (Its action follows a group of workers from Sheffield, from the day they enlist as friends to the day their lives are callously thrown away.) I read all the other war poets, from Siegfried Sassoon to Edmund Blunden to Robert Graves. I could feel all the ballast in my hold turning over as I came to view "The Great War" not as an episode of imperishable valor, celebrated every year on 11 November with the jingoistic verse of Rupert Brooke and Lawrence Binyon, but as an imperialist slaughter that had been ended on such bad terms by such stupid statesmen that it necessitated an even more horrible second round in 1939. Even Winston Churchill and the "Finest Hour," in this perspective, seemed open to question, and if there was one thing that was not open to question, to someone brought up in a British military atmosphere in the 1950s, it was Winston Churchill and the "Finest Hour." When allied with my socialist and Fabian readings in other areas, this soon had me thinking of the Spanish Civil War as the only "just" war there had probably ever been. And so I was fairly soon immersed in *Homage to Catalonia*.

I actually couldn't make head or tail of this book in those days because the ideological battles within the Left were still opaque to me. And I had come to Orwell by an unusual path anyway. We were all expected to read *Animal Farm* and *Nineteen Eighty-four*, which had been placed on the syllabus as part of the curriculum of the Cold War. (I took the opportunity to show off, and to compare and contrast *Animal Farm* to *Darkness at Noon*, which I alone in the class had read.) But I had chanced on Orwell's "social" novels first, and had consumed *Keep the Aspidistra Flying* and *A Clergyman's Daughter* as well as *Coming Up for Air*. In these pages, I found some specimens of exactly the lower-middle-class family that was familiar to me from life: the insecure and anxious layer of old England that strove to keep up appearances and, as Orwell put it, had "nothing to lose but their aitches." I understood that Miss Austen and Mr. Dickens and even George Eliot had written with sympathy about folk of the middling sort, but I still hadn't quite appreciated that actual fiction could be written about morose, proud but self-pitying people like us, and was powerfully struck by the manner in which Orwell mimicked and "caught" the tone. If he was reliable on essentials like this, I reasoned, I could trust him on other subjects as well. Soon enough, I was following Orwell to Wigan Pier (James Hilton, creator of "Shangri-La" as well as Mr. Chips, also came, it may interest you to know, from Wigan) and shadowing him in mind on his other expeditions to the lower depths.

Highly derivative in my approach, I began writing grittily polemical and socially conscious essays and fiercely anti-militarist poems. When these were turned down by the school magazine (which was not every time but often enough to inspire bold thoughts of revolt), Michael Prest and I and a few kindred spirits set up a magazine of our own, cautiously and neutrally called *Comment* to avoid too much official attention, and actually learned to operate a manual printing press in the basement of one of the school buildings. Ink-stained pamphleteer! Very heaven!

Cambridge again—both gown and town—came to my aid. I coolly informed my housemaster that I would no longer be donning the uniform of the school's "Combined Cadet Corps," with its "Queen and Country" ethos. He at first opposed this, on the usual grounds that it would "set a precedent," but yielded to my argument that no, it would do no such thing, since none of the other boys in fact wanted to follow suit.* I already knew this because, instead of reporting for rifle-parades, I had to volunteer to do the alternative, which was "social service" in the back streets of the town, and I knew for damn sure that my schoolfellows would want no truck with any of that. I, however, as the budding socialist, positively enjoyed going into the homes of the poor and helping them fill out questionnaires about their needs.

Joining the high-toned United Nations Association and becoming the school's representative on its Cambridge schools' committee was a shrewd move (and an easy one, given that nobody else wanted the job). It meant that I was allowed to go to meetings with reps from other little academies, which in turn meant the chance to meet girls at the famously intellectual Perse School. Here I had the huge luck to encounter Janet Montefiore, a dauntingly brilliant girl who has since emerged as a distinguished professor of literature. She invited me to come and hear Edmund Blunden read his poetry at the Perse and I sat almost numb with emotion, having shaken the hand of someone who had been a contemporary of Wilfred Owen. She did better than that. Her father, Hugh, a Jewish convert to Christianity, was the vicar of Great St. Mary's, the University Church, and ran a famous program for visiting speakers. One night at her invitation—it seemed like a good enough use for a church—I crammed myself into a pew to hear W.H. Auden read from his poetry, and again was spellbound at the thought of seeing a man who had

---

* At about this time I read *Catch-22* and was thrilled when Yossarian, confronted by Major Danby's version of the old official trick-question "Suppose everybody felt that way?" replied "Then I'd certainly be a damned fool to feel any other way, wouldn't I?"

been in Spain at the same time as Orwell. (I didn't know of their bitter quarrel and wouldn't then have understood it.) I use conventional form when I say that Auden "read from" his poems; actually he *recited* them with great aplomb, and I recall hearing from Hugh Montefiore, long after he himself became a bishop, that he was astounded at how much Auden had been able to drink at dinner beforehand, and still perform this great live act. I can also distinctly remember hearing Auden say that he'd reached a stage where his leathery and runnelled face looked like "a wedding cake that's been left out in the rain." (This was before the release of the horror song "MacArthur Park.")

So that was another version of doomed youth and of once-epicene but now-departed beauty. Perhaps now is the moment at which I should make my own confession here. We were taught the poetry of Owen and Auden at school, and allowed to ruminate on the obsession of Owen with wounded and bleeding young soldiers, as well as on the cunning way in which Auden opened "Lay Your Sleeping Head, My Love / Human on My Faithless Arm." The master who introduced this was dexterous enough to point out that the words could easily be rearranged to make it "faithless on my human arm," and ambidextrous enough to instruct us also in the subtleties of Catullus and his "Vivamus mea Lesbia," but I don't think any instructor was sufficiently phlegmatic to break the news that the two great English poets of the preceding two generations had been *quite* so gay. Lytton Strachey once summarized the boarding-school hothouse dilemma very aptly:

> How odd the fate of pretty boys!
> Who, if they dare to taste the joys
> That so enchanted Classic minds,
> Get whipped upon their neat behinds.
> Yet should they fail to construe well
> The lines that of those raptures tell
> It's very odd you must confess—
> Their neat behinds get whipped no less.

There were two ways in which this hottest of all subjects could "come up" in an all-male school featuring communal showers, communal sleeping arrangements, communal lavatories, and the ever-present threat of an official thrashing on the rear. The first was unambiguously physical. Most boys decided quite early on that, since their penises would evidently give them no rest at all, they would repay the favor by giving their penises no respite in return. The night was loud with the boasts and the groans that resulted from this endless, and fairly evenly matched, single combat between chaps and their cocks. To even the dullest lad, furthermore, it would sometimes occur to think that self-abuse was slightly wasted on the self, and might be better relished in mixed company. Some were choosy about the company, and some less so, but I can only remember a very few boys who abstained from (or to put it more cruelly, were so unappetizing as to be left out of) this compensation for the general hellishness of male adolescence. It was quite possible to arrange a vigorous session of mutual relief without a word being spoken, even without eye contact.

It's very important to understand that ninety percent of these enthusiastic participants would have punched you in the throat if you suggested there was anything homosexual (or "queer") about what they were doing. (When I later read Gore Vidal's distinction between homosexual persons and homosexual acts, I saw the point at once.) The unstated excuse was that this was what one did until the so-far unattainable girls became available. And there were related etiquettes to be observed: a senior boy might well have some sort of "pash" on a much junior one, but any action taken by him would be very strongly deplored. (You couldn't actually treat a boy like a girl, in other words.) Yet the very word "pash" somehow gives the game away. In a minority of "cases"—another word for it, often represented by the = sign between two names written up as graffiti—things were infinitely more serious, as well as more ridiculous, because what appeared to be involved was, of all ludicrous things, the emotions. The routines of the day, from stolen glimpses across the chapel in the morning to a longing glance across the quadrangle as the bells tolled for "lights-out," could be utterly consumed by the presence of "him." One such episode came close to ruining my life, or so I thought and believed at the time.

I had one advantage and one disadvantage in this ongoing monastic sex drama, and the problem was that the advantage and the disadvantage were the same. I was a late developer physically, was quite girlish in my prepubescent years and then later, if I do say so myself, not all that bad-looking once boyishness had, so to speak, "kicked in." This meant that I didn't lack for partners when it came to the everyday (well, not *every* day) business of sheer physical relief. But it also meant that I could become the recipient of attention from older males, attention that could sometimes be very sudden and quite frightening. This perhaps made me additionally vulnerable to the fantasy of the "romantic" idyll.

Mr. Chips's feminist-socialist wife had phrased it in a no-nonsense way by saying that official disapproval of public-school homosexuality was the equivalent of condemning a boy for being there in the first place. She was chiefly right about the sheer physical aspect. I knowingly run the risk of absurdity if I offer the spiritual or the transcendent in opposition to this, but actually it was my first exposure to love as well as to sex, and it helped teach me as vividly as anything could have done that religion was cruel and stupid. One was indeed punishable for one's very nature: "Created sick: commanded to be sound." The details aren't very important, but until this moment I have doubted if I would ever be able to set them down. "He" was a sort of strawberry blond, very slightly bow-legged, with a wicked smile that seemed to promise both innocence and experience. He was in another "house." He was my age. He was quite right-wing (which I swiftly decided to forgive) but also a "rebel" in the sense of being a cavalier elitist. His family had some connection with the louche Simon Raven, whose "Fielding Gray" novels of schoolboy infatuation and later versions of decadence furnished, for me at any rate, a sort of cheap-rate anteroom to the grander sequences of Anthony Powell. The marvelous boy was more urbane than I was, and much more knowing, if slightly less academic. His name was Guy, and I still sometimes twitch a little when I run into someone else who's called that—even in America, where in a way it is every boy's name.

Were poems exchanged? Were there white-hot and snatched kisses? Did we sometimes pine for the holidays to end, so that (unlike everybody else) we actually yearned to be back at school? Yes, yes, and yes. Did we sleep together? Well, dear reader, the "straight" answer is no, we didn't. The heated yet chaste embrace was exactly what marked us off from the grim and turgid and randy manipulations in which the common herd—not excluding ourselves in our lower moments with lesser beings—partook. I won't deny that there was some fondling. However, when we were actually caught it must have looked bad, since we had finally managed—no small achievement in a place where any sort of privacy was rendered near-unlawful—to find somewhere to be alone. The senior boy who made the discovery was a thick-necked sportocrat with the unimprovable name of Peter Raper: he had had his own bulging eye on my Guy for some time and this was his revenge.

The usual "thing" would have been public disgrace followed by expulsion. But "things" were made both more cruel and more arbitrary, and also less so. Various of my teachers persuaded the headmaster that I was a good prospect for passing the entrance exam for Oxford: a statistic on which the school annually prided (and sold) itself. The same could be said of Guy, though he didn't eventually make it. Accordingly, having been coldly exposed to public shame, we were allowed to "stay on" but forbidden to speak to each other. At the time, I vaguely but quite worriedly thought that this might have the effect of killing me. Yet there was something so stupid, as well as so intricate, in the official sadism that I managed to surmount most of its effects. (After all, this was a time when not only was all homosexual conduct illegal in the rest of society, but all contact with members of the female sex was punishable by beating within the rules of my school! You could not win. "Perversion," so often invoked from the pulpit and the podium, was the very word that I personally employed for this sick mentality on the part of the authorities.) Of the reaction of my parents I remember almost nothing. The luckless Commander was summoned and we had a whey-faced interview in some "study" or another until I realized that he was *far* more embarrassed than I was. (And this was a man whose regular standby of stoicism was to intone, unvaryingly, "Worse things happen in big ships.") My mother wisely said nothing and wrote nothing. At the end of the term I didn't go home but went rock-climbing in North Wales with a school group where there was considerable free and emotionless sex among the tents and cooking fires. When I finally did get back, not having advertised my arrival time in advance, I was lucky to find my mother alone in the kitchen. She brilliantly rose and greeted me as if I'd been expected for some brittle and glamorous cocktail party of the sort that she always planned and never quite gave.

Looking back on this, I once again have the feeling that it all happened to somebody else. And yet I can be sure it was to me. Hoping to profit by a "lesson" or two, even from the most dismal and sordid moments, I could nominate perhaps more than a couple. The first is that, though I am generally glad not to be gay, I learned early on that most debates on this question are vapid or worse, since what we are discussing is not a form of sex, or not only a form of sex, but a form of love. As such, it must command respect. Then, and from having been the object of homosexual attention and predatory jealousy—this went on happening to me until I was almost out of university—I believe that the whole experience gave me some sympathy for women. I mean by that to say that I know what it's like to be the recipient of unwanted or even coercive approaches, or to be approached surreptitiously under the guise of friendship. (Assaulted once by a truck driver when I was hitchhiking, and quite lucky to have broken away from him unharmed, I can never listen to any excuses about how the victims of such attacks in some way "invite" it.) I always take it for granted that sexual moralizing by public figures is a sign of hypocrisy or worse, and most usually a desire to perform the very act that is most being condemned.*

I understand in retrospect that this was my first introduction to a conflict that dominates all our lives: the endless, irreconcilable conflict between the values of Athens and Jerusalem. On the one hand, very approximately, is the world not of hedonism but of tolerance of the recognition that sex and love have their ironic and perverse dimensions. On the other is the stone-faced demand for continence, sacrifice, and conformity, and the devising of ever-crueler punishments for deviance, all invoked as if this very fanaticism did not give its whole game away. Repression is the problem in the first place. So, even at the cost of some intense momentary pain, I suppose that I might as well have learned this sooner rather than later.**

In the autumn of 1964, Michael Prest and I managed the Labour

---

* From *King Lear*: "Thou rascal beadle, hold thy bloody hand! Why dost thou lash that whore?...Thou hotly lust'st to use her in that kind, for which thou whip'st her." This is why, whenever I hear some bigmouth in Washington or the Christian heartland banging on about the evils of sodomy or whatever, I mentally enter his name in my notebook and contentedly set my watch. Sooner rather than later, he will be discovered down on his weary and well-worn old knees in some dreary motel or latrine, with an expired Visa card, having tried to pay well over the odds to be peed upon by some Apache transvestite.

** It was Guy, now dead for some time but in his later years an amazingly successful seducer of girls, who first insisted that I read the Greek-classical novels of Mary Renault. If this was all he had done for me, I would still be hoarsely grateful to him. While other boys plowed their way across the puerile yet toilsome pages of Narnia, or sank themselves into the costive innards of Middle Earth, I was following the thread of Ariadne and the tracks of Alexander. *The King Must Die; The Bull from the Sea*: Athens has seldom trumped Jerusalem with greater style or *panache*.

campaign in the school's mock version of the general election. No boy at The Leys had any memory of any government except that of the Tories, who had been in power, with four successive prime ministerships, since Sir Winston Churchill's victory in 1951. But the apparent grandeur of this had sunk into the farcical as the Profumo affair, allied to an infinite number of other scandals from missile procurement to rack-renting in London slums, made the term "the Establishment" (then newly coined by my future friend Henry Fairlie) a byword for "stink." Boldly, Michael and I marched into the town and went to Labour HQ. We got hold of some leaflets to distribute and some posters to nail to the school's trees. We invited a local Labour member of the council—his name, I remember, was Alderman Ramsbottom—to come and speak at lunchtime outside the school's cafeteria or "tuck-shop." I was afraid that the snobs and yobs (then synonymous in my mind) would sneer at him for his name, and so they did. But not for long. With great patience he outlined the achievements of previous socialist administrations and then asked the assembled boys if they could think of anything the Tories had done lately that could match the establishment of the National Health Service and the "granting" of independence to India. Satirically I shouted "Suez!"

Of course, on the day itself, the Tories got an easy majority of the school vote, in fact an overall majority, and I saw my own slender total being cut into by an effective and popular and charismatic Communist boy named Bevis Sale. Still, the Tories lost nationally. And I have to set down the fact that the school's own "establishment" was committed to fair play. The local Tory MP, Sir Hamilton Kerr, came to respond to my plebeian Ramsbottom and made himself look a complete weed and drip by comparison. ("Pompous little ponce," I heard my Scots housemaster distinctly say.) An even more grotesque figure named Sir Percy Rugg, who had been at the school and was the Conservative leader on the London city council, came to lunch after chapel one Sunday, and the headmaster's wife made sure that, as opposition spokesboy, I was invited. The headmaster himself, a man somehow aptly named Alan Barker, sat on the Cambridge city council as an independent—being too right-wing for the official Conservatives—and his wife Jean has since become a national treasure in the massive and flesh-pink form of Lady Trumpington.

So I say again that I believe I benefited more from my public school than many boys who took it for granted. There came a day when the plummy-voiced reactionary Barker called me to his headmaster's library and handed me (1) a copy of Lytton Strachey's *Eminent Victorians* and (2) a copy of Karl Marx and Friedrich Engels's *Communist Manifesto*. He went on to instruct me in the elementary mechanics of dialectical materialism. I am sure that his intention was to inoculate me (the term "tremendously wrongheaded" was certainly used) but, just as Arthur Koestler had given so many good lines to his brutish but shrewd interrogator Gletkin in *Darkness at Noon*, so the dialectic in my churning mind took on a life of its own. It was certainly rather broadminded of old Barker to give me a demolition job on high-Victorian reputations that had been written by a notorious old Fabian socialist queen. And with Marx and Engels, I realized that I was reading a superb paean to revolutionary properties and qualities—but to those of capitalism, not just of the working class.

Before long, I was peeling off the compulsory-wear school tie that made us easily identifiable in the streets of the town, and joining undergraduates at lectures in the history faculty. I heard Herbert Butterfield of Peterhouse, a famous Methodist and critic of the Whig interpretation of history, talk on Machiavelli. I went to Walter Ullman's inaugural lecture on theocratic states. It became possible, in a town with many jovially blind-eyed landlords, to join people for drinks and disputation in pubs afterward. While I was little more than a schoolboy, I was more than ready to be that relatively new thing—a "student."

Other noises, coming from just off the tiny stage of school, had begun to reach me, sometimes by transistor radio. At the Poetry Society one evening, a boy named Mainwaring interrupted our sedate discussion to urge forward a new name that I first registered mentally as Bob Dillon. I was fairly soon hooked on what Philip Larkin called Dylan's "cawing, derisive voice," and felt almost personally addressed by the words of "Masters of War" and "Hard Rain," which seemed to encapsulate the way in which I had felt about Cuba. Then there were the loving and less cawing strains of "Mr. Tambourine Man," "She Belongs to Me," and "Baby Blue"...I've since had all kinds of differences with Professor Christopher Ricks, but he is and always has been correct in maintaining that Dylan is one of the essential poets of our time, and it felt right to meet him in the company of Shelley and Milton and Lowell and not in one of the record shops that were then beginning to sprout alongside the town coffee bars.

A more exotic name was also being wafted through the ether and into my head: the name Vietnam. This did not come freighted with fear like the word "Cuba"; it arrived, rather, as a summary and combination of everything one had ever learned, from Goya to Wilfred Owen, about the horrors of war. There was something profoundly, horribly shocking in the odds and the proportions of the thing. To all appearances, it seemed as if a military-industrial super-power was employing a terrifying aerial bombardment of steel and explosives and chemicals to subdue a defiant agrarian society. I had expected the newly elected Labour government to withhold British support for this foul war (and the amazingly coarse and thuggish-looking American president who was prosecuting it), and when this expectation was disappointed I began, along with many, many of my contemporaries, to experience a furious disil-lusionment with "conventional" politics. A bit young to be so cynical and so superior, you may think. My reply is that you should fucking well have been there, and felt it for yourself. Had the study of life and literature and history merely domesticated me to waste and betray my youth, and to gape at a spec-tacle of undisguised atrocity and aggression as if it should be calmly received? I hope never to lose the access to outrage that I felt then. At Easter 1966 my brother and I joined the annual march of Britain's "stage army of the good": the yearly pilgrimage of pacifists and anarchists and rag-tag Reds that tramped from the nuclear weapons factory at Aldermaston to the traditional center of radical protest in Trafalgar Square. I donned the universal symbol of peace and wore in my lapel its broken-cross or imploring-outstretched-arm logo. I also read Bertrand Russell's appeal to forget about the insipid slogan of "peace" and take the side of the fighting Vietcong. I began to take part in the hot arguments that were latent in these two positions. Singing to the Trafalgar Square crowd, along with various folk-moaners like Julie Felix, was the dynamic, sexy Paul Jones of Manfred Mann. Patrolling the fringes of the demonstration were blue-uniformed figures whom I had been brought up to view as friends and protectors. The first real kick he gets from a cop is often a huge moment of truth to a young member of the middle class...

One should not postpone the raising of a curtain. In my own case, the revelation of "curtain up" was more of a sudden vivid peek from the wings but no less memorable for that. I was back at boarding school, and gritting my teeth to do well in my exams so that I might shed the schoolboy carapace and pupate as a full-fledged "student" at Balliol. It must have been the late summer of 1966, and probably toward the end of term, because otherwise the headmaster wouldn't have given permission for our very own home-grown school "pop" group, harmlessly enough named "The Saints," to give a concert on the cricket field. It was one of those warm and still evenings that in ancient Cambridge stay in the memory for a long time. Boys and masters sat or stood as they would have done for a cricket match, the more senior in comfy seats in the pavilion, the others on benches, the rest on the grass. After taking us through a fairly tame Buddy Holly–style repertoire, the respect-able "Saints" switched to a passably potent and twanging version of "House of the Rising Sun." The amplifiers must have been good and, as I said, the night was soft and still. At any rate, the sound must have carried because very suddenly, and very quietly, the cricket ground of our exclusive private school was overrun by a huge crowd of boys (and even girls) from the town. They had heard the strains of rock, even of mild rock, and they knew about Eric Burdon and The Animals, and they also knew by now that there was noth-ing much their parents or the police could do about it, or about them. They crossed a social and geographic boundary that they had never transgressed before, and suddenly found it to be delightfully easy. Nonetheless, they were civil and quiet and curious, which meant that even my most awful contem-poraries were embarrassingly polite and broadminded in return (as well as nervously aware of being surprised and outnumbered). There was even some mild fraternization before the school authorities saw the way things might go and pulled the plugs that had animated the drums and guitars. Then, but too late, the traditional police constables made their appearance.

As one who had already been employing the town against the school for all kinds of private and public purposes, I was still rather slow to see what had just happened to old Britain in front of my very eyes. The first thought I had was derived from my traditional and classical half: surely this was like those other "animals" of the forest who had been shyly drawn to sit, forgetting their own wildness, when Orpheus began to pluck his lute? It was quite some while later that I thought, no, you sentimental fool, what you were seeing, and hearing, was the opening of "The Sixties."

# The Sixties: Revolution in the Revolution (and *Brideshead* Regurgitated)

Contradiction is what keeps sanity in place.

—Gustave Flaubert

—————◄○►—————

I SUPPOSE YOU KNOW," said the most careful and elegant and witty English poet of my generation when I first took his hand and accepted a Bloody Mary financed from his slight but always-open purse, "that you are the second most famous person in Oxford." We were in the unswept front room of the King's Arms, a celebrated but grim pub which allowed one to wear out the intervals of the day between the drably utilitarian Bodleian Library—open to the public and across the road—and the soaringly beautiful Codrington Library, which was for private members only and formed a part of the sort of upper-crust game reserve that was All Souls. The year was 1969 and I had spent a good deal of time failing to study seriously in either library. I also detected, in James Fenton's rather pointed if not indeed barbed hello, a sort of reproach that I should have squandered so much of my studentship and still ended up as only the *second* most notorious person at the university. Time spent on a second-class degree, it was often said, was time wasted even if it was "an upper second." For this to be said of one's degree was perhaps understandable, even forgivable. But of one's thus-far career?*

Of course I knew without asking who had won the laurel as the most famous person. This was Mike Rosen, a tall and rangy and bushy and charismatic Jewish Communist who could draw all eyes and who had already had a theatrical piece performed at the Oxford Playhouse. It was said that this same play (its name was *Backbone*) might have a season at the Royal Court in Sloane Square, which at that date still possessed the *frisson* that attached to *Look Back in Anger* and countless other dramas that had unsettled London's theatergoing bourgeoisie. So everybody knew who Mike Rosen was. The experts in children's literature—that most exacting form of all writing, to which he has contributed whole shelves—still do. But I bridled nonetheless. Rosen was of the Old Left. His family was fatally compromised by Stalinism. During the Oxford Playhouse version of Günter Grass's play *The Plebeians Rehearse the Uprising*, where the actors in a Bertolt Brecht drama become the sudden participants in real events, Rosen had been more or less compelled to go along with the play-within-the-play that satirized the ghastly East German regime and celebrated the workers' revolt against it that had taken place in 1953. At an early age, then, we all got to know Brecht's mordant line about East German Communism: that if the People had indeed let down the Party—as had actually been said in a Communist leaflet distributed on the Stalinallee or Stalin Street—then the Party might have to dissolve the People and elect a new one. I went to the play and was impressed to see Rosen take the part of the Berlin worker who—in a premonition of November 1989—ripped the red flag off the Brandenburg Gate. It was said that Mike's old father had been very distressed to learn of his son betraying the proletariat in this way.

You may ask what kind of Oxford it was in which an ex-Stalinist and a post-Trotskyist vied for the celebrity that had once belonged to Oscar Wilde and Kenneth Tynan, or more fictionally, Zuleika Dobson and Sebastian Flyte, or more realistically, the supposedly serious politicians who had been

---

* "I think you are going finally to displace me as the most hated man in American life. And of course that position is bearable only if one is number one. To be the second most hated man in the picture will probably prove to be a little like working behind a mule for years..."
Norman Mailer to William F. Buckley, 20 April 1965.

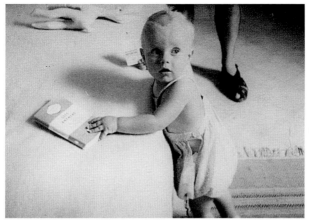

Portrait of the author as a young man. The novel is called *Soft Answers*, and it proved to be second-rate.

With Yvonne.

The Commander.

Yvonne.

King and Country. The Commander *(far right)* welcomes the future King George to the HMS *Ajax*. The woman in the picture was to become the last Empress of India.

Without any previous qualifications, I became a member of the Church of England. Malta, 1949.

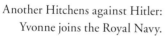

Another Hitchens against Hitler: Yvonne joins the Royal Navy.

Nathan Blumenthal, my
great-great-grandfather.

Sarah Blumenthal.

Nathan and Sarah.

Great-Uncle Harry, posed as
"Young England," 1900.

School general election, 1964. Michael Prest stands guard, while my Communist opponent Bevis Sale dominates the foreground.

Rabble-rousing at Oxford.

Blockading a racist hairdresser, 1968. I am at the back, on the right-hand side. Arrest to follow.

My first television appearance. Balliol's reputation as the college for "effortless superiority" took a long time to recover from this defeat.

With friend and tutor.

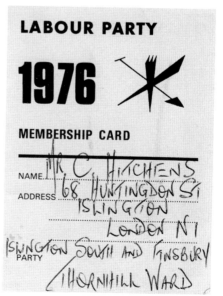

Card carrying.

In Cuba, at a
work camp for
young revolution-
aries, 1968.

Pursuing my studies
at Oxford, 1968.
(© Billett Potter,
Oxford)

On the picket line at a non-
union factory.

at my own college and then gone on to be prime minister, foreign secretary, and all the rest of it. The clue, at least in this decade, lay in a very small distinction. There were people of the Sixties, and then there were the "sixty-eighters" or, if you wanted to be more assertively Marxist and internationalist about it, *les soixante-huitards*. I was one of those who desired to be a bit more assertively Marxist and internationalist about it. After all, to be a mere "Sixties" person, all you needed was to have been born in the right year, and to be available for what I once heard called "the most contemptible solidarity of all: the generational."

Without quite knowing it, I had been rehearsing for 1968 for some time. I attended every demonstration that I could against the war in Vietnam. I joined the Labour Party as soon as I was eligible to do so, and went to branch meetings to agitate against the Labour government's craven support for President Johnson. At that stage I suppose I would have described myself as a Left Social Democrat (or "LSD" in the jargon of the movement). Anyway I know that this was my frame of mind when I went to a meeting at Oxford Town Hall one evening in the winter of 1966.

The main speaker was John Berger, the art critic and novelist who was still, then, a member of the Communist Party. He spoke with some verve about the suffering and the resistance of the Vietnamese. Then we heard from some moon-faced pacifist priest and a Labour local councillor or two, and finally a man who I distinctly remember was called Henderson Brooks. He was evidently a Maoist of some kind and spoke with the sort of sloganized hysteria that I instantly recognized from Orwell's description of the Left Book Club meeting in *Coming Up for Air*. It was fascinating to see that some people still talked like that: Did I dream it or did he actually say "running dogs of capitalism"? Anyway, I was getting better at this sort of thing and in the question period got up and said some satirical things about the Great Helmsman of the Chinese people: a people who were then floundering wretchedly in bankruptcy, famine, and mass murder under the state sponsorship of Mao's "Great Proletarian Cultural Revolution." I don't remember what was said in riposte but as the meeting was breaking up, I was approached by a rather terrier-like man who said he'd admired my remarks and asked me if I'd like to go with him to the pub. If a pint of tepid British beer can be said to have acted as a catalyst, then this encounter changed my life.

My host was named Peter Sedgwick. He was a short, slightly misshapen fellow—I mean by the unkind but indispensable word *misshapen* to convey that his back was slightly hunched—with penetrating blue eyes and thinning wiry curls. He was a specialist in psychiatry. After some general chat he rather diffidently handed me some of the "literature" (the Left always used to speak of its pamphlets and leaflets in this exalted way) of a group called the International Socialists. I promised to take a look, we made an appointment to meet again, and my education in "Left Opposition" Marxism began.

I had been impressed by the essays of Marx to which my headmaster had prophylactically (or so he thought) introduced me. But when applied to the English scene there seemed scant relevance in these texts. Had not the postwar social changes in Britain rendered the idea of "class" somewhat obsolete? Were the trade unions not a self-serving interest bloc? And wasn't the failure of Communism in Russia and Eastern Europe a demonstration in practice of the failure (to put it no higher) of the Communist idea? Only in countries like apartheid South Africa, whose goods I was already boycotting, could anything so dogmatic have a residual appeal. These were among my objections to moving any further to the left than I already had.

From Peter I heard (and read, because he liked to write me letters as well) that by no means was class a dead issue, and that in the workshops and factories of Britain there was a growing shop-floor movement, which sought to democratize the act of labor itself and put an end to the wasteful inequalities of capitalist competition. In contrast, the Labour government was building a corporate state: an alliance between big capital, union bureaucrats, and the government, from which an impermeable hierarchy would emerge. (This had some force in my ear: the car industry was the lifeblood of non-university Oxford, and the Labour government had just spent an immense sum of public money to finance a merger of the two main automobile manufacturers. The tendency of capitalism toward monopoly seemed not to have abated.)

Then, Peter inquired searchingly, what about this same capitalism's tendency to war? Much of the full-employment surge that had followed 1945 and made the Great Depression seem so far away was based on a sort of militarized Keynesianism: an "arms economy" that kept the assembly lines going and the wage-packets full but exposed us all to an unelected and uniformed authority and ultimately to the sheer barbarism that would follow a nuclear "exchange." Still reeling as I was from the Cuban missile moment, and horrified as I had become by the high-tech assault on Vietnam, I was perhaps especially susceptible to persuasion here.

Most important, though, it was from Peter that I acquired a grounding in the alternative history of the twentieth century. Yes, it was true that the Soviet Union and its satellites were a tyrannical empire (in point of fact a "state-capitalist" system, according to the theoreticians of the International Socialists), but did I know what Rosa Luxemburg had written to Lenin, warning him of the tyranny to come, in 1918? Did I know about the epic struggle of Leon Trotsky to mount an international resistance to Stalin? Was I aware that in mutated and isolated forms, that magnificent struggle was still going on? I knew nothing of this, but I became increasingly fascinated to learn of it, and to read more of it.

I was slowly being inducted into a revolution within the revolution, or to a Left that was in and yet not of the "Left" as it was generally understood. This perfectly suited my already-acquired and protective habit of keeping two sets of books.

Thus, by the time that I enrolled as an "undergraduate" at Balliol College, Oxford, I was already a militant "student" member of the International Socialist *groupuscule*, as such factions were to become known after the momentously imminent events in France. That winter of 1967 I doubt that our Oxford branch contained more than a dozen members: perhaps three from the Cowley factories and the rest drawn from the student-teacher-stray-intellectual classes. In a year we had grown to perhaps a hundred, with a "periphery" of many more and an influence well beyond our size. This was because we were the only ones to see 1968 coming: I mean *really* coming.

I can still remember the feelings of mingled exhilaration and vindication that accompanied this. Some premonitory birth pangs had been felt throughout 1967, even as I was learning from Peter Sedgwick how to try and trace the red thread of the anti-Stalinist Left through the bloody labyrinth of the century. In the spring of 1967 had come the atrocious military coup in Greece, making "free-world" NATO complicit in a filthy dictatorship. At about this time it was becoming clear that the American forces in Vietnam had no chance of repressing the southern insurgency and keeping the country partitioned unless they were prepared to redouble their troop presence or else resort to methods of wholesale cruelty and destruction (on which it often seemed that they had decided already). The same was becoming self-evident for another NATO dictatorship: Salazar's bankrupt and odious regime in Portugal, trying in vain to frustrate the forces of liberation in its colonies in southern and western Africa. In Prague, the Czechoslovak Communist Party was morally and intellectually disintegrating, purely because people had been permitted to raise the most elementary questions (about whether they could read Franz Kafka, for example). In a way most stirringly of all, and with that exemplary dignity and courage that truly has passed into history, black America had quietly and simply folded its arms and said "enough" and was prepared to dare and outface any bully who took up the challenge.

There did not seem enough hours in the day, or days in the week, with which to take part in the different movements of solidarity. But I was no longer a boarding-school boy, so I could afford the time. In addition, and rather seductively at that age, one seemed somehow to have become equipped with a special set of spectacles with which to read the newspapers and thereby make unique sense of them. Events in Vietnam and Selma clearly discredited the vaunted "New Frontier" of American pseudo-liberalism, just as the stirrings in Poland and Czechoslovakia demonstrated the historic bankruptcy of Stalinism, while it went without saying that a British Labour government that could not even put down a white settler racist revolt in colonial Rhodesia (we all proudly called it by its true name of Zimbabwe) was showing in practice that Social Democratic reformism had exhausted itself. Soon all humane people would understand the need for a revolution from below, where those who worked and struggled and produced would be the ruling class. Those with eyes to see could detect this with ease, while those whose eyes had yet to be opened could always...well, it was thought that events would also assist in persuading them. I realize that this may sound slightly as if I had joined a cult. There actually was a rival Trotskyist group, later to make itself notorious by recruiting Corin and Vanessa Redgrave, whose depraved "leader" Gerry Healy did in fact teach us all we needed to learn about cultism and the mental and sexual and financial exploitation of the young and the credulous. (I learned a lot about "faith-based" movements from this early instruction.) But the "I.S.," as our group was known, had a relaxed and humorous internal life and also a quizzical and critical attitude to the "Sixties" mindset.

We didn't grow our hair too long, because we wanted to mingle with the workers at the factory gate and on the housing estates. We didn't "do" drugs, which we regarded as a pathetic, weak-minded escapism almost as contemptible as religion (as well as a bad habit which could expose us to a "plant" from the police). Rock and roll and sex were OK. Looking back, I still think we picked the right options. The general atmosphere of intellectual promiscuity and "Third World" romanticism didn't grab us all that hard, either. If there were any two pseudo-intellectuals who really defined moral silliness in that period, they were Herbert Marcuse and R.D. Laing. The first had come up with the lazy concept of "repressive tolerance" to explain how liberalism was just another mask for tyranny, and the second was a would-be shrink who believed schizophrenia to be, rather than a nightmarish yet treatable malady, a social "construct" imposed by the ideology of the family. It so happened that the best critiques of both these frauds (as well as a stringent essay against the marijuana "culture" titled "Flowers of Decay") had been written for the annual *Socialist Register* by my new comrade Peter Sedgwick, who was a qualified expert in mental health as well as in the difference between frantic Frankfurtian illusion and stubborn material reality. So how lucky I was to have been initiated, if that's the word I want, by someone who was a trained and hardened skeptic about the worst of the Left as well as an advocate for the best of it.*

Three major names survive for me from this period (when, so solemnly and suddenly history-conscious, I had not yet ceased to be a teenager). The first is that of Jacek Kurón, who with his colleague Karel Modzelewski had newly written a "socialist manifesto" from within the forbidding walls of a prison in Poland. These two hardy intellectuals had been members of a "Trotskyist" group before being abruptly jailed for their work, and it was one of my jobs to

---

* I can't say that we didn't have to deal with our own cognitive dissonance. The British working class was for the most part entirely unmoved by our exertions. I do remember a demonstration, assiduously prepared for by mass factory-gate leafleting, to which exactly no workers showed up. My theoretician friend David Rosenberg, confronting this daunting result, said to me: "It rather confirms our analysis that the union bureaucrats can no longer truly mobilize their rank and file." True enough as far as it went: but also true that those who bang their heads against history's wall had better be equipped with some kind of a theoretical crash helmet. It was to take me some time to doff my own.

see that their pamphlet got a wide circulation, and that "our" version of anti-Communism was heard as loudly as the commonplace "Cold War" variety. The Polish workers, said this argument, should understand that the Communist Party was their exploiter and not their representative. Did we know that in our tiny way we were assisting at the inception of Polish *Solidarnosc*?

The second name is that of C.L.R. James, one of the moral titans of twentieth-century dissent. In the 1930s he had managed to combine two very attractive positions. He was the main spokesman for the independence of his native Trinidad and the chief cricket correspondent of the *Guardian*. His book on the latter subject, *Beyond a Boundary*, elucidates this recondite sport for the uninitiated and also suggests that in several ways it is not really a "sport" at all, but more of a classical art form that prepares young men for social grace as well as for chivalric heroism. James—whose early short stories, collected as *Minty Alley*, were plainly influential on the early writings of V.S. Naipaul—managed to do without Naipaul's combination of rancor and racial/ethnic resentment. He was an internationalist to his core. His monumental work is *Black Jacobins*, a history of Toussaint L'Ouverture and the slave insurrection in Haiti. This rebellion, taking the slogans of the French Revolution to be universal, ran up against the disagreeable fact that the France of Bonaparte regarded the noble words of 1789 as being, at best, for whites only. James's book—exactly the sort of history that was left out of the school and university syllabus—had a lasting effect on me. So did its author, when I helped arrange a meeting for him at Ruskin College, Oxford, on the fiftieth anniversary of the Russian Revolution. He chose to speak largely about Vietnam, putting it squarely in the context of imperialism and the resistance to it, and his wonderfully sonorous voice was as enthralling to me as his very striking carriage and appearance. He was getting on by then, but the nimbus of white hair only accentuated his hollow-cheeked, almost anthracite face. One had heard of his legendary success with women (all of it gallant and consensual, unlike that of some other masters of the platform) but for me a little crackle of current was provided by the reflection that here stood a man who had, in real time, publicly broken with Stalin and associated with Trotsky, actively taken part in an anti-colonial revolution, and been present (before being hastily deported) in the very early stirrings of the American civil rights movement.

Another important thing about "CLR," as he was known in our little movement, was his disdainful opposition to any Third World fetishism or half-baked *negritude*. He had schooled himself in classical literature and regarded the canon of English as something with which every literate person of any culture should become acquainted. He had a particular love for Thackeray, and it was said that he could recite chapters of *Vanity Fair* by heart. This commitment was important then and was to become much more so as the 1960s fashion turned against "Eurocentrism."*

The third name from the esoteric historical and cultural dimension with which I was becoming so enamored was that of Victor Serge. This Belgian-born proletarian rebel had graduated from embroilment in the politics of Barcelona and harsh experience of the inside of many European jails (episodes which were to help him produce two excellent books in the shape of *Birth of Our Power* and *Men in Prison*) to direct participation in the upheavals of the First World War and the Bolshevik seizure of power. During his work with the Third International he had the opportunity to see the monstrosity of Stalinism in detail, and as it was actually taking shape. It seems possible that he was the first person to use the word "totalitarianism": in any event he was early in apprehending the whole implication of the concept. He had to get out of the Soviet Union in a big hurry, having backed the Left Opposition, and might well have died in the Gulag if it had not been for the intercession of a few of those European intellectuals who had not capitulated to the Red Tsar. His precious papers were all stolen from him by the secret police at the frontier; he was able to republish his poems from memory, and that capacious memory, too, was strong enough to enable him to produce a novel — *The Case of Comrade Tulayev* — which many good judges regard as the earliest and best fictional representation of the show trials and the Great Terror. Ending up in exile in Mexico like some others who had survived what we Luxemburgists and Trotskyists used to call "the midnight of the century" — the dire moment of explicit collusion between Stalin and Hitler — Serge died

---

* I visited CLR on his deathbed in London — on the corner of Shakespeare Avenue and Railton Road — in the late 1980s. He was still quite lucid but hard of hearing. I asked him to inscribe a new edition of *Black Jacobins* and, when he inquired what I'd like him to put on the flyleaf, simply suggested that he use the old Left salutation and put "yours fraternally." He fixed me with a piercing look. "I do not," he said sternly, "believe in eternity." For a moment I was confused and then thought how apt it was that, in mishearing me but repudiating the afterlife, CLR could get fraternity and eternity entangled with one another.

there but not before producing one of the finest autobiographies of that same century: *Memoirs of a Revolutionary*. As it happened, none other than Peter Sedgwick had, when I met him, just edited and introduced a fine edition of this book for Oxford University Press. My headmaster Alan Barker had produced a potted history of the American Civil War, and my English master Colin Wilcockson had edited Langland and *Piers Plowman*, and in my budding-bibliophile way I did possess signed copies of these volumes, but I'd never before had a friend who was in so many ways an actual author and critic, and of the books I've lost in the various moves and mess-ups of my life the one I regret most keenly is the one that Peter Sedgwick gave me. I shall not forget the inscription though. "To Chris," it said, "in friendship and fraternity."

This was my official induction into the comradely manners and addresses of the Left, but it also presented a problem which I didn't particularly like to "raise"—as we invariably said when mounting an objection. The awkward fact was: I simply couldn't bear or stand to be called "Chris."

# Chris or Christopher?

Perhaps I should add that when Christopher Hitchens was still a humble Chris, he and I were comrades in the same far-left political outfit. But he has gone on to higher things, discovering in the process a degree of political maturity as a naturalized citizen of Babylon, whereas I have remained stuck in the same old political groove, a case of arrested development if ever there was one.

— Terry Eagleton, trying to be funny while describing himself accurately in *Reason, Faith and Revolution* [2009]

———◄o►———

THERE WAS A little more to this dislike, of having my name circumcised or otherwise amputated, than may at first appear. "Chris," it seemed to me, was too matey and pseudo-friendly as an abbreviation, even had it gone with another kind of surname. Chris Price, an old comrade of mine and a Labour member of Parliament, almost preferred it. But then his second name began with a "P." Whereas mine began with an "H," and the next thing after "Chris Hitchens" — itself a dreary sound — would be, given this incentive to ditch the aspirate, "Chris 'itchens." All other aesthetic considerations to one side, I knew that this would be more than Yvonne could bear. (What she wanted was to see me represent Balliol on the *University Challenge* team, where I did actually make my first-ever television appearance. I can still remember the name of the captain of St. David's, Lampeter, a theological college in North Wales for heaven's sake, which trounced us in the very first round and demolished the complacent Balliol myth of "effortless superiority." He was called Jim Melican.) My mother had not nurtured her firstborn son in order to hear him addressed as if he were a taxi driver or pothole-filler. And yet, to that son's chosen brothers and sisters of the Labour and socialist movement, it was a part of the warmth and fraternity—part of one's very acceptance—that the informal version be adopted without any further permission or ado. Could I tell Yvonne that so many of my dearest associates were now called names like "Harry" or "Norm"? I couldn't see it softening the blow. She swallowed a bit when someone did call me "Chris" in her presence, and shuddered when I myself used one of the movement's favorite nouns and verbs—the keyword "concern"—with the accent on the first syllable. So help me, I can plead that I hadn't quite known I was doing it.

Oddly enough—as the English say on so many occasions where there is nothing in the least bit odd to relate, as in "I saw old Jorkins the other day, *oddly enough*"—I hadn't ever had to face this problem before. At English boarding schools you are known by your last name, or by your initials if you are very lucky or extremely unlucky. (Yvonne had been vigilant about this too, understanding that one's initials had often to be stenciled on luggage or briefcases, and deploring the thoughtless parents who had baptized their sons with life-threatening initials like "VD" or "BO.") There were always nicknames, but these were mostly infantile, such as "Jumbo" for a fatso. If another boy was addressing you by your actual first name, it often heralded some doomed or farcical romantic proposal. And the time when all my best friends would solve the problem by calling me "Hitch" lay well in the future. Meanwhile, this "Chris/Christopher" business was a torment and, as I say, it symbolized something about the double life that I was trying to lead at Oxford.

I use the words "double life" without any shame. To be sure, I had hoped to re-make myself into a serious person and an ally of the working class and was educating myself with that in view. But I also wanted to see a bit of life and the world and to shed the carapace of a sexually inhibited schoolboy. There was the Oxford of A.D. Lindsay's great anti-Munich and anti-Chamberlain and anti-Hitler election campaign in 1938—Lindsay having been head of my college—and then there was the Oxford of the great steaming and clanging car factories that had been founded by Lord Nuffield (one of the financiers of prewar British fascism). But somewhere there was also the Oxford of Evelyn Waugh and Oscar Wilde and Max Beerbohm and punts and strawberries and enticing young ladies. Occasionally the two aspects overlapped: in the Victorian buildings of the Oxford Union debating society, which I joined on my first day, there were some faded pre-Raphaelite frescoes executed by the aesthete—but the *socialist* aesthete—William Morris. In any case, I was determined as far as I could to have it both ways.

To do otherwise, it seemed, would have been to miss the point of being there. As the head of my college we had Christopher Hill—nobody ever thought of calling *him* "Chris"—who was arguably the most distinguished Marxist historian of his day and certainly the man who had done the most to influence thinking about that English Civil War (or rather, "English Revolution"), which had ended by separating the head of King Charles I from his shoulders in 1649. One could have sherry with this amazing man (who had called his daughter "Fanny" at a time when he thought that eighteenth-century pornography was a rarefied pastime that would never catch up to him) and learn to negotiate his mild, disarming stutter. Or, down the road a bit in Wadham College, there was Sir Maurice Bowra, an inspired classicist around whom the aura of *Brideshead* still clung. (He always had the look, to me, of a near-extinct but still-smoldering volcano: on our first introduction he gave me one of the most frankly appraising "once-over/up-and-down" glances I have ever had. The joke about "Wadham and Gomorrah," apparently, had been his own idea.)

My main tutor was Dr. Steven Lukes, already famous for his study of Emile Durkheim and soon to be more celebrated still for his book *Power: A Radical View.* Thanks to his kind interest in me, I was taken to a private seminar at Nuffield College (yes, named after that fascist-sympathizing automobile tycoon) to talk with Noam Chomsky, who had come to deliver the John Locke lectures. And I was also invited to a small cocktail party to meet Sir Isaiah Berlin.

I hope that by dropping these names I can convey something of the headiness of it. It might have been heady at any time, but in the '68 atmosphere it chanced to coincide with other ferments and intoxications as well. It's trite to say that each generation rebels, and I'd already had the chance to get bored with the late-'50s image of a "rebel without a cause." But it so fell out that we, the so-called boomers or at least the '68 portion of us, were rebels *with* a cause. Thus it happened that one evening in the Oxford Union dining room, when I was still not yet twenty and maybe not even nineteen, I acted as host to Isaiah Berlin, our guest as an invited speaker on the subject of his very first published book, the life and thought of Karl Marx. The sponsor was the Oxford University Labour Club, which had not yet irretrievably split between the Socialists and the Social Democrats, and I had been listed on the club's card as "Secretary: Chris Hitchens (Ball)." This rankled twice: even the name of my ancient college had been pruned and cut back. Still, not much could spoil an evening where one was hosting an eyewitness of the Bolshevik revolution in St. Petersburg: still the only such person I have ever met.

I have to say that the evening was two kinds of shock to me. In the first place, Berlin's urbanity and magnetism were like nothing I had ever met before and vindicated, I remember thinking, the whole point of coming to Oxford in the first place. "Cured me for life, cured me for life," he murmured authoritatively, about the experience of seeing a Communist revolution at first hand. Having had every opportunity to grow weary of undergraduate naïveté and/or enthusiasm, he betrayed no sign of it and managed to answer questions as if they were being put to him for the first time. This I understood as a great gift without being able to define it, just as I who knew nothing of food or wine somehow understood that the dinner we were offering him — a strain on our fiercely straitened socialist budget — was far inferior to the average he could have expected if dining at home or in college, or indeed alone.*

The second shock came when we moved to the seminar room for the talk itself. Though he spoke with his customary plummy authority, and leavened this with a good deal of irony and wit, Berlin clearly didn't know very much about either Marx or Marxism. He woodenly maintained that Marx was a historical "determinist." It's true that the old boy sometimes spoke of "history" itself as an actor, but he actually stressed human agency more than almost any other thinker. It came to me later as quite a confirmation to read, in Berlin's biography, that he had been commissioned to write a

---

* I was later to find that George Orwell, invited by Philip Larkin in 1941 to address a joint meeting of the Labour Club and the English Club, had been given an inedible dinner because Larkin had earlier splurged all the hospitality fund on an ill-advised blowout for Dylan Thomas.

"quickie" book on Marx, and had told the publishers how unqualified he felt to do it. (This was another aspect of his famous insecurity about his own golden reputation: a self-doubt that he could never get his many disciples to take seriously.) But at the time, I was marooned between two almost equally subversive and exciting thoughts. Was it possible that the class of celebrated "experts" were all like this, that there was an academic kingdom of Oz where it was only pretended that the authorities were absolute? Or was I putting on airs and presuming to judge my betters?*

At the somewhat later cocktail party in Beaumont Street, Berlin again lived up to his billing by, first, remembering my name and the circumstances under which we had met, and, second, remembering that I'd said that his talk had made my own Marxism a little more self-confident, and, third, ignoring much more distinguished figures who wanted his company, and telling me quite a long story about Henry James and Winston Churchill. Having told you that much, how can I avoid re-telling it to you? It seems that in the early days of the First World War, both James and Churchill had been invited to a lunch party near one of the Channel ports, James presumably because he lived at Rye and Churchill because he was running the Admiralty. James was all enthusiasm, having applied to become a British citizen and flushed with the zeal of the convert. Churchill, however, had no time for the old man's eager questions about the progress of the war, and rather snubbed him. When the coming statesman had left in his chauffeur-driven car to go back to London, the rest of the company turned to Henry James to see if he could be cheered up after being so crushed. But he brightened on his own account and said: "It is strange with how uneven a hand nature chooses to distribute her richest favors," going on to add "but it rather bucks one up." In that way that was so characteristic of him, Berlin went on to repeat "rather bucks one up" a couple of times.

I had had a *frisson* of another sort when seated in a small Nuffield seminar room with Noam Chomsky. Having attended those John Locke lectures, in which he had galvanized the university by insisting on delivering one of

---

* His very *name* seemed to exude authority: Old Testament conjoined to the brilliant but haunted capital. The only rival in nomenclature I can call to mind is my friend Pascal Bruckner.

the series solely on the question of Vietnam, I knew that he was a highly potent scholar and speaker. (A large number of leftists in those days suddenly discovered a consuming interest in linguistics and the deep structure of "generative grammar.") But up close I realized there was something toneless about him: something indeed almost mechanical, as if he were afraid to show any engagement with the emotions. He wasted, I remember, a huge amount of time on a banal question about the American Maoist sect "Progressive Labor." Through this and other experiences I began to discern one of the elements of an education: get as near to the supposed masters and commanders as you can and see what stuff they are really made of. As I watched famous scholars and professors flounder here and there, I also, in my career as a speaker at the Oxford Union, had a chance to meet senior ministers and parliamentarians "up close" and dine with them before as well as drink with them afterward, and be amazed once again at how ignorant and sometimes plain stupid were the people who claimed to run the country. This was an essential stage of my formation and one for which I am hugely grateful, though I fear it must have made me much more insufferably cocky and sure of myself than I deserved to be. A consciousness of rectitude can be a terrible thing, and in those days I didn't just think that I was right: I thought that "we" (our group of International Socialists in particular) were being damn well *proved* right. If you have never yourself had the experience of feeling that you are yoked to the great steam engine of history, then allow me to inform you that the conviction is a very intoxicating one.

In the early spring of 1968 we saw the valiant guerrillas of the Vietcong carrying their fight to the very doorstep of the American embassy in Saigon. Not long after came the never-to-be-forgotten shots of the Capitol in Washington shrouded in plumes of smoke and flame, as black America refused to sit still for the murder of the gentle Martin Luther King. In Poland, a so-called anti-Zionist purge proved that the Stalinist gerontocrats would stoop even to Hitlerite tactics to repress dissent and prolong their sterile and boring hold on power. The year began to gather pace and acquire a rhythm: in late April (on Hitler's birthday to be precise) Enoch Powell appeared to insult the memory of Dr. King by making a speech warning that "colored" immigration to Britain would eventuate in bloodshed. He succeeded at any rate in igniting a bonfire of rubbishy racism among many elements of the British working class. A few weeks later, the French working class appeared to make a completely different point by joining a revolt against ten years of Gaullism that had originally begun among Parisian students, and by not merely going on strike but occupying the factories that warehoused them for the working day. Many of the Paris '68 slogans struck my cohort as absurd or quixotic or narcissistic ("Take Your Desires For Reality" was one especially silly one), but I shall never forget how the workers at the Berliet factory rearranged the big letters of the company's name to read *"Liberte"* right over the factory gate. Suddenly, it did truly seem possible that the revolutionary tradition of Europe was being revived. How was I to know that I was watching the end of a tradition rather than the resurrection of one?

I kept that transistor radio by my bed and almost every morning I would reach out and turn it on and be forced out of bed by some fresh crisis. Bobby Kennedy slain; the implosion of Lyndon Johnson's "Great Society"; the mass mobilizations of American youth against the draft. When I was eighteen and nineteen and twenty, there was no eighteen-year-old franchise, and the single deadliest and most telling line of Barry McGuire's then-famous song "Eve of Destruction" was "You're old enough to kill, but not for voting."* One was, to a certain degree, compelled to think in generational terms, and in these terms my whole arrival at Balliol, an outcome for which I had worked so hard for so long, had been a disappointment. There were still petty rules and regulations covering one's movements, still a curfew by which time the college gate was locked and all female guests had to be out of one's room, still instructions about what to wear, and still the impression that one's new dons, like one's former teachers, were *in loco parentis* or surrogate parents or guardians. In time, my "generation" was to change a lot of that, too. But we of the International Socialists thought that such alterations were incidental, indeed almost irrelevant, when contrasted to the global struggle of which we quite genuinely believed ourselves to be a part. Let me give an example (I would once have said: "Let me give a *concrete* example").

---

* It's sobering and depressing to reflect that McGuire, who had mainly been influenced by the war in the Middle East the preceding year, is now one of those bards who still likes to sing about the end of days because he is a millennialist and fundamentalist Christian. But by then, I had come to prefer even the hard-line militant verses of Phil Ochs to the more lenient Bob Dylan.

For some time, there had been mounting reports of a rising in Africa against Portuguese colonialism. The senescent dictator António Salazar, a dirty relic from the era of Mussolini and Hitler, held the people of Portugal itself in bondage but also counted among his "possessions" the territories of Angola, Mozambique, and Guinea-Bissau. Angola and Mozambique, if you glance at a map, are like pillars or gates guarding the eastern and western approaches to Zimbabwe (then Rhodesia) and South Africa. Thus it seemed fairly obvious that a victory against Portuguese fascism would also spell the end, in not too much time, of apartheid. Picture then my pride and excitement when it was announced that Dr. Eduardo Mondlane, the founder of the Mozambican movement *FRELIMO* (Front for the Liberation of Mozambique), would be in England and had accepted an invitation from our modest little Labour Club to come and speak. We booked a big hall for him, and a very small room (my own, inside the college, because our resources were exhausted) for a reception. Both events were full, and I shall not forget the immense pride with which I opened my door to this genial and eloquent and brave and modest man. In my lodgings that evening, as I think back on it, the guests (among them Robert Resha, representative in London of Mandela's African National Congress) included the spokesmen for several movements that were later to become governments. After Mondlane's rafter-ringing speech (through which Michael Prest sat by the door determinedly holding a stout and sharp umbrella in case any local fascists tried any rough stuff), we all marched in torchlight procession to lay a wreath for those who had died to free their country. A few weeks later, Dr. Mondlane opened a parcel in his office in Tanzania and was murdered by an explosive charge that had been sent to him by the Portuguese secret police. I have since laid another wreath on his grave in a free Mozambique.

I can't be as proud now as I was then of also hosting Nathan Shamyurira, a spokesman for the black majority in white Rhodesia, for whom we arranged a meeting in the precincts of Rhodes House itself, one of the great imperialist's many endowments to Oxford. He spoke persuasively enough, but the next time I saw him in the flesh he was a minister in Robert Mugabe's unspeakable government. However, and in compensation, I can say that Nelson Mandela, then only at the beginning of his almost three decades of imprisonment, was made an honorary vice president of the Labour Club and had his name put on our membership cards. We wrote to him on Robben Island to inform him of this honor. Decades later when I met him at the British ambassador's house in Washington, I rather absurdly asked him if he had ever received the letter. With that room-warming smile of his, he replied that he had indeed received it, and that he remembered it brightening his day. I didn't really believe this charming pretense, but I did become voiceless for a minute or so.

Just as "Oxford" allowed one to meet near-legendary members of the Establishment's firmament on nearly equal terms, so it enabled encounters with celebrated academic dissidents. One of the achievements of our "year" was to bring the students of Ruskin College, the Labour movement institute for scholarship-minded workers, into the argument. (All right, not to "bring" them but to help them bridge the gap by, for example, demanding that they be made eligible to join the Oxford Union.) At gatherings of the "History Workshop," held on Ruskin's grounds and in nearby alehouses, I heard E.P. Thompson deliver an impromptu lecture on the "Enclosures" of common land in the eighteenth and nineteenth centuries, in which he brought an otherwise unsentimental audience to tears with his recitation of the poems of John Clare. The gentle and humane spirit of the late Raphael Samuel was the animating force in this "higher education": his democratic energy was boundless and his meek, modest appearance always made him a special target for the rough attentions of the police. I can still see him being rudely shoved into a cell where I and others were already penned after a demonstration, his spectacles deliberately broken and his face and hands cut and bruised, for all the world like some luckless Jewish scholar who had been made a plaything by the brown comedians on *Kristallnacht*. Taking his seat on the bare floor and looking myopically and cheerfully about himself, he reconvened the last session of the History Workshop and made us all recollect how even Edward Thompson had left a few things out of the account. Nowadays the very word "Workshop" is an intimation to me of boredom and dogma, and I shall never forget Raphael's honesty when he finally wrote in the 1980s that he didn't really desire to live in a socialist society, but his *Theaters of Memory* is still a potent and eloquent reminder of a braver time, the recollection of which I don't have the right to deny.

All this was very much a part of the "Chris" half of my existence, the

Chris who wore a donkey jacket and got himself beaten up by scabs in a punch-up on the picket line at French and Collett's non-union auto-parts factory. (Fenton swears that I even donned a beret to lead a demonstration: he is quite incapable of an untruth but I am sure I didn't do it more than once.) This was all in a day's work: a day that might include leafleting or selling the *Socialist Worker* outside a car plant in the morning, then spray-painting pro-Vietcong graffiti on the walls, and arguing vehemently with Communists and Social Democrats or rival groups of Trotskyists long into the night. These latter battles were by far the most bitter and strenuous ones, and they often involved disputes that would have seemed ridiculously arcane to the outsider (as to whether the Soviet system was a "deformed" or "degenerated" workers' state, for example, as opposed to our indictment of it as "state capitalist"). However, a training in logic chopping and Talmudic-style micro-exegesis can come in handy in later life, as can a training in speaking with a bullhorn from an upturned milk crate outside a factory, and then later scrambling into a dinner jacket and addressing the Oxford Union debating society under the rules of parliamentary order.

That last example was an instance of the "Christopher" side. It was through the Union, in fact, that I found myself becoming socially involved with an altogether different "set." These were confident young men who owned fast cars, who had "rooms" rather than a room, who wore waistcoats and cravats and drank wine and liqueurs instead of beer. After I'd made some successful sally or other in a Union debate, a group of these closed in on me as the proceedings were ending and more or less challenged me to come and have a cocktail. I couldn't resist: anyway I didn't want to. Here, I thought, might be the *entrée* to that more gorgeous and seductive Oxford of which I'd read so much and (thus far) experienced so little.

Thereby, and perhaps not quite unlike poor, dowdy Charles Ryder in Waugh's masterpiece, I found myself from time to time transported into the world of Christ Church and the Gridiron Club and invited to dine in restaurants which featured tasseled menus and wine lists. This was wholly new to me and potentially very embarrassing, too, since I had virtually no money. (The Commander, when I turned eighteen, had taken me to the bank, opened an account in my name with fifty pounds in it and told me, in effect, that that was my lot.) However, without a word actually being spoken, it was subtly conveyed to me by my new friends that I wasn't expected to reciprocate. I was, instead, expected to sing for my supper. This could have been corrupting, but I justified it to myself by saying that I was learning from, and perhaps even teaching, the enemy camp. In the late Sixties, it wasn't only we who thought there might be a revolution round the corner. Quite a good portion of the Establishment was fairly rattled and apprehensive also, and the Tory press was full of material which — because it tended to exaggerate our influence and numbers — made those of us on the hard Left feel that perhaps we weren't wasting our time. (The university authorities at one time seriously considered paving over the cobblestones in some of Oxford's older streets, lest they be dug up and employed as missiles as had occurred in Paris.)

In case I may seem too opportunistic, let me say that I genuinely came to like some of these gilded and witty reactionaries. One of them, the late David Levy, later quite a celebrated conservative intellectual, was certainly the first protofascist I had ever met, and I would often almost literally pinch myself as he burbled gaily on about Charles Maurras and Action Française, about the beauties of Salazar's Portugal and Franco's Spain, and sang the words of the Mussolini anthem "Giovinezza." "Gaily" might chance to be the apt expression here, because there was a good deal of camp among these young men, and a certain amount of active bisexuality — though I don't think David himself ever even looked at a woman. It makes me blush a bit to say so, but I was still prized for my looks in those days and, from experience at my own much less glamorous boarding school, could read the signs and knew the ropes. Every now and then, even though I was by then fixed on the pursuit of young women, a mild and mildly enjoyable relapse would occur and I suppose that I can "claim" this, if that's the right word, of two young men who later became members of Margaret Thatcher's government.

For this very reason I can't really give any more names, but one oblique consequence was that I got myself invited to meet John Sparrow at All Souls. How to describe "The Warden," as he was universally known? And how to describe his college, a florid antique shop that admitted no students and guarded only the exalted privileges of its "fellows": a den of iniquity to every egalitarian and a place where silver candelabras and goblets adorned a nightly debauch of venison and port. Or so the tales ran. It was in this thick, rich atmosphere that the Munich agreement had partly been hatched: there was a whole book with the simple, damning title *All Souls and Appeasement*. I absolutely could not wait to see the place for myself.

It was by no means a disappointment. Sparrow was hosting a small lunch—"luncheon" might have been more the *mot juste*—and as he took my hand with both of his he summoned a butler named Lane to inquire what I might desire by way of a drink. I had never seen a butler before, and this one had the same name as Algy's manservant in *The Importance of Being Earnest*. I had barely had time to adjust myself when lunch began and I was overwhelmed by the variety and deliciousness of the food and wine, and the splendor of the silver and glass. Sparrow exerted himself to live up to everything one had ever heard about him. He declared that homosexuality ought to be punishable—"gravely punishable," as he put it with purring relish— even though he hoped to remain a member of a sophisticated minority that would be exempt from this very code. Since the law had only recently been changed, I recall myself guessing that there was an element of masochistic nostalgia in this. Sparrow had evidently done some hard thinking about buggery. He had contributed to the last great argument about literary censorship in England, arguing that in a very rugged passage of *Lady Chatterley's Lover* D.H. Lawrence had plainly intended to suggest that the gamekeeper had sodomized his boss's wife. (I must say that I agree with this analysis, though what struck me most about the novel when I last read it was the way in which gruff Nottinghamshire miners say "aks" for "ask," in just the same manner that now marks off the speech of the black American ghetto. Some work here surely for a philologist, but not a project that would have especially amused Sparrow.)

Like Lord Marchmain in *Brideshead*, Sparrow was "everything that the Socialists would have me be." His reactionary style was almost, if not in fact, a self-parody. He had engaged a photographer to walk around Oxford and take discreet photographs, not of the most beautiful and epicene young men, but of the most scrofulous and surly ones. This might have betrayed an interest in "rough trade" and was perhaps not unconnected to it, but when he showed me the resulting album (which contained snatched studies of quite a few of my more disaffected friends), he accompanied my turning of the pages with a reading of Walter Pater on the ephemerality and fragility of youth. I was by then a dinner guest, and even an after-dinner guest over the candles and decanters as they reflected each other in the high polish of the table. One evening I was placed next to that great Cornish queen A.L. Rowse, who had only recently unburdened himself of a new gay theory of the origin and dedication of Shakespeare's *Sonnets* but mainly wanted to tell me what I already knew, that Hitchens was a Cornish name, and positively demanded to be told whether the Mrs. Hitchens who kept sending him such fervent and unwanted love letters was by any chance my mother. He was so lost in conceit that he did not, I remember thinking, completely trust my denial.

For all who try to lead a double life there will eventually be "a small but interesting revenge" as James Fenton later phrased it to me. Mine came when I was addressing a crowd of infuriated students from the steps of the Clarendon Building and denouncing some official infraction of our rights to free sex and free association and free speech. Over the heads of the audience, as I was hitting my peroration, I saw the silvered and saturnine features of "The Warden," who must by then have been the most execrated figure on the Oxford Left. A twitch at the corner of his lip betrayed his design, which I detected almost at the same instant. Making a discreet but determined path through the astonished protestors, he arrived just as I was concluding and said: "My dear Christopher, I am so sorry to have missed most of your speech. I have no doubt it was admirable. But I do hope you haven't forgotten that you promised to look in after dinner tonight." It was a moment of cock-crow. I could have pretended not to understand, but I replied instead that I was looking forward to it and—as he glided away with a sleek air of "game, set, and match" clinging to him—faced the slightly baffled faces of my comrades. I could have taken refuge in some "know your enemy" formulation, but something in me said that this would be ignoble. I didn't want a one-dimensional politicized life.

I sympathized, all the same, with those who were effectively forced to live one. Again to cite James Fenton, who first pointed it out to me, you were compelled to notice something different about the American students. As the rest of us poured out of "hall" after dinner and had a smoke and a drink in the quad, they tended to draw aside and form a huddle, as if hashing over some private matter or specific grief. We all knew what this was. Having been lucky enough to become Rhodes Scholars or in other ways be chosen as

envoys of their country, they found themselves overseas at a time when the
United States was conducting an imperialist war in Indochina and a holding
action against the insistent demands of its own long-oppressed black minority at home. Those things would have been bad enough by themselves, but in
addition it was entirely possible that these young Americans could be compelled to take part in a war they mostly regarded as criminal. Hence those
tight little circles on the lawn as the Oxford dusk came on: Should they defy
the draft and become outlaws, with the choice of prison or exile, or submit
and become obedient and get on with their careers? It's been often said since
that it was only the military draft that stoked anti-war feeling among the relatively privileged American students, and that once the system of conscription was abolished, the feeling of outrage about Vietnam was diminished in
proportion. I was there and I remember clearly, and I feel it a point of honor
to give the lie to this sneer. The young Americans I knew were not afraid of
being killed, or rather, they were very much more afraid that they would be
forced to kill.*

I remember the address—46 Leckford Road—where many of them
shared a house. Frank Aller, for example, a brilliant and conscience-ridden
young man, eventually took his own life because he could not bear the
conflict between his love of his country and his hatred of the war. Another
young man lodging at the same address was Bill Clinton. I don't recollect
him so well though my friend and contemporary Martin Walker, later to
be one of Clinton's best biographers, swears that he remembers us being
in the same room. The occasion was to become a famous one, since it was
the very time when the habitual and professional liar Clinton later claimed
that he "didn't inhale." There's no mystery about this, any more than there
ever was about his later falsifications. He has always been allergic to smoke
and he preferred, like many another marijuana enthusiast, to take his dope
in the form of large handfuls of cookies and brownies. Distributed around
Oxford at the time were many young men—Strobe Talbott, Robert Reich,

---

* I would never have guessed at the time that conscription would be abolished by Richard
Nixon, and still less that he would appoint Milton Friedman and Alan Greenspan to the
Presidential Commission on the subject. The two right-wing libertarians condemned
the draft as "involuntary servitude." Today, almost the only people who call for the return of
the system are collectivists and liberals.

Ira Magaziner—who were later to become members of the Clinton administration. Of these, I remember Magaziner (later the man to ruin American health care on behalf of Hillary Clinton) the best. He had been something of a leader of the anti-war movement at Brown University in Rhode Island. I had written "RING IRA" on a pad by the telephone in a house I was then sharing, and when the police came calling on another matter to do with a public demonstration, they took a lot of persuading that this was not a sinister appointment with Irish Republicanism.

I didn't much like what little I knew of Clinton, and this may have had something to do with my suspicion that he, too, was trying to have things both ways. Someone was informing on the American anti-war students and reporting their activities to Mr. Cord Meyer and the CIA desk at the London embassy in Grosvenor Square (we knew this because the fools once approached the wrong guy as a recruit, and he blew the whistle), and I am not the only person who has sometimes suspected that it was Clinton who was the snitch. On another face-both-ways question, he and I both became peripherally involved (at different times, I hasten to add) with a pair of Leckford Road girls who, principally Sapphic in their interests, would arrange for sessions of group frolic. The men who flattered themselves that they were the desired objective would later discover that they were merely the goats tethered in the clearing, the better to magnetize more women into the trap. I have always thought that to be a deft and sinuous scheme and wish that I had understood its dynamics better at the time. But this is very much like the rest of life, where, as Kierkegaard so shrewdly observes, one is condemned to live it forward and review it backward. If you are going to sleep with Thatcher's future ministers and toy with a future president's lesbian girlfriend, in other words, you will not be able to savor it fully at the time and will have to content yourself with recollecting it in some kind of tranquility.

I tried at the time and have even attempted retrospectively to pretend that I enjoyed Oxford more than I did. For example, my tutor in formal logic was Dr. Anthony Kenny, who was then only beginning to raise the vast architecture of his now-magisterial History of Philosophy. Descending the staircase from his room after a tutorial, I remember thinking that I had finally lodged in my mind the principles of Cartesian reasoning. Kenny had been a Catholic priest in a tough parish in Liverpool before deciding that Thomas

Aquinas's proofs of god's existence were unsatisfactory. He left the ministry and quite some time later got married, at which point the Catholic Church excommunicated him because he had violated his vows as a priest! Many people don't understand that the term "lapsed Catholic" entails the sinister implication that only the Church can decide who leaves it and why, or when. (I had already come across some extreme Communist sects which would insist on expelling anyone who wished to resign.) Anyway, on the evening of my Cartesian tutorial I sat in my room listening to all the bells of Oxford chiming and tolling, and telling myself "Here you are, in a college that has been a great center of learning since the medieval schoolmen. Outside your window is the very place where Bishops Cranmer and Latimer and Ridley were burned at the stake for their principles. You can be the inheritor of all this, and more, and give yourself to the life of the mind." Even as I tried to convince myself, I realized what I have often had to accept since, that if you have to try and persuade yourself of something, you are probably already very much inclined to doubt or distrust it.

Did I really think that my examinations in logic and philosophy didn't matter much, because a revolution was in progress or at least in prospect? I did. Did I ignore my parents and my tutors when they said that my career prospects would suffer unless I applied myself more to my studies? Yes again, and not so much with careless abandon as with the thought that such counterinducements were somehow contemptible. Did I go to a vast demonstration in Grosvenor Square in London, outside the American embassy, which turned into a pitched battle between ourselves and the mounted police, and wonder in advance how many people might actually be *killed* in such a confrontation? Yes I did, and I can still recall the way in which my throat and heart seemed to swell as the police were temporarily driven back, and the advancing allies of the Vietnamese began to sing "We Shall Overcome." I added to my police record for arrests, of all of which I am still reasonably proud. When a charge against me of "incitement to riot" was eventually dropped, I was slightly crestfallen because I had thought it a back-handed tribute to my abilities as an orator. I helped organize a sit-down outside an Oxford hairdressers' shop that refused black female customers. While still on bail for this pending offense, I sat down again on the pitch at a cricket match involving a segregated South African team. In court, I failed to amuse the magistrate when I complained of the brutal behavior of the arresting police officer and gave the number that he had worn on his uniform. "How can you be so sure," snapped the man on the judicial bench, "of that number?" "Merely because, Your *Honor*," I responded sarcastically, "the figures 1389 are the same as the date of the great Peasants' Revolt." The resulting heavy fine reflected the court's view of my impromptu contempt, as well as of my refusal to swear on the Bible when I took my oath. When found guilty, my comrades and I rose to our feet in the dock and sang "The Internationale," fists raised in the approved and defiant manner.

I didn't have the money to pay the fine, but I had been told that there was every chance that John Lennon would shell out for all of us. I later vastly preferred Mick Jagger's "Street Fighting Man," which had been written for my then-friend Tariq Ali, to the Beatles' more conciliatory "You Say You Want a Revolution," but in those days I would also have agreed with one of Lenin's favorite statements (borrowed as I now know from the satirical Juvenal) that *pecunia non olet* or "money has no smell." Anyway I left the court in a hurry because on the following day I was due to board a charter flight that would take me across the Atlantic for the first time in my life and land me in revolutionary Cuba.

# Havana versus Prague

Within the Revolution, everything. Outside the Revolution, nothing.

> —Fidel Castro

Ex ecclesia, nulla salus. [Outside the church, no salvation.]

> —Thomas Aquinas

At the risk of seeming ridiculous, the true revolutionary is moved by true feelings of love.

> —Ernesto "Che" Guevara

Socialism with a human face.

> —Alexander Dubček

———◄○►———

THE EXPEDITION TO CUBA was the toughest exercise in double-accounting that I had so far undertaken. It was only a few months since Guevara had met his pathetic yet stirring demise in the highlands of Bolivia, and the Cuban government had announced that any young leftist who wanted to break the embargo and could get to the island would be a guest in a special camp for "internationalists." This, with its chance to mingle with revolutionaries from all over the globe, was an unmissable invitation. But it was also an opportunity to see whether Cuba's claim to be an alternative "model" to Soviet state–socialism possessed any staying-power. It's difficult to remember today, when Havana itself is run by a wrinkled oligarchy of old Communist gargoyles, but in the 1960s there was a dramatic contrast between the waxworks in the Kremlin and the young, informal, spontaneous, and even somewhat sexy leadership in Havana. Not that we of the International Socialists, who sent our own team of polemicists and dialecticians to the camp, were much impressed by beard-sporting histrionic types, either. It was revolution within the revolution again.

Since I couldn't pay that fine, how had I paid for the flight? Easy. I had just been awarded a Kitchener Scholarship, named for the man whose face adorned the World War One poster admonishing all young Britons to remember that "Your Country Needs YOU!" Available only to the sons of naval and military officers who were obliged to lead low-budget lives at university, this award required an interview with some red-faced old buffers who wanted mainly to reassure themselves about one's general soundness. I had a decent shave and put on a tie and played along. When asked what I did for extracurricular activity, I cited the Oxford Union. "Didn't Her Majesty The Queen," one of the whiskery veterans inquired, "just recently attend a debate there?" This was too good to miss: she had in fact shown up and I had been technically a member of the committee that ran the debate. Modestly, I made the most of this fact and knew in that moment that the scholarship named for the red-coated imperial hero of Khartoum would be mine and would help finance a socialist incendiary. (I think I may also have justified my duplicity by recalling the shameful way in which the Navy had treated my father over his pension. Yes, that's right—they *owe* us. What great self-persuaders we all are.)

At Gatwick Airport I recognized quite a few of the brothers and sisters who turned up to board the scruffy Czechoslovak charter aircraft that was to take us to Havana, and I submitted sullenly to the business of being pulled to one side while plainclothes British policemen rudely grabbed my passport and wrote down all my details in a ledger before letting me proceed. (Who cares? I thought angrily. Their rule won't last much longer.)

"The belly of the beast" was the expression commonly used for the United States in those days, and there seemed something gratifying in the way that our plane made only a brief touchdown in Newfoundland before embarking upon the second leg and setting course for Havana while avoiding the taint of Yanqui airspace. Arrival at the José Martí Airport, with its blinding sunshine and crushing humidity, was an excitement all of its own. We were greeted by smiling and good-looking young comrades who offered a tray of daiquiri rum cocktails: this first impression was as unlike the Berlin Wall version of official Communism as one could wish. But there came at once a slight moment of awkwardness. After handing over my passport, I waited awhile and, having by now heard a couple of rousing speeches of welcome, asked for it back. The hospitable internationalist grin on the face of the Cuban host contracted perhaps a millimeter or so. "We look after it for you." "You do? For how long?" "Until you leave our country." I felt an immediate sense of unease but decided to get over it.

I might perhaps have succeeded in getting over it, were it not for a couple of later developments. The scheme was for our planeload of mainly British internationalists to board the waiting buses that would take us to the *Campamento Cinco de Mayo*, a newly built work-camp in the hilly, verdant province of Pinar del Rio. Here we would join our French, German, Italian, African, and other *compañeros*, and have dialogues with them in the evening while helping to plant much-needed coffee seedlings during the day. In this fashion, we would build links between different insurgencies at the grassroots level while—at the seedling level—helping to rid Cuba of its notorious colonial dependency on the single crop (the infamous "monoculture") of sugar.* What could be more agreeable?

I didn't expect or want luxury at the camp, and I didn't get it. Canvas bunk beds, very early starts, communal showers and meals: these were no sweat and no problem for one who had survived English public school, whereas in contrast to my boarding-school experience the food was excellent and plentiful, and there were females with red scarves in their hair. I didn't especially like the way that uplifting music and hectoring speeches were played all the time on the camp's loudspeaker system, but I was much more alarmed when, deciding on a hike one day to enjoy the surrounding scenery, I began to wave goodbye to the Cuban boys at the gate and was ordered to hold it right there. Where did I think I was going? On a hike. Well, I was told, I couldn't. And why not? Because we say so. Now, I didn't speak much Spanish and I didn't have a

---

* Not unlike the state of Kentucky, which subsists on bourbon, gambling, and tobacco, Cuba's economy rested almost wholly on the manufacture of agreeable toxins like rum and cigars. But even then, its chief export was its own citizens. When I returned to Cuba some years later, there was no trace to be found of the coffee plantation and—in the era of Gorbachev's *perestroika*, which Castro was resisting—about a fifty-fifty chance of getting a cup of actual coffee even in a Havana hotel.

passport (it suddenly came back to me) and I would have had only a vague idea how to negotiate my way to a neighboring village, let alone to Havana. But the guards—as I now thought of them—pointed emphatically back up the trail to the camp. Once you have been told that you can't leave a place, its attractions may be many but its charm will instantly be void. A cat may stay contentedly in one spot for hours at a time, but detain it in that spot by grasping its tail and it will try to tear out its own tail by the roots. I wasn't free to move at all, and the Cubans who wanted to leave Cuba were only free, after a long process, to be expelled from their country of birth and never allowed to return.

Naturally this qualified my attitude to the camp itself but then, I had come with my fellow Trotskyists and Luxemburgists precisely to test the Cuban claim that this was a new revolution, a brave departure from the grim, gray pattern of Soviet socialism. Also, it had to be admitted, Cuba was helping the many rebel forces that were even then fighting so bravely on a Latin American continent that was dominated by cruel and backward military dictatorships. Factional disputes in the camp kept us joyously and passionately awake. Of course we argued about everything from the Paris Commune to the Spanish Civil War, but two critical questions were these: Had Che Guevara been right in proposing that "moral incentives" should replace material ones? And what line should be taken about the increasingly bitter split between the Russian and Czechoslovakian Communist Parties?

On the question of moral incentives and the idea of "the new socialist man," I had nothing but doubts. At the close of his beautiful essay *Literature and Revolution*, Trotsky had spoken lyrically of a future in which "the average man will rise to the stature of an Aristotle, a Goethe or a Marx"; in which his very physique would become "more supple, muscular and harmonious," and had closed by saying that "beyond these hills, new peaks will rise." Myself, I could understand that political and economic conditions could make people very much *worse* (as in the case of Nazism, say) but I had too much English empirical schooling to believe that material circumstances on their own could make people all that much better. And surely, to be a materialist in the first place entailed the acceptance of mankind as a primate species? Karl Marx himself had admired and even hoped to emulate Charles Darwin. Anyway, here was my chance at witnessing a laboratory experiment. Was Cuba producing a more selfless and exemplary human type?

I shan't easily forget the reply I received from a very sweet if slightly slow-spoken Communist Party official. "Yes," he said. "In fact the 'new man' is being evolved in the town of San Andres." As soon as I heard this, I demanded to visit this Utopian commune, as did many of my comrades, but the trip to San Andres was always somehow being postponed while they ironed out the wrinkles in the "new man," and one was forced to wonder why in any case it should only "work" in this particular isolated hamlet. As a consolation prize, perhaps, we were instead invited to see Fidel Castro speak in Santa Clara, at a mass rally on 26 July, anniversary of the beginning of the revolution, in the very city that Che Guevara had personally wrested from the control of the old regime.

Although Guevara's martyred cadaver had been displayed on televisions all around the world, looking more than slightly Christ-like in its defiant and bearded serenity, his actual resting place was—as with the Nazarene, indeed—unknown. (He had in fact been secretly buried by the CIA under the tarmac of a Bolivian airstrip, and after having his hands amputated for fingerprinting purposes, but this grisly detail was not to be uncovered, or the whole reliquary returned to Havana, until the 1990s.) Thus, the yell that "*Che Guevara no ha muerte!*" had a sort of resonance, just as the innumerable images of his living visage possessed an iconic potency. The Cuban leadership declared 1968 to be the "Year of the Heroic Guerrilla" and issued a call to all the schoolchildren in the country that they should live their lives "*Como el Che*" or in the manner of Guevara. It was the impossibility of following this directive that hit me first, even before the realization that the whole thing was borrowed from what Christians called "The Imitation of Christ." So there it was: Cuban socialism was too much like a boarding school in one way and too much like a church in another.

Long lectures from the headmaster were another feature that the two set-ups had in common. (That, and a huge overemphasis on team games and competitive sports of every kind.) I mustn't pretend that it wasn't somewhat thrilling to have a front-row seat and see the young Fidel Castro step up to the microphone and begin to stroke his beard in that way he once had. But after the first couple of hours and the first few standing ovations I felt that I had begun to grasp the main points. And a couple of hours later I was about ready to go and look for a cold beer. This commodity was actually easily come by, and for free, and one cynic suggested to me that that's how so many of the audience had been recruited to the rally in the first place. What hit me even more in my midsection, though, was the astonishing availability of young hookers on the edge of the crowd. One of the claims of the Cuban revolution was to have abolished prostitution and though I had never personally believed this to be feasible (the withering away of the state being one thing but the withering away of the penis quite another), the whore scene in Santa Clara was many times more lurid than anything to be imagined in a "bourgeois" society. The same thing went, by the way, for the regime's much more arrogant and nasty claim to have done away with that other "bourgeois" vice of homosexuality. In such working public lavatories as one could find, the slogan *libertad por los maricons* was frequently chalked or scrawled, to show that the Cuban gays were by no means willing to concur in their own abolition. As the macro address by the Maximum Leader showed signs of drawing to a close, the crowd began to disintegrate into its individual constituents of people hurrying home. The red-scarfed militants near the platform kept up a steady volley of cheers, but the masses were calling it a day. There was a distinct impression that more and better material incentives were what many workers and peasants would appreciate. I won't claim that I saw this all at once, and another part of me was still with the zealous Cubans who wanted to make sacrifices for Vietnam and Angola, and who didn't want a life of ease.

These and other reflections inevitably "raised the question"—as we never tired of putting it—of Czechoslovakia. The Cuban leadership took no decided view on the increasingly public quarrel between Prague and Moscow. The Cuban Communist Party paper *Granma* (later to be described by my Argentine anti-fascist friend Jacobo Timerman as "a degradation of the act of reading") was then printing the communiqués from both Communist capitals. This neutrality was not at all shared by the Cuban in the street, as I was to find out. Perhaps it had something to do with the natural bias in favor of a small country as against a superpower; equally probably, as I was told, it had to do with the arrogant conduct of the many Russian "advisors" in Cuba. Certainly when you have had your European features greeted by little showers of pebbles and dogshit and the taunt "*Sovietico*" from the street urchins of Havana, you have been granted a glimpse or a hint of that very useful thing, an unscripted public opinion. Moreover, the Czech crew of the charter plane that brought me to Cuba had issued an invitation. When we go back, they said, we stop in London to drop you off and we are not allowed to pick up any passengers. In other words, we fly on to Prague with an empty plane. If you care to stay on board, we can show you "Socialism With A Human Face" for no extra charge. I had instantly signed on for this marvelous opportunity. Reporting to the Czechoslovak Airlines office in Havana to reconfirm my ticket, I found that the Czechs and Slovaks of the city had mounted their own demonstration on *La Rampa*, the city's main drag, and had been greeted by enthusiastic applause from average citizens on the sidewalk: another unfakeable test of popular emotion.

Back in the camp, though, it seemed hard to imagine that Party-mindedness would not emerge as the eventual victor. I can remember exactly how I came to realize this. Cuba was famous for its celebration of cinema and its lionization of its revolutionary directors like Tomás Guitiérrez Alea, the great "Titon" (even if his best-known marquee title, *Memories of Underdevelopment*, was perhaps only rivaled in sheer balls-aching tedium of nomenclature by the Czechoslovak masterpiece *Closely Watched Trains*). Almost every night we could sit on a hillside and watch dramatic movies projected onto a huge open-air screen. On one tense and humid evening I watched Pontecorvo's *Battle of Algiers*, completely unaware as were many first-time viewers that the harsh, grainy sequences of street fighting were *not* taken from a documentary, and near-intoxicated (despite my supposedly better ideological training) by the visceral, sordid romance of the urban guerrilla. When it was over I sat around, part-hypnotized by the raw seduction of violence, until they showed it again. (Several of the people I met in the *Campamento Cinco de Mayo* later showed up in the dock in Europe as members of the "Angry Brigade," the "Red Brigade," and kindred nihilist organizations. One of them I had known quite well. I attended his trial at the Old Bailey in the early 1970s and, as an early "Angry Brigade" communiqué was read out by the prosecuting counsel, suddenly realized that it was almost word-for-word what I had heard young Kit actually saying under the palms of Pinar del Rio.)

At all events, to the camp one day, for a seminar on film and revolution, was brought the legendary Cuban director Santiago Alvarez. I had seen some of his stuff and been more impressed by its pace and color than I should have been: I knew perfectly well that the hideous President Johnson had *not* ordered the murders of John Kennedy, Martin Luther King, and Robert Kennedy, but in that frenzied year it was exciting to see a piece of throbbing filmic propaganda called *"LBJ"* (the letters standing for "Luther, Bobby, and Jack" though even the order was weirdly wrong there) which blamed him for all three, and which additionally boasted a piercing soundtrack with the magnificent, defiant wailings of Miriam Makeba, wife of the crazed but charismatic incendiary Stokely Carmichael.

For all this lurid lapse into infantile pre–Oliver Stone leftism, old Alvarez then gave a reasonable-enough talk, and so I put up my hand and asked him a question. How did he find it, as an artist, to be working in Cuba, a state that had official policies on the aesthetic? Alvarez had obviously expected something like this and replied that artistic and intellectual liberty was untrammeled. Were there, I inquired, no exceptions to this? Well, he said, almost laughing at the naïveté of my question, it would not of course be possible or desirable to attempt any attacks or satires on the Leader of the Revolution himself. But otherwise, the freedom of conscience and creativity was absolute.

I do not know if what I next said came from the "Left" or "Right" part of my brain, but I like to think I anticipated at least some of the huge cultural and literary defection that later cost Castro the allegiance of writers as diverse as Carlos Franqui, Heberto Padilla, Jorge Edwards, and many others. I made the mere observation that if the most salient figure in the state and society was immune from critical comment, then all the rest was detail. Ah, please never forget how useful the obvious can be. And how right it is that the image of the undraped emperor is such a keystone of our folklore. I don't think I have ever been so richly rewarded merely for saying the self-evident. There was quite an "atmosphere" until after Alvarez—whose reply, if any, I don't remember—had left, and then this "atmosphere" persisted while I took my metal tray and lined up in the dining hall. When I pretended to ask what was up, one of the Scottish comrades informed me: "The Cuban brothers thought what you said and did was so obviously counter-revolutionary." I was both annoyed and delighted by this obloquy. I certainly considered myself a revolutionary and would warmly have contested the right of anybody to deny me the title, but there was also the sheer pleasure of seeing cliché in action: almost as if one had been called an "enemy of the people," or a "capitalist hyena" or—back to school again—someone who had "let the whole side down." You do not forget, even if you come from a free and humorous society, the first time that you are with unsmiling seriousness called a "counter-revolutionary" to your face.

It cannot have been many mornings later when I was shaken awake and told "Get up, and get up NOW! The Russians have invaded Czechoslovakia." The person who was doing the shaking had bet me a trifling sum that this outcome would not occur, so it was nice of her to bring me the news of her own loss. I had already felt, in the course of the *annus mirabilis* of 1968, the sensation of being somehow involved in a historical moment or conjuncture, but at that instant in Cuba I think I could have been forgiven the self-dramatization. For one thing, and merely because of the time zone, the terrible news from Eastern Europe came to us quite early in the morning. And as I have said, the Castro leadership had as yet taken no public position on what was still an inter-Communist quarrel. It was announced that Fidel would speak that night and give the "line." I was quite sure that I knew what he was going to say (and indeed was frivolous enough to make a few more wagers on the side) but meanwhile one was in the almost unique position of being in a Communist state where for a whole day there was no official position on the most important item of international news.

I was in Havana itself by then, because it was almost time to catch the charter plane home or, in my case, to Prague. The Red Army's first action had been to seize and immobilize the main airports of Czechoslovakia, so our plane hadn't even been able to leave its base. I remember going to the campus of Havana University, where there were a surprising number of students willing to denounce the Russian action without looking over their shoulders or lowering their voices. All dissent had to be couched in Communist terms, so you heard it said that "Che" would never have supported such big-power bullying. (This I then half-believed but now doubt.) The Chinese leadership in Beijing had lost no time in denouncing "Soviet social-imperialism," and there was a demonstration outside the Chinese embassy in support of this position, with people wearing little badges of Mao. I was told by somebody that if you went to call on the Chinese, they would ply you with cocktails and cigarettes while they explained their position, so I posed as an internationalist visitor and found the story to be true...the exquisite cigarettes, I remember, had the name "Double Happiness." The politics weren't so sublime: a tiny diplomatic bureaucrat explained that China had been the first to call for Russian intervention in Hungary to stop counter-revolution in 1956, so had every right to denounce the latest move as "counter-revolutionary" in turn. The logic of this didn't seem exactly beautiful. And there was that unsettling term again...

At lunchtime came the news that Ho Chi Minh and the Vietnamese Communists had supported the Russians. This was enough to sway quite a number of Cubans... then dusk began to draw in and the population mustered around the TV sets. I forget now where I watched the lengthy tirade in which Fidel Castro ended all Utopian babble about Cuba following a different course from the sclerotic Stalinists in the Kremlin, but I think it was in the same pink-façaded Hotel Nacional where Graham Greene's sadistic Captain Segura once received a cold blast of soda-water in the face and shouted "*Cono!*" before he could stop himself. As the speech of the bearded one wore on, the faces of some of my comrades began to take on a startled and upset cold-shower look as well. And by the end of it, as the routine standing ovation of the Central Committee was being shown, the argument in our ranks was already under way.

Apart from those few who stubbornly thought that Castro had done and said the right thing by taking the Brezhnev line, the main division was between those who thought he had acted under duress and those who felt he was expressing his real ideological kinship. I thought it could well be both: it was obvious that Cuban Communism depended upon Soviet oil and weapons to survive but even had this not been so, Castro in his speech had been frigidly unsympathetic to the desire of the Czechoslovaks to live a life that was more open to the market economy, more attuned to the culture of the United States, and more adapted to the open societies of Western Europe.

Once more making the stern attempt to be dialectical about this, I think I concluded without actually admitting it to myself that Castroism might still have a point in Latin America and the Caribbean, where monstrously reactionary dictatorships like those of Brazil and Nicaragua and Haiti were still undergirded by cynical American power. However, in more advanced Europe the impulses of a revolutionary Left could and should be used to erode the Berlin Wall from both sides. There were a number of brave Trotskyists among the Czech resistance, after all, led by the heroic Peter Uhl... Anyway, I do not completely hate myself for attempting this book balancing. And I can say with some pride that our small International Socialist contingent in Havana managed to receive a rolled-up tube of a special edition of *Socialist Worker* from London by way of the mail, and that this edition was headed in big bold black capitals: "**Russians Get Out of Czechoslovakia!**" To have handed this out in Cuba during a world crisis was for me a matter of socialist honor and gave me an irrepressible sense of participating in a genuinely historic moment. It seemed so clear that the ossified, torpid Communist systems and parties had committed a kind of political and moral suicide by their *Panzerkommunismus* (Ernst Fischer's acid phrase) conduct in Prague. Yet this seemed to offer a chance that in France, in Poland and Czechoslovakia, and in the yet-to-be-liberated territories of the "Third World," the brave *soixante-huitards* were clearing the way for a "real" and authentic Left to emerge at last.

The long-delayed Czech charter flight almost failed to clear the palm trees at the fringe of Havana Airport—something to do with a wrong guess about the weight of the luggage—but the expressions of the crew conveyed a generally listless attitude. They were returning to a country where the state-decreed slogan was that of postinvasion "normalization" (one of the most casually ugly phrases of the whole twentieth century). Once again we had a stopover in Canada and on the TV screens saw the Chicago police beating puddles of blood out of the demonstrators who were willing to pit themselves against a filthy war, a racist Democratic Party machine, and a fixed convention. Damn it, I remember thinking. I have missed Prague and now I am missing Chicago.

"Tourist of the Revolution" was a phrase that was later used to ridicule those who went in search of socialist fatherlands, but I truly did not think of myself as a tourist. I simply and exhaustingly and fervently wished I could be in many places at once, so as to lean the uttermost of my slight weight onto the fulcrum. It was years later that I read Thomas Paine saying that to have played a part in two revolutions was "to have lived to some purpose." This was the sort of eloquence that I wish I could have commanded at the time.

However, I was still somewhat imprisoned within the jargon of Left sectarianism. By the time our plane had landed in London, with the Czechs continuing morosely homeward and I myself being subjected to yet another police scrutiny of my passport and my person, the new post-Chicago headline of *Socialist Worker* read like this: "East and West: Tanks and Cops Defend 'Freedom.'" To a point, I approved this moral equivalence. It was at any rate better than those who only moaned painlessly about Prague (which the West had not defended) or those who were only moved to protest about Vietnam. The verbal crudeness of the headline's phrasing bothered me less than it should have done. After all, as our plane had neared London, we had been told that one of our number might possibly be detained and even deported upon arrival. He was a South African exile. Nothing more needed to be said: we all knew that we would form a cluster around him, pile our luggage into the shape of a barricade, raise our fists and utter the most obvious chants of resistance until we could be sure that a proper left-wing lawyer had arrived. The risk of our own detention or blacklisting would have been nothing more than the payment of a duty. Had you then accused me of being "sloganistic" in my politics, I would have considered it no great insult.

As 1968 began to ebb into 1969, however, and as "anticlimax" began to become a real word in my lexicon, another term began to obtrude itself. People began to intone the words "The Personal Is Political." At the instant I first heard this deadly expression, I knew as one does from the utterance of any sinister bullshit that it was—cliché is arguably forgivable here—very bad news. From now on, it would be enough to be a member of a sex or gender, or epidermal subdivision, or even erotic "preference," to qualify as a revolutionary. In order to begin a speech or to ask a question from the floor, all that would be necessary by way of preface would be the words: "Speaking as a..." Then could follow any self-loving description. I will have to say this much for the old "hard" Left: we earned our claim to speak and intervene by right of experience and sacrifice and work. It would never have done for any of us to stand up and say that our sex or sexuality or pigmentation or disability were qualifications in themselves. There are many ways of dating the moment when the Left lost or—I would prefer to say—discarded its moral advantage, but this was the first time that I was to see the sellout conducted so cheaply.

Back in Oxford I ran into "The Warden" in the High Street. He was very much his usual self, bustling and brimming and half-deferential, half-ironic. "My dear Christopher, just the man I wanted to tell. We have a new fellow coming to the college: a new recruit as you would probably say, but a hero, an absolute hero. Bit of a Marxist I'm afraid but it can't be helped. You must meet him." This was my introduction to Leszek Kolakowski, who was then not much known outside his native Poland. He had been one of the "reform Communist" intellectuals of the "Polish spring" of 1956, a moment that had inaugurated a period of relative openness under the Gomulka regime. The reactionary and anti-Jewish crackdown of 1968, presaged by the arrest and imprisonment of Kurón and Modzelewski, had put all this into reverse. Kolakowski had, like so many of the intellectual leadership of Eastern Europe, been partly deported and partly self-exiled. He had at first gone to teach philosophy at the University of California at Berkeley—a campus whose name was near-sacred to those of us who felt we were breathing the pure air of the Sixties—but had evidently tired of this already and was willing to come to All Souls.*

Kolakowski had missed his "formal" education because of the Nazi occupation of his country but had more than made up for it by the hungry ingestion of books during the wartime underground years, during which time he had also become a consecrated Communist. When we eventually met, I was first of all and perhaps rather foolishly impressed by how exactly he looked his part. Victor Laszlo in *Casablanca* simply seems too sleek and well-fed to have been a survivor of Nazi penal institutions (I still shudder when I think how nearly Ronald Reagan came to being cast as Rick in that movie) but Leszek had the ideally gaunt, austere appearance of the dissident who has known what it is to suffer material as well as intellectual deprivation.** His voice and manner, also, were appropriately ironic and sardonic. And he had, in effect, seen all the way through Communism. In my boyish way I thought I had done the same. But—and I cannot tell you how much this argument used to matter—I would not concede that Leninism and Stalinism were the same thing, or that the second logically followed from the first. After much wrestling and juggling, Kolakowski had simply given up on the whole idea of "reform" Communism, or was at any rate in the throes of doing so. I did not believe that Stalin's system could be reformed, but I was quite convinced that

---

* While at Berkeley he had been handed a pamphlet that spoke of the contents of the university's library system as so much "useless white knowledge": this had somewhat put him off the New Left in its then–Bay Area form, where I assure you it can still be met with.

** I was later to find that as a youth he had contracted tuberculosis of the bones.

it could and would only be overturned by, and from, the Left. Kolakowski was quite patient with me. At the time—and how embarrassing I now find it to say this—I thought that it was I who was being quite indulgent to him.

The Polish ambassador to London, a doltish *apparatchik* named Marian Dobrosielski, was invited to Oxford to give a talk. With the help of some Polish leftist friends to act as translators for the Polish press on file at St. Anthony's College, I managed to draft and print a leaflet, in Polish and English, telling the Stalinist envoy that he was not welcome. I asked Kolakowski if he'd come to the event and help to swell our protest. He declined, saying rather drily that there was little point in such commonplace encounters. We went ahead anyway, and gave Ambassador Dobrosielski quite a bad time, and just as the evening was breaking up I saw a bony and quizzical visage peering from a dark corner at the very back of the hall. Leszek had not, after all, been able to resist showing up. At the time, I thought that this was a small triumph for Trotskyism over "mere" anti-Communism. In fact, Kolakowski was just beginning to erect the edifice of his astonishing trilogy *Main Currents of Marxism*. I was fabulously lucky in having met him so early, but much too callow and overconfident to take full advantage of the chance I'd been given. Still, for almost the next two decades of my life I carried on an argument with him, and others like him, about the nature of Communism. Yes, the germ of Stalinism had been in Leninism to begin with. But had there not been other germs as well? And what historical conditions led to the dominance of which germs? I suppose I still hope to show that not everything about this debate was a complete waste of time.

The remainder of my golden Oxford years slid by in this way and, though I was oppressed at the time by a sense of waste—what my fellow Balliolman Anthony Powell had called "the crushing melancholy of the undergraduate condition"*—I do not believe that they were entirely squandered, either. Let us say one quarter of the time allotted to political confrontations and dramas, another devoted to reading books on any subject except the ones I was supposed to be studying, another quarter on seeking out intellectual heavyweights who commanded artillery superior to my own, with the residual twenty-five percent being consumed by the polymorphous perverse.

---

* *Books Do Furnish a Room*, 1971.

It could have been worse. I made a minor discovery which has been useful to me since in the analysis of some larger public figures like my contemporary Bill Clinton: if you can give a decent speech in public or cut any kind of figure on the podium, then you need never dine or sleep alone. I was actually a bit more confident on the platform than I was in the sack, and I can remember losing my virginity—a bit later than most of my peers, I suspect—with a girl who, inviting me to tea at one of the then-segregated female colleges, allowed me to notice that her walls were covered with photographs taken of me by an unseen cameraman who'd followed my public career. Since apparently I could do no wrong with this young lady...

There came also a day when the undergraduate weekly *Cherwell* asked me if I would like to help write the "John Evelyn" gossip column. This was a prestige spot, disapproved of by some of my grimmer and less hedonistic comrades, but a perfect finesse of that problem offered itself at once. I was to be co-author of the column with Patrick Cockburn, whose father, Claud, a Red veteran of the Spanish Civil War, had been one of the great guerrilla journalists of all time. Had been? In the London offices of the great satirical magazine *Private Eye*, he still was a figure of immense authority. His oldest son, Alexander, had left Oxford to become one of the editors of the *New Left Review*, and his middle son, Andrew, an arrestingly handsome boy with a look reminiscent of the young T.S. Eliot, was another of my contemporaries. Anybody who knows anything about the later history of radical journalism will recognize these names, as they will that of the great documentary maker Christo Hird, who became the third member of our "John Evelyn" team and helped us transform it from a mere chronicle of idle and gilded youth into something more mordant and investigative and Swiftian (or so *we* liked to think). Once again, that lure of printers' ink and the word "pamphleteer."

I had better confess, before quitting this, to a "having it both ways" moment that gave me even at the time a twinge of remorse. When Richard Nixon and Henry Kissinger circumvented Congress and the Constitution and the strategic majority of Nixon's own cabinet in 1970 in order to conduct the invasion of Cambodia, I had already been invited to debate with the then–Foreign Secretary Michael Stewart at the Oxford Union on the morality of the war in Indochina. The obscene images of the conflict as they were extended to yet another country were so enraging that I banished all thoughts of scruple. I accepted the formal invitation to take part in the debate, and to attend the dinner beforehand with the foreign secretary. Meanwhile, I intrigued with friends to make sure that there was a large claque of hard-core protestors stationed in the main hall and in the gallery. I made my speech from the dispatch box in the approved manner—it wasn't one of my best but it made a fairly fierce and detailed case against the imperial incursion—and then loudly insulted the government's guest of honor, deserted the other guests, and went to sit with, and shout with, the mob. At a given signal when Stewart rose to speak, a phalanx also rose and simply and repetitively yelled the one word "murderer" in his face. It was horribly gratifying to see the way in which such a leading member of Her Majesty's Government turned so pale under the assault. At another signal, a noose was uncurled from the gallery and fell dangling within inches of the wretched foreign secretary's head. (It was dropped by James Long, later to be a distinguished economics editor at the BBC.) Nobody had ever attempted to abort a debate in these precincts before, and so the pitifully weak staff of the building was at a loss. We could have done almost anything we wanted, including at least roughing up if not lynching the foreign secretary. A sudden consciousness of exactly this ability—both intoxicating and nauseating—is probably what stalled us. We contented ourselves with further deafening insults and marched away. The official Minute Book of our little parliament still records that: "For the first time in the 147 years of the Society's existence, the House voted to stand adjourned *sine die* on account of riot."

The publicity was astounding. An editorial in the *Times* opined that our movement of protest was "one of the nastiest political phenomena that Britain has experienced in this century," which I thought—when one considered only a few of the other "phenomena"—was plainly absurd. We had, in our own opinion, not "silenced" Mr. Stewart, whose views were well known and could easily be broadcast, so much as we had voiced the outrage that should properly be felt at the destruction of Cambodian society. I remember arguing with dexterous casuistry that we had compelled the Establishment press to take notice and had thus, in a way, actually succeeded in *enlarging* the area of free speech. A nice try, I hope you will admit. But however one phrased the case, the only reason for mentioning free speech in the first place was that, however one looked at it, we had in fact shut down a public debate by force.

I had a huge quarrel about it with Jack Straw, then the head of the National Union of Students and a strong opponent of the Vietnam War, who insisted that the right of free expression trumped all other considerations. (It was years before we agreed on anything again, and by that time he was himself the foreign secretary—for Tony Blair—and arguing at the United Nations for the removal of the intolerable Saddam Hussein tyranny from Iraq.)

I remember how we arrived at a higher synthesis: a final justification of our breach of the rules of civility, debate, and hospitality. After all, we had—did we not?—a higher cause and nobler purpose. It was even possible, given the huge media fuss generated by our action, that the people of Indochina would get to hear of it and, as a result, take additional heart from the knowledge of our solidarity. As I write this, I realize that I then truly did believe it. After a mighty demonstration outside the American embassy in Grosvenor Square, Michael Rosen had written a haunting poem, published in the university's literary magazine *Isis*, that hymned a then-famous poster of a Vietnamese woman in a paddy field, with a gun slung over her shoulder. Please let it be, the poem had urged, that some of the news and pictures of our revolt will reach you and put a smile on your face. Next to this imperative, we felt, all lesser reservations were merely pallid and insipid. So, quite hardened as I was to insisting on this point against those who were more tentative, why was it that I could not quite repress the sense of having done something shabby? "I have something to expiate," as D.H. Lawrence put it in his poem "Snake." "A pettiness."

# The Fenton Factor

The friends thou hast, and their adoption tried,
Grapple them to thy soul with hoops of steel.

—*Hamlet*: Act I, Scene iii

————◄○►————

O F COURSE I knew about Fenton, too, when I took that first
cocktail off him in the public bar of the King's Arms. He had already
demonstrated extreme precocity in winning the Newdigate poetry prize for
a sonnet sequence titled *Our Western Furniture*, about Commodore Perry's
historic "opening" of the closed island society of Japan. It had a beauty and
ominousness to it which I shall try to catch by this brief extract:

> I saw the salmon flash, caught in the net.
> It was the only light. It flicked the spray!
> An energy to spawn and procreate!
> The sudden poet's cry—its silver grey
> Dagger-blade flash—a protest yet:
> "I saw the ships in Nagasaki Bay."

On the cover of the first published version was a paragraph from Commodore Perry's report to Congress in 1856 (just one year before India rose in
rebellion against the East India Company). "It seems to me," opined the
gallant Commodore:

that the people of America will, in some form or another, extend their dominion and their power, until they shall have placed the Saxon race upon the eastern shores of Asia. I think too that eastward and southward will her great rival in future aggrandizement (Russia) stretch forth her power to the coasts of China and Siam and thus the Saxon and the Cossack will meet...Will it be in friendship? I fear not! The antagonistic exponents of freedom and absolutism must thus meet at last and then will be fought the mighty battle on which the world will look with breathless interest; for on its issue the freedom or the slavery of the world will depend.

This seemed quite redolent of the huge drama then playing itself out in Indo-china (a comparison to which James himself drew attention), but it came at the subject in a very different and much less propagandistic way than I had been doing. I take down my first edition of this poem, very finely bound by the Sycamore Press (a hand-set-type operation run out of the garage of the poet and tutor of Magdalen College, John Fuller). "To Christopher Hitchens from James Fenton with much love," it says on the flyleaf, the inscription dated "November 1969." When James's first collection of published poems, *Terminal Moraine*, came out in 1972, I have just noticed to my irritation, it was inscribed "To Chris, from the author, with lots of love." I hadn't before registered this qualitative degeneration. What I *had* noticed at the time was an observation by the great Roy Fuller, honored laureate of the 1930s and father of John, at a party at the latter's house in Benson Place. "You're a friend of young Fenton's, then?" he said gruffly. I allowed as much. "I rather think that he writes as well now, if not better, than Wystan did at his age." I knew this would please James, who had first been introduced to Auden and Kallman through some mutual friends in Florence, but I also knew it wouldn't go to his head.

Ah, that head! Redmond O'Hanlon was later to compare it to an owl's egg. It certainly did have the most domed and sapient appearance. And under the arc and curve of that skull lay an extraordinary variety of elements and materials. The first of these was a sort of direct line to the tradition of English poetry, the second was a talent for burlesque and parody, often manifested with an almost manic glee, and the third was a buried seriousness that, as with his mentor Auden, derived from a sort of post-Christianity based on a form of English Protestantism. He also, broke as he was and as we all were, invariably had the price of a drink or a smoke about his person, and I am glad that I loved and love him so, because it was he who awakened my thus far buried and dangerous lust for alcohol and nicotine. Friends, somebody said, are "god's apology for relations." I was one of those who had tended to think of friends at school as comrades or acquaintances or co-conspirators or cronies or sex partners (or an occasional salad of all four). Monastic school and college traditions, I will plead, made this less freakish and grotesque than it may now look on the page. I did have a friend, Michael Prest, my former rescuer from bullying and the only man I still knew from school. And I had a comrade, James Pettifer, who was a playwright and polymath and internationalist. It was so that we could all three find a fourth person to share the expenses of a house in the wastes of Cowley Road that we were meeting Fenton in that pub. All of us, I am sure, would still date our future moments from the one in which this encounter occurred.

It isn't a matter of looking back and thinking: this was when I met the finest English poet of his generation. I already *knew*, or at any rate believed, that he was the finest poet of his generation writing in English. The pressing question was: Could he be induced to write a few stanzas that would be of immediate help to the cause of the socialist revolution? I knew that Auden had been inconvenienced by similar demands but I also believed that I was more persuasive and subtle and less dogmatic than those who had tried to induce him, too, into composing lines that could be employed as weaponry.

James was absolutely ready to do anything he could in order to help the struggling people of Indochina (indeed, in a quieter way he was much more decided upon this than I was), but he thought there were other things in life as well. He liked long walks, and he loved the ancient buildings and antique trees and botany of Oxford. He liked to talk about Italy and Greece and all matters classical. He had a huge talent for rude songs and crude puns, rescued from vulgarity by a sort of innocence. He was tremendously impressed, as well as a bit put off, by the extreme seriousness of George Steiner, who had just published his imposing collection of essays *Language and Silence*. In rather the same way as I had felt a bit overawed by Isaiah Berlin, James was unable to forget the embarrassment of an undergraduate dinner with Steiner, in which he had overdone his own insouciance and had too languidly said that there were no great unifying causes left anymore: no grand subject of the sort that had sent Auden to Spain or China. Steiner had snapped at this Fentonian display of the blasé and told him to take a hard look at what seemed to be happening in Vietnam. And this had certainly worked with James, who was swift on the uptake and who cringed to remember how smug he must have sounded. However, before this full confession could be registered, there was some other business to be done, as we tramped across Magdalen Bridge: the polishing of the rude songs:

> I Am The King of China
> And I Like A Tight Vagina:
> It Lets Me Show The Things I Know—
> Like The Prose Style of George Steiner.

James's "King of China" series—which had to follow the scheme laid out above, where the first line could not be changed at all and the subsequent lines should be obscene and if possible (failing in the above case) mildly homosexual—was obviously a minor-key achievement for the times. However, I would defend it very strongly and believe it has its place in the history of Auden-inspired minor but useful obscenity. The model verse ran like this, and all others had to observe the rules:

> I Am The King of China
> And My Court Is Crammed With Sages.
> But When I Want A Bit Of Bum,
> I Ring Around My Yellow Pages.

I cannot be sure if the Sycamore Press's (very limited and hand-printed and elegant) edition of this collection of trivia yet survives, but if so, there is a sporting chance that my own contribution is still in print:

> I Am The King of China.
> I'm A Patron of the Prize-Ring.
> And Every Time My Man's On Top—
> You Can Feel My Boxer Rising.

I already knew in principle that word games, like limericks and acrostics and acronyms and crosswords, are good training in and of themselves. I could not then guess at the harvest of such marvels that lay ahead, but I did dimly appreciate that the Fenton factor was having the effect of making me somewhat less rigidly disapproving. In his copy of Steiner's *Language and Silence*, though, I found a thumbed-over dog-eared page that fell open at an essay titled "Trotsky and the Tragic Imagination," and realized that my new chum had suggested to me a possible relationship, which was that of politics to literature but this time beginning at the literary end and not at the ideological one.

James was a son of the Church: his father was a leading Anglican divine, the principal of a theological training college in Durham and author of a standard commentary on the Gospel of Luke. James's mother had died suddenly while he was at public school (Repton), and Canon Fenton had remarried, in a reverse-Murdstone-ish kind of way, a woman who could not bear to be reminded of his former life or former wife. This had led to an estrangement from the children—James had an older brother and younger sister—and to their being brought up by a pair of maiden aunts in Wales. This outwardly unlucky experience had made him rather a genius at handling personal relations and improvising surrogate families. (The two aunts, for example, were named Eileen and Noel: rather than have to call them either thing, or to have to address them as "Aunt," James hit on the idea of naming them "E" and "N," which worked brilliantly. In later years, E went back to her prewar work as a teacher in Jerusalem and helped out at the Anglican school at St. George's Cathedral where Edward Said had been a pupil. It used to satisfy me greatly when returning correspondents would tell me that they had "run into Aunt E at the American Colony Hotel." Having a drink with her there myself one day, I heard her say wistfully that she wished she could have been called to the priesthood instead of being limited to being a glorified missionary. On principle I could not care less who took holy orders or who did not, but it did hit me with terrific force what a wonderful minister she would have made.)

This talent of James's for hitting it off with people was immediately evident when we all moved into our "digs." There were in theory four rooms, but one of them gave directly onto the kitchen and it was obvious that whoever slept there would be effectively living in a corridor and at the mercy of the requirements of everyone else. "I'll take that one," said James at once, as if he'd pre-emptively "bagged" the best quarters for himself. I remember thinking that there was a sort of quasi-Christianity in this cheerful self-sacrifice: a thought that James would often give me cause to have again. It was additionally decent of him in that he was the only one of us who didn't at the time have a female companion. (Incidentally, Pettifer's girlfriend and wife-to-be was called Sue Comely. Michael Prest's was named Liz Horn. Mine was named Teresa Sweet. Later, James was to have a walk-out with a Valkyrie look-alike named Elizabeth Whipp, and it was he who first noticed when we were all together that the firm of Comely, Horn, Whipp, and Sweet would make quite a sensational brothel-management team.)

Apart from renewing the interest in poetry that I had been in danger of letting lapse because of my political obsessions, and apart from getting me to smoke the deadly brand of Players Number Six (the "tokens" of which he collected in the hope perhaps of one day buying a gramophone or an electric kettle) as well as to imbibe Teacher's Scotch whisky, Fenton changed my life in two other ways. We were walking along Turl Street one day when he stopped to speak to a small, slightly pouting yet rather stern-looking young blond man, who had on his arm an even more blonde girl. The girl I slightly knew. Her name was Alexandra Wells, known throughout the university as the enticing "Gully," and she was the stepdaughter of Sir A.J. Ayer, also known as "Freddie," whose book *Language, Truth and Logic* had brought the work of the Viennese philosophers to England. A tireless and justly celebrated fornicator, Freddie was the patron of our Labour Club and one of the few senior academics who could be counted on to sign petitions from the insurgent Left. (He's brilliantly caricatured as Sir Roy Vandervane in Kingsley Amis's neglected masterpiece novel *Girl, 20.*) I chatted to Gully, for whom I harbored a keen secret desire — she was later to say to me, on the sole occasion when I have heard the words used literally: "not if you were the last man on earth"*— and who was the only young woman on campus who had dared to try the latest fashion for wearing "hot pants." James briefly made the introduction to her escort, whose hand I no less briefly took. As we passed on, I asked: "Did he say his name was Amis?" "Yes," came the response. "He's called Martin Amis." I inquired slightly indifferently if he was any relation to the famous comic novelist, who had notoriously signed a letter to the *Times*, along with Simon Raven and Robert Conquest and others, supporting the American war on Vietnam.

---

* This declaration on her part was all the more striking for being pre-emptive, in view of the fact that I had never even dared to proposition her.

It sometimes makes me whistle to think about this near-miss. Martin had been born in the same year as Fenton and myself, but had arrived in Oxford a year later because of various disasters (later hilariously narrated in his memoir *Experience*) involving his poor schooling, his chaotic family, and his smoke-wreathed experiments with voyages of the imagination. So he was a year "below" me and—this is why he was lurking in "the Turl"—a member of Exeter College. Alma mater of Richard Burton and Tariq Ali as it may have been, this college was thought even by non-snobs to be a bit on the "minor" side: more for the boat club than the *cognoscenti*. Who knows how many blunders I might have made with Martin if we had chosen that as our moment of first acquaintance? At the very least I would probably have felt compelled to say something disobliging about Kingsley, and that might have been all that it took to cause a lifetime estrangement. At any rate the danger passed, and I was safely out of the university, having almost failed to get a degree of any kind when Martin stepped forward to get the best "First" in English of his year.

Then one day—I can be sure it was in the fall of 1969—Fenton proposed a day off and a day out. The adventurous plan was to board the train to London, take a taxi to Chancery Lane, have a decent lunch with some interesting people, and then see what opportunities presented themselves for the evening. I was agog, but apprehensive. How, first of all, was this to be financed? James assured me that if I was willing to do a little carrying, all would be well. My role as bearer involved the toting of a big bag of books. Once arrived at Paddington Station, we indulged in the luxury of a cab which let us off at a bookshop named Gaston's, on Chancery Lane between Holborn and Fleet Street. There and with a practiced air James traded the books for crisp currency notes. While still an undergraduate he had already become a reviewer for London papers and had learned a cardinal principle of the reviewer's trade—which was that Gaston's would give fifty percent of the cover price of a new volume, always assuming it to be in good condition. I was lost in wonder, both at the sophistication of this, and at the largesse.

I had never seen or smelled Fleet Street or Bloomsbury before, and these totemic names took on life and shape as the luxurious day drew on and became a misty autumnal one. Lunch was with Anthony Thwaite, in a wine bar with sawdust on the floor and—to my fanciful thought—Dickensian and Johnsonian elements in its atmosphere. Thwaite, a diminutive figure with a big thatch of hair, was a poet who had formed part of the "Movement" that comprised such elevated names as Philip Larkin and Robert Conquest. He was also the literary editor of the *New Statesman*, which at that time was certainly the most celebrated of London's intellectual weeklies. I considered myself to be miles to the "left" of it, of course, but still in awe of the review on which I had cut my teeth as a schoolboy, and on whose stairway one might have met Bertrand Russell, say, or George Bernard Shaw. In one room was an old hatstand draped with an ancient raincoat said to have belonged to H.G. Wells. The lore had it that if you donned this totemic Macintosh and ventured out in it, you would make a conquest of the very first woman you met. To be invited back to this famous office in Great Turnstile after lunch and to climb that stairway to Thwaite's aerie was an uncovenanted bonus. To exit the building onto Lincoln's Inn Fields clutching a couple of review copies of my own — "We might like you to take a look at these for us": Surely there had been a misunderstanding? — was to feel that one had drunk far more at that lunch than one actually had.

I can't be sure where we dined or where we slept that night, but I do remember taking James, by way of return as it were, to the Curzon cinema to see Costa-Gavras's film *Z*. The effect of it on both of us was electric. I was trying to recruit James to the International Socialists at the time, and so when he murmured something about how eye-opening a movie it was, I readily and militantly challenged him with a "what are *you* doing about it?" that was, when I think about it, a slightly poor return for the marvelous day he had shown me. Quite taking me at my own face value, however (something that always makes me uneasy), he replied evenly enough: "Oh, I am going to do something about it."

By the end of that year I had been published in the *New Statesman* with my review of Eric Hobsbawm's book on labor militancy in the Victorian epoch ("Hitchens in the *New Statesman*? Hitchens on *Eric Hobsbawm*? Who is this callow youth?" I can still hear these questions) and had been invited to the Christmas cocktail party given in the magazine's boardroom, where the cartoons and caricatures of Bloomsbury were on the very walls. There, I mentally bid farewell to Oxford and to the provinces in general. If ever anyone was "hooked," it was me. The network of streets and lanes and squares roughly between Blackfriars Bridge and Ludgate Circus and Theobalds Road and Covent Garden had me in thrall. So they do still, in their way. This was the district that stretched from the Marx Memorial Library on Clerkenwell Green to the British Museum Reading Room where the old boy had done his best work. Extending itself a bit to the north and colonizing Charlotte Street up to Fitzroy Square, it became the area where Anthony Powell had located some of his more louche scenes of pre- and postwar literary interpenetration. Looping around on itself and doubling back via Shaftesbury Avenue, the neighborhood might be said to "take in" Soho, with its little grid of streets and alleys, containing the offices of *Private Eye* and *New Left Review*, and then Gerrard Street, now "Chinatown," in which Dr. Johnson's "Club" of Burke, Gibbon, Reynolds, and Garrick had met (and near the corner of which I was later to take my last glimpse of my mother). In these and other purlieus was manufactured the journalistic small-arms ammunition that was to be hurled against the gigantic (but inaccurate and poorly commanded) batteries of Fleet Street's Tory newspaper establishment, located farther east as a sort of bulwark to the City of London.

The problem, as usual, was how to be able to play a decent hand on both sides of this street. Peter De Vries, one of my favorite minor novelists (he could make you laugh out loud, as in *Mackerel Plaza*, as well as weep, as with *Blood of the Lamb*), was once asked to name his ambitions as a writer. He replied that he wanted a mass audience for his books, one that would be large enough for his more elite audience to look down upon. I suspect that many authors, if they were honest, would admit to something like the same. My desire at that stage was to make a sufficient living at the business of Grub Street "hackery"—the refreshing term that the English use for the scribbling trade—so as to be able to toil more nobly in the evenings and weekends, both on my literary efforts and on my alliance with the working class.

I wasn't by any means the first person to have thought of this scheme, nor to have run into some of its more immediate obstacles. In order to get a job in "the media" in those days, you had to be a member of a labor union. I thought that that was fair enough, and indeed favored the closed shop, and was anxious to join a union if only so that I could start agitating as a union member, but then there was the difficulty that I couldn't join such a union unless I already had a job. This was a bar to entry, itself based on a double standard, that made one unashamed to play things both ways in one's own turn. One had somehow to get from being the second most famous person at Oxford to being a completely obscure but perhaps "promising" person in the metropolis. Once again, it was a lunch at All Souls that supplied the answer. The London *Times* was starting a new supplement, to be devoted to higher education. It needed a newly created staff, which in turn meant that a job could be awarded without a union ticket being required as a precondition. Thus did I become a "Social Science Correspondent" on a paper that had yet to be printed: a Gogol-like ghost job which I held for about six months before its editor said something to me that made it impossible to go on working for him.* I sometimes wonder what might have become of me if I had been good enough at that job to keep it: the paper could well have become my winding-sheet. Still, I had at least managed to move myself to London and I had become a member of the journalists' union.

I had also managed to negotiate the slight but unmistakable political invigilation that used to be part of the scenery in those days. When applying for a trainee job at the BBC, I had been asked by one member of the interviewing panel: "Do you feel strongly about things? Strongly enough for example to sit down in Trafalgar Square?" I wasn't stupid enough not to realize that he wouldn't have asked that question if he didn't already know the answer to it. I didn't get the job, either—another defeat for which I am eternally grateful. (And this now makes me old enough to remember a time when the BBC tried to *exclude* subversive and resentful types.) A later interview, for that *Times* job, was more typical of British Establishment reserve and understatement at its deadliest. "Just a formality... won't take a second. Need to ask you a few things before we have you on the strength." The interlocutor was a Mr. Grant, a slightly red-faced and portly chap with no special title. This was in the days when the offices of the *Times* were in the magnificently named Printing House Square, just opposite the old Blackfriars Station where on the portico were still incised the names of ancient steam-railway destinations like Darmstadt and St. Petersburg. It was redolent of the time when the young Graham Greene had been a subeditor down the corridor. Mr. Grant asked me a few questions of such apparent innocuousness that I became suitably lulled. Then: "Interested in politics at all?" I decided there

---

* "You're fired" were the exact words as I remember them.

could only be one answer to that. "Good, good. Would you describe yourself as having any special affiliation?" Again on the assumption that he knew the answer, as well as on the conviction that it would be shameful to conceal my stance, I replied: "I am a socialist." "Fine, fine, my dear boy: don't look so defensive. More socialists on the *Times* than you would probably guess. Some of our best people too…" I was just relaxing when he leaned forward slightly and asked, looking me directly in the eye: "By the way, would the Labour Party allow you to join it?"

This, as he must have known, was the very question that I might have hoped to avoid. I was "in" the Labour movement all right, but not at all "of" it.

Let us go then, you and I, to a meeting in a rather dingy and poorly lit union hall in Haringay, North London. The time: the mid-1970s. The place: a run-down but resilient district, with a high level of Irish and other immigrant population. I am the invited speaker and the subject is Cyprus, the former British colony in the Mediterranean which has recently been attacked and invaded by both Greek and Turkish NATO armies. Many refugees from this cruel bombardment and occupation have arrived in London to join the staunchly working-class and left-wing Cypriot community that has been here since the 1930s. My articles on the ongoing imperial crime have won me a certain audience. The brothers and sisters in Haringay aren't easily impressed by visiting talent, and it's unlikely that I'll even get the taciturn treasurer of the local branch to refund my "tube" fare from downtown, but I'm used to this no-nonsense style and have even trained myself to approve of it. Before being exposed to my scintillating rhetoric, the audience will be subjected to a steady series of quotidian preliminaries. There will be an appeal for the strike fund at a neighboring engineering factory, whose workforce has been "out" on the picket line for over a month. There will be an announcement about a regional meeting to discuss resolutions for the forthcoming annual Labour Party conference, scheduled for a distant and dismal seaside resort sometime in the fall. The lady who helps run social services for needy immigrants will make an appeal, couched in that amazing warmth in which some Labour matriarchs specialize, urging Cypriots (who generally prize family values above all else and are leery of charity) to claim their entitlements as Commonwealth citizens. It is stressed that no distinction is to be made between Greek and Turkish Cypriots, none of whom have ever raised so much as a voice or a hand to each other in this old and fraternal borough. A veteran of the bus drivers' union gets to his feet to make a sturdy, ringing call for British workers to take their holidays in democratic and struggling Cyprus, instead of on the so-called touristic Costa Brava that is part of the disgrace that is (still, after all those years and in spite of all our efforts) General Franco's Spain. These are people who shun the gaudy display of supermarkets and spend their hard-earned wages at the Co-Op, with which many of them also bank their small savings.

It's all gone now, or gone to pieces, but this was what we used to call "the Labour movement." Sometimes in elevated May Day rhetoric it was TIG-MOO (This Great Movement Of Ours) and sometimes it was TMAAW (The Movement As A Whole) but even as we mocked this stock speech, we felt a fierce pride at belonging to the ranks that it described. Men and women, "warriors for the working day," who had survived mass unemployment and slum housing and bitter exploitation, stuck together to resist fascism at home and abroad, rebuilt the country after 1945, fought for independence for the colonies, and striven to remove the terrible fear—of illness and penury and a Dickensian old age—that had hagridden the British working class. In 1939, when it had once again become necessary to summon those workers back to the colors and the flag and the defense of the nation (mainly in consequence of the abysmal and shameful capitulations of the ruling class in the face of Nazism), the recruiting officers had been appalled at the human material that was presented to them. Men with crumbled teeth, failing eyesight, wheezing pigeon-like chests, bow-legged and balding; exhibiting symptoms of deficiency diseases like rickets and pellagra that would have shocked some of Britain's Indian and African subjects. As a child born after the war and in the first years of the National Health Service (itself always semireverently capitalized by the people as "the NHS") I was a beneficiary of all this, despite my father's Toryism. Free blackcurrant juice for Vitamin C—making me pee purple—was available at school, as was free milk, from which I first made the nauseating discovery of what is now called "lactose intolerance." A "district nurse" called as a matter of course on any household that had registered the birth of a new baby. If I developed a squint or a toothache, my parents need not fear bankruptcy, but could take me to be fitted with spectacles or healed with a filling. The resulting work is not beautiful (I winced with recognition when I first read the expression "British teeth" in Gore Vidal's *Judgment of Paris*) but it is nonetheless real and tangible and *available* as a kind of right, and a hard-won right at that. Everybody in the hall is proud of the fact that the most elemental thing of all—human blood—is freely donated to the National Health Service, which never runs out of it and never pays a penny to those who line up to give it and expect nothing in return but a strong brown cup of serious proletarian tea.

For me, this "movement" is everything. It contains within itself the germinal hope of a better future where a thinking working class can acquire the faculties of a serious party of government, and can extend these small early "reformist" gains into something more comprehensive—all the while uniting with similar movements in other countries to repudiate the narrow nationalisms and chauvinisms that lead to wars and partitions. To be enrolled in its ranks is to be a part of an alternative history as well as an alternative present and future. Official Britain may have its Valhalla of heroes and statesmen and conquerors and empire-builders, but *we* know that the highest point ever reached by European civilization was in the city of Basel in 1912, when the leaders of the socialist parties of all countries met to coordinate an opposition to the coming World War. The names of real heroes like Jean Jaures and Karl Liebknecht make the figures of Asquith and Churchill and Lloyd George seem like pygmies. The violence and disruption of a socialist transformation in those years would have been infinitely less than the insane sacrifice of culture to barbarism, and the Nazism and Stalinism that ensued from it. This feeling seemed absolutely authentic to me at the time. (As a matter of fact it still does.) The only two immediate difficulties with this idealism are that, first, this same movement is, at least for the time being, expressed politically by a very boring and compromised party known as the Labour Party; and, second, that in the industry where I actually happen to work, the unions are the most hidebound and conservative force of all, which in the newspaper business is saying quite a good deal.

In my efforts to live up to the Peter De Vries maxim, I took various "mainstream" jobs, from being a freelance researcher for the "Insight" team at Harold Evans's *Sunday Times* (then at its zenith), to working at the newly formed London Weekend Television, to being a correspondent for the *Daily Express* and a part-time editorial or "leader"-writer for the old *Evening Standard*. This makes me one of the last of those who can say that they worked for "Beaver-brook Newspapers": the famous old racket, half-magic and half-criminal, that was preserved forever in Evelyn Waugh's portrayal of *The Daily Beast*. Writing my own introduction to the Penguin edition of *Scoop*, I said of Waugh's Fleet Street masterpiece that it perfectly evoked both the fugitive glamour of the business—that pseudo-deco black-glass palace on Fleet Street from which one might take a taxi at short notice to the airport, clutching a brick of traveler's checks, with an exotic visa in one's old blue-gold hardback British passport ("The Street of Adventure")—as well as its irredeemable squalor ("The Street of Shame"). Here is how Waugh introduces a group of veteran British hacks met in some dismal overseas bar:

> Shumble, Whelper and Pigge knew Corker; they had loitered of old on many a doorstep and forced an entry into many a stricken home…

I once had a drink with an *Express* veteran, his face richly veined and seamed with grog-blossom, in the old Punch Tavern opposite the offices, while he explained to me the etiquette of stricken-home violation. The bereaved generally liked to offer a cup of tea, he said, out of immemorial working-class courtesy. Thus, when extracting the maximum of tragedy from the relatives of a recent victim—be it of crime or fire or plane crash—it was always important to take along a colleague. "He offers to help them out in the kitchen while they put the kettle on, and that gives you a nice time to slip into the front room and collar the family photos from off the mantelpiece." Lest I seem to pretend to have been shocked by this, I freely admit that the unofficial motto of our foreign correspondent's desk was, when setting off to some scene of mass graves and riven societies, "Anyone here been raped and speaks English?" In Martin Amis's novel of Fleet Street, *Yellow Dog*, you might think that the contempt shown by the reporters for both their subjects and their readers is overdone, but you would be wrong.*

---

* I appear in some obscure online dictionary of quotations for having said that I became a journalist partly so that I wouldn't ever have to rely on the press for my information.

In many ways journalism was the ideal profession for someone like myself who was drawn to the Janus-faced mode of life. Did I say "profession"? There is something about the craft and practice (better words for it) that is naturally two-faced. One has to pretend to be at least formally polite to the politicians one interviews; one has to be civil and smiling and curious when sitting with criminal lunatic "freedom fighters" and crazed, aphasic dictators.

I can give an example of this from the formative days of my own career in the media racket. In the early 1970s, in what had once been called "the jewel of Africa," there was a state-sponsored pogrom against Ugandans of Asian descent, who were first dispossessed and then deported. The man responsible was the almost pornographically wicked figure Idi Amin (later to become an exiled guest in Saudi Arabia as a heroic son of Islam). His bigotry and greed were two aspects of the same rampant disorder: he wanted the assets of the Asian business community as his political spoil, and he also wanted to be the man who "Africanized" his unhappy country by ethnic cleansing. Most of the Asians had British passports, though it had never been thought that they would employ them for the crassly tactless purpose of (say) coming to live in the United Kingdom. When they did exercise this small legal privilege, there was quite a strong racist reaction to their arrival. One of those who was most demagogic on the point was Sir Oswald Mosley, an ageing figure to whom there still clung the authentic stench of the 1930s, when he had been the black-shirted leader of the British Union of Fascists. Since the end of the Second World War, he had chosen to live in Paris. As it happened, my very amateur network of intelligence and information brought me the news that the old would-be dictator was in London and staying at the Ritz. I decided to see if he would come on the television show for which I was then a researcher and cub reporter.

The first part was easy: I established that he was indeed at the Ritz and that he was willing to be interviewed. The second bit was slightly more difficult: Was I not having to be civil to a man who had had Josef Goebbels as the best man at his wedding to Lady Diana Mitford, with Adolf Hitler (who gave the happy couple a framed portrait of himself as a nuptial gift) in attendance as guest of honor? I decided that the problem could be resolved in the following way: the opportunity was too good to miss but there the formalities ended. I would send him a car, and would greet him in the lobby, but would not extend my hand when he arrived. I rehearsed the moment many times, waking and sleeping, until the limousine drew up and the now-silvered and bull-like figure of the old bastard began to emerge. Somehow I found I was putting out my own hand first and saying: "Sir Oswald, how very good of you to come." In what seemed a volitionless state, I then conducted him to the hospitality suite and poured him a drink.

I can justify this if you like. (It occurs to me now that I could also have justified it then, since Mosley was the model for Sir Roderick Spode, the brutish and ridiculous leader of the "Black Shorts" movement in P.G. Wodehouse's 1938 masterpiece *The Code of the Woosters*, and one doesn't get many chances to meet such an original. But I was far too solemn for that in those days.) Instead, I justified myself tactically. From our ensuing chat I learned that he had never dreaded the Marxist hecklers of the Thirties who had hurled rocks and vegetation at him. The most disconcerting tactic of the Left, he informed me, had been to occupy the first few rows of seats in a town hall and then, as he began speaking, to open newspapers and bury their faces in the pages. It's somehow very hard to whip up a crowd when the front-row seats are thus otherwise engaged. He carried on in this urbane and confessional manner until it was time to put him on the set and begin the serious business. As soon as the studio lights came up and the camera's light began winking red, he seemed to shrug off his previous character and style and to become suddenly lean and hawklike as of yore. The whole timbre of his voice altered, and to the interviewer's first question on Ugandan Asian immigration he returned a rasping, sneering answer that summoned all the old echoes of race and nation. Thus, green and untried as I was, I had the opportunity to notice in one hour what many members of the British upper class had been unable to bring themselves to see in the 1930s: there was one Mosley who acted in a fairly civilized and even amusing way in the drawing rooms and country houses, and another whose relish it was to go down to the slums of the East End and get all dirtied up with those who were so base and stupid as to think that their lives would improve if they were not afflicted with Jewish neighbors.

How I managed the conclusion of the thing I can't now recall: perhaps I was proud and heroic enough to decline a handshake as Sir Oswald departed.

Anyway, it taught me that the moral attitudes that one strikes are often devoid of any significance.*

This was all in "the Seventies." When exactly did we begin to periodize by decades instead of, say, by reigns? Did people in the Thirties know that they were going to be historically collectivized in that way? There were no noughts or tens in the twentieth century, which went straight from Edwardian to the Great War. Hints of an idea of "the Twenties" had been contained in the concept of the Jazz Age. In the spring of 1968 I do remember a revolutionary speaker on the pavement outside the London School of Economics referring to a year that might one day be matched with 1848 and 1917, and we did have a sort of consciousness of living in "the Sixties" while they were still going on. But the Seventies were only the Seventies because they had to have a name. Nullity and anticlimax appeared to close in on all sides. And so did certain kinds of nastiness, often composed of, or distilled from, the worst of the Sixties. The television HQ to which I had invited Mosley was situated

---

* This was perhaps not quite as true for my next confrontation with the old buzzard. In 1980 his wife, Lady Diana—estranged sister of my later friend Jessica Mitford—wrote a review of a book about the Goebbels family for the London sheet *Books and Bookmen*, an outlet to which I also occasionally contributed. Even had I not been appalled by her gushing praise for the delightful Josef and Magda, I would have drawn the line at the metaphor she employed for their murder of their four children. This she called "a Masada-like deed." I thought that crossed a line, and said so in the *New Statesman*, adding an unkind play on the name of the publisher of *Books and Bookmen*, a man named Philip Dosse. Mr. Dosse that week committed suicide and Auberon Waugh accused me in the *Spectator* of having driven him to his death. I both liked and disliked—fortunately I disliked more—the notion that a polemic of mine could have anything like this effect. By the time it was revealed to my relief that Mr. Dosse had killed himself without having read my piece, and because of an impending collision with his creditors and the Inland Revenue, I had opened an envelope from the "Chateau de la Gloire," the rather grotesque address outside Paris which I knew to be the lair of the Mosleys, and convenient for their friendship with their frightful neighbors, the Duke of Windsor and Mrs. Simpson. The enclosed letter was from Sir Oswald, complaining that while he was fair game, it wasn't cricket to be attacking his dear wife. Since she had been a far more active Nazi than he and had invited Hitler to her wedding, I thought this was weak stuff. Later, opening that day's London *Times,* I saw Sir Oswald's obituary notice, which means that it's quite thinkable that I was the recipient of the last missive he ever wrote. Lady Diana was to outlive him for some decades, never uttering a repentant remark about her Third Reich period. When I once asked Decca if she ever had any contact at all with her sister, she replied: "Certainly not! I think I did bow slightly to her at dear Nancy's funeral, but otherwise it's been absolutely *non-speakers* since Munich!"

in a new high-rise on the South Bank of the Thames, with a commanding view of London. Looking out of one of its higher windows after lunch one day, I first saw and then heard a huge explosion. It seemed to be located somewhere near St. Paul's Cathedral. What I had just seen—and was to be seeing at street level within the hour—was the first Irish Republican Army car bomb to detonate on the British mainland. The "target" had been the Old Bailey: the country's supreme court.

I had always been opposed to the partition of Ireland and a strong supporter of the civil rights movement against the Orange sectarian ministate that embodied the petrified, stagnant outcomes of that old and cruel division. My outfit, the International Socialists, had been involved at an early stage in the nonsectarian protests and marches and strikes that had challenged the Ulster "Six County" rump system. Many was the evening, especially after the "Bloody Sunday" massacre by British troops in Derry, and after Britain's imposition of internment, better known as imprisonment without trial (but with some torture), that I had spent in Irish pubs and clubs, making speeches and organizing protests. As a journalist, also, I started visiting Belfast and Derry and Newry and had my first experience of seeing shots fired in anger, as well as nail bombs thrown and gasoline bombs too. As one brought up *inside* the protective womb of the Royal Navy and its bases, it felt very strange to me to see the British Army patrolling streets that were at least constitutionally "British," but while wearing the visors and helmets of occupying space aliens. That was one distinct oddity. The other—in a city like Belfast where there had been almost no Commonwealth immigration—was that if one saw a black face it was almost invariably the face of a British soldier. (Some of the taunts from angry old ladies in Republican slum districts did not fail to make use of this striking contrast. "What'll you do with it, then, soldier boy?" shrilled one banshee as a young squaddie from Barbados flourished a "rubber bullet": a crowd-control device that resembled a Coke bottle sculpted in black. "Post it to your *focken* wife?" I never forgot the look of hurt on his face.)

With James Fenton (whom I had eventually succeeded in recruiting to the International Socialists) I made a few trips to Northern Ireland and collaborated on an article or two for the *New Statesman*. (One of these carried our joint byline: something that still gives me great pride in retrospect.) Our own polemics were of course staunchly nonsectarian, stressing the contribution of Irish Protestants like Wolfe Tone to the long tradition of republicanism, and laying emphasis on historic Irish socialists like James Connolly and Jim Larkin. In the squalid and cramped back streets around the Belfast shipyards, it seemed to us, no better illustration could be found of the need for working people to forget their confessional and national differences and unite in a brotherly fashion. But to say that such appeals failed to achieve locomotive force among the masses would be to understate the case to an almost heroic degree.

I eventually came to appreciate a feature of the situation that has since helped me to understand similar obduracy in Lebanon, Gaza, Cyprus, and several other spots. The local leaderships that are generated by the "troubles" in such places *do not want* there to be a solution. A solution would mean that they were no longer deferred to by visiting UN or American mediators, no longer invited to ritzy high-profile international conferences, no longer treated with deference by the mass media, and no longer able to make a second living by smuggling and protection-racketeering. The power of this parasitic class was what protracted the fighting in Northern Ireland for years and years after it had become obvious to all that nobody (except the racketeers) could "win." And when it was over, far too many of the racketeers became profiteers of the "peace process" as well.

No, what got people going in Belfast in the early 1970s was not humanism and solidarity but rather violence, cruelty, conspiracy, bigotry, alcohol, and organized crime.* I did in fact make friends with a few Protestant workers in the Woodvale District who showed some interest in crossing the divide and having speech with their Catholic brethren, but they developed a depressing tendency to wind up in the trunks of bullet-sprayed cars, or sometimes— I think of Ernie Elliot—to be bullet-sprayed before being stuffed into the trunk. This was all brought home to me with singular force when James failed to turn up for a rendezvous that we had made in Andersonstown, a grit-strewn housing estate dominated by the emerging Provisional IRA. He had gone to the agreed pub and sat down to look at some documents about British Army roundups and internments in the area. This was a mistake, arguably a big

---

* The most witty and penetrating first-hand account of this morbid interlude is to be found in Kevin Myers's memoir *Watching the Door*.

one. Within minutes, a group had joined him and told him to put his hands on the table, under which a gun was pointing at his midsection. Taken to a filthy house and told to lie on the floor, he was kept for several hours while his captors failed to reach the various people in London who could have vouched that he was indeed a reporter and not a spy or a provocateur. But eventually they let him go, and he wrote quite an amusing account of his brush with terror. This was rendered much less risible a few days later, when in a villainous Belfast tavern I chanced to introduce him to a local reporter with known "republican" connections. "Did you say 'Fenton'?" breathed this worthy gent. "Did you know they took a vote about what to do with you? It was just six-to-five against shooting you there and then." That sort of vote was almost the only concept of democracy that some of the denizens of the city were ever able to form. (The woman who had "chaired" the meeting, a haggard crone by the name of Maire Drumm, was later shot in her hospital bed by some no less tender "Ulster Volunteer" Unionist riffraff who were prepared to cross the city's divide just for the chance to enjoy such an atrocity.)

A reprehensible temptation presented itself at once. In places like this, in contrast to the rather dreary precincts of the British urban and suburban and rural mainland, there was drama to be had, and for the asking. Every night and day there were bombs and gunshots and riots and roundups, and it didn't take long to gain a little access to the bars and shebeens where these things were discussed with a certain knowingness. One could do this as a political activist or as a journalist or, as in my case, an amateur combination of both. I have to admit that I sometimes found this double life more than just figuratively intoxicating. I was sufficiently furious, after the British Army massacre of demonstrators on Bloody Sunday, that I once shocked Fenton very much by saying that, if an IRA man were to be on the run and needing no more than a bed for the night and not a word spoken, I myself might be ready to furnish the needful. Of course I knew to beware of this vicarious identification with the "authentic." I had acquired some of that wariness in Cuba. But I hadn't yet quite learned to stay clear of it consistently. And—to mention another expression that annoyed James so much that I often used it merely to tease him—these encounters on the dark side also supplied "good copy." In the weirdly beautiful landscapes along the Irish border, most especially in Derry with its haunting evening light along the Waterside and the old walls, and in rainy Belfast with its nineteenth-century slums and yet its permanent view of the lovely surrounding hills, I saw my first "war" without even needing a passport to travel to it.

One is unlikely to forget the first time that one sees violent death, or feels it graze one's own sleeve. The Europa Hotel in Belfast was for me the first of many journalistic resorts, from the Commodore in Beirut to Meikles in Rhodesia-Zimbabwe to the Holiday Inn in Sarajevo where one was to find "Mahogany Ridge": the hack shorthand for the *Scoop*-like bar where so many war stories were told and written. Here was where one might go to meet surreptitious "sources," to trade tales with rivals and exchange information with friends, to play poker with the employer's money, to rub shoulders and scrape acquaintance with the fringe elements of the demimondes of terrorism and counterintelligence. One evening, when as it happens I was sincerely entertaining some local trade-union men to a nonsectarian supper, there came the crash of an explosion that was near enough to rattle the glasses. Hastening outside and into the warren of little streets across the road, one saw that a renowned local drink-shop named the Elbow Room was no more. Named as much for its position at the junction of two narrow streets as for the bending of the relevant arm joint, it had taken the full force of a car bomb that had been parked in a confined space. The resulting blast had blown everything in and then, it seemed by some evil backdraft, sucked everything out again. The mess of beer and whisky and blood and glass was everywhere, as were some huddled objects that made me wince and flinch. I remember best a Belfast fireman, one of those seemingly seven-foot giants in whom the province specialized, coming out from the ruins with a small figure wrapped in a tarpaulin in his arms. He then sat down on what was left of the steps and began to weep. I had that terrible inward feeling that I have since had at bullfights and executions and war scenes, of wanting this to stop while simultaneously wishing it to go on, and wanting to look away while needing to look more closely. Deciding that the man must be cradling a murdered child, I was bizarrely taken aback to find that he was in fact sobbing over a hopelessly mangled dog. And a Belfast fireman must by then have been exposed to quite a lot...

My own case was much less dramatic but still very vivid to me. Coming back to the Europa one night from checking casualties at the Royal Victoria Hospital, I couldn't find a taxi and decided to hoof it through some of the insurgent-run lanes of the Falls Road district. I hadn't reckoned with the speed of nightfall and found myself alone in the gathering dark: a crepuscular gloom augmented by the local habit of shooting out all the streetlights. A very sudden bang convinced me that a nail bomb had been thrown at a British patrol, and I swiftly decided that the better part of valor was to drop into the gutter and make myself inconspicuous. Judging by the whistling and cracking of nearby volleys, this decision was shrewd enough as far as it went, and I remember thinking how awful it would be to end my career as the random victim of a ricochet. Instead, I nearly ended it as a bloody fool who tested the patience of the British Army. Rising too soon from my semi-recumbent posture, I found myself slammed against the wall by a squad of soldiers with blackened faces, and asked various urgent questions that were larded with terse remarks about the many shortcomings of the Irish. Getting my breath back and managing a brief statement in my cut-glass Oxford tones, I was abruptly recognized as nonthreatening, brusquely advised to fuck off, and off I duly and promptly fucked. Graham Greene writes somewhere about John Buchan that his thrillers—*The Thirty-Nine Steps* being a salient example—achieve some of their effect by the imminence of death in otherwise normal situations, such as right beside the railings of Hyde Park. I wasn't exactly in Hyde Park, but I was still in my own country and the telephone boxes were red and the police uniforms were blue, and the awareness that the distinction between "over here" and "over there," or between "home" and "abroad" is often a false one has never left me.

So, here was how to get through the boring and constipated Seventies. First, adopt the profession of journalism that allowed one to become a version of John Bunyan's "Mr. Facing-Both-Ways." (Northern Ireland was near-perfect for polishing up this act, since in one day one might visit a Republican bar and a Unionist saloon before rounding off the night at an off-the-record dinner with a British intelligence officer.) Second, keep traveling to exotic places that seemed to preserve at least some of the waning promise of 1968. Third, maintain the double life in London as well. I would do my day jobs at various mainstream papers and magazines and TV stations, where my title was "Christopher Hitchens," and then sneak down to the East End where I was variously features editor of *Socialist Worker* and book-review editor of the theoretical monthly *International Socialism*. (On the masthead of the latter, my name stubbornly continued to appear as "Chris," whereas at the *New States-man* I would always insist on it being rendered full-out, even though on the cover this sometimes meant that it was too long to be featured where I most wanted it.) Of the "agitational" rags with which I have been involved, *Socialist Worker* was one of the best. I managed to conscript James Fenton as its film critic; an achievement which turned out a bit too rich for the digestive system of some of the sterner comrades. He contributed an almost lyrically Marxist notice of Pontecorvo's slave-revolt movie *Queimada* before attracting annoyed letters for his slightly camp praise of a then-recent "Carry On" production. Working to improve these dour pages brought me into proper contact with Paul Foot, the scion of one of England's truly great radical families and perhaps the person with whom it was hardest to identify the difference between the way he thought and felt and the principled manner in which he lived and behaved. (When he later became gravely ill and was asked if he would like his hospital bed moved into a private room, he was incapable of speech but fully able to make an easy-to-recognize digital gesture.) He was somewhat older than me, but his reaction to any injustice was as outraged and appalled as that of any young person who has just discovered that life is unfair.* By this I do not at all want to make him sound naïve: I resolved to try and resist in my own life the jaded reaction that makes one coarsened to the ugly habits of power. There were some giants on the Left in those days.

It was becoming reasonably obvious, however, that I wasn't going to be one of them. I knew that with half of myself I was supposed to be building up the Labour movement and then with another half of myself subverting and infiltrating it from the ultra-Left, but then I came across that fatal phrase of Oscar Wilde's that says the problem with socialism is that it wastes too many evenings on "meetings." Boredom has always been my besetting vice in any case. Then, I still wanted some sort of a good time and that definition had to include a variety of acquaintances and a decent if not sumptuous menu. The Central line on the Underground could make the journey from the proletarian East End to the Oxford Circus/Regent Street quarter very smooth: I

---

* When Paul died, the organizer of his memorial meeting invited me to record a video tribute, which I gladly did. In a minor spasm of spite, the gargoyles who by then ran the Socialist Workers Party prevented it from being shown at the event.

remember dashing from the grimy offices of the *Worker* to a job interview in the West End where I (rashly but successfully) tried to sell a freshly printed copy to John Birt, future boss of the BBC, member of the House of Lords, and character in the play and movie *Frost-Nixon*. (He hired me anyway.) The pages of the satirical review *Private Eye* record the early stages of this mutation. Early entries have me as "handsome Christopher 'Robin' Hitchens," yet as the Seventies go by, these soon give way to another staple reference, this time to the "chubby Trotskyist defector." Such photographs as survive tend to confirm the same story.

I mentioned that Fenton had introduced me at Oxford to some of the charms of alcohol and tobacco. This is to give you *NO IDEA* of how much I improved upon his initiation ceremonies. I dare say this might have happened to me anyway, but the discovery that so much of London journalistic life took place in pubs and bars, and that anything absorbed there could be charged to an expense account, caused me to resemble the cat Webster in the imperishable story by P.G. Wodehouse:

> Webster sat crouched upon the floor beside the widening pool of whisky. But it was not horror and disgust that had caused him to crouch. He was crouched because, crouching, he could get nearer to the stuff and obtain crisper action. His tongue was moving in and out like a piston…And Webster winked, too—a wholehearted, roguish wink that said, as plainly as if he had spoken the words:
> "How long has this been going on?"
> Then with a slight hiccough he turned back to the task of getting his quick before it soaked into the floor.

I soon made that fine cat look like the mere beginner that it was. The Commander used to drink too much, and Yvonne was seldom without a lit cigarette ("I lit another cigarette," says John Self in Martin Amis's *Money*, adding "Unless I specifically inform you to the contrary, I am always lighting another cigarette.") As a boy I had disliked the smell of both habits, which I suppose adds to the strong case that genetic predisposition plays a role in these addictions. But my tolerance for alcohol was very much greater than my father's had been, greater indeed than anyone I seemed to run into. It wasn't all that easy to get a reputation for boozing when you worked in and around old Fleet Street, where the hardened hands would spill more just getting the stuff to their lips than most people imbibe in a week, but I managed it. I still have somewhere the memo from Bill Cater at the accounts office of Harry Evans's *Sunday Times*, for whom I had done a story that eventually led to the imprisonment of a corrupt Labour mayor. "I've passed your Dundee expenses," he wrote, "but I couldn't help noticing that almost half the bills were for cocktails. I don't think any newspaper is entitled to this kind of loyalty."

A figure from this period may illustrate how nearly I might have run completely to seed. Since redeemed from an unjust obscurity by Francis Wheen's wonderful biography, Tom Driberg in the last years of his life was still a true legend on the journalistic and cultural Left. In youth, he had been an original member of Evelyn Waugh's *Brideshead* set, while also maintaining good relations with the more radical forces clustered around W.H. Auden and Stephen Spender. He had, indeed, given the young Auden his first copy of *The Waste Land*, and joined him in reading it aloud. Adopted by Edith Sitwell as the coming poet of her own generation, nominated by Aleister Crowley as the successor to his own Satanic role as "The Beast 666," friendly if not indeed intimate with Guy Burgess, the most calcified degenerate of those who had deserted British Intelligence for the embrace of Moscow and the KGB, Tom in his amoral and aloof elegance breathed all of the dubious enchantments of the 1930s and was redolent, too, of all the byways of Bohemia. I knew him by reputation as a leading member of the Left faction of the Labour Party in Parliament, and as the author of some sparkling collections of journalism. (Reporting from Vietnam in 1945, he may have been the first person to assert the extreme unwisdom of trying to restore French colonialism with British troops.) Anyway, he was sometimes invited to contribute the "Londoner's Diary" to the *New Statesman*, and one week issued an appeal to readers to help him complete an indecent limerick the first line of which ran: "There once was a man of Stoke Poges." This highly respectable town in Buckinghamshire seemed to cry out for the rhyme "poke Doges," which in turn meant that the remainder of the limerick would have to be Venetian in flavor.

Fenton and I, assisted by our dear friend Anthony Holden, accepted the challenge and were duly invited to a lunch by old Tom held at the Quo Vadis restaurant in Dean Street, above which Karl Marx had once kept his squalid lodgings. How we completed the task I don't entirely remember ("entirely resolved to poke Doges. So this elderly menace / Took steamship to Venice..." But what *was* the last line?). At all events, by the time the restaurant had finally insisted on throwing us out—this in the days when the pubs in London were not allowed to stay open in the afternoon—Tom simply took me down the street and up a flight of dingy stairs and made me a member of the infamous "Colony Room Club," an off-hours drinking establishment run by a tyrannical Sapphist named Muriel Belcher. Renowned to this day for its committed members, from Peter O'Toole to Francis Bacon, the joint at that epoch gave off an atmosphere of inspissated gloom, punctuated by moments of high insobriety and low camp. Muriel, arguably the rudest person in England ("shut up cunty and order some more champagne"), almost never left her perch at the corner of the bar and was committed to that form of humor that insists on referring to all gentlemen as ladies. Occasionally this routine was still funny. "Yes," she would screech if someone mentioned the London Blitz, "that was when we were all fighting that nasty Mrs. Hitler." O'Toole's favorite was a rejoinder she made when he'd described some ancient and absent member as a bit of a bore. "He was a *very brave lady*," insisted Muriel, "in the First World War!" This Pythonesque drag queenery was all very well in its way, and it was nice to have a boozy hideaway in the afternoons and late evenings, but there were times when it all felt a bit thin and sketchy, and as with some pubs in Fleet Street there seemed to be too many people who were perhaps forty and looked perhaps sixty: awful warnings in fact, splashing their lives up against the porcelain. In time I took heed and mainly confined my drinking to mealtimes, which was at least a start.

Driberg developed a fondness for me which I don't think was especially sexual. He would "try" any male person at least once, on the principle that you never know your luck, but he preferred working-class tough guys (policemen and soldiers an especial treat) and all he really wished was to offer them his version of lip service. I once had to cancel a dinner engagement with him and, being asked rather querulously why this was, replied that my girlfriend was in hospital for some tests and that I wanted to visit her after work. "Ah yes," said Tom with every apparent effort at solicitude, "there's a lot to go wrong with them, isn't there? I *do* so hope that it isn't her clitoris or anything ghastly like that." Not all of this was by any means affectation. For

Tom, the entire notion of heterosexual intercourse was gruesome to the last degree. ("That awful *wound*, my dear Christopher. I just don't see how you *can*." Forced into a marriage of convenience as the price of his early political ambitions, he was said to have accused his bride of attempting to rape him on their wedding night.) In this, he was like Noël Coward, who was once asked by Gore Vidal if he had ever even attempted anything with a woman. "Certainly not," replied The Master. "Not even with Gertrude Lawrence?" Gore inquired. "*Particularly not* with Miss Lawrence," was Coward's return-serve to that. (In something of the same manner, Chester Kallman would sometimes taunt Auden, during domestic disputes, with the fact that Wystan had admittedly slept with Erika Mann. "At least I'm *pure*, dear," he would intone.) Through Tom I was eventually to meet Gore Vidal, and also to learn how when in Rome the two of them would hunt together and organize a proper division of labor. Rugged young men recruited from the Via Veneto would be taken from the rear by Gore and then thrust, with any luck semi-erect, into the next-door room where Tom would suck them dry. It shows what few people understand even now, which is the variety of homosexual conduct. "I do not want a *penis* anywhere near me," as Gore would put it in that terse and memorable way he had. Incidentally, this double act also emphasized another distinction: Tom adored to give pleasure while Gore has always liked to boast that he has never knowingly or intentionally gratified any of his partners. Not even a sighing reach-around by the sound of it.

I am necessarily telling the next story very slightly out of order, but there came a time when Kingsley Amis asked me if by any chance I could intro-duce him to Tom Driberg. He understood that the old cocksucker had a trove of unpublished filthy poetry from W.H. Auden, Constant Lambert, and others, and he (Kingsley) had been commissioned to edit the new *Oxford Book of Light Verse*. Might Tom, in exchange for a good dinner, be induced to share his collection? If so, Kingsley handsomely offered to make a four-some of it at a good restaurant and invite myself and Martin along for the fun. I telephoned Tom and asked him if he would say yes. "I'd be most interested to meet the senior Amis," he murmured. "But do tell me, is he by chance as attractive as his lovely young son?" To this absurd query, from the ever-hopeful old cruiser, the best reply I could improvise was, "Well, Tom, Kingsley is old enough to be his *father*."

# Martin

My friendship with the Hitch has always been perfectly cloudless. It
is a love whose month is ever May.
            —Martin Amis: *The Independent*, 15 January 2007
            [as cited in the National Portrait Gallery catalogue
                                    that reported my death]

————————◄O►————————

E VENTS ONLY ELICITED the above tribute from Martin
when in our real lives it was mid-September and when the press had
been making the very most of a disagreement we had been having in print
about Stalin and Trotsky in the summer of 2001. Looking back, though, I am
inclined to date the burgeoning refulgence of our love to something more like
the calendar equivalent of April. Still, it was actually in the gloomy autumn of
1973, around the time of the Yom Kippur/Ramadan War between Israel and
Egypt, that we actually and properly met. To anchor the moment in time: Salvador Allende had just been murdered by Pinochet in Chile, W.H. Auden had
died, James Fenton (the author of the most beautiful poems to come out of
the Indochina War) had won the Eric Gregory Award for poetry and used the
money to go off and live in Vietnam and Cambodia, and at the age of twenty-
four I had been hired to fill at least some of the void that he left behind at the
*New Statesman*. Peter Ackroyd, literary editor of the rival and raffishly Tory
*Spectator*, was giving me a drink one evening after returning from a trip of his
own to the Middle East, and he said in that inimitable quacking and croaking
and mirthful voice of his: "I've got someone I think you should meet." When

he told me the name, I rather off-handedly said that I believed we'd once met already, with Fenton at Oxford. Anyway, it was agreed that we would make up a threesome on the following evening, at the same sawdust-infested wine bar called the Bung Hole where my *New Statesman* career had begun.

Lovers often invest their first meetings with retrospective significance, as if to try and conjure the elements of the numinous out of the stubborn witness of the everyday. I can remember it all very well: Ackroyd doing his best to be a good host (it's a fearsome responsibility to promise two acquaintances that they will be sure to get along well with one another) and Martin rather languid and understated. He did not, for example, even pretend to remember when I said we had met before with our other mutual friend Fenton.* A verse letter to him from Clive James, published in *Encounter* at about this period, described Martin as resembling "a stubby Jagger," and I remember this because of how very exact it seemed. He was more blond than Jagger and indeed rather shorter, but his sensuous lower lip was a crucial feature (I didn't then know that he thought he was most vulnerable in the mouth) and there was no doubt that you would always know when he had come into the room.

His office performed, Ackroyd withdrew and the remaining pair of us later played some desultory pinball in another bar. I noticed that Martin had the gift of mimicry: he could drop or raise his voice and alter his features and just simply "be" the person we were talking about (I cannot now remember who). He asked me which novelists I enjoyed and I first mentioned Graham Greene: this answer palpably did not excite him with its adventurousness. In answer to my reciprocal question he said he thought that one had to look for something between the twin peaks of Dickens and Nabokov, and it came back to me that Fenton had said to me how almost frighteningly "assured" all Martin's literary essays were turning out to be. I don't recollect how the evening ended.

But some kind of mutuality had been stirred, and we soon enough had dinner with our respective girlfriends in some Cypriot *taverna* in Camden Town, where things went with a swing and I can remember making him laugh. Then Yvonne died and I vanished from London and from life for a bit, to discover on my return that Martin had taken the trouble to write me a

---

* It is characteristic of Martin to have pointed out that Dickens's title *Our Mutual Friend* contains, or is, a solecism. One can have common friends but not mutual ones.

brief, well-phrased, memorable note of condolence. (A lesson for life: always when in doubt please *do* send letters of commiseration; at the very least they will be appreciated and at the best they may even succeed in their apparently futile ambition of lightening the burden of bereavement.) The next I knew, I was invited to a small party to celebrate the publication of Martin's first novel, *The Rachel Papers*.

Chat about this literary debut had been in the wind for a while, and Martin had an editorial position at the *Times Literary Supplement* as well as a mounting reputation as a reviewer and (which of course could be made to irk him) the same surname as one of the most famous novelists writing in English. Thus it seemed rather odd that he should be throwing his own book party, in his own small and shared flat, at his own expense. But I am glad of it, because those of us who had the good luck and good taste to attend were later able to reminisce rather triumphantly.

The 1973/74 apparel was absurd of course: cowboy boots and flared trousers for some of the men (those ill-advised cross-hatched blue jeans, designed to resemble armor, for me in particular) and Christ knows what for the girls. Sobriety and corduroy were supplied, however, by Amis senior and by his friend Robert Conquest, the great poet and even greater historian of Stalinism. In the International Socialists we made his book on *The Great Terror* required reading, but that didn't mean I didn't suspect him—and Kingsley too—of pronounced reactionary tendencies. This was mainly because of the reprehensible line they had both taken over Vietnam. Yet I was queasily aware that Kingsley's *Girl, 20*, with its ridiculing of "Sixties" morality and mentality, was rather hard to laugh off. Then there was Clive James, dressed as usual like someone who had assembled his wardrobe in the pitch dark, but always "on" and always awash in cross-references and apt allusions. The presence of these few but gravity-donating figures, plus the climb up the stairs from Pont Street on the fringes of Chelsea, made me conserve my breath for a time. I had in fact met both Kingers and Conkers—as they were sometimes known—before, but I was very aware that my roadworthiness (Martin prefers the term "seaworthiness") in real grown-up company was not to be assumed: at any rate not by me.

The main event of my evening turned out in any case to take place at the opposite end of the age and gender scale. It suddenly seemed to me that Martin's sister Sally did not perhaps find me entirely repulsive. As the evening gently evaporated I found myself taking her arm in the street and seeing—through quite a lot of fog, I now remember—the looming bulk of the Cadogan Hotel. Perhaps a little flown with wine, I suddenly and confusedly felt that it might be a fine thing to take her to the very place where Oscar Wilde had been arrested. I couldn't possibly afford it but then, as I thought about it, I couldn't possibly afford not to do it once I had thought about it. The Wilde suite itself was not available but we did procure a decent room and things proceeded happily enough. Ghost of Oscar or no ghost of Oscar, I did briefly allow myself to wonder if there was anything remotely subliminal or oblique in what I was doing: Sally had rather the same coloring as the brother I was beginning to adore though not at all the same face (it was years until it was established that she was not Kingsley's daughter, but that's another tale altogether).

I find now that I can more or less acquit myself on any charge of having desired Martin carnally. (My looks by then had in any case declined to the point where only women would go to bed with me.) What eventuated instead was the most *hetero*sexual relationship that one young man could conceivably have with another. As the days became weeks, and the months became seasons, and as we fell happily into the habit of lunching and dining and party going *à deux*, there began an inexhaustible conversation, about womanhood in all its forms and varieties and permutations, that saw us through several episodes of sexual drought as well as through some periods of embarrassment of riches.

It was not, or not by any means *all*, the locker-room talk that you may imagine (though any reader of Martin's novels will know how brilliantly inventive is his capacity for bawdry: I refuse to say "obscenity" because the obscene is too easy and besides, it is always either quite humorless or too dependent for its humor on the knowledge that mere infants have of the human anatomy).* It might have been anyone—actually I am sure it was our

---

* The crudest thing that comes to mind—because it is such a cliché element of male fantasy—was our word, annexed from something said by Clive James, for the possibility of enjoying two young ladies at the same time. The term for this remote but intriguing contingency, which I still think was at least partially redeemed by its inventiveness, was "a carwash." Think about it, or forget it if you can. Incidentally, Kingsley's novel *The Green Man* contains the best-ever depiction of one of the many ways that this much-rehearsed ideal can go badly wrong in practice.

poet friend Craig Raine—who came up with the appalling yet unforgettable idea that there is a design flaw in the female form, and that the breasts and the buttocks really ought to be *on the same side*. But it was Martin who went to all the trouble, with dead-pan and dead-on acuity, of arguing the respective merits of *which side that ought to be*. (One doesn't necessarily want to see both features walking toward one, for example, but then again it might be dispiriting to see them both simultaneously marching away…) As for metaphors, everybody has at one point seen men standing in front of the pornography section, in either a magazine store or a video emporium, but it was Martin who observed these swaying and muttering figures pulling out and then replacing the contents and compared it to "the Wailing Wall." He had an instinctive understanding of the relationship between Eros and Thanatos: one winter he was suffering quite badly from flu and left the *New Statesman* office early to go home. I agreed to walk an abnormally subdued and mufflered Martin down the gelid street to Holborn tube station: as we trudged along there was a girl in front of us who looked as if she was walking on beautifully fluted stilts. "How might it be…?" he murmured thoughtfully with absolutely no leer or salacity. At once, it seemed, he had brightened and straightened and ceased to snuffle.

This was a tiny aspect of an elaborate and detailed investigation of the feminine mystique: a scrupulous weighing of evidence and comparing of notes. I would love to be able to give the impression that it was a relationship between equals but, if represented in cartoon form, the true picture would be closer to one of those great white sharks that evolution has fitted out with an accompanying but rather smaller fish.* I would turn up at parties with Martin, to be sure, but with a rather resigned attitude. At one *soirée* in Holland Park, he was introduced to a young woman with a result that was as close as made no difference to witnessing a lightning strike or a thunderbolt. His then-girlfriend was present at the party, as I think was the other young lady's husband, but what then happened in the adjoining room was unstoppable and seemed somehow foreordained. We both knew that the subsequent

---

* Picture my mixed emotions at appearing in his novel *The Pregnant Widow* in the character of his elder brother.

pregnancy was almost certainly also a consequent one, but so gentlemanly was the husband in the case that it was not until two decades later that Martin received the letter from his missing daughter, the lovely Delilah Seale, his "bonding" with whom—there doesn't seem to be another word for it—is one of the most affecting things I have ever chanced to see. (And she, the offspring of that thunderbolt moment, has now become the mother of Martin's first grandchild: another thought that gives me a reflective but piercingly sweet pang. Pasternak was perhaps not such a fool when he wrote in *Dr. Zhivago* that all conceptions are immaculate.)*

I could tell that Martin was fitted for glory in work as well as life and, when *The Rachel Papers* was a huge critical and commercial grand slam, I sent him a long telegram. It was a stave from F. Scott Fitzgerald's *Early Success*. Of course in some ways this was inappropriate—"Scottie" burned out and died at forty-four and is buried, along with poor mad Zelda, not far from me in Rockville, Maryland—but to us then, the age of forty lay well over the horizon. It wasn't really true of Martin, as Fitzgerald had put it, that "premature success gives one an almost mystical conception of destiny as opposed to will power—at its worst the Napoleonic delusion." However, there was a paragraph that did seem to meet the case and this I sent him:

> The compensation of a very early success is a conviction that life is a romantic matter. In the best sense one stays young. When the primary objects of love and money could be taken for granted and a shaky eminence had lost its fascination, I had fair years to waste,

---

* As I write this I have just read a "round-up" of authorial opinion printed by a London Sunday newspaper to coincide with Martin's 60th birthday. It's one of the most dispiriting things I have ever seen in print. With a few exceptions the contributors seem provincial and resentful and sunk in their own mediocrity. After all this time, they are obsessed with Martin's supposed head start in having had a distinguished father, and with the question of whether or not he is a "misogynist." On the first point he has answered quite well for himself—"Yes, it's just like taking over the family pub"—and on the second I have to reconcile myself with much annoyance to the fact that most people never saw him with his sister, will never see him with his daughters, or his legion of female friends, not by any means all of whom are former "conquests." So far from being some jaded Casanova, Martin possesses the rare gift—enviable if potentially time consuming—of being able to find something attractive in almost any woman. If this be misogyny, then give us increase of it.

years that I can't honestly say I regret, in seeking the eternal Carnival by the Sea.

Over the course of the next several years, we were still able to indulge in creative time-wasting by talking—always with ardent respect, but always exhaustively and until there was absolutely nothing left to say—about women, different women, and sometimes the same woman. I remember being rather relieved when, of one of those women, it could be said that it was I who had featured with her, so to speak, first. It seemed only fair...And then the talk would turn to other things. Martin never let friendship take precedence over his first love, which was and is the English language. If one employed a lazy or stale phrase, it would be rubbed in (there, I have done it again), no, it would be incisively *emphasized*, with a curl of that mighty lip and an ironic gesture. If one committed the offense in print—I remember once saying "no mean achievement" in an article—the rebuke might come in note form, or by one's being handed a copy of the article with a penciled underlining. He could take this vigilance to almost parodic lengths. The words "ruggedly handsome features" appear on the first page of *Nineteen Eighty-four* and for a while Martin declined to go any further into the book. ("The man can't write worth a damn.") He was later to admit that the novel did improve a trifle after that. Years later, when I gave him the manuscript of my book on Orwell, he brought it to our next rendezvous at a Manhattan bistro and wordlessly handed it back. He had gone through it page by page, painstakingly correcting my pepper-shaker punctuation.

He seemed to have read everything and he had the rare faculty of being able to quote longish staves of prose from memory. A passage about Sir Leicester Dedlock and gout from *Bleak House*; a spine-tingling rendition of Humbert Humbert's last verbal duel with Quilty; a pararaph or two about Alexander Portnoy's mother (the latter perhaps not so astonishing now I think about it: in his work as well as in his life, Martin has done the really hard thinking about handjobs, and put us all very sincerely and gratefully in his debt). In this area, too, I felt myself the junior. It was he who got me to read Nabokov and to do so with care as well as with awe, if only because I knew I would be asked questions. However, I was able to return the favor in a way which was to help change his life in turn, by pressing on him a copy of *Humboldt's Gift*.*

Loved by women while also being adored by men—shall I say "no mean achievement"?—Martin also has a way of attracting fathers. He once went to meet John Updike at the Massachusetts General Hospital and told me that, when he'd said goodbye, had felt oddly as if waving farewell to a male parent. I happened to be interviewing John Updike a year or so later and mentioned that I knew his great admirer the younger Amis. With an extraordinarily gentle expression on his face, Updike recalled the meeting at "Mass Gen" and said: "It was the strangest thing watching him walk away—almost as if he were my son." And nobody who has read Martin on Saul Bellow, let alone seen him in the company of the old man, can doubt for a second that his combination of admiring and protective feelings had eventually become fiercely filial. He said indignantly to me, when I gave Bellow's *Ravelstein* a slightly disobliging review, "Don't cheek your elders." I waited for something else—some hint of the ironic, perhaps—but with perfectly emphatic gravity he repeated the admonition. This from the one-time *enfant terrible* could mean only one thing.**

But I was also lucky in meeting Martin when his relationship with his true

---

* In 2008, when I finally had a best-seller hit of my own, it was from the pages of Bellow's great book that Martin sent me a sort of return compliment for my Fitzgerald telegram of 1974:

> It was my turn to be famous and to make money, to get heavy mail, to be recognized by influential people, to be dined at Sardi's and propositioned in padded booths by women who sprayed themselves with musk, to buy Sea Island cotton underpants and leather luggage, to live through the intolerable excitement of vindication. (I was right all along!) I experienced the high voltage of publicity...

This, too—the Sea Island gear and the musky women, for example—was quite imperfect as an analogy while still conveying an atmosphere.

** There was also a time when he might have adopted Vladimir Nabokov, posthumously as it were, as a proxy parent. He made himself master of the subject matter, got to know surviving members of the family, wrote an essay on *Lolita* that was frighteningly exact, did everything except take up *Lepidoptera*. But the more Martin absorbed himself in the man's work, the more it was borne in on him that the recurrent twelve-year-old-girl theme in Nabokov's writing was something more alarming and disturbing than a daring literary one-off. See, for his stern register of this disquieting business, the *Guardian* 14 November 2009.

father was at its absolute best. I remember envying the way in which the two of
them could tell jokes without inhibition, discuss matters sexual, and compete
only over minor differences about literature or politics. There had once been a
bad time when Martin and his siblings (and his mother) had been abandoned
by the old man, and there was to come a moment when that same old man
metamorphosed into an elderly man, querulous and paranoid and devoid of
wit. But in between there was a wonderful golden late summer. "Dad, will you
make some of your noises?" It was easy to see, when this invitation was taken
up, where Martin had acquired his own gift for mimicry. Kingsley could "do"
the sound of a brass band approaching on a foggy day. He could become the
Metropolitan line train entering Edgware Road station. He could be four
wrecked tramps coughing in a bus shelter (this was very demanding and once
led to heart palpitations). To create the hiss and crackle of a wartime radio
broadcast delivered by Franklin Delano Roosevelt was for him scant problem
(a tape of it, indeed, was played at his memorial meeting, where I was hugely
honored to be among the speakers). The *pièce de résistance*, an attempt by
British soldiers to start up a frozen two-ton truck on a windy morning "somewhere in Germany," was for special occasions only. One held one's breath as
Kingsley emitted the first screech of the busted starting-key. His only slightly
lesser vocal achievement—of a motor-bike yelling in mechanical agony—
once caused a man who had just parked his own machine in the street to turn
back anxiously and take a look. The old boy's imitatation of an angry dog
barking the words "fuck off" was note-perfect.*

Evenings at his home in Flask Walk (the perfect address) were of Fal-
staffian proportions, with bulging sacks of takeaway food and continual

---

* I am aware at all times, gentle reader, of the "perhaps you had to be there" element in a memoir. I strive to keep it permanently in mind. In the case of Kingsley, you *don't* absolutely have
to have been there. Try this, from one of his many wonderful letters to Philip Larkin. Amis
is imitating the ingratiating announcer of the BBC's condescending weekly program *Jazz
Record Requests*: "...Archie Shepp at his most exhilarating. Now to remind us of jazz's almost
infinite variety, back almost fifty years to Nogood Deaf Poxy Sam and *One-Titted Woman
Blues*: 'Wawawawa wawawaa wawa wawa wa wa Oh ah gawooma shony gawon tia waah, wawa
wa yeh ah gawooma shony gawon tia wawawwa waah wa boyf she ganutha she wouno where
to put ia.'" I was reading this late one night, several years after Kingsley's death, and once I'd
tried it out loud a couple of times I felt, through my hot tears of astonished laughter, that it was
as if he were in the room. And he went to all this trouble for a private letter!

raids on the rightly vaunted arsenal of his cellar. "Hitch," he said to me once. "You have been here before and you know the rule of the house. If you don't have a drink in your hand it's your own fault." Noises might or might not be part of the entertainment: he had a tendency to the gross and evidently thought that a belch (say) was a terrible thing to waste. I remember his unscripted trombonings and trumpetings, his cigars and his Macallan single malt, his limericks and his charades, just as I remember sitting quietly while he talked with authority about why Jane Austen was not all that good. The word "good," in all its variations (see the blues in the footnote preceding), was almost all that this man of immense vocabulary required as a shorthand critical tool. I don't know whether the concept hailed from the "Newspeak" dictionary in *Nineteen Eighty-four*, where the choices range from "plusgood" to "doubleplusungood," but "bloody good" from Kingsley was authoritatively affirmative, "good" was really pretty good, "some good" wasn't at all bad, "no good" was applied very scathingly indeed and a three-sentence six-word pronouncement which I heard him render upon Graham Greene's then-latest novel *The Human Factor* ("Absolutely no. Bloody good. AT ALL!") was conclusive.*

I shall try and be brief about the sorry way in which things "ended up." After I had left for America, Kingsley wrote a novel called *Stanley and the Women*. This failed to get itself published in New York, and word reached me that objections from feminists had prevented it from getting adopted by any major house. (There were also those who claimed to find it anti-Semitic, though the only "offensive" remarks in its pages were made by a young man who was clearly out of his mind.) I launched a campaign in my column in the *Times Literary Supplement*, against what was just then becoming widely known as "political correctness." I kept on being boring about this, until eventually I received a letter from an editor—a Jewish woman as it happened—who said in effect, Okay, you win, we'll save the honor of publishing by "doing" *Stanley*.

Kingsley, whom I hadn't seen for years, invited me to a celebration of this

---

* I write this in a week where I have been re-reading *Northanger Abbey*, and reflecting once again on the sheer *justice* of Kingsley's verdict on Miss Austen's "inclination to take a long time over what is of minor importance and a short time over what is major."

small victory on my next visit to London. We were to meet at the Garrick Club, be joined by Martin, see a movie, and then have a lavish dinner. I still shrink from recalling it: as soon as I arrived at the Garrick's bar he told me a joke I'd heard before and could obviously see that it hadn't "worked." His choice of film was an Eddie Murphy insult that seemed to contradict his increasing contempt for American culture: he appeared genuinely offended that we thought so little of it. Martin and I kept nervously behaving as if he must somehow be joking—"flawless masterpiece," he kept energetically insisting—and this was a mistake. Not only was he not joking, he was in every other way failing to be amusing. In an alarming reversal of his earlier Falstaffianism, he also managed to look both corpulent and resentful: "surfeit swell'd" to be sure, but quite without mirth. I think he may have managed one of his riffs about Nelson Mandela being a terrorist. Most painful of all, and somehow rendering rather pointless the original "point" of the evening, he had abandoned his old liking of the United States and passed the test of the true reactionary by becoming a sulphurous anti-American. (Every modern American novelist, he ended up by telling Martin once, and subverting my defense of him, "is either a Jew or a hick.") I was never to see "Kingers" again and, when I was almost the only person given kindly treatment in his notorious *Memoirs,* felt oddly discriminated against. That last evening of ours was the very definition of having no fun: we were no longer drawing on a common store of comic gags and literary allusions.

I boldly assert, in fact I think I know, that a lot of friendships and connections absolutely depend upon a sort of shared language, or slang. Not necessarily designed to exclude others, these can establish a certain comity and, even after a long absence, re-establish it in a second. Martin was—is—a genius at this sort of thing. It arose—arises—from his willingness to devote real time to the pitiless search for the apt resonance. I don't know quite why this lodges in my mind, but we once went to some grand black-tie ball that had been slightly overadvertised and proved disappointing. The following morning he rang me. "I've found the way to describe the men at that horror-show last evening... *Tuxed fucks.*" As this will illustrate, he did not scorn the demotic or the American: in fact he remains almost unique in the way that he can blend pub-talk and mid-Atlantic idiom into paragraphs and pages that are also fully aware of Milton and Shakespeare. I am morally certain that it's this combination of the classical with the wised-up and street-smart, most conspicuously with *Augie March*, that made it a sure thing that he and Saul Bellow would one day take each other's hands. Martin had a period of relishing the Boston thug-writer George V. Higgins, author of *The Friends of Eddie Coyle*. Higgins's characters had an infectious way of saying "inna" and "onna," so Martin would say, for example, "I think this lunch should be onna Hitch" or "I heard he wasn't that useful inna sack." Simple pleasures you may say, but linguistic sinew is acquired in this fashion and he would not dump a trope until he had chewed all the flesh and pulp of it and was left only with pith and pips. Thus there arrived a day when Park Lane played host to a fancy new American hotel with the no less fancy name of "The Inn on The Park" and he suggested a high-priced cocktail there for no better reason than that he could instruct the cab driver to "park inna Inn onna Park." This near-palindrome (as I now think of it) gave us much innocent pleasure.

Not all of our pleasures were innocent. There came the day when we were both in New York, and both beginning to feel the long, strong gravitational pull of the great American planet, but where a slight chore meanwhile required itself to be performed. In the midterm churnings of what was to become his breakout novel *Money*, Martin required his character to visit a brothel or *bordello*. He even had one all picked out: its front-name was the "Tahitia," a dire Polynesian-themed massage parlor, on lower Lexington Avenue. "And you," he informed me, "are fucking well coming with me."* I wanted to say something girlish like "Have I ever refused you anything?" but instead settled for something rather more masculine like "Do we know the form at this joint?" I could not possibly have felt less like any such expedition: I had a paint-stripping hangover and a sour mouth, but he had that look of set purpose on his face that I well knew, and also knew could not be gainsaid. How bad could it be?

Pretty damn bad as it turned out. Of the numerous regrettable elements that go to make up the unlawful carnal-knowledge industry, I should single out for distinction the look of undisguised contempt that is often worn

---

* I was later rather startled, not to say impressed, when I learned that he had "cleared" all this "research" with his then-wife, the fragrant and lofty Antonia. He telephoned her in London and, rather than temporize, informed her right away that: "I'm going to a handjob parlor with the Hitch."

on the faces of its female staff. Some of the working "hostesses" may have to simulate delight or even interest—itself a pretty cock-shriveling thought—but when these same ladies do the negotiating, they can shrug off the fake charm as a snake discards an unwanted skin. I suppose they know, or presume, that they have already got the despised male client exactly where they want him. As it happens, this wasn't true in our case—I would gladly have paid *not* to have sex at this point, and Martin needed only to snap his fingers in order to enjoy female company—but the cynical little witches at the "Tahitia" were not to know that they were being conscripted into the service of literature. It was well said—by Jean Tarrou in *The Plague*, I think—that attendance at lectures in an unknown language will help to hone one's awareness of the exceedingly slow passage of time. I once had the experience of being "waterboarded" and can now dimly appreciate how much every second counts in the experience of the torture victim, forced to go on enduring what is unendurable. But not even the lapse of time between then and now has numbed my recollection of how truly horrible it was to be faking interest in someone who was being paid—and paid rather more, incidentally, than I could afford—to feign a contemptuous interest in me. The multiplier effect of this mutual degradation gave me dry-heaves and flop-sweats and, I began to fear, conveyed the entirely misleading impression of my being a customer who was convulsed by the hectic sickness of lust. The seconds went limping and dragging by on absolutely leaden feet.

It was the cash question, though, that saved me. With some presence of mind, I had for once pre-empted Martin in the "bar" of the dump, where the gruesome selection process began, by swiftly pointing to the prettiest and slenderest of those available (who also possessed one of the most vicious-looking smiles I have ever seen on a human face). Once removed to her sinister cubicle, we commenced to bargain. Or rather, in a sort of squalid reverse-haggle, every time I agreed to the price she added some tax or impost or surcharge and bid me higher. Clad by now only in some sort of exiguous sarong, and equipped only with a dank Ziploc bag containing my credit cards and money (one was obliged to "check" everything else before entering the humid "bar") I wearily started to count out the ever-steepening fee, which was the only thing in the room that showed any sign of enlarging itself. It turned out that, what with tips and percentages and what-not, the avaricious bitch had contrived a figure that was not just more than I could afford, but more than I had on me. I was down to the quarters and nickels, and it showed. She had, I will say for her, more pride than that. A handful of change thrown in...No. No one can be expected to take this. So I took her cue of rage and stood up with about as much self-esteem as I could wrap around myself. Here was a two-faced coin of luck: I not only didn't have to go through with it, but I didn't have to shell out the dough, either.

I lurked torpidly in the recovery room or whatever they call it, and was eventually joined by a rather reduced and chastened Martin. If you want to know what happened to him, the whole experience enriched and enhanced by what I confessed to him of what had happened to me, you must read pages 98–104 of the Penguin edition of *Money*, where John Self tries to get laid for pay "under the bam, under the boo," at a perfectly foul establishment named "The Happy Isles." There are many, many reasons why *Money* is the Great English Novel of the 1980s, to which I am able to add this ensuing insight. Out of our grim little encounter (where he, poor bastard, actually had to part with the cash *and* endure a sexual fiasco) came several paragraphs of pure reality-based fantasy that make me twist and snarl with laughter every time. And no, you most definitely did not have to have been there. We went off to recuperate at a lunch with Jane Bonham Carter and Ian LeFresnais, at which I remember using hot Japanese *sake*, by no means for the first time, as an expedient solvent for my still-clinging hangover. Seldom can a midmorning have been so ill spent, yet (which perhaps goes to show) seldom can such rank dissipation have yielded so many dividends on the page.

In all of Martin's fiction one finds this same keen relish for, and appreciation of, the multiple uses of embarrassment. The bite of his wit redeems this from being mere farce or humiliation. When fused with his high seriousness about language, the effect is truly formidable. He once rebuked some pedantic antagonist by saying that the man lacked any sense of humor, but added that by this accusation he really intended to impugn his want of seriousness. In a completely other incarnation, I have often thought that he would have made a terrifying barrister. Once decided on mastering a brief, whether it be in his work on nuclear weapons, the Final Solution, or the Gulag, he would go off and positively saturate himself in the literature, and you could always tell there was a work in progress when all his conversation began to orient itself to the master-theme. (In this he strangely resembled Perry Anderson, the theoretician of *New Left Review*, with whom I also became friendly at about this time. Perry's encyclopedism extended well beyond ideology: he introduced me to the great social comedy of Anthony Powell's *Dance* sequence, of which he possesses a matchless understanding.) Like Perry, Martin contrived to do this without becoming monomaniacal or Ancient Mariner–like. There was a time when he wouldn't have known the difference between Bukharin and Bakunin, and his later writing on Marxism gets quite a few things wrong, including some things about me, and about James Fenton. Uncharacteristically for Martin, his labor on the great subject of Communism is also highly deficient in lacking a tragic sense, but he still passed the greatest of all tests in being a pleasure to argue with.

Back to my point about shared language: this gradual thickening of mutual experience became its own *patois*, as *Money* shows. Only recently, I found myself smirking in a foolish manner as a *New York Times* profile of Martin referred to the words "rug" (for hair-do) and "sock" (for loathsomely inadequate bachelor accommodations), that he had popularized for a generation. I played my own small part in this, with "sock" as I recall, as also with the then-overused word "re-think" to describe any wearisomely necessary and repetitive activity (such as a haircut or a bathroom trip). But it was not until Martin had put it into circulation that a coinage of this sort could hope to acquire any real currency.*

Something of the same was true of the "Friday lunch" that has now become the potential stuff of a new "Bloomsbury" legend. I find I want to try to limit myself on this subject, because the temptation to be "in" ought be resisted, and also because in this instance you probably did indeed have to "be there." I also bear in mind what Fenton once told me about the first Bloomsbury: in the early days of tape-recording it was decided to make a

---

* The only time that he ever seemed at all literal to me was in his absorption with soccer games. He would even buy tabloid newspapers on the following day, "to read accounts of previously played football matches" as I tried discouragingly to put it. From him I learned to accept, as I have since learned to accept from my son and my godson Jacob Amis and their friends, that there are men to whom the outcome of such sporting engagements is emotionally important. This is a test of masculinity, like some straight men's fascination with lesbianism, which I simply cannot seem to pass.

secret tape of the brilliant conversation of Raymond Mortimer and others. All who were "in" on the plan were later agreed that Mortimer and the others had been at their most scintillating on the afternoon concerned. But when replayed, the tape was as dull as rain. So the first thing to say about this luncheon circle was that, like Topsy in the old folk-story, it "just growed." There was never the intention or design that it become a "set" or a "circle," and of course if there had been any such intention, the thing would have been abortive. The Friday lunch began to simply "occur" in the mid-1970s, and persisted into the early 1980s, and is now cemented in place in several memoirs and biographies. Let me try and tell you something of how it was.

It began, largely at Martin's initiation, as a sort of end-of-the-week clearinghouse for gossip and jokes, based on the then-proximity of various literary magazines and newspapers. Reliable founding attendees included the Australian poets Clive James and Peter Porter, Craig Raine (T.S. Eliot's successor as poetry editor at Faber and Faber), the *Observer*'s literary editor Terry Kilmartin (the re-translator of Scott Moncrieff's version of Marcel Proust, and the only man alive trusted by Gore Vidal to edit his copy without further permission), the cartoonist and rake and dandy Mark Boxer, whose illustrations then graced (for once the word is quite apt) all the best bookcovers as well as the *Times*'s op-ed page. Among those bookcovers were the dozen volumes of Anthony Powell's masterwork and among Mark's aesthetic and social verdicts the one I remember being delivered with the most authority was his decided and long-meditated conclusion that: "It's the *height* of bad manners to sleep with somebody less than three times." (Once, planning a party with Martin and myself, he had completed the formal task of inviting all those who simply had to be asked, and exclaimed with relief and delight: "From now on, we should go on the basis of *looks alone*.") The critic Russell Davies, the then-rising novelists Ian McEwan and Julian Barnes, James Fenton and Robert Conquest when they were in England, Kingsley when he wasn't otherwise engaged with yet more lavish and extensive lunches, and your humble servant help to complete this *dramatis personae*. There were no women, or no regular ones, and nothing was ever said, or explicitly resolved, about this fact. Between us, we were believed to "control" a lot of the reviewing space in London, and much envious and paranoid comment was made then, and has been made since, to the effect that we vindicated or confirmed Dr. F.R.

Leavis's nightmare of a conspiratorial London literary establishment. But I can only remember one occasion when a book was brought along to lunch (to be given to me, so that I could "fill in" for some reviewer who had failed at the last moment), and I truly don't think that this "counts."

Time spent on recollecting our little Bohemia confirms three related but contrasting things for me. The first was the pervasive cultural influence of Philip Larkin. The second was the importance of word games and the long, exhaustive process that makes them both live and become worthwhile. The third was the gradual but ineluctable rise of Margaret Thatcher and her transatlantic counterpart Ronald Reagan. These, then, will be my excuses and pretexts for "letting in daylight upon magic," as Walter Bagehot phrased it.

Unspoken in our circle was quite a deep divide between Left and, if not exactly Right, yet increasingly anti-Left. Fenton and I were still quite Marxist in our own way, even if our cohort was of the heterodox type that I tried to describe earlier. Kingsley had become increasingly vocally right-wing, it often seeming to outsiders that he was confusing the state of the country with the condition of his own liver (but please see his diaries of the time to notice how cogent he often still was). Clive and Martin had been hugely impressed—as who indeed had not?—by the emergence of Alexander Solzhenitsyn as a moral and historical titan witnessing for truth against the state-sponsored lie. In between, men like Terry and Mark found it difficult to repudiate their dislike for a Tory Party that had been the main enemy in their youth. Robert Conquest was and still is the most distinguished and authoritative anti-Communist (and ex-Communist) writing in English, but if this subject was excluded, his politics tended toward something fairly equably Social Democratic in temper. He and I agreed that the Moscow Olympics should be boycotted after the Soviet invasion of Afghanistan, and of course it was he who noticed that some of the aquatic events were being held in the Baltic states, the Russian annexation of which had never been recognized by the post-Yalta agreements that defined the Cold War. At the last lunch I ever attended before emigrating for the United States, a toast was raised to Bob's impending fourth or was it fifth marriage. "Well," he replied modestly, "I thought perhaps 'one for the road.'" Philip Larkin wrote gloomily to Kingsley that the new Texan spouse would probably make their old friend move permanently to America, "as Yank bags do." And so indeed it proved.

Elisabeth—or "Liddie"—is a bit more than the "other half": she is a great scholar in her own person and the anchor of one of the most successful late marriages on record. Once Martin and I had also married Americans, she printed a T-shirt for all concerned that read "Yank bags club."

I learned appreciably from registering the crosscurrents that underlay this apparently light but really quite serious lunch. Our common admiration for Larkin, as a poet if not as a man, arose from the bleak honesty with which he confronted the fucked-up—the expression must be allowed—condition of the country in those years. It was his use of that phrase—"They fuck you up, your mum and dad," as the opening line of his masterly "This Be the Verse"—that put him outside the pale of the "family values" community. At one of my first encounters with Martin, when we discovered a common affinity for the man, I put my own main emphasis on his poem "Going, Going," which was a non-lachrymose elegy for the seaside and countryside of England, increasingly vandalized and paved and polluted by a combination of plebeian litter-louts and polluting capitalists. The poem had actually been commissioned by the Tory government of Edward Heath, to accompany the publication of a "White Paper" on the environment, but had then been censored because of a verse about the greedy businessmen who filled the estuaries with effluent. Larkin's innate pessimism, his loyalty to the gritty northern town of Hull (where lay the provincial university that employed him), and his hilarious interest in filth of all kinds were attractive to all of us: likewise his very moving, deliberate refusal of the false consolations of religion (beautifully captured by his "Aubade" and "Churchgoing") on which not even Kingsley disagreed. However, Larkin's pungent loathing for the Left, for immigrants, for striking workers, for foreigners and indeed "abroad," and for London showed that you couldn't have everything.

From Larkin's own emphatic use of it, a common-enough idiom, that of the "fool," was also evolved so as to try and make it as capacious as Kingsley's variation on the ordinary word "good." Thus there were of course, and as ever in English, plain fools and damn fools. But trying extra hard to be stupid could get you "bloody fool," and real excellence and application in the willful led to the *summa* of "fucking fool." This last title corresponded to Orwell's definition of something so simultaneously dumb and sinister that only an intellectual could be capable of uttering it. One lunchtime attempt to draw up a "Fucking Fools' First Eleven" of current greats attracted various nominations, John Berger being unanimously chosen as captain.

As for the word games, just bear with me if you would. Try, first, turning the word "House" into "Sock." OK: *Bleak Sock, Heartbreak Sock, The Fall of the Sock of Usher, The Sock of Atreus, The Sock of the Seven Gables, The Sock of the Rising Sun*... This can take time, as can the substitution (a very common English vulgarism) of the word "cunt," for the word "man." Thus: *A Cunt for All Seasons, A Cunt's a Cunt for All That, He Was a Cunt: Take Him for All in All, The Cunt Who Shot Liberty Valance, Batcunt, Supercunt* (I know, I know but one must keep the pot boiling) and then, all right, a shift to the only hardly less coarse word "prong," as in *The Prong with the Golden Gun, Our Prong in Havana, Prongs without Women, Those Magnificent Prongs in Their Flying Machines*, and so forth. These and other similarly grueling routines had to be rolled around the palate and the tongue many a time before Clive James suddenly exclaimed: "'A Shropshire Cunt.' By A.E. Sockprong." This symbiosis seemed somehow to make the long interludes of puerility worthwhile.

Clive was in some ways the chief whip of the lunch and would often ring round to make sure that there was a quorum (though I noticed that whenever Martin was away his enthusiasm waned a bit, as did everyone else's). He needed an audience and damn well deserved one. He beautifully illustrated my Peter De Vries point by having an absolutely massive following on television while slaving until dawn in Cambridge to produce gem-like essays for no-readership magazines like the *New Review* or, as his later anthologies of criticism and poetry have amazingly proven, for no immediate audience except himself: a fairly exacting one at that. His authority with the hyperbolic metaphor is, I think, unchallenged. Arnold Schwarzenegger in *Pumping Iron* resembled "a brown condom stuffed with walnuts." Of an encounter with some bore with famous halitosis Clive once announced "by this time his breath was *undoing my tie*." I well remember the day when he delivered his review of Leonid Brezhnev's memoirs to the *New Statesman* and Martin read its opening paragraphs out loud: "Here is a book so dull that a whirling dervish could read himself to sleep with it... If it were to be read in the open air, birds would fall stunned from the sky." One could *hear* his twanging marsupial tones in his scorn for this world-class drone and bully (whose work was being "published" by the ever-servile and mercenary tycoon Robert Maxwell, one of the Labour Party's many sources of shame). Clive had given up alcohol after a long period of enjoying a master-servant relationship with it, in which unfortunately the role of the booze had been played by Dirk Bogarde. He thus threw in money only for the food part of the bill, until one day he noticed how much the restaurant charged for awful muck such as bitter lemon and tonic water. At this he moaned with theatrical remorse: "I owe you all several hundred pounds!" But not all was geniality and verve: the only rift in the Friday lute came when Clive took huge exception to Fenton's review of his (actually quite bad) verse-play about the rise of Prince Charles. The expression complained of, I seem to recall, was "this is the worst poem of the twentieth century." The ensuing chill went on for a bit.

Ygael Gluckstein, the theoretical guru of the International Socialists, whose "party name" was Tony Cliff, used to tell an anecdote that I came to regard as an analogy for this sort of wordplay. Rosa Luxemburg, our heroine in the struggle against German imperialism (and the woman who had told Lenin that the right to free expression was meaningless unless it was the right of "the person who thinks differently") had once satirized the overcautious work of the German reformists and trade unionists as "the labor of Sisyphus." Whenever she approached the podium of the Social Democratic conventions before 1914, and before they proved her right by siding with the filthy kaiser on the crucial vote for war, she would be jeered at as she moved her lamed body toward the platform, and catcalled as "Sisyphus" by the union hacks. "So maybe Sisyphus was wasting his time," Gluckstein would say, hesitating for emphasis: "But maybe from this he still got some good muscles!"

If this historico-materialist point could be adapted for literary weight-training purposes, I would feel compelled to place on record the marginal question of the Tupper family. Everything depended, in this otherwise undistinguished imaginary dynasty, on your nickname. Thus, you might be an overeager salesman known to his colleagues as "Pushy" Tupper. You might even be a pedantic and donnish fellow saddled with the tag of "Stuffy." The opium-addict "Poppy" was about as far as most of us were prepared to last on this short-lived expedition, but Robert Conquest, the king of the limerick (and the dragon slayer of the Stalinoid apologists) always thought that if a job was worth doing it was worth doing well. He went off and brooded, and came back with Whirly, the helicopter pioneer, as well as the two hopeless boozers Whisky and indeed Rye Tupper. Ought one to blush, and to admit that some of these went straight into print as the questions-and-answers of the *New Statesman* weekend competition? Well, so did other things no less trivial that are now the stuff of *New Yorker* profiles, such as new equivalents for the old phrase "cruising for a bruising." ("Angling for a mangling," "aiming for a maiming," "strolling for a rolling" and — my own favorite — "thirsting for a worsting.") There was also the time that competitors were asked to submit a paragraph of a Graham Greene parody: Greene himself entered under a pseudonym and placed third. More demanding still was the restless quest, again chiefly led by Conquest, to inscribe the names of obscure and lowly, unenviable, and ultimately poorly rewarded occupations. Thus: one employed as a disciplinarian of last resort in a turbulent kitchen: "Cook-sacker." As a disciplinarian of last resort in an ill-run lunatic asylum: "Kook-socker." As the man in the bottling plant who keeps things moist: "Cork-soaker." As a sectarian pyromaniac in the Scots wars of religion: "Kirk-sacker." As one who has the lonely task of interrupting boat races by leaning over the bridge to snatch up the steersman with rod and line: "Cox-hooker."

Simple "versified filth" — Amis senior's crushing condemnation of most popular limericks — was not allowed.*

---

\* Indeed, insistence upon the capacious subtleties of the limerick was something of a hallmark. Once again Conquest takes the palm: his condensation of the "Seven Ages of Man" shows how much force can be packed into the deceptively slight five-line frame. Thus:

> Seven Ages: first puking and mewling
> Then very pissed-off with your schooling
> Then fucks, and then fights
> Next judging chaps' rights
> Then sitting in slippers: then drooling.

This is not the only example of Conquest's genius for compression. The history of the Bolshevik "experiment" in five lines? Barely a problem:

> There was an old bastard named Lenin
> Who did two or three million men in.
> That's a lot to have done in
> But where he did one in
> That old bastard Stalin did ten in.

One of Kingsley's letters from this period may show the way things were tending, and certainly makes me remember the atmosphere as it then was. He is writing to Robert Conquest on 7 April 1977:

> The swing to the right here is putting the wind up the lefties. At the Friday lunch the other day they, chiefly Hitchens and Fenton, were saying that chaps were getting fed up about stuff that may not be Labour's fault, but is associated with them rather than the Tories: porn and permissiveness generally, comprehensivization, TUC bosses, terrorism, and the defence run-down.

In cultural-political terms that's much as I remember it myself: an expiring postwar Labour consensus, increasingly dependent upon tax-funded statism yet actually run by the union-based, old-line right wing of the Labour Party machine. "A Weimar without the sex," as I once tried to phrase it at the time. Except that in the rest of society there was sex aplenty, with the hedonism of "the Sixties" almost officially instated as dogma, and the slow, surreptitious growth of this consensus to the then unguessed-at status of "correctness."

There could have been no bad time to meet him, but this in retrospect seems to have been the perfect moment to become acquainted with Ian McEwan. It was Martin who brought us together (Ian having succeeded him as the winner of the Somerset Maugham Award). By then, "everyone" had been mesmerized by Ian's early collections of short stories, *First Love, Last Rites* and *In Between the Sheets*. Met in person, he seemed at first to possess some of the same vaguely unsettling qualities as his tales. He never raised his voice, surveyed the world in a very level and almost affectless fashion through moon-shaped granny glasses, wore his hair in a fringe, was rail-thin, showed an interest in what Martin used to call "hippyish" pursuits, and when I met him was choosing to live on the fringes of the then weed-infested "front-line" black ghetto in Brixton. "What he wrote, you could see," as Clive James put it when using Ian's character in a novel, and when it came to fiction he seemed to have contact with other, remoter spheres. (He could and still can, for example, write about childhood and youth with an almost eerie ability to think and feel his way back into it: a faculty that many superb writers are unable to recruit in themselves.) I was sitting at my *New Statesman* desk one afternoon when the telephone rang and a strange voice asked for me by name. After I had confirmed that it was indeed me, or I, the voice said: "This is Thomas Pynchon speaking." I am glad that I did not say what I first thought of saying, because he was soon enough able to demonstrate that it *was* him, and that a mutual friend (make that a common friend) named Ian McEwan had suggested that he call. The book of still another friend, Larry Kramer's ultrahomosexual effort *Faggots*, had been seized by the British Customs and Excise and all the impounded copies were in danger of being destroyed. Mr. Pynchon was somewhere in England and was mightily distressed by this. What could be done? Could I raise an outcry, as Pynchon had been assured by Ian I could? I told him that one could protest hoarsely and long but that Britain had no law protecting free speech or forbidding state censorship. We chatted a bit longer, I artlessly offered to call him back, he laughingly declined this transparent try-on and faded back into the world where only McEwan could find him. (Ian seemed to be able to manage this sort of thing without ever boasting of it: he also formed a friendship with the almost-impossible-to-find Milan Kundera.)

From this you may surmise that Ian was not part of any pronounced drift to the political or cultural Right. But nor was he someone who had stopped reflecting at approximately the time of Woodstock. His father had been a regular officer in a Scottish regiment. He had a serious working knowledge of military history. His love of the natural world and of wildlife, leading to the arduously contemplative hikes about which we teased him, was matched by an interest in the "hard" sciences. I think that he did, at one stage in his life, dabble a bit in what's loosely called the "New Age," but in the end it was the rigorous side that won out and his novels are almost always patrolling some difficult frontier between the speculative and the unseen and the ways in which material reality reimposes itself. When not talking with penetration about literature and music, he was in himself an acute register of the stresses, cultural and moral, that were remaking the old British political divide.

One day, or actually one night, I made another saunter across the bridge of that divide in order to test the temperature and conditions on the other side. The circumstances could hardly have been more propitious for me: the Tories were having a reception in the Rosebery Room of the House of Lords, in order to launch a crusty old book by a crusty old peer named Lord Butler, and there was a rumor that the newly elected female leader of the Conservative Party would be among those present for the cocktails. I had written a longish article for the *New York Times* magazine, saying in effect that if Labour could not revolutionize British society, then the task might well fall to the Right. I had also written a shorter piece for the *New Statesman*, reporting from the Conservative Party conference and saying in passing that I thought Mrs. Thatcher was surprisingly sexy. (To this day, I have never had so much anger-mail saying, in effect, "How *could* you?") I felt immune to Mrs. Thatcher in most other ways, since for all her glib "free-market" advocacy on one front, she seemed to be an emotional ally of the authoritarian and protectionist white-settler regime in Rhodesia. And it was this very thing that afforded me the opportunity to grapple with her so early in her career.

At the party was Sir Peregrine Worsthorne, a poised and engaging chap with whom I'd had many debates in Rhodesia itself, both at the celebrated colonial bar of the Meikles Hotel and in other more rugged locations. I'd even taken him to meet Sir Roy Welensky, the tough old right-wing white trade unionist and former prime minister of Rhodesia who had broken with the treasonous pro-apartheid riffraff around Ian Smith. "It's always seemed perfectly simple to me, Mr. Verse-torn," this old bulldog growled in the unmistakable accent of the region: "If you don't *like* blick min, then *don't* come and live in Ifrica." Perry had granted the justice of this, as how could he not, and now felt that he owed me a small service in return. "Care to meet the new Leader?" Who could refuse? Within moments, Margaret Thatcher and I were face to face.

Within moments, too, I had turned away and was showing her my buttocks. I suppose that I must give some sort of explanation for this. Almost as soon as we shook hands on immediate introduction, I felt that she knew my name and had perhaps connected it to the socialist weekly that had recently called her rather sexy. While she struggled adorably with this moment of pretty confusion, I felt obliged to seek controversy and picked a fight with her on a detail of Rhodesia/Zimbabwe policy. She took me up on it. I was (as it chances) right on the small point of fact, and she was wrong. But she maintained her wrongness with such adamantine strength that I eventually conceded the point and even bowed slightly to emphasize my acknowledgment. "No," she said. "Bow *lower*!" Smiling agreeably, I bent forward a bit farther. "No, no," she trilled. "*Much* lower!" By this time, a little group of interested bystanders was gathering. I again bent forward, this time much more self-consciously. Stepping around behind me, she unmasked her batteries and smote me on the rear with the parliamentary order-paper that she had been rolling into a cylinder behind her back. I regained the vertical with some awkwardness. As she walked away, she looked back over her shoulder and gave an almost imperceptibly slight roll of the hip while mouthing the words: "Naughty boy!"

I had and have eyewitnesses to this. At the time, though, I hardly believed it myself. It is only from a later perspective, looking back on the manner in which she slaughtered and cowed all the former male leadership of her party and replaced them with pliant tools, that I appreciate the premonitory glimpse — of what someone in another context once called "the smack of firm government" — that I had been afforded. Even at the time, as I left that party, I knew I had met someone rather impressive. And the worst of "Thatcherism," as I was beginning by degrees to discover, was the rodent slowly stirring in my viscera: the uneasy but unbanishable feeling that on some essential matters she might be right.

# Portugal to Poland

———◄○►———

I N RETROSPECT it seems to have been more conscious on my part than perhaps it was at the time, but there came a stage where I took refuge in travel. To adapt what Cavafy says about the barbarians, this was a solution of various kinds. It removed me from a London that was often dank and second-rate. It kindled in me a resolution which I have tried to keep ever since: to spend at least once every year a little time in a country less fortunate than my own. (If this doesn't stop you getting fat, it can at least help prevent you from getting too soft.) And, in the period I am writing about, it allowed me to continue seeing the Left as a force that was still struggling for first principles against the traditional foes.

I would be indignant if anyone were to describe this as "romantic"—a term that we were especially educated to despise in the International Socialists, even though I now think that there may be more reprehensible words. But, if you exempt a solidarity trip that I took to express support for the Icelandic socialists who were fighting to stop British trawlers from hoovering up all their fish (and Iceland is an exotic locale all of its own, with its moonscape interior and geyser-supplied hot water with the ever-present diabolical whiff of sulphur), it is true that the impulse generally led me to the south and to the Mediterranean and to the Levant.

One of the many great hopes of 1968 had been to complete the unfinished business of the Second World War and cleanse Spain and Portugal of their antique fascist regimes. Not only had this ambition not been realized, but another dictatorship of the Right had been imposed on Greece and then spread, with calamitous results, to the independent republic of Cyprus. The drama extended across both sides of the Pillars of Hercules: Franco's Spain made a free gift of its Western Sahara colonial possession to the absolutist monarchy in Morocco, leaving the population voiceless in its own destiny. It also extended to the extreme opposite end of the Mediterranean, where an Israeli Jewish opposition to the occupation of Palestinian land was beginning to take shape, and where in Lebanon an alliance of secular and Palestinian forces was emerging to challenge the old confession-based hierarchy.

A whole anthology of images survives vividly in my mind from this time. A spontaneous riot on the broad Ramblas of Barcelona, after the last-ever use of the hideous medieval *garrotte* for the judicial murder of a Catalan anarchist named Salvador Puig Antich: the illegal Catalan flag proudly flown and a shower of gasoline bombs falling on Franco's military police. A journey to Guernica—a place name that I could hardly believe corresponded to an actual living town—to rendezvous with Basque activists. A weekend in the Latin Quarter in Paris, complete with telephone "passwords" and anonymous handshakes in corner *zinc* bars, so that I could meet a Portuguese resistance leader named Palma Inacio who was engaged in organizing an armed battle against the dictatorship in Lisbon. Some long, hot, and fragrant days in Tyre and Sidon and points south of Beirut, meeting with militants of the "Democratic Front" who, over lunch in the olive groves, would patiently explain to me that Jews and Arabs were brothers under the skin and that only imperialism was really the problem. Standing in Freedom Square in Nicosia among a roaring crowd of demonstrators, many of whom had recently fought with gun in hand against the Greek junta's attempt to annex Cyprus, but whose voices could also be heard over the impermeable wall that the invading Turkish army had built right across a free city.

I liked all this for its elemental headiness (it seemed to go so well with different blends of wine and *raki*) but also for its seriousness—politics in these latitudes being a game played for keeps—and for its immediate and intense connection to history. I felt I knew the Ramblas from Orwell's *Homage to Catalonia*: in Algiers after returning from an expedition with the Polisario guerrillas fighting in the Sahara, I thought I also had at least a vicarious glimpse of the continuation of an old struggle for the soul of North Africa that had once involved Camus and Sartre. As for Cyprus, where I fell so hard in love with the island and the people—and with the very place names: Famagusta, Larnaca, Limassol, Kyrenia, and with one very dramatic and life-altering Cypriot—was not the philhellenic tradition the very one that had helped revive British radicalism more than a century before? (Today I want to puke when I hear the word "radical" applied so slothfully and stupidly to Islamist murderers; the most plainly reactionary people in the world.)

The alteration of perspective was the most useful thing. In northern Europe it was, roughly speaking, a case of the free West versus the "satellite states" of the East. In Cyprus, though, the illegal occupying power was a member of NATO. In Portugal, the fascist regime itself was a member of NATO. Likewise in the case of Greece. In Spain, the main external relationship of the system was with Washington. Thus it was possible to meet Communists who, in these special circumstances, not only made sense but had heroic records and were respected popular figures. In Cyprus, at a very red-flag rally where I was among the platform speakers, I had the distinct honor of shaking the hand of Manolis Glezos, who had given the signal for revolt in Athens in 1944 by climbing up the Parthenon and tearing the swastika flag from the pediment. Not a bad day's work, I think you'll agree.*

However, of Comrade Glezos it also had to be said that he had once run a bookstore in Athens that largely featured the work of Enver Hoxha of Albania, possibly the most Aztec-like of all Europe's remaining Stalinists. And I hadn't forgotten the second great promise of 1968, which was that of solidarity with the forces of dissent in "the other Europe," the nations of the East and the Baltic who had been stranded and frozen in time ever since the Yalta agreement permitted the partition of the continent. Thus for me the three most important episodes from this epoch are the stirrings of revolution in Portugal and in Poland, and the experience of counter-revolution in Argentina.

---

* A comparable if not equivalent consideration sometimes applied in the "other" case: for all his indomitable moral courage Solzhenitsyn had already begun to show signs of being an extreme Russian nationalist and partisan of religious orthodoxy. The synthesis for which one aimed was the Orwellian one of evolving a consistent and integral anti-totalitarianism.

# Lusitania

Mediterranean though it can feel, Portugal is the only European country that has the Atlantic Ocean lapping around the inner harbor of its capital city. Its amazing mariners took its oddly inflected language as far away as East Timor and Macao though King Henry "the Navigator" probably never actually boarded a ship. As soon as I could manage it after the revolution of April 1974, I arrived ordinarily enough by air, and was then told to wait in the customs area. Was I perhaps on some list of undesirables, as I had found myself to be at other airports? A lanky, white-haired official, proffering a card that proclaimed his name to be Viera da Fonseca (just like the delicious port wine), extended a hand. He was to escort me to a hotel. It appeared that I was an honored guest. For the first time in my life, I was on a list of desirables. When the files of the former secret police of the Salazar/Caetano dictatorship had been broken open, it was found that I was listed as a particular foe of the *ancien régime*. Having imagined myself dossing down happily with my comrades on the floor of some left-wing slum apartment, I was promoted to a fairly elevated floor of the Tivoli Hotel on the Avenida Libertad, with a view of the city's captivating harbor. It all seemed too much, as if one had suddenly received the profits and dividends of an investment that had barely been made. I formed a private resolution not to become too used to it.

But the fall of fascism in Lisbon in April 1974 was the occasion for an almost perfect storm of radical desires. The overthrow of the Caetano dictatorship was not only part of the long-postponed business of cleansing Europe of pre-1939 fascism, it was also a sort of revenge for the destruction in the preceding autumn (on 11 September to be precise) of the Allende government in Chile. There were other happy convergences at work, also. With the old gang removed, the grip of Portugal on its African colonies was broken, and this meant not only the emancipation of Angola and Mozambique and Guinea-Bissau but also an acceleration of the process that would eventually terminate racist rule in Rhodesia and South Africa. Other revolutionary ripple effects might be expected in Portuguese-speaking Brazil, the largest and in some ways the most vicious of the authoritarian military regimes of the Southern Cone of the Americas, while the effect on neighboring Spain surely had to be a demoralizing one from the viewpoint of Franco's military and religious allies. A whole series of fault lines radiated away from this Lisbon earthquake, all of them shivering the structures of traditional order. And this was simply to speak politically. The cultural element made it seem as if the best of 1968 was still relevant. One of the precipitating prerevolutionary moments had been the publication of a feminist manifesto by three women, all of whom were named Maria, and "The Three Marias" became an exciting example of what womanhood could do when faced with a theocratic oligarchy that had treated them as breeding machines not far advanced above the level of chattel. Sex, long repressed, was to be scented very strongly on the wind: I remember in particular the only partly satirical Movimento da Esquerda Libidinosa or "Movement of the Libidinous Left," with its slogan *Somos um partido sexocratico*," whose evident objective was the frantic making-up of lost time. The best revolutionary poster I saw—perhaps the best I have ever seen—expressed this same thought in a rather less erotic way: it showed a modest Portuguese family in traditional dress, being introduced to a receiving line of new friends who included Socrates, Einstein, Beethoven, Spinoza, Shakespeare, Charlie Chaplin, Louis Armstrong, Karl Marx, and Sigmund Freud. (There are many people in much richer countries who are still putting off this rendezvous.)

As well as being a colonial power, Portugal under fascism had managed also to let itself become a semi-colony, whose main export was cheap labor to the rest of Europe and whose illiteracy rate was about thirty percent. The resulting division of the country, between the boss class and the officer class and the rank-and-file, was very striking. The astounding thing, in the mass demonstrations that thronged the Avenida Libertad and the Rossio Square, was to see the squads of uniformed young sailors and soldiers joining in with the workers and the students: to my eyes an almost literal replay of the scenes from *Battleship Potemkin* or the storming of the Winter Palace. And, once I had cleared my eyes by drying them, I noticed that the parallel with St. Petersburg could be drawn in other ways, too.

In 1968 the ferment of revolution had taken the ossified French Communist Party completely aback, forcing it in effect to line up with de Gaulle. This it had done, partly to protect its position as "the party of order" and partly to obey Soviet instructions that the anti-NATO and anti-American regime of the Gaullists be left as far as possible unmolested. In Portugal no such inhibitions were in play, because the old order had irretrievably vanished like breath off a razor blade, and there was a good old-fashioned power vacuum or, as we used to say in factional meetings, a "situation of dual power." Workers' committees were forming embryo soviets, soldiers' and sailors' collectives had whole ships and regiments under their temporary command, landless workers in the countryside were taking over abandoned farms and properties. There were two things to notice about this. One was that hardly a shot was fired: the Portuguese may have exported a good deal of their violence overseas to Africa but in the country itself the rhythms were—when compared to neighboring Spain, say—remarkably gentle. (As a possible metaphor, in Portuguese bullfights the bull is not tortured or killed: the matador tests only his own agility and bravery against the noble beast.) The second thing to absorb was that, behind all the spontaneity and eroticism and generalized "festival of the oppressed" merrymaking, a grim-faced Communist *apparat* was making preparations for an end to the revels and a serious seizure of the state.

"The USSR is the sun in our universe," proclaimed Alvaro Cunhal, leader of the Portuguese Stalinists, who had returned from exile in Moscow to direct operations. The tactics were more those of 1948 in Prague than St. Petersburg in 1917, consisting of the slow acquisition of positions in the army and the police, and the application of what used to be called "salami tactics" against other parties. The Portuguese Socialist Party enjoyed the support of a majority of the people, so it was not by coincidence that one of its main newspapers, *La Repubblica*, became the target of a "spontaneous" takeover by the print-workers, which their Communist union bosses endorsed as if butter would not melt in their mouths. Nor was it by coincidence that the Chemical Workers' Union, which had a latent socialist majority among its membership, found some of its Communist officials oddly reluctant to hold a ballot. The emergency nationalization of the banks meant opportunities, in a state that had formerly been corporatist and monopolistic, for the bureaucratic "new class" to become the owners of large tracts of Africa, and the proprietors of seats on the boards of newspapers and television stations. The leader of the Socialist Party, Mario Soares, a man whom I would normally have regarded as a pallid and compromising Social Democrat, summarized the situation with some pith. I still have the question he put to me, double-underlined in my notebook from Lisbon. "If the army officers are so much on the side of the people, why do they not put on civilian clothes?" It was a question not just for that moment.

I began to be extremely downcast by the failure, or was it refusal, of my International Socialist comrades to see what was staring them right in the face. Intoxicated by the admittedly very moving attempts at personal liberation and social "self-management," they could not or would not appreciate how much of this was being manipulated by a dreary conformist sect with an ultimate loyalty to Russia. Thus I found myself one evening in late March 1975 at a huge rally in the Campo Pequeno bullring in Lisbon, organized by the distinctly cautious Socialist Party but with the invigorating slogan: "*Socialismo Si! Dictatura Nao!*" The whole arena was a mass of red flags, and the other chants echoed the original one. There were calls for the right of chemical workers to vote, a banner that read "Down With Social Fascism" and another that expressed my own views almost perfectly in respect of foreign intervention in Portugal: "*Nem Kissinger, Nem Brezhnev!*" I took my old friend Colin MacCabe along to this event. For his numberless sins he was at the time a member of the Communist Party, and at first employed an old Maoist catchphrase—"waving the red flag to oppose the red flag"—to dismiss what he was seeing. But gradually he became more impressed and as the evening began to crystallize he unbent so far as to say: "Sometimes the wrong people can have the right line." I thought then that he had said more than he intended, and myself experienced the remark as a sort of emancipation from the worry, which did still occasionally nag at me, that by taking up some out-of-line position I would find myself "in bed with," as the saying went, unsavory elements. It's good to throw off this sort of moral blackmail and mind-forged manacle as early in life as one can.*

The sequel takes very little time to tell: the Communists and their ultra-Left allies hopelessly overplayed their hand by trying for a barracks-based coup, the

---

* Colin, who went on to become a distinguished author of books on James Joyce and Jean-Luc Godard, years later called me from China where Deng Xiaoping had just announced that his reforms would mean that all would get richer but some would get richer than others. "So it looks as if your pal Orwell was on to something after all." I thought that was a handsome enough concession. It was rather a poor return, when his friend the grim and fraudulent Stalinist philosopher Louis Althusser was convicted of murdering his wife, for me to say, "I see Comrade Althusser has been awarded the electric chair of philosophy at the Ecole Abnormale."

more traditional and rural and religious elements of Portuguese society rose in an indignant counter-revolution, a sort of equilibrium was restored and— *e finita la commedia*. The young radicals who had come from all over Europe to a feast of sex and sunshine and anti-politics folded their tents and doffed their motley and went home. It was the last fall of the curtain on the last act of the 1968 style, with its "take your desires for reality" wall posters and its concept of work as play. For me, it was also the end of the line with my old *groupuscule*. I had developed other disagreements, too, as the old and open-minded "International Socialists" began to mutate into a more party-line sect. But Portugal had broken the mainspring for me, because it had caused me to understand that I thought democracy and pluralism were good things in themselves, and ends in themselves at that, rather than means to another end.

In his superb collection of essays *Writers and Politics*, which influenced me enormously when I first found it in a public library in Devonshire in 1967, Conor Cruise O'Brien had phrased it better than I could then hope to do:

> "Are you a socialist?" asked the African leader.
>
> I said, yes.
>
> He looked me in the eye. "People have been telling me," he said lightly, "that you are a liberal..."
>
> The statement in its context invited a denial. I said nothing.
>
> And yet, as I drove home from my interview with the leader, I had to realize that a liberal, incurably, was what I was. Whatever I might argue, I was more profoundly attached to liberal concepts of freedom—freedom of speech and of the press, academic freedom, independent judgment and independent judges—than I was to the idea of a disciplined party mobilizing all the forces of society for the creation of a social order guaranteeing more real freedom for all instead of just for a few. The revolutionary idea struck me as more *immediately* relevant for most of humanity than were the liberal concepts. But it was the liberal concepts and their long-term importance—though not the name of liberal—that held my allegiance.

One can read such things and understand and even appreciate them, and one can undergo experiences that recall one to the original text as if in confirmation. I cite O'Brien not as an argument from authority, for I was to have many disputes with him down the years, but as a man of considerable mind who brilliantly summarized the contradictions with which I had been living, and with which in many ways I was condemned to go on coexisting for some time to come.*

## Liberté à la Polonaise

I was to have the same contrasts emphasized for me in a different way at the opposite end of Europe over the Christmas of 1976. The previous summer I had been very intrigued by reports of a small-scale but suggestive workers' revolt in Communist Poland, where Party property and several stretches of railway line had been extensively damaged in rioting against a sudden announcement from on high of a steep rise in the price of food. Some protestors had been killed and the rest dispersed and several put on trial—nothing exceptional in that—but a new element had intruded itself. Petitions had been circulating in Warsaw, soliciting money for a legal defense of the accused workers. Voices had been raised, demanding an inquiry into the conduct of the police and militia during the disturbances. Was it possible that, twenty years after the Polish "spring" of 1956, the *Germinal* of another movement from below was under way?

Interviewing one of the former leaders of the Portuguese fascist system, Dr. Franco Nogueira, in his office at the amazingly titled Banco Spiritu Santu e Comercial (Bank of the Holy Spirit and Commerce, its grotesque moniker partly explained by a family name), I had been informed by him that it was relatively easy to keep Portugal and its people contained and under control

---

* O'Brien's definition of liberalism as a position "that made the rich world yawn and the poor world sick" is a phrasing that older readers may remember if only because of Phil Ochs's bitingly satirical song "Love Me, I'm a Liberal." Arrested once in Oxford for disrupting a cricket match with an apartheid South African team, I was able to get myself acquitted of the police frame-up because a bystander came forward and offered himself as an impartial witness. He was a highly respectable citizen and cricket-watcher and the treasurer of the local Liberal Party. Attending the trial and after giving his testimony, he saw me refuse to take my oath on the Bible and heard me tell the bench as my reason that I was "an atheist and a Marxist." After the hearing was over, he came up to me and said that if he had known that I was *that* kind of person, he would never have volunteered to testify. For many years, this well-meaning but invertebrate figure was my ideal type of the "liberal" mentality, and he still comes back to me at odd moments.

because the country was peculiar in Europe in only having one land frontier. Poland's problem is the exact opposite. It is condemned by geography to live between Germany and Russia, and has been repeatedly invaded, occupied, and partitioned. Not an entirely blameless country—its forces took part in the dismemberment of Czechoslovakia after the British sell-out in Munich— in 1939 it was attacked and overrun by both Hitler and Stalin acting in concert. Its borders were redrawn again after 1945—I was late in life to discover that those frontier territories had been the home of my mother's ancestors— and in 1976 the eventual results of the Hitler-Stalin rapacity could be seen in a dingy Russian-backed Communist bureaucracy sitting atop a sullen and strongly Catholic people who perhaps only agreed with their rulers in distrusting Federal Germany. (An old national chestnut asks the question: If the Russians and Germans both attack again, who do you shoot first? Answer: "The Germans. Business Before Pleasure." You can also deduce something about a Pole who answers this question the other way around.)

My business, however, was not with the Communists or the nationalists but with the democrats and the internationalists. At the time, these seemed to be about ten or twenty in number, barely enough to constitute a *minyan* had they been Jewish, which a few of them—however secular and non-Zionist—actually were. The one I most wished to meet was Jacek Kurón, author of the Trotskyist manifesto against the regime that I had so eagerly hawked around Oxford. He was still going, and strongly at that, in a tiny apartment much invigilated by the "U.B." or Polish secret police. Out of this cell of an apartment and other cells like it was to come a replicating system—the Workers Defense Committee/Komitet Obrony Robotnikow or KOR—which would eventually multiply and divide and evolve (perhaps paradoxically) into something more basic and simple: the elementary word—and movement—*Solidarnosc* or "Solidarity."

Rabbi Tarfon says somewhere that the task can never be quite completed, yet one has no right to give it up. Of the comrades I met that bleak winter, many of them veterans of the extemely nasty Polish prison system, none really expected to make more than a small dent in the regime. Yet to an outsider like myself, there did seem to be a faint nimbus of optimism, visible on the very edge of a dark and cold star. It was, to put it another way, quite astonishing to see how much, and to what an extent, the party-state depended on lies. Small lies and big lies. Petty lies hardly worth telling, that would shame a nose-picking, whining, guilty child, and huge lies that would cause a hardened blackmailer and perjurer to blush a bit.

To give an example of the paltry sort: the Chilean Communist leader Luis Corvalán had recently been "swapped," in a piece of overt Cold War horse-trading, for the Soviet dissident Vladimir Bukovsky. No evident disgrace in that, perhaps, but the Polish Communist press insisted only on reporting the release of Corvalán, and only as the outcome of a campaign of inter-national proletarian solidarity. In a time of BBC and other broadcasts, and with many Poles having family overseas, the chances of such a falsification being believed were exactly nil. Yet such crass falsification was the everyday currency of the Polish media.

On the macro scale, it was still officially "true" that the mass graves of Katyn, across the Belarus border, in which the corpses of tens of thousands of Polish officers had been hastily interred in the 1940s, were the responsi-bility of the Nazis. But there simply wasn't a single person in the whole of Poland who credited this disgusting untruth. Not even those paid to spread it believed it.*

My American Trotskyist girlfriend and I had been told by friends that the thing to take to Warsaw was blue jeans, which had totemic value on the black market. We accordingly packed several old, patched, worn-out pairs. We scrounged a bed from my old Oxford comrade Christopher Bobinski, who was then just beginning his stellar career as a reporter from his home-land. As an interpreter he provided us with the lovely Barbara Kopec, who held down a daytime job in the "Palace of Culture" that dominated the main square of the city. It had been built as a personal gift from Joseph Stalin to the people of Poland, and in its form and shape expressed all the good taste and goodwill that such benevolence might have implied. It wasn't much fun working inside the building, as Barbara remarked, but at least it meant she didn't have to look at the damn thing.

When we went to meet Jacek Kurón in his tiny cluttered apartment, this

---

* The British Foreign Office may be an exception here. Its bureaucrats continued to spout the lie, born of the wartime alliance with Stalin, until the Soviet Union beat them to it under Mikhail Gorbachev and officially accepted responsibility for Katyn in 1990.

tough and stocky fellow punctured one of my illusions right away, by saying that he no longer had any illusions about Trotskyism. The real terrain
of struggle was for democratic liberties and the rule of law. And, even as we
spoke, we were continually reminded of the distance to be traveled toward
this goal. At regular intervals, Kurón's phone would ring and he would be
subjected to "spontaneous" abuse. In an effort to spook him, a death threat
had been anonymously delivered, with a countdown of a hundred days. It
stood at sixty-five to go on the day of our visit. And the besetting sin of Polish public life, anti-Semitism, was in evidence as well. He showed and read
me a violently Jew-hating letter, sent to him by registered mail. The sender
had then delivered another letter, this time by hand, confessing that the first
missive had been dictated to him in a police station! This showed a real
sickness in the Communist system, not just because of the use of bigotry as
a provocation, but because anti-Semitism had historically always been used
by the Polish right wing against the Reds. It took real calcified cynicism to
employ such a weapon of reaction against dissent. (It would have been even
nastier if Jacek Kurón had actually been Jewish, but the fact is that he wasn't:
Polish and other Jew-baiters have been known to operate without possessing
the raw material of any actual Jews to "work" with.)

In their pedantic way, the postwar Communists had tried to rebuild
Warsaw as an exact replica of its prewar self. Some of this was soulless and
dull, but there was heavy snow that Christmas, and I found the icy city rather
hypnotizing. We went to the nearby township of Kazimierc, once a center
of Jewish life before the nearly "clean" sweep that had been made of Polish
Jewry. We attended a midnight Mass in Vilanow, where the congregation was
so densely packed that it spilled out of doors, with worshippers kneeling in
the drifts. I could not understand much of the sermon, but it didn't seem to
be delivered in the emetic, emollient tones of the Second Vatican Council.
Polish Catholicism, often a historic ally of extremist politics, also had its col-
laborationist side with a semi-official group known as Pax Christi sitting in
the rubber-stamp parliament. But that Christmas Cardinal Wyszynski gave
a rather decent and spirited sermon, making quite strong statements about
the repression of strikers. Everybody got to hear about it, but the official
press didn't report a single line of the homily, thus underlining yet again the
self-defeating character of lying and censorship. "Self-sabotaging" might be

a better term: one of the strikes in the port city of Stettin had been provoked when the shipyard workers read in the Communist Party paper that they had all "volunteered" to work longer hours in the interests of production. One of the leaders of that strike, a man named Edmund Baluka, later told me that he had been sent as a soldier into Czechoslovakia during the Warsaw Pact aggression of August 1968. He had been told, and had believed, that he was going to repel a West German invasion of Prague. Discovering a complete absence of Germans in the country—except for East German soldiers who were also taking part in the Russian-sponsored occupation—had destroyed his entire faith in anything the Party ever said. (Baluka, too, was for some time to associate himself with Trotskyism.)

Our young friends in the KOR invited us for a Christmas Eve feast in a cold but cheery apartment. There was a great deal to eat and drink, but I suddenly noticed with an inner qualm that everything—every loaf and sausage and cheese and bottle—was the last third or quarter of itself. It was clear that in the interests of hospitality, all the odds and ends and saved-up leftovers were being deployed. I was glad to be able to produce the parcel of blue jeans. And I don't remember a gift ever going over so well. "Are you sure you can spare *all* of these?" we were asked, as if we were parting with a fortune. "On the black market, this can raise a *huge* amount for the committee." There was also the eagerly discussed hope that KOR could start an underground publishing house, to print among other things the works of George Orwell. (This did later happen, with a *samizdat* imprint called *NOWA*.) Even so, and keen as I was on the latter idea especially, I urged them to keep back at least something of our gift for themselves. They remained self-denyingly serious, though I think it was decided that Barbara should have a pair of her very own, if only to show off a bit of style in the Stalinist wedding cake that was her office building. In later years, as the strikes burgeoned and spread and the Polish working class outlived both the Polish Communist Party and—as in Portugal—the attempt of that party to stay in power by using the army, I liked to imagine those blue jeans as having acted as one of the pebbles that began the historical avalanche.

My ability to carry my liquor was very useful on that trip, as it has been on several other voyages. The hearteningly jovial and inspiring evening ended with a drinking-bout challenge to me from a young comrade named Witold. Two lines of shot glasses were arranged down each side of the dining table, and filled to the brim with different flavors of Polish vodka, including my own then-favorite Zubrovka, tinted a pale-ish green by the buffalo grass that grows in the east of the country. Last man to the finish-line was a sissy. I do not actually remember whether I beat Witold or whether it was a dead heat, but I remember a rush of pride at his fraternal embrace, and also his exclaiming: "*Christophe, tu es un* vrai *Polonais!*" It was a title of honor.

This trip was also to yield me another of those life-altering *aperçus*. It came from Adam Michnik, one of the founders of the KOR and later one of the chief intellectuals of Solidarnosc and later still—and to this day—a leading figure in the academic and publishing life of his country. When I met him, he was already a veteran of numerous victimizations and imprisonments. His troubles had begun in 1966, when he was expelled from the university for organizing a seminar for Professor Leszek Kolakowski. Having a Jewish father but not a Jewish mother he could easily have "passed" but preferred to describe himself as a Pole of Jewish descent. He was then definitely of the secular Left, and had been impressed by the way that, in Franco Spain, "civil society" had been able to build up parallel institutions that could gradually and organically replace the deliquescent absolutist state. This was very much the model that many of Poland's oppositionists were to follow. I mentioned to him at our first meeting that Jacek Kurón thought the next wave of protests wouldn't be very "socialistic," because the word had been so much discredited by Communist rule. Michnik wasn't so sure. "After all, 'freedom' and 'democracy' are words that have been discredited by governments as well, but we do not abandon them for that reason. *The real struggle for us is for the citizen to cease to be the property of the state.*" I knew as I wrote it down and underlined it that that last sentence was a pregnant one, that its implications for all political positions were enormous and that in order to stay true to the principle—once again, the principle of consistent anti-totalitarianism—one might have to expose oneself to steadily mounting contradictions.

I was to see Adam Michnik on and off through the long transformation of Poland and watch him emerge as an honored historian and politician as well as the editor of perhaps the country's most respected newspaper, *Gazeta Wyborzka*, which had begun life as an illegal strike-sheet. One of the juiciest pleasures of life is to be able to salute and embrace, as elected leaders and honored representatives, people whom you first met when they were on the run or in exile or (like Adam) in and out of jail. I was to have this experience again, and I hope to have it many more times in the future: it sometimes allows me to feel that life is full of point.

## Argentina: Death and Disappearance (and an Infinite Library)

At a lunchtime reception for the diplomatic corps in Washington, given the day before the inauguration of Barack Obama as president, I was approached by a good-looking man who extended his hand. "We once met many years ago," he said. "And you knew and befriended my father." My mind emptied, as so often happens on such occasions. I had to inform him that he had the advantage of me. "My name is Hector Timerman. I am the ambassador of Argentina."

In my above album of things that seem to make life pointful and worthwhile, and that even occasionally suggest, in Dr. King's phrase as often cited by President Obama, that there could be a long arc in the moral universe that slowly, eventually bends toward justice, this would constitute an exceptional entry. It was also something more than a nudge to my memory. There was a time when the name of Jacobo Timerman, the kidnapped and tortured editor of the newspaper *La Opinion* in Buenos Aires, was a talismanic one. The mere mention of it was enough to elicit moans of obscene pleasure from every fascist south of the Rio Grande: finally in Argentina there was a strict "New Order" that would stamp hard upon the international Communist-Jewish collusion. A little later, the mention of Timerman's case was enough to derail the nomination of Ronald Reagan's first nominee as undersecretary for human rights; a man who didn't seem to have grasped the point that neo-Nazism was a problem for American values. And Timerman's memoir, *Prisoner without a Name, Cell without a Number*, was the book above all that clothed in living, hurting flesh the necessarily abstract idea of the *desaparecido*: the disappeared one or, to invest it with the more sinister and grisly past participle with which it came into the world, the one who has *been* "disappeared." In the nuances of that past participle, many, many people vanished into a void that is still unimaginable.

It became one of the keywords, along with *escuadrone de la muerte* or "death squads," of another arc, this time of radical evil, that spanned a whole subcontinent. Do you know why General Jorge Rafael Videla of Argentina was eventually sentenced? Well, do you? Because he sold the children of the tortured rape victims who were held in his private prison. I could italicize every second word in that last sentence without making it any more heart-stopping. And this subhuman character was boasted of, as a personal friend and genial host, even *after* he had been removed from the office he had defiled, by none other than Henry Kissinger. So there was an almost hygienic effect in meeting, in a new Washington, as an envoy of an elected government, the son of the brave man who had both survived and exposed the Videla tyranny.

I had four ambitions when I disembarked in the extravagantly lovely city of Buenos Aires in December of 1977. The first was to see if I could discover what had happened to Jacobo Timerman. The second was to interview the president, who was then General Videla. The third was to see the pampas, and the fourth was to meet my literary hero Jorge Luis Borges. I failed — though not completely — with the first. And I succeeded with the other three, though not in quite the ways I had anticipated.

Clichés, as the late William Safire was fond of saying, should be avoided like the plague, yet one stale journalistic standby — the "pall of fear" hanging over the city — seemed to be warranted. People spoke to foreigners with an averted gaze, and everybody seemed to know somebody who had just vanished. The rumors of what had happened to them were fantastic and bizarre though, as it turned out, they were only an understatement of the real thing. Before going to see General Videla in Perón's old pink presidential palace at the Casa Rosada, I went to deliver some letters from Amnesty International to a local human rights group, and also to check in with *Los Madres*: the black-draped mothers who paraded, every week, with pictures of their missing loved ones in the Plaza Mayo. (*"Todo mi familia!"* as one elderly lady kept telling me imploringly, as she flourished their photographs. *"Todo mi familia!"*) From these and from other relatives and friends I got a line of questioning to put to the general. I would be told by him, they forewarned me, that people "disappeared" all the time, either because of traffic accidents and family quarrels or, in the dire civil-war circumstances of Argentina, because of the wish to drop out of a gang and the need to avoid one's former associates. But this was a cover story. Most of those who disappeared were openly taken away in the unmarked Ford Falcon cars of the Buenos Aires military police. I should inquire of the general what precisely had happened to Claudia Inez Grumberg, a paraplegic who was unable to move on her own but who had last been seen in the hands of his ever-vigilant armed forces.

Escorted into Videla's presence, I justified my politeness and formality by telling myself that I wasn't there to make points but to elicit facts. I possess a picture of the encounter that still makes me want to spew: there stands the killer and torturer and rape-profiteer, as if to illustrate some seminar on the banality of evil. Bony-thin and mediocre in appearance, with a scrubby moustache, he looks for all the world like a cretin impersonating a toothbrush. I am gripping his hand in a much too unctuous manner and smiling as if genuinely delighted at the introduction. Aching to expunge this humiliation, I waited while he went almost pedantically through the predicted script, waving away the rumored but doubtless regrettable dematerializations that were said to be afflicting his fellow Argentines. And then I asked him about Senorita Grumberg. He replied that if what I had said was true, then I should remember that "terrorism is not just killing with a bomb, but activating ideas. Maybe that's why she's detained." I expressed astonishment at this reply and, evidently thinking that I hadn't understood him the first time, Videla enlarged on the theme. "We consider it a great crime to work against the Western and Christian style of life: it is not just the bomber but the ideologist who is the danger." Behind him, I could see one or two of his brighter staff officers looking at me with stark hostility as they realized that the general — *El Presidente* — had made a mistake by speaking so candidly. (I was later to find that I was being followed around the city, which caused me many a fearful moment.) In response to a follow-up question, Videla crassly denied — *"rotondamente"*: "roundly" denied — holding Jacobo Timerman "as either a journalist or a Jew." While we were having this surreal exchange, here is what Timerman was being told by his taunting tormentors:

> Argentina has three main enemies: Karl Marx, because he tried to destroy the Christian concept of society; Sigmund Freud, because he tried to destroy the Christian concept of the family; and Albert Einstein, because he tried to destroy the Christian concept of time and space.

Punctuated by thrusts of the cattle prod, it wasn't difficult to determine the direction that such a clerical-fascist interrogation was taking. And Senorita Grumberg, too, was a Jew. We later discovered what happened to the majority of those who had been held and tortured in the secret prisons of the regime. According to a Navy captain named Adolfo Scilingo, who published a book of confessions, these broken victims were often destroyed as "evidence" by being flown out way over the wastes of the South Atlantic and flung from airplanes into the freezing water below. Imagine the fun element when there's the surprise bonus of a Jewish female prisoner in a wheelchair to be disposed of... we slide open the door and get ready to roll her and then it's one, two, three... go!

Many governments employ torture but this was the first time that the element of Saturnalia and pornography in the process had been made so clear to me. If you care to imagine what any inadequate or cruel man might do, given unlimited power over a woman, then anything that you can bring yourself to suspect was what became routine in ESMA, the Navy Mechanics School that became the headquarters of the business. I talked to Dr. Emilio Mignone, a distinguished physician whose daughter Monica had disappeared into the precincts of that hellish place. What do you find to say to a doctor and a humanitarian who has been gutted by the image of a starving rat being introduced to his daughter's genitalia? Like hell itself the school was endorsed and blessed by priests, in case any stray consciences needed to be stilled. The Catholic chaplain of ESMA, Father Christian von Wernich, was three decades later convicted of direct complicity in murder, torture, and abduction. The Papal Nuncio, later to become Cardinal Pio Laghi, was the sleek tennis partner of Admiral Emilio Massera, the supervising member of the Argentine Navy's whole sadistic enterprise. Here's Timerman again, on the details and elaborations of his own electric-shock torture:

> Now they're really amused, and burst into laughter. Someone tries a variation while still clapping hands: "Clipped prick... clipped prick." Whereupon they begin alternating while clapping their hands: "Jew... Clipped prick... Jew... Clipped prick." It seems they're no longer angry, merely having a good time. I keep bouncing in the chair and moaning as the electric shocks penetrate...

And here he is again, on a truly ingenious element of the inferno, when suspects are brought in and tortured *en famille* and where:

> The entire affective world, constructed over the years with utmost difficulty, collapses with a kick in the father's genitals, a smack on the mother's face, an obscene insult to the sister, or the sexual violation of a daughter. Suddenly an entire culture based on familial love, devotion, the capacity for mutual sacrifice collapses. Nothing is possible in such a universe, and that is precisely what the torturers know... From my cell, I'd hear the whispered voices of children trying to learn what was happening to their parents, and I'd witness the efforts of daughters to win over a guard, to arouse a feeling of tenderness in him, to incite the hope of some lovely future relationship between them in order to learn what was happening to her mother, to get an orange sent to her, to get permission for her to go to the bathroom.

I borrow Jacobo's words here because they are crystalline authentic and because my own would be no good: Flaubert was right when he said that our use of language is like a cracked kettle on which we bang out tunes for bears to dance to, while all the time we need to move the very stars to pity.

For all its outwardly easy Latin charm, Buenos Aires was making me feel sick and upset, so I did take that trip to the great plains where the *gaucho* epics had been written, and I did manage to eat a couple of the famous *asados*: the Argentine barbecue fiesta (once summarized by Martin Amis's John Self as "a sort of triple mixed grill swaddled in steaks") with its slavish propitiation of the sizzling gods of cholesterol. Yet even this was spoiled for me: my hosts did their own slaughtering and the smell of drying blood from the abattoir became too much for some reason (I actually went "off" steak for a good few years after this trip). Then from the intrepid Robert Cox of the *Buenos Aires Herald* I learned another jaunty fascist colloquialism: before the South Atlantic dumping method was adopted, the secret cremation of maimed and tortured bodies at the Navy School had been called an *asado*. In my youth I was quite often accused, and perhaps not unfairly, of being too politicized and of trying to import politics into all discussions. I would reply that it wasn't my fault if politics kept on invading the private sphere and, in the case of Argentina at any rate, I think I was right. The miasma of the dictatorship pervaded absolutely everything, not excluding the aperitifs and the main course.

It even made its sickening way into the bookish, secluded atmosphere of Apartment 6B on Calle Maipu 994, just off the Plaza San Martin, where lived Jorge Luis Borges. I was extremely shy of approaching my hero but he, as I found out, was sorely in need of company. By then almost completely blind, he was claustrated and even a little confused and this may help explain the rather shocking attitude that he took to the blunt trauma that was being inflicted in the streets and squares around him. *"This was my country and it might be yet,"* he intoned to me when the topic first came up, as it had to: *"But something came between it and the sun."* This couplet he claimed (I have never been able to locate it) was from Edmund Blunden, whose gnarled hand I had been so excited to shake all those years ago, but it was not the Videla *junta* that Borges meant by the allusion. It was the pre-existing rule of Juan Perón, which he felt had depraved and corrupted Argentine society. I didn't disagree with this at all—and Perón had victimized Borges's mother and sister as well as having Borges himself fired from his job at the National Library—but it was nonetheless sad to hear the old man saying that he heartily preferred the new uniformed regime, as being one of "gentlemen" as opposed to "pimps." This was a touch like listening to Evelyn Waugh at his most liverish and bufferish. (It was also partly redeemed by a piece of learned philology or etymology concerning the Buenos Aires dockside slang for pimp: *canfinflero.* "A *canfinfla,* you see," said Borges with perfect composure, "is a pussy or more exactly a cunt. So a *canfinflero* is a trafficker in cunt: in Anglo-Saxon we might say a 'cunter.'" Had not the very *tango* itself been evolved in a brothel in 1880? Borges could talk indefinitely about this sort of thing, perhaps in revenge for having had an oversolicitous mother who tyrannized him all his life.)

He wanted me to read aloud to him and this I gladly did. I most remember his request for Kipling's "Harp Song of the Dane Women," a poem that employs mainly Anglo-Saxon and Norse words (Borges's own talk was spiced with terms like "folk" and "kin") and which opens so beautifully and hauntingly with the Viking wives as they are keening:

What is a woman that you forsake her
And the hearth fire and the home acre
To go with that old grey widow-maker?

For every author and topic Borges had a crisp summation. G.K. Chesterton: "Such a pity that he became a Catholic." Kipling: "Unappreciated because too many of his peers were socialists." "It's a shame that we have to choose between two such second-rate countries as the USSR and the USA." The hours I spent in this anachronistic, bibliophile, Anglophile retreat were in surreal contrast to the shrieking horror show that was being enacted in the rest of the city. I never felt this more acutely than when, having maneuvered the old boy down the spiral staircase for a rare out-of-doors lunch the next day—terrified of letting him slip and tumble—I got him back upstairs again. He invited me back for even more readings the following morning but I had to decline. I pleaded truthfully that I was booked on a plane for Chile. "I am so sorry," said this courteous old genius. "But may I then offer you a gift in return for your company?" I naturally protested with all the energy of an English middle-class upbringing: couldn't hear of such a thing; pleasure and privilege all mine; no question of accepting any present. He stilled my burblings with an upraised finger. "You will remember," he said, "the lines I will now speak. You will always remember them." And he then recited the following:

What man has bent o'er his son's sleep, to brood
How that face shall watch his when cold it lies?
Or thought, as his own mother kissed his eyes,
Of what her kiss was when his father wooed?

The title (Sonnet XXIX of Dante Gabriel Rossetti)—"Inclusiveness"—may sound a trifle sickly but the enfolded thought recurred to me more than once after I became a father and Borges was quite right: I have never had to remind myself of the words. I was mumbling my thanks when he said, again with utter composure: "While you are in Chile do you plan a call on General Pinochet?" I replied with what I hoped was equivalent aplomb that I had no such intention. "A pity," came the response. "He is a true gentleman. He was recently kind enough to award me a literary prize." It wasn't the ideal note on which to bid Borges farewell, but it was an excellent illustration of something else I was becoming used to noticing—that in contrast or corollary to what Colin MacCabe had said to me in Lisbon, sometimes it was also the right people who took the wrong line.*

Two small sequels complete this episode in my life, which turned out to be a sort of hinge. After returning to London via Chile, I wrote a long-ish report for the *New Statesman* about the American-backed dictatorships of the Southern Cone. This drew two invitations. The first came from Kai Bird, writing on behalf of Victor Navasky, the new editor of *The Nation* magazine in New York. My article was much admired at their office: Might I consider writing for them in the future? ("Dear Ms. Bird," I ignorantly wrote back to the future Pulitzer-winning historian and biographer, read-ily accepting his offer.) The second invitation was from my old comrade Denis Matyjascek, by now renamed MacShane because the BBC wouldn't let him use an unpronounceable Polish name on the air, and also by then the leader of the National Union of Journalists. Would I speak with him at a public meeting, to enlighten all the reporters who would be covering the upcoming soccer World Cup in Argentina, and to encourage them to make inquiries about the human rights situation? Naturally I would, I replied to Tony Blair's future deputy foreign minister. If there was one thing of which my Argentine experience had convinced me, it was that for all its hackery and cynicism, the profession of journalism did still have its aspect of nobility. Jacobo Timerman, some time after his release, was to praise Robert Cox of the English-language *Buenos Aires Herald* as a natural English gentleman. Timerman himself struck me as a vivid example of the great tradition of secular Jewish dissent. Both had testified to the health of the written word and its salutary effect upon diseased and disordered societies. I was renewed in believing in what I wanted to do.

The MacShane-sponsored solidarity evening came: I made my pitch and told my tales, the turnout was good, the questions were of a fairly high stan-dard and then up got a man in a three-piece suit who in a very plummy accent identified himself with a double-barreled name. Here it comes, I

---

* In justice to Borges it has to be added that a few years later he came to realize that he had been duped by the junta, and did sign a rather courageous petition about the *desaparecidos*. Men like him often, and in spite of their inclinations, have a natural "gold standard" when it comes to questions of principle.

thought, there's always some bleeding Tory trying to put a veneer on military rule. The gentleman proceeded to give high praise to my speech. He underlined the fascistic nature of the junta and went on to call attention to its aggressive design on the Falkland Islands, where lived an ancient community of British farmers and fishermen. In 1978 this didn't seem to be a geopolitical detail of any consuming interest, but I do remember agreeing with him that when challenged about its own depredations, the Argentine Right invariably tried to change the subject to the injustice of British possession of the Falklands (or Las Malvinas as they were known locally).

As a consequence, I was invited to an evening event thrown by the Falkland Islands Committee in the garden of Lincoln's Inn. I asked if I might bring my father, who had himself briefly been stationed on this desolate archipelago. The reception was a distinct success, if somehow quaint in its almost antique Englishness. I have often noticed that nationalism is at its strongest at the periphery. Hitler was Austrian, Bonaparte Corsican. In postwar Greece and Turkey the two most prominent ultra-right nationalists had both been born in Cyprus. The most extreme Irish Republicans are in Belfast and Derry (and Boston and New York). Sun Yat Sen, father of Chinese nationalism, was from Hong Kong. The Serbian extremists Milošević and Karadžić were from Montenegro and their most incendiary Croat counterparts in the *Ustashe* tended to hail from the frontier lands of Western Herzegovina. Falklands nationalism was too mild to stand comparison with any of these toxic movements, but the loyalist atmosphere on the lawn that night, with a Navy band playing and ancient settler families inquiring after one another's descendants, was of an unquestioning and profound and *rooted* kind that one almost never encountered in the rest of a declining and anxious Britain. It was a bit much even for Commander Hitchens, who privately thought the islands slightly absurd and probably undefendable. When the time came when his old Royal Navy was sinking and shattering the Argentine fleet, the cadet school of which was a training camp for torture and rape, I was one of the very few socialists to support Mrs. Thatcher and he was one of the very few Tories to doubt the wisdom of the enterprise. So it goes.

I may seem to be getting ahead of my story there—it can happen to the best and the worst raconteur—but in fact the remaining short time of my life in England was becoming more and more overshadowed by that same

Iron Lady. I didn't really like anything about her, except, that is, for the most important thing about her, which was that she was "a conviction politician." In the Labour Party, this sort of principled character had effectively ceased to exist. The closing years of "Old Labour" in Britain were years laced with corruption, cynicism, emollience, and drift. I tried my best to maintain my old commitment, but the effort was too much. In the area where I did my actual work, the printing trade unions were not much better than a protection racket for a privileged guild. In the rest of the country, Labour had become a status quo party, hostile to the union with Europe, suspicious of technological innovation, inward-looking, and envious. Striking workers were too easily emboldened because they were inconveniencing, not the capitalist and the owner and the scab, but the vulnerable remainder of the working public.

My last-ditch moment, though, was the official defense of torture in Northern Ireland. Labour's "responsible" minister in the province, a bullying dwarf named Roy Mason, had both denied and excused (perhaps you notice how the denial is so often the preface to the justification) the use of atrocious methods. Everybody knows the creepy excuses that are always involved here: "terrorism" must be stopped, lives are at stake, the "ticking bomb" must be intercepted. That after so many years of unhappy engagement with Ireland we should imagine that *torture* should be given another try...and that I should know people in the government who would defend it. I had a friend-losing and tearful dinner with a brilliant young junior minister who would not repudiate methods that were bursting the eardrums and fracturing the limbs of Irish prisoners. In the election campaign of 1979 I wrote as much as I could about this for the *New Statesman*. The election itself had been precipitated by a vote of confidence in the House of Commons, when the Irish Left and Republican members had furiously refused to vote to keep Labour in office. To this day, I find, many habitual Labour supporters have succeeded in forgetting that shame. I was in the press gallery that night, and I remember thinking that it would be a long time before there was another Labour government, and that if it came to that I didn't really care.

Decades earlier, in some essays (boldly titled "Origins of the Present Crisis") that had been one of the founding documents of the New Left, Perry Anderson and Tom Nairn had anatomized the British disease as that of an intransigent *ancien régime* whose pathologies were as much institutional as economic. A stringently Marxist conclusion from this would have been that if Labour and "the Left" could not or would not confront the ossification of the past, then the historic task would fall to a newly dynamic "Right." Christopher Hill was later to say to me, half-admiringly, that Mrs. Thatcher had not just chosen to face down the outmoded syndicalism of the trade unions but had also "taken on" corporate-state ideas among business people, and picked fights with the House of Lords, the ancient universities, the traditional Conservative Party, the Church of England, and even the House of Windsor. Moreover, in the two most hidebound areas of old-style British authority, Northern Ireland and Southern Rhodesia, she was also able to enforce some of the constitutional revolutions that Old Labour had been too cowardly and too deferential to impose. She went barmy in the end and even attempted to keep the Berlin Wall as a part of the status quo but at the time she made me suffer from the same *odi et amo* complex that I'd begun to develop on the night of the spanking...

It took me years to admit it to anybody, but when the election day came I deliberately did not vote to keep Labour in office. I had various private excuses: I lived in a part of London where Labour didn't need my franchise because it had long held the district as a rotten borough. Then: Why should I swallow my vomit when Gerry Fitt and Frank MacManus, the Irish MPs who had made the difference in Parliament, had been unable to swallow theirs? On and on I went in my own mind, increasingly expert in self-persuasion. But in truth, I secretly knew quite well that I wasn't merely registering an abstention. I was in effect voting for Mrs. Thatcher. And I was secretly, guiltily glad to see her terminating the long reign of mediocrity and torpor. On top of this, I was becoming increasingly aware that that other old Tory, Dr. Samuel Johnson, had been quite wrong when he pronounced that a man who was tired of London was tired of life. With me, it was if anything the reverse. If I was ever going, it was time for me to go.

# A Second Identity: On Becoming an (Anglo) American

Who are you indeed who would talk or sing to America?
—Walt Whitman: *Leaves of Grass*

We go to Europe to be Americanized.
—Ralph Waldo Emerson

The American who has known Europe much can never again see his country with the single eye of his ante-European days.
—Henry James: *The Ambassadors*

It did not cause me any trouble to become an Italian, but my becoming an American is my own work.
—Max Ascoli

———◄◦►———

IT DOESN'T HAPPEN to me anymore, because a fresh generation of Africans and Asians has arisen to take over the business, but in my early years in Washington, D.C., I would often find myself in the back of a big beat-up old cab driven by an African-American veteran. I became used to the formalities of the *mise-en-scène*: on some hot and drowsy Dixie-like afternoon I would flag down a flaking Chevy. Behind the wheel, leaning wa-aay back and relaxed, often with a cigar stub in the corner of his mouth (and, I am not making this up, but sometimes also with a genuine porkpie hat on the back of his head) would be a grizzled man with the waist of his pants somewhere up around his armpits. I would state my desired destination. In accordance with ancient cabdriver custom, he would say nothing in response but simply engage the stickshift on his steering wheel and begin to cruise in a leisurely fashion. There would be a pause. Then: "You from England?" I would always try to say something along the lines of "Well, I'm in no position to deny it." This occasionally got me a grin; in any case, I always knew what was coming next. "I was there once." "Were you in the service?" "I sure was." "Did you get to Normandy?" "Yes, sir." But it wasn't Normandy or combat about which they wanted to reminisce. (With real combat veterans, by the way, it almost never is.) It was England itself. "Man did it know how to rain...and the warm beer. Nice people, though. Real nice." I would never forget to say, as I got out and deliberately didn't overtip (that seeming a cheap thing to do), how much this effort on their part was remembered and appreciated.

It is not at that level that the Anglo-American "special relationship" is usually celebrated. It tends to be more consecrated by meetings of the Churchill Society, by the queen's visit to horseflesh haciendas in Virginia and Kentucky, by ceremonies with flags and drums and national banners. But I think that the above element of it deserves to be better remembered. For many of these brave gentlemen, segregated in their U.S. Army units, England was the first picture they ever saw of how a non-segregated society might look. In my hometown of Portsmouth there was a riot in 1943, with the locals scorning attempts by American military policemen to enforce a color bar in the pubs. The young Medgar Evers apparently told his English friends that after what he'd seen and learned, when he got back to Mississippi he wasn't going to put up with any more of this garbage. On my very first trip through the Deep South, in 1970, I stopped at some tiny Greyhound bus waystation in Alabama to have a glass of refreshment, and a young black man hearing my voice came up to be hospitable and said: "We here greatly admire the stand of you-all in the Second World War." It stuck in my mind because it was the first time I had ever actually heard someone say "y'all" — it seemed to take slightly longer to say in this part of Alabama — and because I could be fairly sure that on this occasion it must actually mean *all* of us rather than just the person being addressed. (I now appreciate the difference between "y'all" and "all of y'all.")

Americans. They came right out with things. Hitchens family lore related the tale of how once, when I was but a toddler, my parents were passing with me through an airport and ran into some Yanks. "Real cute kid," said these big and brash people without troubling to make a formal introduction. They insisted on photographing me and, before breaking off to resume their American lives, pressed into my dimpled fist a signed dollar bill in token of my cuteness. This story was often told (I expect that Yvonne and the Commander had been to an airport together perhaps three times in their lives) and always with a note of condescension. That was Americans for you: wanting to be friendly all right, but so loud, and inclined to flash the cash.

Parental views diverged a bit at this point, precisely because of the same wartime memory that the old grunts in D.C. had been recalling. The Commander tended to stress the deplorable tardiness of American entry into the Second World War and the exorbitant price exacted by Mr. Roosevelt for the superannuated ships he had offered to Britain under his Lend-Lease program. Yvonne's memory of the same conflict was more indulgent: American servicemen in wartime Britain were openhanded and warm, and to a date could bring along things like nylon stockings and chocolate and smoked salmon. (Those very factors helped explain the gender difference in attitudes to "Yanks": British fighters drew much smaller wages and had scant access to frills and luxuries. It wasn't very long before our guests and deliverers from across the Atlantic were being sourly described as "overpaid, oversexed, and *over here*," though it was generally agreed, as George Orwell noted at the time, that the black or "Negro" soldiers were the most courteous and gallant among them.)

So I was brought up, at home and at school, with an ambivalent view of "our American cousins." Like many poor relations, we consoled ourselves Englishly with the thought that we made up in good taste and refinement for what we increasingly lacked in money and influence. Americanism in all its forms seemed to be trashy and wasteful and crude, even brutal. There was a metaphor ready to hand in my native Hampshire. Until some time after the war, the squirrels of England had been red. I can still vaguely remember these sweet Beatrix Potter–type creatures, smaller and prettier and more agile and lacking the rat-like features that disclose themselves when you get close to a gray squirrel. These latter riffraff, once imported from America by some

kind of regrettable accident, had escaped from captivity and gradually massacred and driven out the more demure and refined English breed. It was said
that the gray squirrels didn't fight fair and would with a raking motion of
their back paws castrate the luckless red ones. Whatever the truth of that, the
sighting of a native English squirrel was soon to be a rarity, confined to the
north of Scotland and the Isle of Wight, and this seemed to be emblematic,
for the anxious lower middle class, of a more general massification and de-
gentrification and, well, Americanization of everything.

This was the same tendency that Orwell thought he had noticed two
decades earlier, with British comic papers being driven out by coarse American
"mags": tales of chivalry and derring-do replaced with sexual and even sadistic themes and the decent English boy-hero deposed in favor of the wised-up
thug. Comic-books were certainly my own introduction to the Yank style: in
spite of endless parental disapproval and discouragement I would sneak off to
the corner shop and waste my pocket money on cheap Western and gangster
stuff. It was easy to read, rather more "real" than Rupert Bear or Dan Dare
or the other insipid English equivalents, and it made America seem huge and
violent and coarse, and in places half-wild. The newspapers and TV made it
seem like that, too. Presidents got shot. People got lynched. A man named
Caryl Chessman—a bizarre enough name as it seemed to me—was put to
death for rape after a long legal wrangle in California and (this being the
detail that held my youthful attention) put to death in "a gas chamber." I
mean, I had had no idea...Mrs. Moss, the first American I ever consciously
met, was one of my history teachers when I was about twelve, and she had a
real flair for igniting interest in her subject. But she also wanted to stray into
the awkward territory of "modern" history, which broke the usual bounds
and challenged the idea that the past was a pageant—of one damn king after
another—culminating in the map of the world (still displayed in my boyhood), which showed the British Empire in majestic red. This new American
postwar atmosphere was a direct challenge to one's sense of security.

Such an impression wasn't corrected even by reading Mark Twain, who
was presented to us as a children's writer only and who seemed to be depicting conditions of near-primeval backwardness, or by watching the input that
made the early days of television so exciting: *The Lone Ranger*, or Clint East-
wood as Rowdy Yates in *Rawhide*. So many cattle, so much emptiness, so

many displays of homicidal ill-temper. A little later I was captivated by *West Side Story* and wrote home from school giving my parents a detailed summary of the plot, but they chose to pretend that I hadn't sent this, and on reflection I had to agree that the picture of New York wasn't a very alluring one at that. America seemed either too modern, with no castles or cathedrals and no sense of history, or simply too premodern with too much wilderness and unpolished conduct.

One also, in our milieu, simply didn't meet enough Americans to form an opinion. And when one did — this was in the days of crew-cuts and short-legged pants — they, too, often really did sport crew-cuts and trousers that mysteriously ended several inches short of the instep. Why *was* that? It obviously wasn't poverty. A colleague of my father's had a daughter who got herself married and found that an American friend she had met on holiday had offered to pay the whole cost of the nuptial feast. I forget the name of this paladin, but he had a crew-cut and amputated trouser-bottoms and a cigar stub and he came from a place called Yonkers, which seemed to me a ridiculous name to give to a suburb. (I, who had survived Crapstone...) Anyway, once again one received a Henry Jamesian impression of brash generosity without overmuch refinement. There was a boy at my boarding school called Warren Powers Laird Myers, the son of an officer stationed at one of the many U.S. Air Force bases in Cambridgeshire. Trousers at The Leys School were uniform and regulation, but he still managed to show a bit of shin and to buzz-cut his hair. "I am not a Yankee," he informed me (he was from Norfolk, Virginia). "I am a CON-federate." From what I was then gleaning of the news from Dixie, this was unpromising. In our ranks we also had Jamie Auchincloss, a sprig of the Kennedy-Bouvier family that was then occupying the White House. His trousers managed to avoid covering his ankles also, though the fact that he shared a parent with Jackie Kennedy meant that anything he did was accepted as fashionable by definition. The pants of a man I'll call Mr. "Miller," a visiting American master who skillfully introduced me to J.D. Salinger, were also falling short of their mark. Mr. Miller's great teacher-feature was that he saw sexual imagery absolutely everywhere and was slightly too fond of pointing it out (oversexed and over here: I suppose it figured). Meanwhile, and as I mentioned much earlier, the dominant images projected from the United States were of the attack-dog-and-firehose kind, with swag-bellied cops lying about themselves and the political succession changed as much by bullets as by ballots.

Yet when I had been to hear W.H. Auden recite his poems at Great St. Mary's Church in 1966, I had noticed that he closed with the words "God bless the USA, so large, so friendly, and so rich." (I now believe that that evening I was privileged to hear the first public rendering of "On the Circuit," of which that is the last line. It's a poem I have come to adore as I go around the United States as an itinerant lecturer.) Come to think of it, hadn't Auden actually *chosen* to live in America, even to become an American? As I went further into the question, and consulted my favorite authors, it kept recurring more and more insistently. Oscar Wilde had loved America and even believed it capable of settling the age-old Irish problem. P.G. Wodehouse had emigrated there and seemed happy as a clam. (Why a clam? one sometimes wanted to know.) One of my heroines, Jessica Mitford, had written a hilarious book about the floridly ghastly and exploitative American funeral industry—fully the nonfiction equivalent of Evelyn Waugh's *Loved One*—but then again she had long domiciled herself in Oakland, California. American movies seemed much more vigorous and colorful and adventurous than their British counterparts. Groups like the Beatles and the Rolling Stones didn't appear to have "made it" until they had been on American TV or been ratified by an appearance in a huge American stadium.

I couldn't quite square this at first with my revulsion from the America of drawling and snarling accents, and cheap fizzy softdrinks and turbocharged war and racism, but my two-track system must have begun churning away again, because not long after leaving Cambridge and arriving in Oxford I began to have a recurrent dream. There was nothing especially subtle about it from the imaging point of view. I simply found myself somewhere in Midtown Manhattan, looking up at the skyscrapers. But the illusion was always accompanied by a feeling of profound happiness, and a sensation of being free in a way I had never known before. American music and American culture were much more pervasive in England by then, and much more nonconformist than they had been in the early days of TV, so that I had an early exposure to the great conundrum that has occupied me since: How is the United States at once the most conservative and commercial AND the most revolutionary society on Earth? I may as well confess another thing: the Mamas and the Papas had produced an album called *If You Can Believe Your Eyes and Ears*. Many, many fans were ravished by "California Dreamin'" and "Monday, Monday," and also by the bewitching sexuality of the female lead singer, Michelle Phillips, but there was a single track called "Go Where You Wanna Go," which, when I played it alone in my Balliol garret quarters, would almost guarantee that I would have to go out and walk restlessly around the quad before I could sleep. And then I would be very liable to dream the dream again...

By then I was getting to know a good number of Americans and it now seems odd and even sad to me that our engagement with one another was so purely politicized. I never asked them, for example, what life and culture were like in Ohio or Rhode Island or California, and they never seemed interested in saying. The war—the bloody war all the time—and the civil rights struggle were the beginning and end of all conversations. The most charming and eloquent of the black Americans was a loquacious Panther (who later became "head of protocol" for the city of Philadelphia). So, while I did my stuff in helping my American comrades discredit first President Johnson and then President Nixon, I quietly opened another front and applied for the Coolidge Atlantic Crossing or "Pathfinder" Scholarship, awarded by Balliol College every year so that about ten of us could be introduced to the American Way. The endowing patron of this award, Mr. William Appleton Coolidge, was a direct descendant of Thomas Jefferson through the Randolph family of Massachusetts. He was an ancient, who had been at Balliol two generations previously. He had a sentimental attitude toward the college and, if I may so phrase it, toward young Englishmen in particular. I was one of the winners of one of his scholarships. He crossed the seas, as he did every year, to run his eye over the new crop. A meeting was arranged in the Master's lodgings. Coolidge was an imposing and craggy man whose trousers, mercifully, seemed equal to the task of shielding his shin and ankle from the vulgar gaze. I rather stupidly asked him if he was related to the president of the same name. "Why no," replied Bill. "I believe that he was one of the working Coolidges." Once again, one found oneself dealing with something, or someone, "so large, so friendly, and so rich."

A little later, the Apollo mission was consummated and there were Americans on the moon. I remember distinctly looking up from the quad on what was quite a moon-flooded night, and thinking about it. They made it! The Stars and Stripes are finally flown on another orb! Also, English becomes the first and only language spoken on a neighboring rock! Who could forbear to cheer? Still, the experience was poisoned for me by having to watch Richard Nixon smirking as he babbled to the lunar-nauts by some closed-circuit link. Was even the silvery orb to be tainted by the base, earthbound reality of imperialism?

At around this time I also met my first U.S. senator. Hugh Scott, the Republican from Pennsylvania, had been seconded to Balliol for some "special relationship" purpose and was occasionally wheeled out to put a respectable face on things. He's rather forgotten now, but Norman Mailer had caught the tailor's-dummy, all-things-to-all-men aspect of the senatorial mien in a thumbnail sketch from the fateful Nixon convention in Miami in 1968:

> Scott had modest but impeccable aplomb as he explained that since only 12 per cent of the delegates had been in San Francisco in 1964, he did not expect bitterness from old Goldwater followers to hurt Rockefeller's chances now. A fine character actor had been lost when Hugh Scott went into politics: he could have played the spectrum from butler to count.

Alarming though American politics and politicians seemed—especially as one devoured Mailer's punchy and instant-paperbacked reporting from the street fights outside the Pentagon and the party conclaves—I didn't fail to register the note of thwarted patriotism that he sometimes sounded when he was writing about himself in the third person:

> A profound part of him detested the thought of seeing his American society—evil, absurd, touching, pathetic, sickening, comic, full of novelistic marrow—disappear now in the nihilistic maw of a national disorder.

In one way, this reeked of Mailer's showbiz reluctance to lose a country that supplied him with such good copy. But I thought I could detect the pulse of patriotic sympathy in him, too, if only because I also felt it latently in myself. Experience with Communists and fellow travelers in Cuba and elsewhere had made me somewhat immune to the sort of propaganda that emphasized "Uncle Sam" or "the Yanqui," let alone the sort that burned the American flag. This style, which usually warned one of the presence of the "peace-loving and progressive forces," also reminded me of the snobbish and even chauvinistic anti-Americanism that I'd overheard on the British Right. Trying to keep all these reflections in balance, in late July 1970 I bought a bucket-shop ticket for a charter flight via Iceland to John F. Kennedy Airport.

Sometimes an expectation or a wish does come true. I have no faith in precognitive dreams or any patience for "dream" rhetoric in general, yet Manhattan was exactly as I had hoped it would be. I had to survive some very discouraging first impressions: the airport café where I ate my first breakfast was a nothingness of plastic and formica and the "English muffin" was a travesty of both Englishness and muffindom. Outside stood a paunchy cop with, on his heavy belt, an accoutrement of gun and club and handcuff of a sort that I had never seen in real life and had believed exaggerated in the movies. The bus into the city was sweaty and the Port Authority Terminal is probably the worst possible place from which to take your original bearings on Midtown. The next thing I actually saw in the city was a flag-bedecked campaign headquarters for the ultraright candidacy of James Buckley (brother of William F.) for the Senate. "Join The March For America!" it yelled. But I was near-delirious. Gazing up at the pillared skyline, I knew that I was surveying a tremendous work of man. Buying myself a drink in the smaller warrens below, in all their ethnic variety (and willingness to keep odd and late hours, and provide plentiful ice cubes, and *free matchbooks* in contrast to English parsimony in these matters), I felt the same thing in a different way. The balance between the macro and the micro, the heroic scale and the human scale, has never since ceased to fascinate and charm me. Evelyn Waugh was in error when he said that in New York there was a neurosis in the air which the inhabitants mistook for energy. There was, rather, a tensile excitement in that air which made one think — made me think for many years — that time spent asleep in New York was somehow time wasted. Whether this thought has lengthened or shortened my life I shall never know, but it has certainly colored it.

In the streets and avenues of this amazing city, there was barely a crew-cut to be seen, and everybody's trousers — if they wore any trousers — seemed

In Babylon, Iraq, 1975.

In Iraq with a Ba'athist banner, 1975.

Striking an attitude in Kurdistan with Saddam's enemies during the first Gulf War.

With Jalal Talabani at his mountain HQ in 1991: then the leader of a murdered and dispossessed people, and now the first-ever elected president of Iraq.

Liberating Iraq.

In Iraq with Paul Wolfowitz, 2003.

Swallowing vomit while greeting General Videla of Argentina in Juan Peron's old palace, 1977.

In Zimbabwe, 1977.

With the only priest I've ever liked, Archbishop Makarios, President of Cyprus.

In the Sahara with Polisario guerrillas around a captured Moroccan tank, 1977.

With an extremely moderate Muslim in Malaysia.

With Sayeed Khomeini, courageous foe of his grandfather's theocracy, in Qum, Iran, in 2006.

With Ugandan soldiers pursuing the Lord's Resistance Army, 2007.

Getting to know the General: in Venezuela with Sean Penn, Douglas Brinkley, and the dictator, October 2008.

The Romanian Revolution, 1989.

In Nicaragua with Vice-President Sergio Ramirez, a Sandinista and novelist.

equal to the task of covering the ankle if not indeed the entire shoe. (Bell-bottoms may have been involved.) With skirts, though, the reverse process applied. In some manner, the whole place was redolent of sex, but in a natural rather than a leering way. Three big differences between this culture and the English one began to disclose themselves at once.

The first was the extraordinary hospitality. Balliol College had equipped me with a list of former alumni who were willing to "put me up" and this comprised some fairly solid citizens all across the USA. But Americans to whom one had barely been introduced would also insist that one came for a weekend "on the shore," or "upstate," and would actually mean it. On the way to any destination, if you put out your thumb on the roadside you would almost immediately get a lift or a "ride" (to set this down now makes me bite my lip as I mourn the lapse of time and the passing of hitchhiking) and very often the driver would go out of his or her way to drop you where you wanted to go. Music on the radio would be loud and various as the trip progressed, and if there was any song more evocative of those days than "Go Where You Wanna Go" it was the schmaltzy, haunting "Leaving on a Jet Plane." Should you happen to be in need of a jet plane, you could go to the airport and try your luck. It cost nothing to acquire a standby "YouthFare" card and, once equipped with this proof of mere youthfulness, you could wait in the boarding area and snap up any unbought seat for a few dollars. I first flew across the Great Lakes from New York to Chicago in this manner, in brilliant sunshine, on a plane where I was the sole passenger and the tawny, lissome American Airlines hostesses treated me as if I had paid for First Class. In Britain, "inter-city" travel meant crummy station platforms and delayed and dirty trains run by resentful oldsters. To really feel the connection between youth and freedom (and somehow, nothing did this for me more than the experience of flight), I had also had to flee.

My trip to Chicago, where I was rather chilled to see the egotistic, mina-tory signs on the airport road welcoming me in the name of "Richard J. Daley, Mayor," also happened to coincide with the first celebration of International Women's Day. All through the downtown "Loop," one sun-drenched lunchtime, a great avalanche of pulchritude filled the plazas just as music and fighting speeches moved the air. I felt the stirrings and yearnings of another civil rights movement, triggered by an earlier one that still had some distance to run. (In a distant undertone, I also felt the premonition of "identity politics" but believe me, to see the womanhood of Chicago *en fête* in all its bird-of-paradise variety that day was not something to give you any pinched or narrow conception of things.)

Hospitality, easy riding, and easy flying: Could it get any better? Mr. Coolidge had decreed that all those accepting his scholarship money should be unaccompanied by females. After voyaging up to stay with him in his magnificent home in Topsfield, Massachusetts, and putting in my time lying on his pool-patio and being discreetly growled and purred at, I felt somewhat released from this obligation. (He threw an all-male lunch which included the then-president of Harvard, a man with the near-perfect New England name of Nathan Pusey and perhaps a hint of austere attenuation in his gray pants-leggings.) My girlfriend was coming to the United States anyway, and in those days if you bought the ticket outside the country you could travel on the Greyhound bus system for ninety-nine days for ninety-nine dollars. This was even better than YouthFare. I told her to buy and bring two tickets. Seeing America by road turned out to be even finer than gazing at it from the sky.

For all the indifference I felt toward the shallow concept of a "Woodstock Nation," there was in those days a sort of "underground" vernacular for people under the age of twenty-one. A brisk flash of the "peace" sign would get you a roadside lift even more quickly than the showing of a mere thumb, and if you needed to borrow a floor or a bunk there was a similar idiom, often to do with the verses of Bob Dylan. (It comes back to me that on one of those big smooth rocks on the edge of Central Park, someone had painted in giant letters: "He Not Busy Being Born Is Busy Dying," and underneath it the deranged Weatherman flash of a "W" with a superimposed lightning bolt and then the subtitle: "Make The Pigs Pay!"*)

It was possible to voyage all over the United States for a few dollars a day, sometimes sleeping a night on the bus when it was crossing the emptier bits,

* I still know someone who was at the very, very far-out meeting that founded the "Weatherman" faction. He too was strongly for a Bob Dylan sloganography but held out for the sect to be named "The Vandals," because in another and equally telling "underground" line of Dylan's "Subterranean Homesick Blues," is it not truly said: "The pump don't work 'cos the vandals took the handle"? Get sick, get well...my friend's recovered now.

but then getting off and staying, not just with the list of Balliol alumni, but with individuals and even "collectives" on the informal list of the American branch of the International Socialists. This double act worked well enough in Detroit. We stayed with a snowy-haired ramrod-straight old union man named Carl Haessler, who had been at Balliol before the First World War and in jail with Eugene Victor Debs, grand old man of American Socialism, during and after it. From his home we got ourselves introduced to the "Black Caucus" on the assembly line at the Hamtramck and Flint auto plants (these hard guys were extremely scornful of the "petit-bourgeois adventurism" of the Black Panthers) and were taken to a free rock concert on a vacant lot not far from the headquarters of General Motors itself. In those days there were several cities where you could still smell the riots and burnings of not so very long before, and Detroit was one of them.

But it didn't work so well in Salt Lake City, say, where Balliol men and Trotskyists alike were as rare as rocking-horse droppings and one had little choice but to take the tour of the Mormon Tabernacle and notice the John Birch Society bookshop that was right next door to it. Beautiful as Salt Lake City was, with its street plan leading to white-topped horizons in every direction, and lovely as Utah was, with its main church having only just had the needful "revelation" that black people might have human souls after all, it was a slight relief to cross the frontier of Nevada and breathe the bracingly sordid and amoral air of Reno and Las Vegas. The variety and scope and contrast of this country seemed limitless. And then the bus began to cruise lazily through Sacramento toward the Bay Area, and into the then-mecca of the radical style.

The best of that scene was probably over, because by the time you have heard of such a "scene" it has almost invariably moved on or decayed, but I had already formed a sharply new picture of life in the United States, and exposure to California did little to dull my enthusiasm. Here was a country that could engage in a frightening and debilitating and unjust war, and undergo a simultaneous convulsion of its cities on the question of justice for its oldest and largest minority, *and* start a national conversation on the rights of women, *and* turn its most respectable campuses into agitated seminars on right and wrong, *and* have a show trial of confessed saboteurs in Chicago where the incredibly guilty defendants actually got off, *and* put quite a lot of this onto its television and movie screens in real time. This seemed like a state of affairs worth fighting for, or at least fighting over.

There was a lot of nonsense talked, to be sure, much of it drug-sodden. But the note of generosity never seemed to be absent. In this part of California, one could hitchhike not just between towns but between city blocks, as if there were a free taxi service. One man took us, for a lark, on a vertiginous detour down the same hairpin San Francisco helter-skelter street that had featured Steve McQueen's celebrated car chase in *Bullitt*. Over at City Lights bookstore in North Beach you could see a man chatting with customers and looking like Lawrence Ferlinghetti: it was Lawrence Ferlinghetti. Haight-Ashbury and the flower-power district were getting truly tawdry but this was also in obedience to the iron law which states that once you have to call something a "historic district" or a "popular quarter" then, just like the Wild West, it loses whatever character gave it the definition in the first place. Berkeley, however, perhaps because it bore the name of a distinguished philosopher who had predicted a great future for America, still managed to remain itself (as in many ways and through many "Berserkely" metamorphoses it still does). During the showing of a film in a movie theater on Telegraph Avenue, the projector broke down, and the manager came to the front of the house and made the following offer. We could all wait while he "rapped with" us for a while about Hitchcock's career as an *auteur* (the movie was *The Thirty-nine Steps*). If, after that, the projectionist still couldn't fix things, we could have our money back. And anyone who didn't want to join the rap session could claim their money back right away. Fair enough? *Fair?* I was thunderstruck, if only by trying to picture this happening in a British cinema. (Of course it would be tough to imagine it happening in a New York or Cleveland one, either, but a crucial part of seeing America was also seeing how many Americas there were.)

For all this seductive open-arms aspect, and while we were all grooving away, the bombs were still falling and the shipments of weaponry to dictators were punctually leaving the docks at nearby Oakland. I went to see the Black Panthers, whose "breakfast program" for poor ghetto kids had degenerated into a shakedown of local merchants and whose newspaper now featured paeans to North Korea. I went to call on David Horowitz at the offices of the legendary radical glossy *Ramparts*, where he inaugurated what was to be four decades of commingled love/hate/respect between us by sneering humorously at my faith in the revival of the working class and recommending that I go call on the International Socialists, which I had already done. Our local Berkeley guru was Hal Draper, twin brother of the more famous historian Theodore and also one of the world's experts on the poetry of Heinrich Heine. He was suitably contemptuous of the prevailing "left" fashions and illusions. But there was work to be done down in the Salinas Valley where César Chávez was organizing the grape pickers and lettuce workers out of their state of un-unionized peonage. In Europe I had been told by sapient academics that there wasn't really any class system in the United States: well, you couldn't prove that by the conditions in California's agribusiness, or indeed its urban factories.*

I joined the picket line on a very spirited strike, set to start at midnight, against the General Motors plant at Fremont. Just before the deadline the company tried to get some blackleg supply trucks through the gate: these were intercepted and burned and gave a lovely light. On the front page of the rather awful Communist *People's Daily World* the following day, there appeared a headline that can still make me think "Late Sixties" just by remembering it. It showed the blazing trucks and it read "Fremont: *At The Midnight Hour.*" (Down the page was a shorter report, announcing that Salvador Allende on the previous evening had won the election to become the first socialist president of Chile.)

The summer began to lengthen a trifle—not that one notices the seasons all that much on the West Coast—and with regret I began to work my way back east, following the perimeter of the country rather than crossing its heartland. I made as many stops as possible, in La Jolla where an old friend of mine was studying under the legendary if posturing Herbert Marcuse (and where I belatedly and self-consciously added the Pacific to the list of oceans in which I had swum), in El Paso where I made my first venture south of the Mexican border to Juarez, and in New Orleans where Bourbon Street hadn't yet

---

* An old joke has an Oxford professor meeting an American former graduate student and asking him what he's working on these days. "My thesis is on the survival of the class system in the United States." "Oh really, that's interesting: one didn't think there was a class system in the United States." "Nobody does. That's how it survives."

become completely kitsch and could still seem quite startlingly and encouragingly obscene. I still regret passing so little time in the rest of the Deep South, but I really wanted to be back in New York as the leaves turned.

I had by then more or less made up my mind to overstay my visa and apply for a work permit. All I needed was a sponsor, either at a magazine or newspaper or publishing house. I had already been published in the *New Statesman*, which then had a bit of a following among the U.S. intelligentsia. I had already had a friendly interview with Carey McWilliams, the extraordinary and gentlemanly radical veteran who edited *The Nation* (still in my future) and whose history of modern California, *Island on the Land*, was, and still is, considered more or less the book to beat. He had given me a list of people to see in the Golden State, including Lou Goldblatt, the stout longshoremen's union leader who had been one of the gutsy few to denounce the round-up and internment of Japanese-Americans in 1942. Now I was looking feverishly for anyone who would take me on, on any terms.

Again, and considering that I was a twenty-one-year-old stripling with only a very few decent magazine clips to his name, I was overwhelmed by how many people were willing to give me the time of day. An editor at Random House had me to a big lunch and gave me a letter that promised a contract if I could furnish a synopsis. (This would have been for a *very* solemn book on the intersections of race and class.) Agents made room for me in their crowded days: I had the chance to see Midtown Manhattan from high-level corner offices, which is an experience I still find captivating but I then thought of as near-orgasmic. Life in Britain had seemed like one long antechamber to a room that had too many barriers to entry; here in the USA it seemed to be true that if you dared to give things "your best shot" then the other much-used phrases like "land of opportunity" would kick in as well.

I did have one difficulty. It sometimes seemed as if my attempts at nuanced response were falling a trifle flat. It had happened to me in the Midwest, when a chance neighbor on a bus or a plane would say: "Of course, we're Baptists," and I would soothingly say, "Of course," as if in confirmation. It had occurred in California also, when people I had barely met would tell me what their "shrink" thought of them, and I would do my damnedest to wear an encouraging face. But even in sophisticated New York I found myself occasionally unmanned. For example, I remember a female editor saying to me over a generous cocktail: "Of course the difference between us and you Brits is that you have irony and we don't." I decided to smile and murmur, "Well, apparently not," and she looked at me as if a trick cigar had just exploded in her face. At all costs I didn't wish to seem "superior"—I hadn't read *The Loved One* for nothing—but the price of being literal seemed too steep. In my eagerness to scrape acquaintance I dug that list of potential blue-chip Balliol hosts out of the bottom of my bag and noticed that it contained the name of Penn Kimball, listed as "Professor of Journalism" at Columbia University. Surely this was a mistake or a misprint? Journalism was a state of mind: it wasn't the sort of thing that could be taught, or in which one could get an academic qualification. But within a short time of making my call to him, I was ascending the steps of a pseudo-Athenian building which actually and quite unironically housed a "School of Journalism." And within a day or so of that experience, I had accepted an invitation to stay in Westport, Connecticut, with Professor Kimball and his sharp, knowing wife.

There—within a bull's roar of the house occupied by Paul Newman and Joanne Woodward—I was taken to my first Democratic Town Committee meeting, and introduced to the sort of decorous yet vigorous New England local democracy that I was later to try and intuit again from the work of John Updike. This was as different from Berkeley and Oakland, let alone Chicago and Detroit, as one could easily get. But it was pluralism and it was transparent. The biggest and most passionate of the side arguments, I still remember, was between those who still thought it had been OK to vote for Gene McCarthy over Hubert Humphrey in 1968, and those who thought that this leftist self-indulgence had held open the door for Richard Nixon and his goons. So I was given a vivid preview of a dispute that has raged in different forms for the rest of my life. Kimball was a New Deal–type liberal with an elevated contempt for my own leftism, and I remember him disagreeing with special scorn when a truly striking but hysterical brunette (who also happened to be a local realtor) described the USA as "fascist." I was rather intrigued to discover that in snow-white Connecticut there were such sultry and subversive females. Later in his life, Penn was to discover that he and his wife had been under almost permanent police surveillance since the onset of the Cold War, and that this explained many denials of many employment opportunities: his ensuing book *The File* is a well-controlled masterpiece of frigid outrage at America's betrayal of a loyal citizen. The man who had falsely ratted him out, it emerged, was Arthur Schlesinger Jr., famous Kennedy suck-up and believer in "the vital center."

One always has the vague illusion of taking or making one's own decisions, the illusion itself running in parallel with the awareness that most such calls are made for you by other people, or by circumstances, or just made. I didn't have the wherewithal to stay on in New York. I didn't have the heft to get a lawyer who would help me overstay my student visa and fight for a work permit. Feeling weak but happy, because it had after all been a hell of a ride, I went to a travel agent near the old Pan Am Building and booked another bucket-shop charter home. During the wait, I was exposed to a near-perfect rapid-fire duet between the salesman of the cheap tickets and his partner: a sort of *West Side Story* except in Yiddish-English or I suppose Hebronics. ("Explain to me something. Why should I need you on my vacation?") I had thought this style came from some kind of expired vaudeville and was impressed to find that it took place in real life and in muscular, humorous English idiom.

*Rolling Stone* gave a party at Orsino's to mark the opening of its "Straight Arrow" book imprint and I was somehow invited to this, and went from there to the midnight jet plane from JFK. My retrospective excitement and sadness meant that I slept not at all and drank the foul cocktail known as a "Manhattan" to such an extent that I have never needed to touch it again. My welcome home was everything I could have asked for, and the wonderful warm bath of England enveloped me again, as it does if you let it. Soon enough, I was swallowed up in the exigencies of making a living, trying to write, negotiating a move from Oxford to London, all of that. I gave a series of talks and lectures to the comrades, explaining to them that there was a revolutionary character to the United States. And every now and then, I would wake up early and remember things like the wobbling sirens in Detroit, or the guitarists in Washington Square, or the contours of the Guggenheim Museum, or the "ping" in the metal cup as the Bell Telephone operator refunded you your lost dime if the connection hadn't worked. Songs that were loved in England, like Simon and Garfunkel's lines about "counting the cars on the New Jersey Turnpike," or Judy Collins's or Bob Dylan's version of "Lost in the Rain in Juarez," could now be visualized by me as poems and pictures of real places.

I was hooked and felt the occasional tug and twitch upon the thread, but the line was a long one and I could often swim with the lazy English current for months at a time without remembering my New World.

I shared a house on my return with Richard Parker, a brilliant California radical (and future biographer of John Kenneth Galbraith) who had been one of the commanding figures in the Bay Area Left. He was at the center of a group of radical American political economists at Oxford, who included one of my former tutors, Keith Griffin. Together, we distributed anti-war leaflets at the U.S. Air Force base in Upper Heyford and befriended a number of disaffected servicemen who were stationed there. From then on, my life was always to contain many American friends and, as I moved to London and began to try and make a mark as a journalist, I invariably felt it a distinction to be invited to write for any American magazine or newspaper. I was especially pleased with myself later on when the *New York Times* magazine asked me to profile the emerging Mrs. Thatcher, of whom I wrote—very much against the general expectation—that she would probably be the next prime minister.

Almost all my American acquaintances took the same attitude of visceral hatred toward Richard Nixon as I did, so there was no evident conflict between our friendship and an attitude that essentially characterized the United States as an evil empire. In the countries I was beginning to visit as a reporter—Spain, Portugal, Greece, Cyprus, later Chile—it was often American power that in the last resort guaranteed the forces of reaction. At home, Nixon had staged something very like a coup, running a parallel regime of bagmen and wiretappers behind the façade of the legitimate government. "Big Brother and the Holding Company" was, I remember, one of the better titles of a pamphlet about the Watergate gang. Overseas, his indescribably loathsome deputy Henry Kissinger felt free to suborn murder and sponsor military coups. A vast system of nuclear weaponry meanwhile meant that—as Martin Luther King had phrased it—we were ever ready to commit suicide and genocide at the same time. The colossal expense of this military-industrial system was also a theft from the world's poor. I began to read quite a lot of Hunter Thompson, and when Nixon finally went down, I celebrated as if I'd defeated a personal enemy.

In the aftermath of that very thing, though, I had to reflect a bit. After all, the American legal system and the U.S. Constitution had survived Nixon's attempt to undo it. Congress had held wide-open hearings, of a kind it was very hard to imagine taking place in the Palace of Westminster, and summoned important witnesses to testify. The Justice Department had resisted the president's lawless attempts to purge it. The special-prosecutor system had proved itself. The American press, led by the *Washington Post*, had penetrated the veil of lies and bribery and—despite crude threats from the White House—had eventually named the main perpetrators on the front page. And all of this in a time of continuing warfare in Indochina.

A great number of the "issues" that I confronted in the 1970s, both as a journalist and as a political activist, had to do with censorship and press freedom and public information. Reporters in Britain were arrested for trying to investigate matters touching on "national security": the Official Secrets Act had a clause that even made the "collection" of information an offense. In the United States there was a Freedom of Information Act that at least made the presumption of innocence when it came to disclosure. In London, an editor could be served by the state with a "D-Notice," preventing him or her from publishing a story that might embarrass the government. In the United States, the First Amendment to the Constitution—as had been reaffirmed in the case of the Pentagon Papers—forbade "prior restraint" of the press. As for Parliament, its efforts to circumscribe the executive were little short of pathetic. Anyone who had watched or read the Fulbright or Church committee hearings in Washington could only moan with contempt when a Westminster "select committee" made a feeble attempt to find out how British policy in Cyprus, say, had amounted to something between a betrayal and a fiasco.

In the late 1970s I nearly went to jail for revealing, on a television program, that the government had pre-vetted a London jury in an Official Secrets Act trial and, not content with excluding in advance anyone it suspected of sympathy with the defense, had also planted a former member of the elite Special Air Services regiment in the box. The judge in the case halted the trial and summoned me for contempt of court. I carried a toothbrush around in my top pocket for a day or so, but His Worship meanwhile succumbed to a stroke, the principal effect of which was amnesia, and so the danger passed. In America, as I kept pointing out, it would have been those who had interfered with the jury, not those who had caught them in the act, who would be the ones in danger of imprisonment.

One more episode may also illustrate my gradual enlightenment on these points. In the 1970s there was considerable nuisance from fascist and neo-Nazi groups in Britain, which mounted disgusting attacks on emigrants from the Commonwealth and began the recirculation of moth-eaten (or rather vermin-infested) anti-Semitic and Holocaust-denying screeds. It was one of one's standard duties as a leftist to turn out on weekends and block the efforts of this rabble to stage a march or to put up a platform in a street market. Stones and fists would fly, posters would be ripped down: it was all part of a storied social-ist tradition that went back to street combat with the Blackshirts in the 1930s. The police often seemed to me partial to the fascists: you could be arrested "for your own protection" if you even looked as if you were going to make a fight of it. Then one day I read in an American newspaper that, in the town of Skokie, Illinois, the American Nazi Party was going to hold a swastika-flourishing parade. They had chosen this particular suburb of Chicago because it had an unusually large population of Jewish refugees from Germany. Nice work. A temporary ban on the march had, I read, been imposed. But the same injunction was being contested in court by...the American Civil Liberties Union! That had to be some kind of mistake. *Socialist Worker* (which I still read though I no longer helped to edit or sell it) published a viperous paragraph saying that this exposed the empty sham of American liberalism. I went into the thing more closely, out of curiosity, and read an excellent defense of the ACLU by its direc-tor, Aryeh Neier, himself a refugee from Nazism. The First Amendment to the Constitution, he said, enshrined the right of all citizens to free expression and to free assembly. If this protection was withdrawn from anybody, perhaps espe-cially somebody repulsively unpopular, then it would be weakened or diluted in general. It took me a space of time to assimilate this simple Jeffersonian point, if only because I had been raised in a culture where the law governing free speech and free assembly was whatever the nearest policeman happened to say it was.*

---

* In my first months of living in Washington, D.C., I went to a Ku Klux Klan rally where the sheeted marchers were protected from furious counterdemonstrators by phalanxes of imper-turbable black policemen who saw to it that the constitutional rights of those who detested them were duly and good-humoredly upheld.

Then there was the American embassy. With its horrible defacement of the west side of Grosvenor Square it had served in the Sixties as an aesthetic target as much as a political one. But after the eviction of Nixon from the White House, this same neo-brutalist London fortress began to mount a sort of charm offensive. Elliot Richardson, the dignified attorney general who had refused Nixon's peremptory order to fire Special Prosecutor Archibald Cox ("Sack the Cox-Sacker," as a friend of mine had written on a placard outside the White House at the time, as if borrowing from Bob Conquest's most painstaking work), became ambassador and took an early opportunity to come and have lunch at the *New Statesman*. I hadn't seen liberal Republicanism up close before and though it did appear a touch self-satisfied, I felt I had met less attractive kinds of politics. Then, after an interval, the State Department gazetted Dr. Kingman Brewster to become its envoy. As president of Yale during the fabled Black Panther trial in New Haven, he had attracted huge obloquy for apparently saying that a black man might be unable to receive a fair trial. Actually, he had only asked if this might be the case, rather than stated that it really was so, but once a bogus story has been printed for the first time, it will be reprinted again and again by the lazy and/or the malicious. Ambassador Brewster and his wife gave a number of striking evenings at Winfield House in Regent's Park—Barbara Hutton's gift to both London and Washington—where there were after-dinner seminars on everything from affirmative action to El Salvador. The guest list was, I thought, consciously weighted to the left of center. (In due time, Ambassador Brewster agreed to sponsor me for a green card.) Once again, the inescapable American note seemed to be that of generosity and large-mindedness.

I'd be coy if I failed to mention another thing, which was American women. How can one phrase this delicately? English womanhood was, of course, adorable, and the idea of the "English rose" had not yet acquired the sickliness of the Diana epoch, but it did have a slight tendency to leave the initiative to the male. My besetting weakness in this department has always been that I like to know that initiatives are already welcome, if you catch my drift. (This was one of the many differences in style between myself and young Amis, who quite correctly reasoned that neither party could be entirely sure of this welcome until one of them—and he was perfectly willing to volunteer for any ice-breaking duty—had put matters to the proof.) American girls, I came to find, were more…*forward*. They would come right out with it, and would give direct voice, sometimes in a tone of near-command, to their desires. I don't think that I can even begin sufficiently to express my gratitude. It was one such fling that reunited me with the United States after almost seven years absence from it: she met me in London but she lived in New York and when I boarded Pan Am to catch up with her, let alone when I saw again the Pan Am Building from high up on Park Avenue, I had a non-platonic hint of that platonic ideal whereby two separated spheres have been happily conjoined once more. This conviction outlasted the affair. From then on, every time I flew back to England, I was mentally busy with the idea that I would soon return to New York, this time on a one-way ticket.

Thus when I began to publish a few more pieces in *The Nation*, and on one such visit went to call on Victor Navasky at the magazine's downtown offices, and heard him inquire if I ever felt like coming over permanently, I felt I had flung a proper grappling hook across the water. All the awful business of visas, immigration forms, work permits (so very much worse now than it was then) would yield a little if I had a patron or sponsor. So on 9 October 1981 I bought that one-way ticket and barely looked behind me as I went to Heathrow and flew west to see again what had become my favorite sight: Manhattan in early evening as viewed in anticipation from the tip of Long Island. I had perhaps one suitcase, one half-offer of part-time work at the *Nation* office, a truly saintly offer of a long-term stay in the West Village from my old Hitch-proof Oxford friend Gully Wells and her husband, Peter, and a few thousand dollars in the bank.

There is of course a much-derided way for Englishmen to try and "make it" in America, and perhaps especially in New York and Los Angeles. They charm their way into publishing, say, or advertising, or the movies, by the mere attitude and plausibility that's represented by their famous "accent." And then at weekends they get together and have Marmite and Earl Grey and discuss cricket scores and have a good snigger at the gullibility and sappiness of their American hosts. (Really and truly "hosts," as in the relationship with the parasitic.) Waugh had lampooned it in his description of the Hollywood cricket players in *The Loved One* (which I forgot to mention is subtitled *An Anglo-American Tragedy*):

For these the club was the symbol of their Englishry. Here they collected subscriptions for the Red Cross and talked at their ease, out of the hearing of their alien employers and protectors.

Shortly after I arrived in New York, Tom Wolfe claimed to have diagnosed the same syndrome in *The Bonfire of the Vanities*:

One had the sense of a very rich and suave secret legion that had insinuated itself into the cooperative apartment houses of Park Avenue and Fifth Avenue, from there to pounce at will upon the Yankees' fat fowl, to devour at leisure the last plump white meat on the bones of capitalism... They were comrades in arms, in the service of Great Britain's wounded chauvinism.

I was offended, when this fiction first came out, to read third-hand speculation that I was myself the model for the venal English hack and social climber Peter Fallow. True, I had deliberately offended Wolfe—who knows how to take an underhanded revenge—but not by haunting the penthouses of Park or Fifth. To the contrary, I had written disobligingly about his reactionary affectations in a small West Coast leftist magazine called *Mother Jones*. This was hardly *arrivisme* on my part: I was "down" with my fellow American radicals, not conspiring with a bunch of aristos and expats. Yet there is something about the English voice that can still catch some Americans—even outwardly assured white-suit-wearing Virginians—on the raw. More democratic Americans were happier with the sound of it. I resolved neither to exploit this nor to over-assimilate. When the young ladies of AT&T would say: "Just keep talking. I love your accent," I would respond: "But my dear, I don't *have* an accent. It's *you* who has the accent, and a very nice one, too." Five times out of ten I would then be told I sounded like Richard Burton, which I do quite understand was kindly meant.

Actual class struggles apart, one of the aesthetic ways you could prove that there was a class system in America was by cogitating on the word, or acronym, "WASP." First minted by E. Digby Baltzell in his book *The Protestant Establishment*, the term stood for "White Anglo-Saxon Protestant." Except that, as I never grew tired of pointing out, the "W" was something of a redundancy (there being by definition no BASPs or JASPs for anyone to be confused with, or confused about). "ASP," on the other hand, lacked some of the all-important tone. There being so relatively few Anglo-Saxon Catholics in the United States, the "S" was arguably surplus to requirements as well. But then the acronym AS would scarcely do, either. And it would raise an additional difficulty. If "Anglo-Saxon" descent was the qualifying thing, which surely it was, then why were George Wallace and Jerry Falwell not WASPs? After all, they were not merely white and Anglo-Saxon and Protestant, but very emphatic about all three things. Whereas a man like William F. Buckley, say, despite being a white Irish Catholic, radiated the very sort of demeanor for which the word WASP had been coined to begin with. So, for the matter of that, did the dapper gentleman from Richmond, Virginia, Tom Wolfe. Could it be, then, that WASP was really a term of class rather than ethnicity? Q.E.D. Those other white Anglo-Saxon Protestants of the less polished kind had long enjoyed a colloquial description all of their own. It was the good old word "redneck," and those it described were concentrated in what H.L. Mencken had unfeelingly called "the hookworm and incest" belt of Anglo-Saxondom. Thus, to be English in America was, if one had enjoyed something like an Oxbridge education and spoke in tones acceptable to the (then) BBC, to be in the upper middle class almost by defi-nition. As Sir Ambrose Abercrombie explains the system of stratification in America later on in *The Loved One*: "You never find an Englishman among the underdogs — except in England, of course."

There's an interesting corollary to this, which is that the hyphenation question is, and always has been and will be, different for English immi-grants. One can be an Italian-American, a Greek-American, an Irish-American and so forth. (Jews for some reason prefer the words the other way around, as in "American Jewish Congress" or "American Jewish Committee.") And any of those groups can and does have a "national day" parade on Fifth Avenue in New York. But there is no such thing as an "English-American" let alone a "British-American," and one can only boggle at the idea of what, if we did exist, our national day parade on Fifth Avenue might look like. One can, though, be an Englishman in America. There is a culture, even a litera-ture, possibly a language, and certainly a diplomatic and military relation-ship, that can accurately be termed "Anglo-American." But something in the very landscape and mapping of America, with seven eastern seaboard states

named for English monarchs or aristocrats and countless hamlets and cities
replicated from counties and shires across the Atlantic, that makes hyphenation redundant. Hyphenation—if one may be blunt—is for latecomers.
It's been very absorbing (the term I hope is the apt one) to see the emergence
of another non-hyphenated immigrant group. Those from south of the Rio
Grande are now seldom if ever known as Mexican-American, say, let alone
Salvadoran-American. They are, instead, "Hispanic" or "Latino." And they,
too, were in many ways forerunners rather than latecomers.

The two things that my English background and youth had most
featured—anxieties about class and the decline of empire—helped me to
negotiate and explicate these subjects, both of which lay under a certain ban
of "denial" or reticence, to an American readership. It so happened that as
I was finding my feet in New York, the Public Broadcasting System (sometimes known as "Petroleum's British Subsidiary" because of the salience of
its *Mobil Masterpiece Theatre*) was screening *Brideshead Revisited* with none
other than William F. Buckley occupying Alistair Cooke's customary leather
armchair by the fireside. So, though there were large events unfolding in
the political world, from the application of the Reagan doctrine in Central
America to the drama in Poland and the clash over missile deployment, the
first really long considerations that I wrote for *The Nation* and *Mother Jones*
were about the intersections of class and empire. I drew on what I knew best,
to stress that behind the manorial glamour of Brideshead Castle there lay the
deep melancholy caused by the imperialist slaughter of 1914–1918, and that
much of Tom Wolfe's celebrated "style" was part of a revival of a right-wing
politics based on the defensive class-consciousness of the well-off.

Having sponged on my unimprovable friends Gully and Peter for long
enough, I became the tenant of a walk-up on East Tenth Street, on the north
side of Tompkins Square, found for me by the seemingly omni-connected
Ian McEwan, and there I had a desk with a view across town of the Twin
Towers of the World Trade Center. My landlord had a good library in this
small apartment, and the neighborhood, then very poor and grungy and
old-style ethnic with a traditional emphasis on Ukrainians, also featured several decent writerly cafés and restaurants. There was a coffeehouse called Di
Roberti's, to which W.H. Auden had been known to shamble in his carpet
slippers from St. Marks Place. (Auden: almost the only Englishman to have

successfully mutated into an American, or at any rate certainly into a New Yorker. A previous occupant of his rather ramshackle old apartment building had been Leon Trotsky, who could have made a considerable American if things had been very, very different. One day, perhaps, we will uncover some of those old New York movies in which he was cast as an extra.) I felt I had accomplished one rite of New York passage myself, by getting horribly mugged on my own front steps within a few months of moving in. I can still remember the burning shame of having not resisted, despite the assurances of the girl I was escorting that I had done the sensible thing. I shall never forget the choking horror of seeing the knife-wielding psycho turning back, having had second thoughts about not stabbing us after he realized that we had seen him too closely for too long, and the desperate haste with which we slammed the street door behind us just in time, seeing him still menacing us and snarling through the glass. I coldly knew at that moment that if I had had a weapon on me, I would unhesitatingly have shot him dead. He was white, incidentally, though at the police-precinct the surly cops laboriously showed me a whole album of deep-black perps, before asking me if I was sure the assailant hadn't been "light Hispanic." By the time I'd said "no" to that, too, they obviously suspected me of being a bleeding-heart liberal.

The tempo of life in Manhattan seemed something like twice what it had been in London and, however late I went to bed, I invariably woke up early and couldn't get back to sleep. I was reading more and writing more, and furthermore writing for a new audience (of both editors and subscribers) after the over-familiar clientele of the United Kingdom. Yet I was also getting asked more, by papers "back home" (as I swore to try not to think of it) to write about the United States. And what a subject America was: an inexhaustible one in fact, begun by written proclamations and assertions that were open to rewriting and revision and amendment, and thus constituting an enormous "work-in-progress" in which one might hope to play a tiny part. It came to me that this was perhaps why I had felt such a strong push and pull of both emigration and immigration: that the need to write and the magnetic attraction of America had been two versions of the same impulse.

One reason for my varied nightlife in New York was my friendship with Brian and Keith McNally, the two brothers who had opened the Odeon restaurant (now and always to be immortal in a certain *zeitgeist* because it's the luminous illustration on the jacket of *Bright Lights, Big City*). Just as you can't picture McInerney without that cover shot, so it suddenly seemed that you couldn't picture the background of it without the McNallys. I felt awkwardly proud of having been friendly with them before they became so sought after: there had been a time when, of these two rather contrasting East Enders, Keith had been the suave maitre d' and Brian a bit more the combo of barman and—if it absolutely came to it—bouncer. They were both accomplished autodidacts. Keith concentrated on the aesthetic and the theatrical (he was adored as a discovery by both Alan Bennett and Jonathan Miller) while Brian was more riveted by history and ideology. Without our ever making too much of actually saying so, we realized that in England we would probably never have met, or not on such socially easy terms.

Brian it was who woke me very early one morning, sounding almost like a movie version of a Blitz-era Ealing Studios Cockney and inveighing against a "fuckin' diabolical liberty." This turned out to be, once my disordered senses had cleared, the Argentine invasion of the Falkland Islands. Far from home and fairly far from being Thatcherites, we were at one in the belief that under no circumstances could anybody put up with being pushed around by a crew of Buenos Aires brownshirts.

The aggression, for which my still-vivid visit to Argentina had helped prepare me, was the occasion for a fascinating division of forces and clash of opinions on both sides of the Atlantic. It seemed obvious to me that the military junta would never have dared attack a British territory unless it had been given some sort of "green light" from Washington. Indeed, it was at once reported that Jeanne Kirkpatrick, Reagan's UN ambassador and a leading apologist for anti-Communist dictatorships, had graced an Argentine diplomatic reception on the very night of the invasion. General Alexander Haig, Ronald Reagan's vain, preposterous secretary of state, was also in his usual engorged condition of being crazy for anything that was militaristic, sadistic, and butch in a uniform. But the assurances given to Haig's equivalents in Buenos Aires had all been predicated on the assumption that the British would not fight for a stony archipelago at the wrong end of the world. I abruptly realized, for reasons that I believed had little if anything to do with my blood and heritage, and despite the impediment placed in the way of my becoming more American, that I would be unable to bear the shame if this assumption proved to be correct.

In my new cohort around *The Nation*, the sending of a British naval expedition to recover the islands was mostly greeted with mirth and incredulity. Surely this wasn't serious? The British mood wouldn't outlast the shipping home of the first "body bag" (a term that was to become more wearisome to me with each passing year). At first I tried opportunistically to accommodate this mentality and split the difference, and even wrote an editorial mocking the "Rule Britannia" jingoism that seemed to be spoiling the show back home. My cheeks still inflame a bit to remember it. And then Alexander Chancellor, editor of *The Spectator*, gave me a call. His correspondent in Washington, an otherwise lovely man, was also having trouble taking the thing seriously and was filing copy that was "frankly a bit 'flip.'" Would I mind surging down to the capital and seeing if I could hold the fort for a while? I didn't hesitate. Never mind its ostensible Toryism: Chancellor's *Spectator* had been outpacing my old stable at the *New Statesman* for some while, recruiting some of the latter's best talents; it was a distinction even to be asked. I was soon on the shuttle, for what was really my first-ever Washington assignment.

It was a tremendous introduction to the "class" and "empire" dichotomies I mentioned above. On the one side was the very ugliest bit of the new American empire, represented by the Haig-Kirkpatrick alliance of uniformed bullies and power-sucking pseudo-intellectuals. They spoke for the Argentine torturers who were — as they then well knew but we did not — already acting as the herders and trainers for a homicidal crew that the world would soon know as the Nicaraguan *contras*. (It really counts as an irony of history that it was Mrs. Thatcher's bellicosity that robbed the neo-cons of their favorite proxy, compelling the then-unknown Oliver North to finance the *contras* from hostage trading with the Iranian mullahs instead, and very nearly demolishing the presidency of her adored "Ronnie.") On the opposing side stood the most traditional and apparently superannuated but also in a way the *classiest* bit of the old British Empire, given a near-ideal embodiment in this case by Sir Nicholas "Nico" Henderson, lodged as he was in the spacious ambassadorial residence designed by Sir Edwin Lutyens (architect of New Delhi) on the great western sweep of Massachusetts Avenue.

I dare say that, like many Foreign Office types, Sir Nicholas had his doubts about the prudence of sending the Royal Navy so far from home base on an obscure point of principle, but I can testify that it took him about three days to knock the creepy Argentine envoy right off the court and hound him from decent Georgetown society. A tubercular shoulder in youth had given "Nico" a hard time getting dressed in the morning: he was always well turned out but just very slightly rumpled and was by this stage in his life described as looking a bit like "a ruined country house." This he regarded as no insult. Indeed, he undoubtedly made good use of the way in which it caused superficial characters to underestimate him. By judicious leaking, he also managed to make *la* Kirkpatrick and her associates look rather unsavory. And, by calling in a number of markers, he induced Caspar Weinberger to throw the Defense Department onto the British side of the scale. I didn't care for Weinberger either, or for what I regarded as the American cult of Winston Churchill that he represented, but for me the main objective couldn't be in doubt. At all costs the United States should not salvage yet another filthy Latin American *caudillo*. Eventually Reagan sided with Weinberger and Thatcher against Haig and Kirkpatrick, and Argentina itself was liberated along with the tiny British archipelago it had tried to steal. I could not have had a better introduction to Washington and its power struggles.

He might have done the right thing on that occasion, but I did not at all like Ronald Reagan, and nobody then could persuade me that I should. Even now, when I squint back at him through the more roseate lens of his historic compromise with Gorbachev, I can easily remember (which is precisely why one's memoirs must always strive to avoid too much retrospective lens adjustment) exactly why I found him so rebarbative at the time. There was, first, his appallingly facile manner as a liar. He could fix the camera with a folksy smirk that I always found annoying but that got him called "The Great Communicator" by a chorus of toadies in the press, and proceed to utter the most resounding untruths. ("South Africa has stood beside us in every major war we have ever fought," he declared while defending a regime whose party leadership had been locked up by the British for pro-Nazi sympathies in the Second World War. "The Russian language contains no word for 'freedom'" was another stupefying pronouncement of his: Who knows where he got it from, or who can imagine a president whose staff couldn't tell him of the noble word *Svoboda*? On two separate occasions, he claimed that, having never quit the safety of the Los Angeles movie backlots, he had been present for the liberation of the Nazi death camps. It could get worrying.) Up close, at press conferences, the carapace of geniality proved to be flaky: I was once within a few feet of his lizard-like face when he was asked a question that he didn't care for—about the theft of President Carter's briefing book by Reagan campaign operatives during the 1980 elections—and found myself quite shaken by the look of senile, shifty malice that came into his eyes as he offered the excuse that the *New York Times* had also accepted stolen property in the case of the Pentagon Papers. Nobody was less surprised than I when Reagan was later found to be suffering from Alzheimer's disease: I believe it will one day be admitted that some of his family and one or two of his physicians had begun to suspect this as early as his first term.

The Leader of the Free World was frequently photographed in the company of "end-times" Protestant fundamentalists and biblical literalists like Jerry Falwell and Pat Robertson: tethered gas-balloons of greed and cynicism once written up by Martin Amis as "frauds of Chaucerian proportions." The president found time to burble with such characters about the fulfillment of ancient "prophecy" and the coming Apocalypse. He also speculated drivellingly that the jury might yet return an open verdict on the theory of evolution. He was married to a woman who employed a White House astrologer. He said that the Abraham Lincoln Battalion had fought on "the wrong side" in the civil war in Spain, which logically meant that there had been a "right" side and that it was the Francoist one. (When the last attempt at a fascist coup was made in Spain, in the early 1980s, the Reagan administration was asked for comment, again in the person of the Strangelovian freak Alexander Haig, who flabbergastingly said that the armed attack on Spain's elected parliament was a purely internal Spanish affair.) With Haig, Reagan also gave permission to Menachem Begin and Ariel Sharon to invade Lebanon in 1982, and to take their incursion as far as Beirut to do the dirty work of the Catholic Phalange. In order to gratify Chancellor Helmut Kohl of West Germany, Reagan agreed to visit an SS cemetery in Bitburg (*Ich bin ein Bitburger*) and, as if that in itself was not bad enough, to declare that those interred there were not just "victims," but victims "*just as much*" as the civilians they had slaughtered. He made stupid, alarming on-air jokes about pre-emptively bombing the USSR. He pardoned the convicted FBI agents Felt and Miller, who had been prosecuted and fired for illegal break-ins and wiretaps directed at the anti-war movement. In a really sweet irony, one of these men (Mark Felt), as I was to learn, had been the "Deep Throat" whose torpedoes had sent the previous elected Republican administration to the floor of the sea.*

Introduction to the Federal City had been so engrossing that, when Victor Navasky and Kai Bird asked me if I would consider moving there permanently for the magazine, I scarcely hesitated. On my departure for Washington, Victor bought me a farewell lunch at a restaurant near Pennsylvania Station. Known as the "wily and parsimonious" Navasky, in consequence of an imperishable column by Calvin Trillin in which the latter had recorded his being hired for a payment "somewhere in the low two figures," Victor may have been narrow with the magazine's money but he was always very generous with his own and it was a pretty decent snack. A different kind of wiliness had also helped him persuade me to move south: he had remarked casually that *The Nation* hadn't had a regular Washington columnist since I.F. Stone. This name was magic to all Sixties radicals and to earlier generations too: Stone had published his own weekly sheet of investigations and polemics, exposing the warmakers and the segregationists, and actually made a living out of being an independent non-alienated producer of printed words on the page. The good life of the pamphleteer. So flattered and excited was

---

* I was to learn this earlier than most people by a piece of induction of which I am still faintly proud. Bob Woodward and Carl Bernstein had both sworn that they would never reveal Deep Throat's identity until he died, or until he gave them further notice. But Carl Bernstein had been married to the tempestuous Nora Ephron, and I believed from knowing both of them slightly that it was impossible for Nora not to have asked, and even more impossible for Carl not to have told her. Nora's best friend was Annie Navasky, adorable wife of Victor. I therefore evolved the plan of asking Annie. She said—this, by the way, was at a dinner for Alger Hiss—that she *had* been told the name but that it didn't ring a bell and wasn't exciting and that she'd forgotten it. Overcoming my discouragement at this, I adopted the more direct approach of asking Nora straight out. She also said that it wasn't sensational—this was in the days when crazy people thought Deep Throat might have been Henry Kissinger—but told me that to the best of her recollection it was an FBI man called Felt. For quite a while I myself could not believe that it was the same one, so I missed yet another chance for a scoop.

I by this latent comparison that I fell into the Trillin trap and forgot to ask about an exact salary figure until it was very slightly too late…

I was looking forward to fighting back against the Reaganites in their capital city, and in such distinguished company as Izzy Stone's at that (he had promised to host a reception in my honor when I got there), but I still registered a twinge at quitting Manhattan, and this twinge became a pang as, moving toward the door of the restaurant, I had an alluring glimpse of Susan Sontag taking her lunch with Roger Straus. I knew Susan slightly by then: she was a sovereign figure in the small world of those who tilled the field of ideas. She didn't have any boss, but she did have a distinguished book publisher who was also a friend and who was proud to print anything she wrote. Obviously my "pang" was part envy. Susan, political as she was, didn't have to lead the very politicized life that I was about to embark upon.*

To become a Washingtonian is to choose a very odd way of becoming an American. It felt at first like moving to a company town where nothing ever actually got itself made. The typical local "look" was that of a lawyer (almost indistinguishable, in both the male and female cases, from that of the legislative aide). Dowdiness was a theme: on the streets of New York one's visual sense was constantly assailed and tortured by a fiesta of distraction: in my new home I found I could walk almost the whole length of Connecticut Avenue without having to turn my head for a second look. So much the better, perhaps, since for the first time in my working life I wasn't going to an office where there were congenial fellow scribblers, but was having to evolve a stern daily and weekly discipline of my own, and at home.

In my search for an inexpensive place to live, I soon discovered that there was a very stark discrepancy between the city's neighborhoods, and that this discrepancy was no less starkly demarcated. In 1982 and for some years afterward, you could still see the scarred and burned-out area, from eastern downtown to the districts behind the then-dilapidated and disused Union Station and right up through Capitol Hill, that dated from the riots in 1968. The smallness of D.C. made it an additional shock to realize quite how close,

---

* I am sometimes asked about the concept or definition of a "public intellectual," and though I find the whole idea faintly silly, I believe it should ideally mean that the person so identified is self-sustaining and autonomously financed. Susan was pre-eminently one such.

to the White House and to the Dome, that righteous mayhem had come. After staying for a bit with a Zimbabwean friend at the World Bank, and then with a British correspondent of some standing, I came to appreciate that I couldn't and perhaps shouldn't afford their leafy neighborhoods of the Northwest. I found a row house in northeast Capitol Hill, where if I wanted to cab it home late at night from Dupont Circle, African-born taxi drivers would sometimes decline to take me (on the unarguable—at least by me with them—grounds that it was "a black area"). I have never since been able to use the word "gentrification" as a sneer: the unavoidable truth is that it's almost invariably a good symptom.

Other areas of the city were being cheered up at a more rapid rate. Dupont Circle itself was being redone by an immigration of gay couples with spending money, who fixed up the housing stock and opened cafés and specialty stores. In Adams-Morgan, the city's little Latin Quarter, there was some music to hear and an ethnic mix from Ethiopian to El Salvadoran where nobody predominated unduly. Georgetown still had its hostesses in those days, and I was somewhat befriended by one of the very nicest of them, Joan Bingham. In this female-dominated circle, which had always formed a part of the Anglo-American "special relationship" and which eventually went into eclipse along with it, there were still to be found *grandes dames* like Katharine Graham and Susan Mary Alsop and Evangeline Bruce and Kay Halle, and as Oscar Wilde once remarked of Frank Harris, I was invited to all of these great salons—*once.*

Since I was in the city to work for an American magazine (while all of my British friends were naturally enough writing for London ones), my perspective had perforce to alter and my personal way of becoming Americanized was to remain a blood brother of the American Left. I felt a kinship with this in any case: the tradition of Marx's great solidarity with Lincoln in the Civil War; the great and humane figure of Eugene Debs; the mighty class battles of the 1930s that baptized the labor movement—which then helped co-sponsor the March on Washington in 1963. Through men like Izzy Stone I was introduced to some veterans of these heart-stirring episodes. Then Ralph Nader invited me to lunch (and offered me the strange sum of seven thousand dollars if I would give up smoking, which I didn't, or didn't then).

The taunt against us by the Reagan-Kirkpatrick faction was that we were "anti-American" and, when we criticized Israeli expansionism, anti-Semitic. In parallel with this came the accusation that, in the Cold War, we regarded the United States and the USSR as "morally equivalent." One grew used to countering this line of attack and adept at saying that America was being untrue to itself when (say) it tolerated death squads in El Salvador. In the Israeli case, as Stone was fond of pointing out, there was more criticism of government policy in the Jerusalem press than in the American one. Jewish leftist critics of Zionism were to be found all over the American scene, and nothing about them was "self-hating" (the other fork of the "anti-Semitic" indictment). On the "moral equivalence" charge I had a little more difficulty: my old Trotskyism had taught me to be much more anti-Soviet than many of my comrades, and I was often made aware in *Nation* circles that there really were people who did think that Joseph McCarthy had been far, far worse than Joseph Stalin. But on thermonuclear weapons, for example, I did feel that there was an approximate moral equivalence, which got worse as American strategists began to use exterminist phrases such as "launch on warning." And I thought South Africa more nearly met the definition of a "totalitarian" state than did, for example, Hungary. I fell into correspondence with Noam Chomsky on some of these points, and used to go and visit him up in Cambridge, on one occasion speaking on the same platform in defense of Cyprus. He worried me once by saying that as far as he could see, the "moral equivalence" calculus favored the Soviet Union, but I filed this under another heading. My much-admired Gore Vidal worried me once or twice, too. I went down to Lynchburg, Virginia, in the early Reagan days, to see him trail his coat and tease the faithful at a public lecture in Jerry Falwell's hometown. This he did brilliantly. I took young Amis along for the ride, and we all three had dinner. As if helpfully introducing an innocent Martin to the native loam of America, Gore happened to mention the FBI and broke off to tell him confidingly: "You know—that's our KGB." I could feel Martin resisting this glibness: he later wrote that Gore, while a great performer, needed to know that there was something radically, nay terminally, wrong with his smile. Not very much later, I was made to cringe myself by Vidal's response to a bitter charge of anti-Americanism from Norman Podhoretz. He began well enough, by saying airily that he could hardly be accused of hatred for a nation of which he was the "official biographer." That was a fair-enough

riposte, in view of the body of fiction about the life and history of the republic that he had so carefully and lovingly composed.* Things got a touch less
lofty when Gore then rounded on Podhoretz and accused him of being an
Israeli rather than an American. This chanced to be in a special edition of
*The Nation* about patriotism and internationalism: it upset Alexander Cockburn and myself enough for us to express our reservations to Navasky. With
one of the shrugs for which he was famous, Victor (who secretly welcomed
the notoriety that it would bring the magazine) said: "Well, Gore is Gore."
This I was later to find true enough.

---

* I was once seated in a television studio with Newt Gingrich, waiting for the debate between
us to get going, when the presenter made an off-air remark that was highly disobliging to
Gore. The former Republican Speaker abruptly became very prim and disapproving, and
said that he would prefer not to listen to any abuse of the author of *Lincoln*: a novel that he
regarded as being above reproach. I conveyed this news to the author himself, who took the
tribute as he takes all tributes: as being overdue and well deserved.

# Changing Places

All the essentials of humanity's artistic treasures can be found in
New York.

—Claude Lévi-Strauss

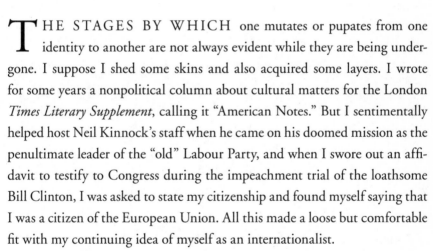

THE STAGES BY WHICH one mutates or pupates from one
identity to another are not always evident while they are being undergone. I suppose I shed some skins and also acquired some layers. I wrote
for some years a nonpolitical column about cultural matters for the London
*Times Literary Supplement*, calling it "American Notes." But I sentimentally
helped host Neil Kinnock's staff when he came on his doomed mission as the
penultimate leader of the "old" Labour Party, and when I swore out an affi-
davit to testify to Congress during the impeachment trial of the loathsome
Bill Clinton, I was asked to state my citizenship and found myself saying that
I was a citizen of the European Union. All this made a loose but comfortable
fit with my continuing idea of myself as an internationalist.

I might have gone on in this way more or less indefinitely, keeping my
European but also British passport and my trusty green card, which was so
old by now that it was blue, but which counted as platinum because it was
one of those beauties that didn't carry an expiration date. The immigration officers had started to say "welcome home" when I presented it, and I
would reply: "nice to be back." I had long since ceased to notice—or do I
mean to care about?—things like the stubborn American belief that "hot
tea" is made with lukewarm or formerly boiled water, rather than water that

is actually boiling. I now took it for granted that perfect strangers would mention their preferred churches or even—at least in New York and California—their shrinks. I had slowly realized that when male neighbors on airplanes or bar stools struck up conversation by asking about "the playoffs," I didn't actually have to know or care anything about sports: it was merely an initial Y-chromosome attempt at an opening and one could get straight to sex or politics (or silence if desired) by acknowledging this and cutting out the middle-man subject.

Speaking of airplanes...on a day in early September 2001 I got up at a decent hour on a morning that simply had to be described as golden and crisp, went out through the blazingly autumnal Virginia woods to Dulles Airport and boarded a flight for Seattle. It was one of those days when everything went right and America again seemed full of light and space and liberty and good fortune: my upgrade on United cleared the waiting list and I ate a packed lunch with a good book, taking time every now and then to look down on the superbly cultivated munificence of American agriculture, contrasting as it did with the great scapes of wooded and mountainous wilderness. On top of all this, I was going so luxuriously west in order to be paid money to deliver an attack on Henry Kissinger. Whitman College, in the town of Walla Walla in Washington State, was associated with the late Senator Henry "Scoop" Jackson, a man who despite his supposed "neoconservatism" had always detested Kissinger's willingness to adjust himself to the convenience of Leonid Brezhnev and other despots. To complete my near-perfect day, the Walla Walla campus was a sylvan delight, the student body immaculate and receptive, while the faculty club knew how to throw a proper dinner, and I had a "scoop" of my own to contribute. On the following morning, the family of a murdered Chilean general was to be given leave to bring suit against Henry Kissinger in a federal court in Washington, D.C. The news was about to be transmitted on the BBC and would, I knew and could disclose, be on the front page of the following day's *Washington Post*. I delivered a not-bad speech, rounded it off with this exciting news and received a standing ovation—including from some of Henry Jackson's family—after which I wound up by saying: "So, comrades and friends, brothers and sisters, we shall be able to say that tomorrow—September 11th 2001—will long be remembered as a landmark day in the struggle for human rights." I shook a lot of hands, kissed a few cheeks, signed quite a number of my Kissinger books, and retired (as Lord Rochester once said, as if breaking the rule of a lifetime) "early, sober and alone."

Very early next morning my wife, Carol, had me lifting the phone before I could quite appreciate the fact. From the East Coast, she had a three-hour time-zone advantage. "If you turn on the TV," she said with her not-unknown dryness and economy, "you may find that the war-crimes trial of Henry Kissinger has been slightly postponed." I found a remote-control device, which gave me the Weather Channel as such things always do, but even the Weather Channel had the "breaking" story.

"Breaking" was about right. I felt myself rending internally as I was forced to watch—that's how it felt, as with being made to witness a torture or an execution—the scenes I don't have to describe to you. Or perhaps you will forgive me one exception to that resolution. As I saw the first of the towers begin to dissolve and lose its shape and outline, I was alerted to what was imminent by the abrupt sinking and sagging of the big antenna on the roof. I can only phrase this by saying that I was very suddenly and very overwhelmingly actuated by pity. I know that this is the pathetic fallacy at work and I dare say I knew it then, but it was like watching the mute last moments of a dying elephant, say, or perhaps a whale. At any rate, the next emotion I felt was a rush of protectiveness, as if something vulnerable required my succor. Vulnerable? This commercial behemoth at the heart of an often-callous empire? Well, yes, at the risk of embarrassment. And my protective feelings were further engaged and enlisted as, on this most fault-less of September days, the whole southern tip of Manhattan was suddenly engulfed in a rolling, boiling cloud of filth that blotted out the sun. And in that filth was contained the pulverized remnant of many of my fellow creatures. In a first-reaction report I wrote that it was as if Charles Manson had been made god for a day.

More Mansonism was in store. My hometown was under attack as well. The next time Carol called, she wasn't quite so wry and detached. The Defense Department was on fire. She could not get across town to collect our daughter, who had just been dropped at school. Chaos was official. There were hysterical and false reports of explosions near the White House and the State Department. The wonderful spaces and distances of America feel fractionally less glorious when a husband and father is on the wrong side of the Continental Divide and can't do a thing. It transpired that, if not for the gallant action of the passengers on United Flight 93, and the traditional tardiness of air-traffic control at Newark Airport, which gave those heroes and heroines their time lag, another plane would have gone sailing through the blue of that day, arrowing right behind the coiffed heads of the TV newscasters, and burst into a gorgeous ball of red and yellow and black against the dome of the Capitol.

From an early age, I had dreamed of Manhattan and identified it with breadth of mind, with liberty, with opportunity. Now it seemed that there were those who, from across the sea, had also been fantasizing about my longed-for city. But fantasizing about hurting it, maiming it, disfiguring it, and bringing it crashing to the ground. "Let it come down!" as the first murderer says in *Macbeth*, expressing in those four words a whole skullful of nihilism and resentment. Before the close of that day, I had deliberately violated the rule that one ought not to let the sun set on one's anger, and had sworn a sort of oath to remain coldly furious until these hateful forces had been brought to a most strict and merciless account.

And what of my other adopted city? How often had I laughed or even sneered at Washington, sometimes saying (echoing a smart friend) that it was New York's nicest suburb, and at other times mocking it in various tones as "provincial" or a "company town." Should I now also feel protective about that other behemoth, the Pentagon? Well, into its outer walls had been flown a nice acquaintance of mine, a feisty Republican lady named Barbara Olson. She had managed to get her husband on her cellphone to say she had been hijacked, and to him had fallen the task of telling her that she was mistaken about that. She was not a hostage. There were not going to be any "demands." She was to be murdered in order that others, too, might die. As I tried to picture her reaction, I hit a barrier that my imagination was unable to cross. Also, when you have seen the Pentagon still smoldering across the river, from the roof of your own apartment building, you are liable to undergo an abrupt shift of perspective that qualifies any nostalgia for Norman Mailer's "Armies of the Night" or Allen Ginsberg's quixotic attempt to levitate the building. In his book *The Company of Critics* the Social Democratic intellectual Michael Walzer says that most of his friends and colleagues have never

even visited Washington except to protest. I was to find this thought, about the mentality of America's intellectuals, recurring to me as the days went by, but meanwhile my feeling for the city became distinctly more tender, and I began to value more what I had become used to taking for granted: the openness and greenery, the nexus of friends and contacts, the wonderful museums and galleries and concert halls, the two Shakespeare theaters, and the way that one could walk right up to the railings of the White House. And then another filthy miasma arrived, this time in the form of anthrax spores stuffed into envelopes. A well-liked mailman on our route was one of the casualties, and our downstairs mailroom was briefly closed. This is the sort of phenomenon that breeds paranoia and hatred and fear, yet I was above all struck, throughout that month, by the calm and dignity with which New Yorkers and Washingtonians were conducting themselves. Every now and then, some nervous official would broadcast an appeal to people NOT to go and launch random attacks on Arab-run groceries or local mosques; these appeals grated on me as being superfluous and patronizing. There were a very few abject morons out in the boondocks who summoned the courage to attack anyone wearing a turban—they usually managed to pick Sikhs or Tibetans—but this was hardly a police-blotter blip.

Two things began to contend for mastery in my head. At first, I was most afraid of an orgiastic flag-waving unanimity, in which the press and media would congeal into an uncritical mass, as if "we" all lived in a one-party consensus. But then a chance encounter crystallized quite another fear. I was still stuck out at Whitman College, waiting for the airports to reopen, and went into a store to buy some overnight supplies. I was approached by a young woman who had been at my Kissinger lecture, and we chatted briefly about it before turning to the inescapable topic. "You know what my friends are saying?" she inquired. "They are saying it's the chickens coming home to roost."

I have always had a dislike for that rather fatuous and folkish expression, and this dislike now came welling up in me with an almost tidal force. (What bloody "chickens"? Come to think of it, whose bloody "home"? And, for Christ's sake, what sort of "roost"?) And I could suddenly visualize, with an awful and sickening certainty, what we were going to be getting by way of comment from Noam Chomsky and his co-thinkers in the coming days.

This realization helped me considerably in sorting out the discrepant and even discordant discussions that were taking place in my interior, and I soon enough sat down to write my regular column for *The Nation*. I titled it "Against Rationalization." I did not intend to be told, I said, that the people of the United States—who included all those toiling in the Pentagon as well as all those, citizens and non-citizens, who had been immolated in Manhattan—had in any sense deserved this or brought it upon themselves. I also tried to give a name to the mirthless, medieval, death-obsessed barbarism that had so brazenly unmasked itself. It was, I said, "Fascism with an Islamic Face." In this I attempted to annex Alexander Dubček's phrase about Czechoslovakia adopting "Socialism with a Human Face," and also to echo Susan Sontag's later ironic re-working, following the military coup in Poland, of the idea of Communism going the other way and degenerating into "Fascism with a Human Face." Obviously, this concept is too baggy to be used every time, so I am occasionally "credited" with coining the unsatisfactory term "Islamofascism" instead.

Anyway, I didn't have long to wait for my worst fears about the Left to prove correct. Comparing Al Quaeda's use of stolen airplanes with President Clinton's certainly atrocious use of cruise missiles against Sudan three years before (which were at least ostensibly directed at Al Quaeda targets), Noam Chomsky found the moral balance to be approximately even, with the United States at perhaps a slight disadvantage. He also described the potential civilian casualties of an American counterstroke in Afghanistan as amounting to "a silent genocide." As time had elapsed, I had gradually been made aware that there was a deep division between Noam and myself. Highly critical as we both were of American foreign policy, the difference came down to this. Regarding almost everything since Columbus as having been one continuous succession of genocides and land-thefts, he did not really believe that the United States of America was a good idea to begin with. Whereas I had slowly come to appreciate that it most certainly was, and was beginning to feel less and less shy about saying so. We commenced a duel, conducted largely in cyberspace, in which I began by pointing out the difference between unmanned cruise missiles on the one hand and crowded civilian airliners rammed into heavily populated buildings on the other. We more or less went on from there.

Gore Vidal, also, could hardly wait to go slumming. He took the earliest opportunity of claiming that, while Osama bin Laden had not been proved to be the evil genius of the attacks, it was by no means too early to allege that the Bush administration *had* played a hidden hand in them. Or at least, if it had not actually instigated the assault, it had (as with Roosevelt at Pearl Harbor!) seen it coming and welcomed it as a pretext for engorging the defense budget and seizing the oilfields of the southern Caucasus. His articles featured half-baked citations from the most dismal, ignorant paranoids. President Bush had evidently forewarned himself of the air piracy in order that he should seize the chance to look like a craven, whey-faced ignoramus on worldwide TV. Vidal's old antagonist Norman Mailer was largely at one with him on this, jauntily alleging that endless war was the only way to vindicate the drooping virility of the traditional white American male. Thus did the nation's intelligentsia, and a part of the mental universe of the *New York Review of Books*, show its readiness in a crisis. I thought I had to say a word for the fortitude that the rest of society was manifesting.

I had another motive that is perhaps plainer to me now than it was then. I could not bear the idea that anything I had written or said myself had contributed to this mood of cynicism and defeatism, not to mention moral imbecility, on the Left. I did not want that young lady at Whitman College to waste her time drawing facile and masochistic conclusions. I had said all I could about American policy in South Africa and Chile (Salvador Allende had been overthrown and murdered on another 11 September twenty-eight years before) but as I asked an audience in Georgetown in a later debate with Tariq Ali, could anyone imagine Mandela or Allende ordering their supporters to use civilian airliners to slaughter more civilians? Any comparison of that kind, or any extension of it to Vietnam, was—quite apart from anything else—vilely insulting to the causes and struggles with which it was being compared.

I went up to New York as soon as I could, and I got my editors to send me off to the Pakistan/Afghan/Kashmiri frontier as soon as possible after that. In Manhattan, it was both upsetting, and yet confirming, to see my favorite poet becoming the unofficial laureate of the moment. Auden's "September 1, 1939" had by some unspoken agreement been sent all around the Internet, and was to be found pasted or stapled to public surfaces in the city.

Its early-warning couplet, "The unmentionable odor of death / Offends the September night," began to materialize itself, especially as one worked one's way south below Union Square and began to feel the nostrils actually dilate with the miasma. (Ever since, the lovely coincidence of the words "fall" and "New York" has always had a wretchedly double meaning for me.) I contrived to get very close to Ground Zero and had to send all my clothes to be cleaned immediately afterward. I talked to my graduate class at the New School for Social Research — itself partly founded as a haven for refugees from fascism — where a few of our downtown dorms had been converted into shelters. The parents of some students had urged them to desert the stricken city and head home. I told them that they'd never forgive themselves if they left New York now. I saw the improvised photo notices of the "missing" and the "disappeared" taped to walls and shop windows downtown, using every language from Spanish to Armenian, and heard again the echo from the victims of the death squads. I saw the awakening of a new respect for the almost-eclipsed figure of the American proletarian, who was busting his sinews in the rubble and carnage of downtown while the more refined elements wrung their hands. What an opportunity for the Left to miss, there, and what an overbred and gutless Left it had proved to be. "Into this neutral air," Auden had written on the eve of destruction in 1939, from his barstool eyrie on 52nd Street:

> Where blind skyscrapers use
> Their full height to proclaim
> The strength of Collective Man,
> Each language pours its vain
> Competitive excuse.

Even as the whining and the excuse making began, Auden's lines were being reborn and recirculated, as if to emphasize that while the great edifices of New York may indeed be "capitalist," they also represent a triumph of confidence and innovation and ingenuity on the part of the workers who so proudly strove to build them. There was for me a narrow but deep contrast between that ethos and the "Strawberry Fields" or "Candle in the Wind" flavor of the vigils downtown. There was something else from the "Devil's Decade" of the 1930s that I was struggling to remember and soon enough it came to me. Remembering the last moments of the *Titanic*, George Orwell had written that:

> In all the long list of horrors the one that most impressed me was that at the last the *Titanic* suddenly up-ended and sank bow foremost, so that the people clinging to the stern were lifted no less than three hundred feet into the air before they plunged into the abyss. It gave me a sinking sensation in the belly which I can still all but feel. Nothing in the [First World] War ever quite gave me that sensation.

"Look, teacher," the *New York Times* reported a child shrilling as the Twin Towers were becoming pyres: "the birds are on fire." Here was a sweet, infantile rationalization of an uncommon sight: human beings who had hesitated too long between the alternatives of jumping to their deaths or being burned alive, and who were thus jumping *and* burning, and from much more than three hundred feet. Nothing that I have witnessed since, including Abu Ghraib and Guantánamo and various scenes in Afghanistan and Iraq, has erased those initial images of the deep and sick relationship between murder and suicide, or of the wolfish faces of those who gloated over the horror. I have just looked up the little piece that I wrote at the time for my editors at *Vanity Fair* (which they titled "For Patriot Dreams") and I now see that I ended it like this, with another closing stave from Auden and then a few clumsy lines of my own:

> Defenseless under the night
> Our world in stupor lies;
> Yet, dotted everywhere,
> Ironic points of light
> Flash out...

I don't know so much about "defenseless." Some of us will vow to defend it, or help the defenders. As for the flashes of light, imagine the nuance of genius that made Auden term them "ironic." It would be a holy fool who mistook this for weakness or sentimentality. Shall I take out the papers of citizenship? Wrong question. In every essential way, I already have.

Introducing the same essay, which he honored me by anthologizing in a collection that he edited just before his distressingly early death, the late Stephen Jay Gould wrote: "I loved the juxtaposition of David Halberstam's and Christopher Hitchens's essays, the first from a longtime New Yorker who used 9/11 to make some kind of peace that he had not found with his life, the second from an Englishman who used the same event to come to terms after decades of struggle." Flattered as I was to be chosen by such a distinguished educator and explicator (Gould's understated Marxism was still unmissable in his great works on evolutionary biology), I found that I didn't quite like the idea that I was starting to "come to terms" or hang up my gloves or in any other sense cool off. In truth, a whole new terrain of struggle had just opened up in front of me. I also noticed another thing, which was the title of that Orwell essay from 1940, written only a few short months after Auden's poem, which I had looked up for its reference to the *Titanic*. It was called "My Country Right or Left." I slightly recast this to say to myself, about the USA: *My country after all.*

I was still only offering a general solidarity without paying the full price of the ticket. Two things had not yet happened. The fantastic, gigantic international campaign of defamation and slander of the United States had not yet got under way, and the argument about the deployment of its sons and daughters to the frontiers had not begun to take on the shape that it has since assumed.

It's only with a conscious effort now that one can recall the supposed moment of international pro-American solidarity that ensued from the September 11 assault. There were vigils and candles, solemn editorials and sonorous pronouncements. President Bush (who had run away and disappeared on the day itself) did his best to muddy the waters by saying that it was a matter of "Amurrka" versus "the terrists" (sometimes he seemed almost to say "tourists") and didn't appear to acknowledge, or even to know about, the huge number of non-American citizens who had perished in downtown New York. But even without this clumsiness on his part, I believe that the venomous propaganda would still have been coming. Within a few days, the Muslim world had been infected by the base, hysterical lie that all Jews had left the World Trade Center just in time to avoid the airstrike. At the New York film festival, held while lower Manhattan was still giving off evil-smelling fumes, I debated with Oliver Stone, who expressed the cheery view that the "uprising" that had occurred downtown would soon link up with a generalized anti-globalization movement. Next up was my magazine *The Nation*, whose publishing wing cashed in with a hastily translated version of a deranged French best-seller, alleging that the Pentagon had not been hit with a civilian plane carrying my friend Barbara, but rather by a cruise missile fired by the Bush administration. The disgusting "Reverends" Pat Robertson and Jerry Falwell were also on hand to announce that the United States had merited the devastation because of its willingness to tolerate sexual deviance. Here was an unexampled case of seeing all one's worst enemies in plain view: the clerical freaks and bigots of all persuasions and the old Charles Lindbergh isolationist Right, the latter sometimes masquerading as a corny and folksy version of a Grassy Knoll conspiracist "Left."

I took it upon myself to defend my adopted homeland from this kind of insult and calumny, the spittle of which was being gigglingly prepared even as the funerals and commemorations were going calmly forward. I was impressed to see who rallied and who did not. Salman Rushdie, Ian McEwan, and Martin Amis all wrote outstanding articles, expressing the support of non-Americans for the United States against this unashamed cult of death. Norman Mailer, John Updike, and even Susan Sontag—to say nothing of Noam Chomsky—appeared to be petrified of being caught on the same side as a Republican president, and often contented themselves with inexpensive, unserious remarks about American *machismo* or Bush's "cowboy" style. It was fatalistically agreed in almost all polite circles that even if one could kill or capture Osama bin Laden, it would only mean that others would spring up in his place (and that's if you believed, unlike Gore Vidal or Michael Moore, with whom I also debated later on this point, that he was in fact the culprit).

I decided to venture back to the epicenter of *jihad* and wrote an essay—"On the Frontier of Apocalypse"—which said that the problem country was actually not so much Afghanistan but Pakistan: our oldest regional ally and the working model for a nuclear-armed, failed-state "Islamic republic." I am still fairly proud of that article. I also began to hear more from my Iraqi and Kurdish friends about the very mad, menacing way in which the Saddam Hussein regime was celebrating and even praising the 9/11 attacks. Ba'athist rhetoric was frequently a matter of dementia, as I well knew, but this was at a time when even Iranian and Saudi Arabian circles were trying to look and sound sympathetic. Amid all this chaos on the various frontiers what I increasingly thought was: thank whatever powers there may be for the power of the United States of America. Without that reserve strength, the sheer mass of its arsenal in combination with the innovative maneuvers of its special forces, the tyrants and riffraff of the world would possess an undeserved sense of impunity. As it was, the Taliban were soon in full flight from the celebrating people they had for so long oppressed, and Al Quaeda was being taught to take heavy casualties as well as inflict them. I was not against this.

I can identify the moment when I decided to come off the fence and to admit that I felt that I had been cheating on my dues. I was keener on the foreign policy response of the administration than on its crude and hasty domestic measures, telling amused audiences that as long as green-card holders could be imprisoned without trial by Attorney General John Ashcroft, I felt I couldn't pass up that chance. But the whole atmosphere was becoming less flippant by the day, especially as the United States began to ask the United Nations to live up to its resolutions on Iraq and on terrorism. One night I was coming back from a TV debate and talking to my Bosnian Muslim driver, who considered his own country of birth to have been rescued from dismemberment and genocide by an earlier American military intervention. "You citizen yet?" he asked me. I made some temporizing reply. "You should get on with it: America needs us." For emphasis, he pressed on me the name of a good immigration lawyer. In a couple of days I called the number, to be greeted by a female voice which was as purely Irish as the summer day is long. I gave her my name. "And was it you that wrote that book about Mother Teresa?" Reckoning the chances that such an Irish tone would track with a Catholic girlhood, I confirmed that this was so and made ready to call another attorney. "That being the case," said the disembodied loveliness, "this firm will be happy to take your own case *pro bono* and without a fee at all." Not bad, I thought to myself: a pure coincidence between a secular Bosnian Muslim and an anti-clerical Hibernian. Only in America… When I went round to the office itself I was sure I recognized the lady but couldn't quite "place" her, and she told me that if I'd ever been in the old Class Reunion saloon down by the White House, she'd once been the barmaid. That was in fact the true explanation, but by this stage I was almost beginning to feel that the warmth and geniality of the USA was beginning to overdo itself a trifle.

That was premature. The American bureaucracy very swiftly overcompensates for any bright-eyed immigrant delusions. *Nihil humanum a me alienum puto,* said the Roman poet Terence: "Nothing human is alien to me." The slogan of the old Immigration and Naturalization Service could have been the reverse: To us, no aliens are human. When folded—along with the Bureau of Alcohol, Firearms, and Tobacco, the only department of state I had ever hoped to command—into the vast inner space of the Department of Homeland Security, the resulting super-ministry was more like the Circumlocution Office than a reformed bureaucracy. My Canadian friend David Frum, who was actually working in the White House and had had a hand in writing the famous "axis of evil" speech, had his personal paperwork lost when he applied to become an American. Ian McEwan was put under close arrest and hit with an indelible "entry denied" stamp while trying to cross from Vancouver to Seattle for a big public reading: it would have been of little use to him to plead that the First Lady had recently asked him to dinner. A Muslim professor of my acquaintance, a permanent resident of many decades' standing, was detained and asked "Are you a Sunni?" When he replied in the affirmative, he was asked "Why are you not a Shi'a?" (Not something that Muslims get asked every day, and a question requiring quite a lot of time for reflection, an interval for which the interrogating officer had no patience.)

Innumerable times I was told, or assured without asking, that I would hear back from officialdom "within ninety days." I wasn't in any special hurry, but it grated when ninety days came and went. Letters came from offices in Vermont and required themselves to be returned to offices in states very far away from the Canadian border. Eventually I received a summons to an interview in Virginia. There would be an exam, I was told, on American law and history. To make this easier, a series of sample questions was enclosed, together with the answers. I realized in scanning them that it wouldn't do to try and be clever, let alone funny. For example, to the question: "Against whom did we fight in the revolution of 1776?" it would be right, if incorrect, to say "The British" and wrong, if correct, to say "The usurping Hanoverian monarchy." Some of the pre-supplied Qs and As appeared to me to be paltry: to the question: "Name one benefit of being a citizen of the United States?"

the printed answer was: "To obtain Federal Government jobs, to travel with a U.S. passport, or to petition for close relatives to come to the United States to live." This had a rather cheap and unimaginative, indeed rather Tammany tone to it. Q: "What did the Emancipation Proclamation do? A: "It freed the slaves." No it didn't: that had to wait until the Thirteenth Amendment, the first United States document to mention the actual word "slavery" (and not ratified by the State of Mississippi until 1995).

Having previously been made to go to a whole separate appointment in deepest Maryland just to be fingerprinted, I sat up on the night before my Virginia one, and decided to read slowly through the Constitution. I wasn't especially nervous about flunking. I just felt like re-reading it. There are very few worthwhile documents in human history that are or were the product of a committee. I suppose that the King James or "Authorized" Version of the Bible is the best. Next to that—and of course very much shorter and rather less monarchical and tyrannical—the American Declaration of Independence and the preamble to the United States Constitution seem to me to rank exceedingly high. I sipped my wine and let the small hours advance as I read, and consulted the supporting case law from the great attendant volume of Professors Lockhart, Kamisar, and Choper. To study the amendments—the Bill of Rights and its successor clauses—is to read the history of the United States in miniature. Here were all the measures that set out to distinguish the new United States from the arbitrary and corrupt practices of the Hanoverian usurpers: amendments abolishing the established church, postulating an armed people, opposing the billeting of soldiers upon civilians, limiting searches of property and persons and in general setting limits and boundaries to state power. One had to admire the unambivalent way in which these were written. "Respecting an establishment of religion," said the very first amendment, drawing on Jefferson's and Madison's Virginia Statute For Religious Freedom, "Congress shall make *no* law." Little wiggle room there; no crevice through which a later horse-and-cart could ever be driven. Alas for advocates of "gun control," the Second Amendment seems to enshrine a "right of the people to keep and bear arms" irrespective of whether they are militia members or not. (The clause structure is admittedly a little reminiscent of the ablative absolute.) And the Eighth Amendment, forbidding "cruel and unusual punishments," is of scant comfort to those like me who might like that definition stretched to include the death penalty. If the Founders had wanted to forbid capital punishment (as, say, the state constitution of Michigan explicitly does), they would have done so in plain words.

The least plain words are probably those of the Emancipation Proclamation, which show that Abraham Lincoln's years as a country lawyer and rhetorical pedant were not wasted. But in splitting the difference between a war-winning measure and a liberating one, he nonetheless achieved magnificence, by demonstrating to those who had seceded from the protection of this document the folly and wickedness of what they had done. To have stood as straight as a spear and as hard as a rail through four years, and to have insisted every single day, often against his own generals, that the writ of the United States Constitution still ran in every tiny county of the remotest part of the indissoluble and above all undissolved Union: it's almost forgivable that people confuse it with the Thirteenth Amendment because when scrutinizing the moment you actually *do* hear the sound of a "trumpet that can never call retreat," and you do understand why Hegel said that history was the story of freedom becoming conscious of itself.

Inching along less dramatically and agonizingly through 1865 and 1870 come the workaday, necessary amendments finally doing away with involuntary servitude and racism in the franchise. Direct election of senators arrives in 1913. One step forward, one step back: 1919 sees Prohibition but then only the next year the Nineteenth Amendment extends suffrage to women. In 1951 the Twenty-second Amendment, limiting presidential terms to two, reflects the vindictiveness of a Republican Congress after the three drubbings taken by the GOP at the hands of FDR. Things go quiet for a bit until in 1964 the poll tax is abolished as a test of eligibility to vote, and in the dry words of this constitutional guarantee one can detect all the distilled spirit of *Shuttlesworth v. City of Birmingham* (which I then re-read, marveling again at the nerve of the fifty-two poor parishioners led by the Reverend Shuttlesworth on that Good Friday, little knowing that their church would soon be dynamited), and of other landmark cases like my personal favorite, *Loving v. Virginia*, which in 1967 struck down the law forbidding "mixed" marriages. The Twenty-sixth Amendment, setting the voting age at eighteen in 1971, is the way in which I suppose my own "generation" has engraved itself on this great tablet of freedom under the law.

The next day was a Day of the Beast (the 6th of June 2006 or 6/6/06) and this seemed auspicious enough as I drove out to Fairfax County and stopped just off the highway named for Robert E. Lee. In the waiting room, under portraits of George W. Bush and Homeland Security Director Michael Chertoff, there sat the sort of rainbow constituency that I had become used to joining on the various stages of my application. A woman from Barbados recognized me from the TV and asked shyly if I knew how soon she could hope to get a passport since she needed to travel. We chatted about the fact that both our current countries had the same Queen. Husbands and wives were testing each other on sample questionnaires. There were some basic toys on the floor for the many children who had to be brought along. For some reason cellphone use was forbidden. I picked up a leaflet which explained naturalization procedures, including the posthumous ones for military per-sonnel who had died before getting their citizenship papers. (This had been true for many Hispanic soldiers in Iraq and Afghanistan, though usually the grant of citizenship had been made automatic and retrospective for such men and women and for their families.) Finally Ms. Lopez was ready for me.

The questions didn't take very long: I can boastfully say that I got top marks on the history and Constitution test. I decided not to show off: when asked who said "Give Me Liberty or Give Me Death!" I replied "Patrick Henry" even though I strongly suspect, and have written, that the line comes from Addison's play *Cato*, which was vastly popular with American audi-ences at the time of the Revolution. There were then a few loose ends: I had listed all the political organizations of which I had been a member, including quite recently the "Committee for the Liberation of Iraq." Asked about this I said I technically was no longer a member, since the Committee had been wound up. "I suppose," said Ms. Lopez matter-of-factly, "it's not needed now that Iraq has been liberated." I wished I could share her certainty there.

She left the room and came back. "Congratulations!" she said. I stood up to shake her hand. "You have passed the examination. But unfortunately I cannot welcome you as a citizen today. You will be notified in due course by mail." No explanation was forthcoming for this disappointment. It was a moment of bathos and anticlimax; a poor sequel to my smoke-ringed, vinous reverie on American grandeur the previous night. Could I stand yet another pointless ninety-day delay, perhaps to be extended again even as it expired?

Yes, in point of fact I could, if it came to it, but what about the lady from Barbados who had started the day so full of American expectation?

Not very many nights later I ran into Michael Chertoff, the head of the Homeland Security Department, at a reception at the embassy of Kuwait. (It's only a detail, but in 1990 all the embassies of Kuwait were demanded by Saddam Hussein as his personal property, as part of his annexation of the country, so I always feel a slight *frisson* when on Kuwaiti soil.) As we were introduced, he said that he'd heard somewhere that I was becoming an American. Now, at the time, I was also a named plaintiff in a major lawsuit against the National Security Agency and the Department of Justice, petitioning the courts to put a halt to the warrantless wiretapping of American residents and citizens. So I thought of unsettling him and asking how on earth he knew my movements and plans so well. But it seemed more opportune and more serious to say a word about how tough a time good people were having, backed up in apparently endless lines, as they tried to negotiate the "golden door" that is mentioned on the Statue of Liberty. In fact, probably making him regret that he had ever asked, I gave the examples of several friends who had been abysmally hampered and insulted, and who wanted only to be allies of the USA.

It wasn't an absolute or mathematical consequence, but the next time I ran into him he again asked me how it was going and I said, look, the waiting in my case is the closest I have attained to a truly Zen experience of boredom and absurdity. Did I need anything? Well, sure, since he asked, I would like a personal citizenship ceremony at the Jefferson Memorial on the Tidal Basin, replete with cherry blossoms, on 13 April next, which would be my fifty-eighth birthday and would have been Thomas Jefferson's two hundred and sixty-fourth.*

The first trip I had taken, after arriving in the United States in 1981, had been down to Charlottesville to see Jefferson's house at Monticello: perhaps the most interesting private home in America. Here the great polymath had done the two things I most wished to do for myself if I ever became a house

---

* In fact Jefferson was born under the old calendar, on 2 April 1743, and had to change his birthday to the thirteenth when the historic Gregorian calendar date-shift was ordained. Both dates appear on his memorial obelisk at Charlottesville. I have often wondered what the racketeers of astrology and the zodiac did when everybody had to change birthdays and many people had to change their "sign." No doubt they managed to adjust suavely enough.

owner. He had designed and indexed a personal library and created a proper store of wine (some of it made with his own grapes). In a public dialogue between Susan Sontag and Umberto Eco I had once heard the latter define the polymath as someone who was "interested in everything, and in nothing else." Jefferson might have excelled as a lawyer, an architect, an engineer, a draughtsman, a botanist, an agronomist, a literary critic: almost anything in fact except a public speaker. At a time when smallpox vaccination was being denounced by leading men of god like Dr. Timothy Dwight of Yale as an interference with god's design, Jefferson helped devise a method of keeping Jenner's life-saving physic cool for conveyance over long distances, taught Lewis and Clark to administer it during their long trek across the interior, and saw to it that all his slaves were inoculated against the scourge. Mention of the system that underwrote his prosperity (and that I suppose had at a great remove also helped underwrite the scholarship that his descendant Mr. Coolidge had provided for me) was still slightly hushed when I first toured Monticello and asked to see the "servants' quarters."

But by 2007, when I had published my Jefferson biography, we had essentially ventilated the whole matter. Thanks to my friend Annette Gordon-Reed, the whole story of Jefferson's other family had become an open page for any reader, and one could even begin to dare see Sally Hemings as one of the unacknowledged "founding mothers" of that multiethnic American republic that Jefferson himself could never have foreseen. So the author of the Declaration of Independence and the Virginia Statute on Religious Freedom was a man who owned other people. (Part of my education in the subtleties of racism had been learning to cope with American historians who could easily accept that Jefferson had *owned* Sally Hemings and had indeed acquired her as a wedding present from a man who was his father-in-law and her actual *father*—this making the girl his wife's half-sister—but who could not bring themselves to believe that in addition to inheriting her and owning her, our third president had also gone so far as to have fucked her.) In taking on American citizenship, I was not invoking some sentimental Emma Lazarus idea of a country of refuge from the houses of bondage. I was consciously accepting that many people who later asserted themselves as Americans had originally, as James Baldwin phrased it, been brought here not from but *to* a house of bondage. Thus, when Michael Chertoff rather generously called and said: all right, we'll see you at the Jefferson Memorial after lunch on 13 April, I gave some thought to the guests I would have at my ceremony.

I first invited Ayaan Hirsi Ali, the heroine of feminine resistance to the living death known as *sharia*. I had met her at a conference in Sweden when she was still a relatively unknown Dutch dissident member of Parliament, trying to warn Western liberals against the sick relativism which had permitted them to regard "honor" killings and genital mutilation as expressions of cultural diversity. Since September 2001 she had taken ever more forward and courageous positions, and seen her friend and colleague Theo van Gogh (distant descendant of the painter) ritually murdered in the streets of Amsterdam as an obscene vengeance for the film about Muslim female "submission" that they had jointly made. The knife that burst the ventricles of Theo's heart also pinned to his body a barbaric message that told Ayaan that she was next. Ever since then her life had been one of those "maximum security" nightmares where an over-nervous state had overcompensated for its previous negligence in confronting theocratic terrorism. And then the Dutch government, tiring of its strenuous commitment, had abandoned Ayaan to the tender mercies of the free market, while her pious Amsterdam neighbors demanded that she be evicted from her home lest she spoil their chances of a quiet life. What was left for her, after this double European betrayal, but to turn to the United States? When we met again, her magically beautiful face was alive with humor. Before escaping from Somalia she had survived brutal circumcision as a child, numberless beatings from clan members, the dull horror of an arranged and forcible marriage, the misery of tribe-based civil war and religion-based domestic tyranny, and the arduous transition from refugee to exile status. Yet she was — in all the right senses — glad to be alive. "You'll be pleased to hear, Christopher, that I am no longer a Muslim liberal but an atheist." I told her that I was indeed happy to learn of this. "Yes, I find that it obviates the necessity for any cognitive dissonance." Pure music. Edward Gibbon once wrote that if all of European civilization were to be destroyed, it could be reconstituted from what had been transferred across the Atlantic: this now holds true for other societies as well.

My old Oxford comrade Andrew Cockburn and his wife, Leslie, had been allies and friends of mine in every sort of crisis and companions at every sort of celebration from the births of our children to the nuptials of theirs. Both as writers and as makers of documentaries they had expanded the frontiers of radical investigative journalism: the sort of work that the First Amendment and the Freedom of Information culture makes possible. For another Irishman I chose Captain Seamus Quinn of the U.S. Marine Corps. "Tell it to the Marines" had been an insult in my father's house and it's amazing how durable the taunts of interservice rivalry can be, but the U.S. Marines I have met have been exceptional in their mental breadth and their ability to be self-critical. Stationed in Anbar province during the hottest and nastiest period of the war against "Al Quaeda in Mesopotamia," Seamus had given me regular email updates on the death-grapple with these foulest of the foul, and thanks to him I'd had some advance intelligence of what later became known as "the surge": the combination of deadly force and political agility that had not only defeated Al Quaeda on the battlefield but discredited it in a region of Iraq that it had once dared to think that it might own.

Ever since I had been in Washington, Professor Norman Birnbaum had been a sort of mentor to me. Indeed, he had been a teacher to my earlier mentor Steven Lukes. He was a real veteran, present at the creation of the Old New Left, as he put it, and influential on the New New Left as well. If ever I needed an old copy of *Partisan Review*, he would either have it in his possession or in his memory, which was and is an institutional one. Internationalism is in Norman's blood, as the Left used to like to say of itself, and if I was ever visiting any European country in crisis I would call him up to find the name of that local Jewish *savant* who had in his time done battle against both sides of the Hitler-Stalin pact. ("You're going to Zagreb…Well you've certainly picked a nice time [this was in 1992, when the men in black shirts were openly back on the streets]…I should call up old Professor Rudi Supek if I were you." The good professor turned out (a) to possess a good cellar and (b) to have been the elected leader of those Yugoslav partisans who had been deported to a German camp. "So you see, Mr. Hitchens, I cannot truly call myself Croat or Serb because it would betray those brave Yugoslavs whom I had the honor of representing in Buchenwald." Yes, yes, I quite understand, but…) I was worried for a moment or two that Norman would not approve of my new friend Michael Chertoff, but he was as usual more than equal to the occasion, and told a surprised director of Homeland Security that he was sure he had known his father at City College in New York in the 1930s. It turned out that this was entirely possible. This was another moment at which to say "Only in America." And then we were all bolstered by Susan Schneider, the glamorous and loquacious wife of Mark, whose career as a human-rights champion, from Edward Kennedy's senatorial staff to the chairmanship of the Peace Corps, is barely to be equalled by any living person. (In El Salvador, there is a bridge named for Mark and Susan by a grateful citizenry. In Chile, if you get lost anywhere, just mention their names and people will instantly supply you not just with directions but with goods and services.)

There was a very stiff breeze blowing across the Tidal Basin but it served to give a real smack and crackle to the Stars and Stripes that Chertoff's people had brought along. It didn't take very long to administer the oath, or for me to swear allegiance and to declare that America's enemies, foreign and domestic, were also mine. Nor did I take very long to give my little acceptance speech, merely noting Mr. Jefferson's birthday and mentioning that, on his own tombstone, he had not cared to recall that he had been president, vice president, and secretary of state of the United States. Instead, he had asked to be remembered as the author of the Declaration of Independence, the founder of the University of Virginia, and the drafter of the Virginia Statute on Religious Freedom. For a writer to become an American is to subscribe of his own free will to a set of ideas and principles and to the documents that embody them in written form, all the while delightedly appreciating that the documents can and often must be revised, so that the words therefore *constitute*, so to say, a work in progress.

This was all rather well set out in the passport that I immediately went to acquire. When I first came to know young Americans at Oxford, the British passport was a many-splendored thing: a blue-gold hardback emblazoned with heraldry and speaking grandly in the tones of Her Britannic Majesty's Secretary of State for Foreign Affairs. The American passport was a limp paperback by contrast, and spoke in costive Cold War terms of the number of countries, from Cuba to North Korea, where it could not be lawfully taken. The new-look United States travel document makes a real effort. On the inside front cover is an old engraving of what must be Francis Scott Key observing the siege of Fort McHenry in Baltimore, with the words of *The Star-Spangled Banner* inscribed in manuscript form. On the opposite page are the closing words of the Gettysburg Address, delivering the ringing triune phrasing "of," "by," and "for" the people. On succeeding pages appear the Preambles to the Constitution and the Declaration, and brave words from Dr. Martin Luther King, the Kennedy inaugural, and a Mohawk chieftain. The illustrations maintain the note of uplift, with the Statue of Liberty, the Atlantic-Pacific railroad, and the spacecraft *Voyager* as it pushes beyond the edge of our solar system. The whole is a nice combination of the civically religious — only Jefferson and King mentioning a "creator" — with the great American accomplishments in mechanical and scientific innovation. It is possible to imagine handing it over, when one is being held up by some festering thug at some scrofulous checkpoint, and loftily asking to see his proof of identity in return. But more than that, it is possible to imagine the unfortunates, whose lives are temporarily under the command and control of this festering thug, aspiring one day to carry this same passport themselves. Human history affords no precedent or parallel for this attainment. On the day that I swore my great oath, dozens of Afghans and Iranians and Iraqis did the same. A few days later, I noticed that I had sloppily gummed a postage stamp onto an envelope with the flag appearing upside down. I am the most frugal of men, but I reopened the letter, tore up and threw away the envelope, invested in a whole new stamp and sent Old Glory on its way with dignity unimpaired. A small gesture, but my own.*

---

* There is flag-waving and flag-waving. When the giant statue of Saddam Hussein was pulled down from its plinth in Baghdad in April 2003, I was annoyed to see an American soldier step forward and drape a Stars and Stripes flag over the fallen visage of the dictator. This clearly disobeyed a standing order prohibiting display of the American colors. But then I learned that the overenthusiastic soldier was Marine Corporal Edward Chin, an ethnic Chinese volunteer both of whose parents had escaped the hell of Burma and begun a new life in Brooklyn. The offense might have been worse.

# Salman

A poet's work is to name the unnameable, to point at frauds, to take sides, start arguments, shape the world and stop it from going to sleep.

— Baal the Poet in *The Satanic Verses*

Where books are burned, people will next be burned.

— Heinrich Heine, on the burning of the Koran by the Inquisition, in his *Almansor* [1821]

———◄o►———

NOTTING HILL has always been my particular London. When I was eighteen, I signed up for an American-style "summer project" in the area, collecting data and raising consciousness in the "inner city." The old 'hood had got a name for itself in the late 1950s as the site of Britain's first race-riot,* and as I unrolled my sleeping bag amid the guitars and duffels on the floor of the run-down school where the volunteers slept, I could still see some of the traces. (The lightning-flash symbol of Sir Oswald Mosley's fascist party, which had attempted to profit from the localized hatred, was often to be seen whitewashed and chalked on crumbling local walls. One of my contributions to the project was to organize teams to go up the Portobello Road rubbing these out or painting them over: a contribution to improving

---

* Very well captured by Colin McInnes in his contemporary novels *City of Spades* and *Absolute Beginners*.

the atmosphere that was my first intuition of the "broken windows" theory of community policing.)

Padding around Notting Hill was an education in cheek-by-jowlery. Spicy Indian restaurants along Westbourne Grove, the West Indians and their ganja funk around the Mangrove in All Saints: Irish pubs where the regulars were not entirely thrilled by the arrival of the latest immigrants. Multiculturalism was a new thing in those days and even then could take aberrant forms. A ludicrous but menacing local figure had named himself "Michael X" in the hope of attracting some cross-Atlantic street cred: as a Trinidadian pimp and hustler called Michael de Freitas he had won notoriety as an especially nasty enforcer of evictions for a rack-rent landlord named, in one of those Dickensian coincidences, Mr. Rachman. The soi-disant X had a group—actually a gang—called RAAS. The letters were supposed to stand for Racial Adjustment Action Society and some white liberal clergymen and similar dupes were induced to take it seriously, but in Caribbean patois, as one soon discovered, a "raas" was a used tampon. How the gang must have cackled when they saw this filthy word solemnly printed in the newspapers. John Lennon fell for the con, as did some other gullible showbiz types. Years later, reporting on the murders that eventually saw the grisly Mr. X go through the trapdoor of a Trinidadian execution shed, I found myself on many a celebrity doorstep, including that of Corin Redgrave, of those who had been in his star-periphery. At Oxford in my first term, a rather silly Catholic bleeding-heart don named Michael Dummett managed to use his privileges to get X to speak in the All Souls dining room. The *New Statesman*, by some frightful miscalculation, found that a block of its shares had been acquired by the head of RAAS, who could in theory have turned up to vote at board-meetings. The air of Notting Hill was thick with bullshit on the racial question, and some other questions too, and it was sometimes a relief to walk over to Holland Park and sit on the grass for some of the free open-air summer concerts. As always in London, it was astonishing to see how swiftly one could make the transition from a slum quarter to a green one. There were still private gardens in the middle of some of the crumbling old stucco squares, accessible only to lucky residents with keys. We briefly campaigned to have some of these gardens opened to local children, who got knocked down by traffic while playing in the street. I can't imagine what we thought we were doing: this much-restored housing stock went on to furnish a backdrop for Hugh Grant's oleaginous talents and later for the hardly less slithery emergence of David Cameron as the hip Tory.

It was in an early stage of this metamorphosis of the 'hood that I made a visit to London in the mid-1980s, and went back as I always did to Notting Hill. It was carnival time: the time of that great non-bullshit event where London's West Indians compete to flaunt the finest floats and to deploy the steel bands with the most stamina. Some of the indigenous bourgeoisie take that weekend off and flee to Dorset or Wiltshire, leaving their keys and their viewing balconies to trusted friends, while others "stay on" and maintain every appearance of ultra-coolness and empathy. It was in John Ryle's more-than-cool mews house that I was introduced to Salman Rushdie, who was scanning the external world with an ironic gaze shaded by the brim of a flat cap.

It would be trite to say that I already knew him by reputation. Who didn't? If *Midnight's Children* had not won the Booker Prize, and won it fairly early in that prize's career, then the Booker might have been the sort of prize won by its first winner, John Berger. But in proposing himself as the product of a simultaneous parturition and partition, the offspring of a country that had had to undergo amputation and mutilation in order to achieve independence, Salman had managed to represent as well as record all the ambivalences of the postcolonial. To phrase it another way, he had come via Rugby School and King's College Cambridge to remind the British that they had betrayed the very people they had claimed to be schooling for nationhood: tossed away the "jewel in their crown" like some cheap piece of paste.

One great fictional chronicler of this sell-out had been Paul Scott, whose *Raj Quartet* had spoken to my depths because it understood that the treason at midnight in 1947, and the monstrous birth of a spoiled theocracy in Pakistan, was a tragedy for the English too. I knew that Rushdie had written scornfully of the reception of Scott, at least on the screen, viewing this as an old-style wallow in sentiment and nostalgia. I knew also that he hung around with a somewhat "Third World" and even black-power crew in north London. In a celebrated broadcast about the way that Britain treated its internal colony—the immigrants—Salman had quoted warmly from the above-mentioned silly-clever Catholic don Michael Dummett of All Souls (he of the warm collegial welcome for Michael X) about "the will not to know—a chosen ignorance, not the ignorance of innocence" where British attitudes to the "other" were involved. "Four hundred years of conquest and looting, four centuries of being told that you are superior to the fuzzy-wuzzies and the wogs, leave their stain," as he had pugnaciously put it. So I was prepared to be slightly Mau-Mau-ed if I said anything that wasn't all OK and on the up-and-up about the racial correctness question. But this turned out to be a needless and groundless fret. We burbled a bit about Pakistan and about Benazir Bhutto, whom we had both known in different ways, and I didn't quite tell him what I thought, which is that his novel *Shame*, anatomizing the heap of madnesses and contradictions that went to make up the nightmarish state of Pakistan, was the superior in wit and depth even of *Midnight's Children*.

We kept up a kind of touch after I went back to Washington. He wrote a book about a voyage to revolutionary Nicaragua, called *The Jaguar Smile*, which was unfairly attacked in America as a credulous work of revolutionary tourism. I defended it in print, saying that it seemed to me he had gone to Nicaragua knowing perfectly well in advance the dangers of excessive idealism. (Salman later confounded me by saying that he thought the Sandinistas *had* succeeded in deceiving him about a few things, but I think that makes the same point in a different way.) I published my first collection of essays, titled *Prepared for the Worst*, which contained a short critique of his attack on Paul Scott, and asked him for a jacket blurb. After a short pause, back came a very handsome endorsement with the proviso that it didn't apply to "the inexplicable wrongheadedness on pages 225–227."

Salman had not been at our table in the days of the Bloomsbury kebab joint, but he soon started to feature in all my conversations with, and letters from, Martin and Ian and Colin MacCabe. We began to meet during the permanent floating crap game of book launches and book fairs, and tended to sign the same petitions. But the first great qualitative change Salman brought was in the level of the after-dinner word games. I have already offered the excuse that the puerility of these was at least a muscle-building dress rehearsal for a higher form. You may think it absurd or pathetic, for example, to see what happens when you subtract the word "heart" from any well-known title or saying and then substitute the word "dick." Some of the results are in fact mildly funny ("I Left My Dick in San Francisco," "Bury My Dick at Wounded Knee," "Dick of Darkness," "The Dick of the Matter," and so forth), and others can recur to one at absurd moments ("Dickbreak Hotel," "The Sacred Dick," "The Dick and Stomach of a King," "The Jack of Dicks," "An Affair of the Dick," "The Dick Has Its Reasons," "The Dick Is a Lonely Hunter") where they even threaten to be apposite. You can—I warn you—spend years working on a coal-face like this before hitting an unlooked-for seam. How were we to know that Woody Allen, when questioned about his decision to run off with his adopted teenage daughter, would so tonelessly say: "The heart wants what it wants"? Much the same can be said of changing the word "love" (as a verb, that is) to "fuck." Then you can get to "The Fucked One," "The Man Who Fucked Women," "Fuck, Fuck Me Do," "She Fucks You," "Fucked Not Wisely But Too Well," "Fuck Thy Neighbor," and numberless similar instances of harmless pleasure. As a noun, and perhaps marginally more ambitiously, the word was to be dropped and replaced with "hysterical sex" thus: "The Allegory of Hysterical Sex," "Hysterical Sex Is a Many-Splendored Thing," "What Is This Thing Called Hysterical Sex?" "Hysterical Sex in a Cold Climate," "Hysterical Sex, Actually," "Free Hysterical Sex," "Hysterical Sex Story," "Hysterical Sex Potion Number Nine" (which has only just occurred to me), and "A Fool for Hysterical Sex" as well as "Ain't No Cure for Hysterical Sex." In spring a young man's fancy lightly turns to thoughts of...

One might also instance the time when Martin returned from interviewing the pornographer John Staglione. This transcendent Californian director had scrubbed almost all "normal" sex from his "Buttman" productions, in favor of a near-exclusive emphasis on heterosexual sodomy. Martin, inquiring about this aesthetic *auteurism,* had been informed that, in the new age of filth, "pussies are bullshit." This was a facer and no mistake. How to draw the nasty sting from something so profane? We proceeded carefully with the substitutions. "Bullshit Galore," "What's New Bullshitcat?" "The Owl and the Bullshitcat Went to Sea..." "Ding Dong Bell, Bullshit's Down the Well," "Bullshit in Boots" (a bit of a stretch). Salman it was who redeemed the occasion by casually tossing in "Octobullshit," which had the looked-for and healing effect.

At all events there came a time when someone arrived late at a dinner party, complaining of having been stuck at an airport with nothing to read but a Robert Ludlum–style novel. This didn't seem worth pursuing until the complaint was refined somewhat: "I mean it's not just that the prose is so bloody awful but that the titles are so sodding pretentious... *The Bourne Inheritance, The Eiger Sanction*; all this portentous piffle." Again, not a subject to set the table afire, until someone idly said they wondered what a Shakespeare play would be called if it were Ludlum who had the naming of it. At once Salman was engaged and began to smile. "All right, Salman: *Hamlet* by Ludlum!" At once—and I mean with as much preparation as I have given you—"The Elsinore Vacillation." Fluke? Not exactly. Challenged to do the same for *Macbeth*, he produced "The Dunsinane Reforestation" with hardly a flourish and barely a beat. After this it was plain sailing through "The Kerchief Implication," "The Rialto Sanction," and one about Caliban and Prospero that I once knew but now can never remember.

There seemed to be no book or poem in English that he hadn't read, and his first language had been Urdu. This was of course the tongue of the camp followers of the Mughal Empire, who had brought Islam to India and to Salman's best-beloved native city of Bombay. At Cambridge he had studied the Koran as a literary text on some optional course, now no longer taught. To his reflections on this I paid not enough attention. Nobody in our world was religious; even India was basically secular, surely, and when white racists attacked British Asians they called them all "Pakis" without, if you like, discrimination. (The one thing that the racist can never manage is anything like discrimination: he is indiscriminate by definition.) The mosque was at the margin of English life: there was quite a nice-looking one as you took a taxi round Regent's Park to watch England play Pakistan at cricket.

In the larger world, I knew well enough, there was a challenge from Islamic extremism. It had, for example, destroyed the promise of the great Iranian revolution that pitted masses of unarmed civilians against an oil-crazed megalomaniac with a pitiless network of secret police and a huge, purchased army which in the end was too mercenary and corrupt to fight for him. At the moment when Iran stood at the threshold of modernity, a black-winged ghoul came flapping back from exile on a French jet and imposed a version of his own dark and heavy uniform on a people too long used to being bullied and ordered around. For the female population of the country, at least, the new bondage was heavier than the old. And for my friends on the Iranian and Kurdish Left it became an argument as to which model of repression and imprisonment and torture was the harshest.

In New York my friend Edward Said had written a book—punningly titled *Covering Islam*—which partly sought to explain these unwelcome developments away. It was Western presumption, he argued, to regard Islam as a problem of backwardness. It led to our first major disagreement, which was still conducted in a friendly key. How, I demanded of him as he sat wreathed in fragrant pipe smoke and dressed in the most impeccable tweed, would a person like himself expect to fare in an Islamic republic? He had a most engaging crinkle around the eyes when he smiled, which he did as he told me that the more pressing question was the misrepresentation of Muslims by the "orientalist" and all-conquering West. The cloud that overshadowed our conversation was, then, no bigger than a man's hand.

But I wasn't conscious of any impending cloud on a later evening in late 1987 or early 1988, when I was dining at Edward's table, overlooking the Hudson on Riverside Drive, and a courier came bustling up from the Andrew Wylie Agency in Midtown. He bore a large box, which contained the manuscript of a forthcoming novel by Salman Rushdie. A note came along with it, which I remember very well. Dear Edward, it said in effect, I'd be obliged to have your view on this, because I think it may upset some of the faithful... Edward himself was a Christian from Jerusalem—indeed, by birth an Anglican however secular he had since become. (In a public dialogue with Salman in London he had once described the Palestinian plight as one where his people, expelled and dispossessed by Jewish victors, were in the unique historical position of being "the victims of the victims": there was something quasi-Christian, I thought, in the apparent humility of that statement.)

I mention this episode because it was later to be insinuated that Salman was himself the author of the fanatical response to his book, and that—in a phrase fashionable at the time—"he knew what he was doing." Well, no doubt he did know what he was doing (no disgrace there, one might hope) and he certainly understood that he would attract attention if he took what was claimed as holy writ and employed it for literary purposes. In doing this when he did, he ignited one of the greatest-ever confrontations between the ironic and the literal mind: a necessary attrition that is always going on in some form. But he undertook it with care and measure and scruple, and nobody could have foreseen that he would be hit by simultaneous life and death sentences.

When the *Washington Post* telephoned me at home on Valentine's Day 1989 to ask my opinion about the Ayatollah Khomeini's *fatwah*, I felt at once that here was something that completely committed me. It was, if I can phrase it like this, a matter of everything I hated versus everything I loved. In the hate column: dictatorship, religion, stupidity, demagogy, censorship, bullying, and intimidation. In the love column: literature, irony, humor, the individual, and the defense of free expression. Plus, of course, friendship— though I like to think that my reaction would have been the same if I hadn't known Salman at all. To re-state the premise of the argument again: the theocratic head of a foreign despotism offers money in his own name in order to suborn the murder of a civilian citizen of another country, for the offense of writing a work of fiction. No more root-and-branch challenge to the values of the Enlightenment (on the bicentennial of the fall of the Bastille) or to the First Amendment to the Constitution, could be imagined. President George H.W. Bush, when asked to comment, could only say grudgingly that, as far as he could see, no American interests were involved...

To the contrary, said Susan Sontag, Americans had a general interest in defending free expression from barbarism, and also in defending free citizens from state-supported threats of murder accompanied by sordid offers of bounty. It was providential that she was that year's president of PEN, because it quickly became evident that by no means everybody saw the question in this light. There were those who thought that Salman in one way or another deserved his punishment, or had at any rate brought it on himself, and there were those who were quite simply scared to death and believed that the Ayatollah's death squads could roam and kill at will. (Rushdie himself disappeared inside a black bubble of "total" security, and as time went on his Japanese translator was to be murdered, his Italian translator stabbed, and his Norwegian publisher shot three times and left for dead.)

Of those who tended to gloat over Salman's fate, a surprising number were on the Right. I say "surprising" because the conservatives had lamented the fall of the Shah and been appalled by the rise of Khomeini, and were generally the most inclined to lay emphasis on the term "terrorism" when confronted by violent challenges from the Third World. But in America the whole phalanx of neoconservatives, from Norman Podhoretz to A.M. Rosenthal and Charles Krauthammer, turned their ire on Salman and not on Khomeini, and appeared to relish the fact that this radical Indian friend of Nicaragua and the Palestinians had become a victim of "terrorism" in his turn. They preferred to forget how their hero Ronald Reagan had used the profit of illegal arms dealing with the Ayatollah to finance the homicidal *contras* in Nicaragua: but they did not forgive Salman for having written *The Jaguar Smile*. In Britain, writers and figures of a more specifically Tory type, like Hugh Trevor-Roper, Lord Shawcross, Auberon Waugh, and Paul Johnson, openly vented their distaste for the uppity wog in their midst and also accused him of deliberately provoking a fight with a great religion. (Meanwhile, in an unattractive example of what I nicknamed "reverse ecumenicism," the Archbishop of Canterbury, the Vatican, and the Sephardic Chief Rabbi of Israel all issued statements to the effect that the main problem was not the offer of pay for the murder of a writer, but the offense of blasphemy. The British Chief Rabbi, Immanuel Jakobowitz, aiming for a higher synthesis of fatuity, intoned that "both Rushdie and the Ayatollah have abused freedom of speech.") This sort of stuff was at least partly to be expected. Rushdie was a bit of a Leftie; he had contrived to disturb the status quo: he could and should expect conservative disapproval.

More worrying to me were those on the Left who took almost exactly the same tone. Germaine Greer, always reliably terrible about such matters, again came to the fore, noisily defending the rights of bookburners. "The Rushdie affair," wrote the Marxist critic John Berger within a few days of the *fatwah*, "has already cost several human lives and threatens to cost many, many more." And "the Rushdie affair," wrote Professor Michael Dummett of All Souls, "has done untold damage. It has intensified the alienation of Muslims here...Racist hostility towards them has been inflamed." Here we saw the introduction—and by a former promoter of "Michael X," do not forget—of a willful, crass confusion between religious faith, which is voluntary, and ethnicity, which is not.* All

---

* It can and should be remembered that many religious texts, not least the sacred *hadith* of Islam, prescribe horrible penalties for those who apostasize from religion, even if they were only born into it without their own consent. This does somewhat qualify the "voluntary" principle and it, too, had its part in the campaign to murder Salman. Nonetheless, I insist on my distinction between this man-made phenomenon and that of "race."

the deaths and injuries—*all of them*—from the mob scenes in Pakistan to the activities of the Iranian assassination squads, were directly caused by Rushdie's enemies. None of the deaths or injuries—*none of them*—were caused by him, or by his friends or defenders. Yet you will notice the displacement tactic used by Berger and Dummett and the multi-culti Left, which blamed the mayhem on an abstract construct—"the Rushdie affair." I dimly understood at the time that this kind of postmodern "Left," somehow in league with political Islam, was something new, if not exactly New Left. That this *trahison* would take a partly "multicultural" form was also something that was slowly ceasing to surprise me. In his *Diaries*, the Labour Left leader Tony Benn recorded a meeting of like-minded members of Parliament the day after the *fatwah*, and mentioned the contribution of one of Britain's first black MPs:

> Bernie Grant kept interrupting, saying that the whites wanted to impose their values on the world. The House of Commons should not attack other cultures. He didn't agree with the Muslims in Iran, but he supported their right to live their own lives. Burning books was not a big issue for blacks, he maintained.

And then there were those who, at a time of moral crisis for free expression, simply looked for a neutral hiding place. I remember it as at once the most depressing and the most inspiring month. The most depressing, because the centers of several British cities were choked by hysterical crowds, all demanding not just less freedom for the collective (they wanted more censorship and more restriction and the extension of an archaic blasphemy law, and more police power over publication) but also screaming for a deeply reactionary attack on the rights of the individual—the destruction of an author's work and even the taking of an author's life. That this ultrareactionary mobocracy was composed mainly of people with brown skins ought to have made no difference. In Pakistan, long familiar with the hysteria of the *Jamaat Islami* and other religio-dictatorial gangs, it would have made no difference at all. But somehow, when staged in the streets and squares of Britain, it *did* make a difference. A pronounced awkwardness was introduced into the atmosphere: a hinting undercurrent of menace and implied moral and racial blackmail that has never since been dispelled. It took me a long time to separate and classify the three now-distinctive elements of the new and grievance-privileged Islamist mentality, which were self-righteousness, self-pity, and self-hatred.

So that was what some Notting Hill–ers would once have called a downer. Even more of one was the decision by the two main American bookstore chains to stop displaying or selling *The Satanic Verses*. This capitulation, justified in the name of "security" like almost every cowardly idiocy before and since, was reported on the day that I learned that certain usually trusty literary figures—Arthur Miller among them—had declined Susan Sontag's invitation to come and read publicly from Salman's novel in a downtown New York auditorium. Some of these veteran petition signers had openly said they were physically afraid, and one or two had added that their Jewishness ought to excuse them from endorsement or attendance, since their Semitic signatures could only make matters worse! That this kind of thing should be said, and by the author of *The Crucible*, was, to an infinite extent and degree, lowering to the spirit. It seemed that the assassins were winning without a fight, and that those who should be defending the citadel were weeping and scattering before they had even heard a shot or felt a wound.*

Susan Sontag was absolutely superb. She stood up proudly where everyone could see her and denounced the hirelings of the Ayatollah. She nagged everybody on her mailing list and shamed them, if they needed to be shamed, into either signing or showing up. "A bit of civic fortitude," as she put it in that gravelly voice that she could summon so well, "is what is required here." Cowardice is horribly infectious, but in that abysmal week she showed that courage can be infectious, too. I loved her. This may sound sentimental, but when she got Rushdie on the phone—not an easy thing to do once he had vanished into the netherworld of ultraprotection—she chuckled: "Salman! It's like being in love! I think of you night and day: *all the time*!" Against the riot of hatred and cruelty and rage that had been conjured into existence by a verminous religious fanatic, this very manner of expression seemed an antidote: a humanist love plainly expressed against those whose love was only for death.

---

* Later on, the working staff of these bookstores passed a resolution saying that they were not selling bananas or condoms, and would honor the professional duty to provide any customer with any book. And they were the ones standing by the plate-glass windows. I wish this example were better remembered, and more emulated, than it is.

Two ominous modern phenomena began to make their appearance in that time of the toad. The first was the employment of pre-emptive censorship-by-force, as mentioned above, whereby the mere threat of violence was enough to make editors and publishers think twice, or rather think not at all. The second, if anything even more worrying, was the mobilization of foreign embassies to intervene in our internal affairs. All of a sudden, accredited diplomats of supposedly sovereign nations like Pakistan and Quatar were involving themselves in matters that were none of their concern, such as the publication or distribution or even paperback printing of works of fiction. And this unheard-of arrogation was none too subtly "meshed" and synchronized with the cruder potency of the threat, as if to say in a silky tone that you might prefer to deal with us, the envoys of a foreign power, rather than with the regrettably violent elements over whom we have, needless to say, no control... In recent years this awful picture has become so familiar as to be dreary, most recently in the case of the caricatures of Islam's prophet that were briefly published in Denmark and reprinted nowhere else, while unchecked violence against a small Scandinavian democracy was seen as something for which it was *the Danes* who should be apologizing.

I felt then as I feel now: that this was a test. I saw Salman every time I went to London, getting gradually used to the moment at the end of the meeting when he would cram on some shades and a bush-hat or some other improvised disguise and slide into a waiting car that would take him to a secret destination. (This, in the middle of England, after the Cold War. The sting of that humiliation is with me still, and I fight against its ever being thought of as "normal.") I sat with him through some of the other humiliations whereby he was offered a shameful deal by the British authorities and the religious bullies whom they (still) like to promote by recognizing them as "negotiators." If Salman might perhaps undertake some sort of grovel, it was insinuated, if he might care to disown his own work and make a profession of faith, things might possibly arrange themselves, or be arranged. It was additionally put to him, by the pliant and sinuous men of Her Majesty's Foreign Office, that if he declined this magnanimous offer he might be protracting the misery of the Western hostages who were then being held, by Iranian-paid kidnappers, in filthy secret dungeons in Lebanon. So that Salman, who had done nothing except read and write, was to be declared the hostage of the hostages. The life of the torturer and the blackmailer is always made that little bit easier—not to say more enjoyable—by the ability to offer his victim what looks like a "choice." One of the worst mornings of my life came in the cold winter of 1990 when I read that Salman Rushdie had written a short article titled "Why I Have Embraced Islam."

There were two or conceivably three things that could be said about this. The first was said by my friend Ben Sonnenberg, who opined that it was no worse than Galileo's *pro forma* renunciation, designed only to save his own skin from the instruments of rending and tearing and burning which he had been shown by the Inquisition. The second was said by Carol, who pointed out that the relationship between the sun and the earth was unchanged by anything said or unsaid by Galileo, whereas Salman had made a direct, brave connection between his own work and life and the wider battle for free expression. ("This issue is more important," he had said on television on Day One, "than my book or even my life.") Thus, in a way, he had no right to withdraw his original statement. The third thing was said by Salman himself at our next meeting: that his awful article had been "the price of the ticket." I didn't exactly feel I had any right to tell him that he owed it to the cause of free expression to risk immolating himself, but then he did at least have the grace, as he was saying this thing, to look somewhat abashed. Anyway, as it turned out, there was no "ticket." The preachers at the Regent's Park Mosque, so fawning and pleasant when it came to the posturing Islamophile Prince Charles and so vicious when it came to Salman, may have pronounced the word "faith" to the point of nausea, but the concept of "good faith" was foreign to them, and not even the craven Foreign Office could hold them to a crummy bargain they had never intended to honor.

It's arduous in the extreme to have a disagreement, on principle, with someone who embodies what is to you the most important of all principles, but fortunately this tension didn't endure. Salman began making ventures in travel, testing the walls of the prison that he had to cart, almost tortoise-like, around with him. Vaclav Havel agreed to receive him in Prague. President Mary Robinson of Ireland had him to Dublin. He continued pushing at the bars and restrictions, refusing to allow himself to be immured or obliterated.

(It was at about this time that he took the "Proust Questionnaire" for *Vanity Fair*. One of the regular questions is: "What do you most dislike about your appearance?" His response: "Its infrequency.")

Having been repudiated by George H.W. Bush on a previous trip to Washington—"just another author on a book-tour," as the White House spokesman put it—he wanted to see if the newly elected Clinton administration would follow the Havel-Robinson lead. I have never felt more as if my life and my "job," or my work, were the same thing. My immediate job was to make sure that the Iranian mullahs could not say that Rushdie had come back to Washington and been turned away yet again. I was ready for a certain amount of temporizing and hairsplitting and throat-clearing, but not for as much of it as I got. Every "official" human-rights committee in the nation's capital turned me down flat when I asked them to sponsor a visit by Salman or to lend their help in getting him invited to the Oval Office. I was looked at with incredulity and even hostility, as if I had proposed something insanely dangerous as well as latently "offensive." It was, if anything, even worse than the atmosphere of panic and capitulation in New York three years before.

The Susan Sontag role was now taken up by George Stephanopoulos. Again, it was striking to see how much difference a bit of character and guts and integrity could make. I telephoned him at the White House, presuming on a not very old or strong acquaintance, but he came right on the line and said immediately that he could guess why I might be calling. "Also," he added, "it's extremely clear what the obviously right thing is. Let me tell him that and see what I can do." The Clintonian "him" in this case was his usual triangulating and vacillating self and would not make a definite commitment, but by the time Salman landed and had established himself in our apartment, which had been turned into an armed command post by the security services, it had been agreed that he could meet Tony Lake, Clinton's chief of staff, and Secretary of State Warren Christopher, and that the meeting would take place at the White House. The excellent Sir Robin Renwick had also offered to give a later reception at the British embassy with Katharine Graham of the *Washington Post* as co-host. Honor was reasonably satisfied. Even if Clinton would not commit, it wasn't going to be a hole-and-corner visit as in the Bush years.

It was Thanksgiving. The city was rather still. Salman was disposed to chat, and to chat about anything but the inevitable topic. One evening I told him that I had a slight column to write, for the upcoming "Black and White" issue of *Vanity Fair*. I simply had to produce, I said, about three thousands words *à la* Truman Capote on exclusively black and white themes. Might he care to free-associate? He looked at me and lowered his very heavy lids: these later became so heavy that they needed a slight surgical correction but in those days he could adopt the gaze of what Martin unforgettably called "a falcon looking through a Venetian blind." This meant his attention was engaged. For the next twenty or thirty minutes he poured out a spate of closely connected allusions, from the photographic-negative techniques of Eadweard Muybridge to a projected jet-black version of the Taj Mahal that Shah Jahan had planned but failed to build on the opposite side of a reflecting pool. My little essay was essentially written for me. More than that, though, was the intuition it gave me. People who knew Mozart said that he was not so much composing music as hearing it and then writing it down. On a previous visit, I had arranged for Salman to be given a private tour of the Folger Shakespeare Library, which has in its vaults an unrivaled collection of the playwright's First Folios as well as — something we know he must have actually handled — the title deed to his house in Stratford. At lunch afterward, Salman had talked in an unstoppably poetic way about all matters Shakespearean: unstoppable in the sense that nobody present wanted to stop him. And again, it was more than a show of erudition. This was the Salman I wished the world could see, and hear. Paul Valéry said that poetry is not speech raised to the level of music, but music brought down to the level of speech. This was also the Salman who went beyond Valéry's thesis and made me think that there might exist a deep connection between music and literature.

Although I am capable at a stretch of writing a short story or faking up a mock-sonnet, I soon enough realized when young that I did not have the true "stuff" for fiction and poetry. And I was very fortunate indeed to have, as contemporaries, several practitioners of those arts who made it obvious to me, without unduly rubbing in the point, that I would be wasting my time if I tried. Now, listening to Salman "compose," as it were, I suddenly wondered if this was related to my near-total inability with music, itself quite possibly linked with my incapacity in chess and mathematics. Thinking quickly and checking one by one, I noticed that all my poet and novelist friends possessed at the very least some musical capacity: they could either play a little or could give a decent description of a musical event. Could it be this that marked them off from the mere essayist? I hit one iceberg-size objection right away. Vladimir Nabokov, perhaps the man of all men who could make one feel embarrassed to be employing the same language (English being only his third), *detested* music: "Music, I regret to say, affects me merely as an arbitrary succession of more or less irritating sounds... The concert piano and all wind instruments bore me in smaller doses and flay me in larger ones." Ah, but that needn't mean he wasn't *musical*. He wrote a story in 1932 called "Music," in which the protagonist is trapped at a recital with his former wife. ("Any music that he did not know could be likened to the patter of a conversation in a strange tongue.") However, the chords and notes come to exert a healing power and he realizes suddenly "that the music, which before had seemed a narrow dungeon, had actually been incredible bliss, a magic glass dome that had embraced and imprisoned him and her." Another guest at the party speculates that what they have just heard might be the *Kreutzer* Sonata, which was the title of Tolstoy's own personal favorite among his own works. And in the New York Public Library there rests a case of written material— "Nabokov Under Glass"—in which the great lepidopterist attempted a form of notation that could run along the top of his holographs. What is this if not a form of musicality? I feel certain that I was on to something. And at least a negative corollary seemed to be furnished by the Taliban in Afghanistan: they allowed the existence of prose and poetry only to the extent of the enforced recitation of one book, but all music they forbade outright.

The pressure of security around the apartment became almost farcically insupportable as the time came for Salman to be taken by armored vehicle to the White House. ("Is your secret guest your prime minister?" inquired my Filipina housekeeper in a reverent whisper. It turned out that the man she had identified as this key figure was Salman's intrepid agent Andrew Wylie, who had joined us late one night.) As Salman eventually left for the appointment, there was still no word on whether the president would consent to meet him. But Stephanopoulos was on the phone in a half an hour or so, to say "The Eagle Has Landed" and the presidential hand had been outstretched. Later we celebrated this triumph at a press conference and later—after Clinton had basely and typically insisted that the meeting had been unofficial and accidental and off-the-record, with no photograph—we slightly uncelebrated. But it was still no defeat. At dinner I made a point of inviting Kemal Kurspahić, the editor of the Bosnian resistance's daily paper *Oslobojenje* (Freedom): Muslim Bosnia was a site of daily slaughter by Christians and we had also been trying to get Clinton to take some kind of intelligibly vertebrate position on that. It may have been after that dinner that Salman began to evolve and improvise a new word game, this time of book titles that had almost but not quite made it to acceptance by publishers: *The Big Gatsby, A Farewell to Weapons, For Whom the Bell Rings, Good Expectations, Mr. Zhivago, Two Days in the Life of Ivan Denisovitch...*

Talking of "vitches" I noticed again not long ago that the patronymic middle name of Nicholas Rubashov in Koestler's *Darkness at Noon* is "Salmanovitch." Interesting to think of him being a son of a Salman: I don't think it completely fanciful to imagine Rushdie as being the lineal descendant of all those who have had to confront the totalitarian idea physically as well as morally.* He would, I am sure, make light of this and pooh-pooh any comparison between himself and a Gulag victim. But it's still quite something to be told, by the armed, hoarse enforcers of a murder-based regime, that you are yourself "a dead man on leave." And the claustrophobic world in which he had to live for some years was a prefiguration of the world in which we all, to a greater or lesser extent, live now. I mean to say a world in which a fanatical religion, which makes absolutist claims for itself and promises to supply—even to *be*—a total solution to all problems, furthermore regards itself as so pure as to be above criticism. I had a small foretaste of how this world feels when, after Salman's departure from Washington, I received a summons from the head of the Department of Narcotics and Counterterrorism ("Drugs and Thugs" as it is known at Foggy Bottom) at the State Department.

---

* "Salmanovitch," I have since learned, was Koestler's rendition into Russian of "Solomonovitch," the surname of an Israeli-Jewish editor he had known, and a great foe of the Jabotinsky-Begin ultranationalists. Staying with nomenclature for a bit, "Rushdie" itself was derived as a family name by Salman's father, who annexed it from Averroes ibn-Rushd, the great medieval scholar of the Jewish-Christian-Muslim synthesis that flourished in Andalusia before the zealots and dogmatists extinguished that brief candle.

Having overseen Salman's visit, this man now told me, he and his people had been in receipt of "believable chatter" from Iranian sources, indicating an intended revenge on myself and my family for helping to host the trip. I took this in and asked what I was supposed to do. "We suggest changing your address." But would not any Iranian state-directed agent who knew where I lived also be able to find out where I had moved? "Very well, might you at least consider changing your phone number?" Suddenly I "got it." The State Department, like the British Foreign Office, had done its "due diligence." It had called me in, warned me, and could now file the thing away. Already well-covered behinds had been given further protective clothing. But in truth I didn't think my own rear end was any more exposed than anyone else's.* And the time was soon to come when the mentality of the *fatwah*, allied to the ideology of *jihad*, would arrive in Washington by unscheduled civilian air transport and almost demolish a building far better armored than the Department of State.

I don't think it's possible to overstate the importance of the Rushdie case. Along with the reference to Koestler that I have already ventured, I did at one time propose another comparison that you may choose to think is almost as portentous. The Ayatollah's *fatwah* had included in its condemnation all those "responsible for the publication" of *The Satanic Verses*. The night before I was due to speak at Susan Sontag's solidarity meeting in New York, in the first week of the drama, I was striving to think of something that might go beyond the usual petition-signing and letter-writing routine, something that would mark this assault on our liberties and our principles as something out of the common, to be met with no ordinary response. I thought: What if we all declare ourselves "co-responsible for its publication"? This was the principle of solidarity introduced by the followers of Spartacus and taken to a still higher level by those Danes in 1941 who (not, alas, including their king: that story is a beautiful myth) voluntarily donned the yellow star as a gesture to those who were compelled to wear it. On the following morning I made the proposal in my speech and was agreeably surprised by how well it went over: the petition was drawn up

---

* Since I speak and write about this a good deal, I am often asked at public meetings, in what sometimes seems to me a rather prurient way, whether I myself or my family have "ever been threatened" by jihadists. My answer is that yes, I have, and so has everyone else in the audience, if they have paid enough attention to the relevant bin-Ladenist broadcasts to notice the fact.

there and then in that form, and signed by a pretty solid collection of authors from Norman Mailer* to Diana Trilling to Don DeLillo. It was then put out for general circulation and garnered widespread endorsement, though I moaned with disgust when it was eventually printed in the *Times Literary Supplement*, because meanwhile some quavering, cretinous hand had inserted the weasel words "while we regret any offense caused" into the preamble. I know I am not the only one who did not mind in the least if religious delusions were ridiculed, but if I had been the only one, I still wouldn't have given a damn.

And what of Salman himself? He made, I will always feel, the ideal protagonist for this drama. If literature and the ironic mind are to be defended to the death, then it is as well to have a superbly literate and ironic individual as the case in point. I cannot remember any moment when he said or did anything crass, or when he raised his voice unduly or responded in kind to those who were taunting or baiting him. He was at one time very concerned that he would dry up as a writer because of being moved from one safe house to another, but in practice produced several first-rate fictions and many brilliant essays and reviews,** thus disproving Orwell's fine but fallacious dictum that "the imagination, like certain wild animals, will not breed in captivity." I was going to say that he never lost his sense of humor, but this would be to miss the one great exception, which was the awful and unctuous and convoluted prose of his declaration of adherence to Islam. It really

---

* I had thought I might never see Norman Mailer again after I had asked him, on a TV show with Germaine Greer, whether he'd ever wondered about his apparent obsession with sodomy and its male occasions (the barracks, the prison, the boxing gym, even in *Harlot's Ghost* the interstices of the "intelligence community") as well as its more notorious female ones. In the "green room" afterward, he reacted extremely badly, seizing a copy of *Tough Guys Don't Dance* and inscribing it to me with a minatory sentence that told me to beware of his next interview. When that was eventually published, in a London magazine called *The Face*, it contained his accusation that the London literary scene had been rigged against him by a homosexual coterie dominated by Martin Amis, Ian Hamilton, and myself. Martin and I dallied briefly with the idea of writing in to say that this was *very unfair*—at least to Ian Hamilton. After the *fatwah*, though, Mailer became more friendly. Never to be outdone when the electricity of violence was in the air, he initially had to be talked out of a hyper*macho* scheme to raise money for a retaliatory "hit" against the Ayatollah but renewed contact with me because, I suppose, my own position made me look a bit less like a faggot.

** Including one favorite of mine, *The Ground Beneath Her Feet*, which is almost written to music.

read as if written at gunpoint, which of course it had been. It also read as if it were written by someone else. During his stay with us at Thanksgiving, while he was signing a few books for his newly born "un-goddaughter," he seized the volume of essays in which this literary abortion was preserved like a nasty freak in a bottle, and wrote across the title "Why I Have Embraced Islam" the additional and expressive words: "No! Aargh!" He then carefully crossed out every page of the "offensive" piece, signing each one to confirm his own authorial deletion. It was as near to the defacement of a book—or to an auto-da-fé—as I could imagine him getting.

To proceed with that religious imagery, though, there was perhaps something fine to be salvaged even from this preceding degradation. By trying his best to compose matters with the mullahs, he had sincerely shown that he did not seek a violent collision, and he had gone a long way to ask that the bitter cup—of having to live the rest of his life under threat of death—might be allowed to pass from him. Who can fail to sympathize? But, having been made to understand that there was no path of compromise, Salman has become one of the world's most reliable defenders of the free expression of others. The sad paradox is that while he and his book both survived and flourished, nobody in the Anglo-American publishing business would now commission or print *The Satanic Verses*. Indeed, the whole cultural and media industry has become, where reactionary Islam is concerned, one long profile in prudence. The other paradox is that the very multiculturalism and multiethnicity that brought Salman to the West, and that also made us richer by Hanif Kureishi, Nadeem Aslam, Vikram Seth, Monica Ali, and many others, is now one of the disguises for a *uni*culturalism, based on moral relativism and moral blackmail (in addition to some more obvious blackmail of the less moral sort) whereby the Enlightenment has been redefined as "white" and "oppressive," mass illegal immigration threatens to spoil everything for everybody, and the figure of the free-floating transnational migrant has been deposed by the contorted face of the psychopathically religious international nihilist, praying for the day when his messianic demands will coincide with possession of an apocalyptic weapon. (These people are not called nihilists for nothing.) Of all of this we were warned, and Salman was the messenger. *Mutato nomine et de te fabula narratur*: Change only the name and this story is about you.

# Mesopotamia from Both Sides

> Terror, the most abject terror, is in the atmosphere about us—a consuming passion, like that of jealousy—a haunting, exhausting specter, which sits like a blight upon life. Such a settled state of terror is one of the most awful of human phenomena. The air holds ghosts, all joy is dead; the sun is black, the mouth parched, the mind rent and in tatters.
>
> —H.F.B. Lynch: *Armenia: Travels and Studies* [1901]

I N JULY OF 2007 my old magazine the *New Statesman* made an attempt to embarrass me by reprinting an article I had written from Iraq in early 1976. In those days, ran the snide prologue to the reproduction, "Young Hitchens saw Saddam as an up-and-coming secular socialist who would transform Iraq into a progressive model for the rest of the Middle East." The implied accusation—of a U-turn or even of a turned coat—bothered me not at all. I had long since learned to ask John Maynard Keynes's question: "When the facts change then my opinion changes: and you, sir?" But I was nonetheless conscious of two conflicting desires. The first was to point out that my original essay hadn't got it all *that* wrong. The second was to give an account of how I had, in fact, almost completely reversed my opinion— and of how long such a process can take, and how painful it can be.

Iraq in March of 1976 was eight years into the rule of the Ba'ath Party. The nominal president Ahmad Hassan Abu Bakr, whose ugly face was on all the posters and banners, was understood to be terminally ailing from diabetes. Now and then, and always phrased in careful and oblique tones, one heard talk of his vice president Saddam Hussein, seemingly the head of the party's security apparatus. "Make a note of the name," I wrote in my dispatch, adding that "as the situation grows more complicated Saddam Hussein will rise more clearly to the top." I am not so embarrassed to have written that—unless it be embarrassment for my rather leaden prose. But leaden prose always tends to be a symptom of other problems and if I am honest I think I can reconstruct the cause of my own *langue de bois*.

It was my second visit to Iraq and I knew approximately four things about the country. The first was that it had been a British colonial invention, carved out between the other arbitrary frontiers of the post-Ottoman Middle East, between Turkey, Iran, Jordan, Saudi Arabia, and Kuwait. This meant that, as a British socialist, I had an instinctive sympathy with its national-ists. The second thing I knew was that it had a large Kurdish minority, and that the rights of this minority had long been a major cause of the Left. The third thing I knew was that the Ba'ath Party, which called itself socialist, was at least ostensibly secular and not religious. The fourth thing I knew was that the casinos and brothels and nightclubs of London, just then awash in Gulf Arab clientele after the free-for-all of the post-1973 oil embargo, did not tend to feature droves of greedy Iraqis throwing their country's wealth away on drink and harlots. On the visible evidence, partly confirmed to me by guarded British diplomats at the Alwiyah Club near the River Tigris, Iraq was using its immense national income to create a serious infrastructure—of building and development, but also of health and welfare.*

My friend Gavin Young, the great travel writer and gay ex-Guardsman, had told me of the Marsh Arabs of the southern wetlands, pursuing an antique manner of life that still had strong biblical trace elements to it, but when I mentioned my wish for a visit down there, the relevant Iraqi officials steadfastly stonewalled me and tried to put me off. "Why do you want to see backwardness? We are a modern country now." This dimly jogged my memory of visitors to the USSR being taken to see tractor factories while

---

* Recently declassified papers show the British embassy in Baghdad reporting back to Lon-don in these terms: Saddam's accession to office was "the first smooth transfer of power since 1958" and, though "strong-arm methods may be needed to steady the ship, Saddam will not flinch."

collectivization was ravaging the countryside, but in truth I slightly prefer the city to the countryside and meanwhile I had found myself an extraordinary companion of the urban sort.

My first meeting with Mazen al-Zahawi was, I would say, unpropitious. In return for a visa, the Ba'athists insisted on providing me with a "guide." Many regimes do this as a means of keeping visiting scribes under control: you may sometimes escape a "minder" but there's an art and a science to it and it can take time. As I stood in line at Baghdad Airport for my passport to be stamped, I could see a group of people waiting on the other side of the barrier and instantly made up my mind which one I hoped would *not* be for me. He was sallow, morose-looking, and wearing dark glasses indoors: a thoroughly bad sign. A secret-police or *Mukhabarat* type, bored and resentful and hard to shake. As I passed through the barrier he stepped softly forward and gave me a soggy, insipid handshake.

I can't remember how we passed the time in the car—there was a chauffeur, in front of whom he was icily silent—but we got to the hotel and he said he'd let me check in and then meet me in the bar. I took my time. When I eventually pulled myself onto the neighboring stool, it was in order to feign exhaustion and to see if perhaps I might take an uninvigilated walk in the city while he thought I was napping. But he took off his shades, leaned toward me, placed his hand firmly on my knee and said: "I believe we are going to be *such* friends. My own little circle tells me that I am an *exact* blend of Adolf Hitler and Oscar Wilde." If I say that I suddenly noticed how faultless his English was, I say the least of it. "Are you a member of the drinking classes?" he went on, gesturing effectively to the attendant. "I thought so. Later on we shall repair to my home. I shall play you my personal tape of *The Importance of Being Earnest*. I am of course Gwendolyn. The part of Lady Bracknell is taken by Gavin Young." I think I can claim this as one of the more original introductions of an outsider to Ba'ath Party internal affairs.

Mazen did not at all disappoint. He took me to his family home near the banks of the Tigris, which proved to be the former house of Hitler's envoy to Iraq at the time of the pro-Nazi coup in favor of Rashid Ali in 1941, a coup that, as I was to learn, had been supported by the political ancestors of the Ba'ath. There was a rather squawking home-made recording of Wilde's three-act masterpiece, in which Gavin's booming baritone and Mazen's lilting

response could be discerned. It all rather conformed to Susan Sontag's speculations about "camp" and "fascinating fascism." I wondered uneasily what
Gavin had told Mazen about me: Young was one of those old queens who
believes that deep down all men are queer as clockwork oranges. But Mazen's
own double life proved to be much more subtle and convoluted than that.

For one thing, he was by ancestry half-Kurdish. This was nothing special on its own; intermarriage between Arabs and Kurds in Iraq, as between
Sunni and Shi'a, used to be a commonplace. But Iraq had just emerged from
a bitter border war with the Shah of Iran, in which Henry Kissinger had
used the Kurdish militias in the north as a proxy against Baghdad and then
famously abandoned them, to be massacred on the hillsides, in order to seal a
deal with the Shah. This had opened Iraqi Kurds to the charge of disloyalty,
bad enough at any time, and also of being tools of Iran and its ally Israel,
which was even worse. But it wasn't enough for Mazen to be half-Kurdish
and (by night) all gay. During the rest of the working day he was on call to be
one of the interpreters for Saddam Hussein. I had frequently met homosexu-
als who liked to live dangerously or on thin ice but this was the most daring
feat of sociopolitical cross-dressing I had encountered to date.

Together we went to visit factories and dams and ministries—and
mosques and museums and ziggurats—by day, and Baghdad's demimonde
at night. My friend Marina Warner, back in London, was thinking of writing an opera about the Gilgamesh legend, and Mazen arranged for me to
meet a keeper of antiquities at Gertrude Bell's National Museum to see if he
might have anything useful to impart. ("Don't be too *tarty*," he warned me, I
thought and hoped superfluously.) He repeated the same injunction when he
asked me casually if I would care to meet Iraq's nominee for the leadership of
the Palestinian struggle.

I was increasingly sympathetic to the Palestinians by then, and was
hoping that if any Arab state would outgrow the humiliation of the 1973
defeat by Israel, it would be a secular one and not a Saudi-type or otherwise
theocratic manifestation, so I said "yes" without any particular reflection.
Accordingly, I was taken to a villa to meet Sabri al-Banna, known as "Abu
Nidal" ("father of struggle"), who was at the time emerging as one of Yasser
Arafat's main enemies. The meeting began inauspiciously when Abu Nidal
asked me if I would like to be trained in one of his camps. No thanks, I

explained. From this awkward beginning there was a further decline. I was then asked if I knew Said Hammami, the envoy of the PLO in London. I did in fact know him. He was a brave and decent man, who in a series of articles in the London *Times* had floated the first-ever trial balloon for a two-state solution in Israel/Palestine. "Well tell him he is a traitor," barked my host. "And tell him we have only one way with those who betray us." The rest of the interview passed as so many Middle Eastern interviews do: too many small cups of coffee served with too much fuss; too many unemployed heavies standing about with nothing to do and nobody to do it with; too much ugly furniture, too many too-bright electric lights; and much too much *faux bonhomie*. The only political fact I could winnow, from Abu Nidal's vainglorious claims to control X number of "fighters" in Y number of countries, was that he admired the People's Republic of China for not recognizing the State of Israel. I forget how I got out of his office.

Somewhat more intellectually testing was my encounter with the Iraqi Communist Party, then a real power in the state and in the society (and the only faction in Iraq which for secular and internationalist reasons *did* recognize the State of Israel). I was taken to its downtown offices, there to meet Dr. Rajim Ahina. It was amazing to see how closely he stuck to the party line on every detail. When I asked why the Communists had agreed to sit on the governing council with the Ba'athists who used to shoot them and torture them, he replied that Iraq under the Ba'ath had become the only Arab state to give diplomatic recognition to East Germany: a response almost as boring and dank as Abu Nidal on Beijing. But at this point Mazen did me a favor and left the room, abdicating for a while the role of "minder." Dr. Ahina suddenly became less wooden and more animated. Many of the Party's leaders and activists were being secretly arrested, he told me. Here was a list of their names, in English. Could I take it back with me to London? I slid the folded piece of paper into my inside pocket. A moment like that is obviously very much more eloquent and informative than any amount of choreographed question-and-answer.

Later that night Mazen took me to dinner on a houseboat on the Tigris to meet a man named Yahya Thanayan who owned his own printing press. This old boy, as I thought of him, had been in prison under every regime in Baghdad since the British. The worst of all, he told me, had been his imprisonment under the current one. He had received the personal attentions of the dreaded Nadim Kzar, head of the secret police (who had recently been executed as part of the process by which Saddam Hussein was annexing all such powers to himself). However, Thanayan went on, he nonetheless believed that the Ba'athist government was the best that the unhappy country had yet had to endure. He was a cultivated man and did not seem to be suffering from any gruesome repressed masochism. And Mazen, too, half-Kurdish as he was and absolutely not cut out for life in any sort of Sparta, seemed genuine in acknowledging the regime's achievements. Oil had been nationalized and was not, as in neighboring Saudi Arabia or Iran, the property of a horde of venal monarchs and their princelings. Arab unity and secularism were being preached in the face of a tide of reaction sweeping the region.

So the article which I eventually wrote, while it certainly emphasized political repression, attempted to be fair on these points. Iraq was investing in its people; its constitution at least formally defined it as an Arab and Kurdish state (which was more than its NATO neighbor Turkey had ever done for its largest minority); it was modernizing and non-Islamic in its rhetoric. Yet I still grimaced when I re-read the piece, because what I left out was the most important thing of all: the X factor that was later summarized so well by the Iraqi dissident Kanan Makiya in the title of his book *The Republic of Fear*. What I omitted, because I didn't really understand it, was the sheerly irrational. What I should have been noticing was hidden in the spaces between the ostensible words. I should have paid more attention to the way Dr. Ahina's expression had changed when he found himself unobserved. I should have registered the way that people almost automatically flinched at the mention of the name Saddam Hussein. I should have been more observant when, taken to one of the vaunted new clinics of Baghdad after I briefly became ill, I had not been alone with the young doctor for upward of a minute when he asked me in a whisper if I could help him get out of the country. (Later on, reporters who had been in Baghdad would debate whether the fear was so palpable that you could cut it with a knife, or so thick that you could actually *eat* it.)

I followed developments in Iraq after I got home, and began belatedly to appreciate that I had been shown the way things were actually pointing. Saddam Hussein soon made himself president and not long after that launched an all-out assault on the Iraqi Communists, smashing his main

rival to the Left with a campaign of arrests and torture that was a mere foretaste of things to come. He began to spend more of his country's vast wealth
on re-armament, clearly not intending to abide by the border truce he had
signed with Iran. He also began to make Baghdad a haven for international
gangsters. Just after New Year's Day in 1978, hugely to my horror and dismay, an agent of Abu Nidal's walked into the office of Said Hammami in
Hay Hill in Mayfair and shot him dead. I had in fact gone to see Hammami
on my return from London, and told him that this obscure Palestinian in
Baghdad was making threatening noises at him. Said had shrugged—he had
heard this kind of nasty bravado before. Now I was in the position, not just
of having delivered a warning from a terrorist, but of having seen the threat
explicitly carried out. This was the opening of an astonishing spree of murder
and mayhem: in his day Abu Nidal's name was almost as notorious as Osama
bin Laden's was later to become. He went on to bomb Rome and Vienna
airports, and to assassinate several of Arafat's more negotiation-minded lieu-
tenants. Issam Sartawi, the PLO delegate to the Socialist International, was
gunned down while talking to my friend Vassos Lyssarides, leader of the
Socialist Party of Cyprus. Every time a possible "back channel" was opened
between Israelis and Palestinians, a long arm would reach out from Iraq, and
the Palestinian interlocutor would be slain.

Even Iraqis in London lived under the Republic of Fear. My main contact at the embassy was the cultural officer, Naji Sabry al-Hadithi. He was a
fairly literate and civilized fellow with a wonderful feeling for English, and he
would invite me to lavish lunches and once to an Iraqi *soirée musicale* at his
home. I invited him to dinner in turn at my crummy apartment in Islington
and noticed after he had departed that he had left a bag behind. It turned
out to contain a small rug, some Cuban cigars, some top-dollar single malt
Scotch and a few other classy items: I could of course return them if I felt
high-minded enough (I meant to, but I didn't). This was interesting: I was a
fairly junior writer on a small socialist weekly. What did the Iraqis do when
they wanted to butter up more senior members of the media, or of other elements of the Establishment? I was later to find out. But before I could decide
to start reducing my contact with Naji, he was recalled to Baghdad where
first one and then two of his brothers had been accused of plotting against
"the leadership." One of them, a former envoy to Moscow, was very painfully

killed. The other was very painfully treated but survived. Naji, who had such love for English, was put in charge of the regime's English-language *Baghdad Observer*, an illiterate rag given over to the diffusion of menacing gibberish and abject leader-worship.

A small further inducement was offered to my magazine. The Iraqi embassy paid for a full-page advertisement, in which the Ba'athist regime offered all Iraqi Jews the right to come home and reclaim their property and citizenship. This attempt at restitution for the deportations and confiscations that had followed 1948—and the public hangings of Jews that had followed Israel's victory in 1967—was no doubt as hypocritical as Saddam's pro forma recognition of the Kurds. But at least it was the compliment that vice paid to virtue. In Baghdad I had sometimes teased Mazen by asking him how many Jews had accepted the offer and come back. "A trickle," was his invariable reply, until one day he couldn't keep it up anymore and said "not even Mr. Ben-Trickle has exercised his right of return."

As the repression and terror in Iraq became more theatrically cruel, a group called CARDRI (Campaign for the Restoration of Democratic Rights in Iraq) was founded, by an old Communist friend of mine from Oxford named Fran Hazelton. It joined the list of many good causes from Chile to South Africa that drew the signatures of "Left" members of Parliament and intellectuals. I still have its archives and membership lists in my possession. But I admit that I let my own interest lapse a bit and that I wasn't in any case able to get another visa to visit the country. I also stopped hearing from my former Iraqi friends as the pall over the country thickened and as the long insane war with Iran, launched by Saddam in 1979, with the support of the pious born-again creep Jimmy Carter, went pitilessly on. Under cover of this war, Saddam made a deliberate attempt at the extirpation of the Kurdish people by deploying weapons of mass destruction. He also began the building of a nuclear reactor at Osirak, badly hit but not destroyed by the Israelis in 1981. I kept in occasional touch with the Kurdish exile office in Washington, where by then I lived, and with some elements of the Iraqi Left. (My old Communist acquaintance Dr. Rajim Ahina managed to escape from Baghdad and died in London, where he is buried next to Karl Marx in Highgate Cemetery.)

In the spring of 1990 I flew from Washington to Aspen, Colorado, to attend a summit meeting between George H.W. Bush and Margaret Thatcher. Mrs. Thatcher arrived seeming distinctly frazzled and out of sorts: the Bush administration was clearly leaning toward Chancellor Kohl's reunified Germany as its new best friend in Europe, and her own good friend Ian Gow had been blown up by the Provisional IRA a few nights before. And then the entire picture was altered by one bold stroke: Saddam Hussein announced that the state of Kuwait, a member state of the United Nations, the Arab League, and many other international assemblies, had overnight become the nineteenth province of Iraq.

I spent that extraordinary weekend at Aspen in two minds and in two places. This was plainly a case of undisguised aggression and annexation, and one quaked to think what the civilians of Kuwait were undergoing. The Iraqi general in charge of the "operation," I soon enough learned, was Ali Hassan al-Majid, known as "Chemical Ali" for his atrocities in Kurdistan. On the other hand, the Bush administration had been telling the Iraqis that it was neutral in the long-standing border dispute between Baghdad and the Kuwaiti royal family, and as between Ba'athists and feudal emirs there didn't seem to be that much worth fighting over. It was true that Saddam Hussein had not long before employed poison gas against what President Bush insultingly persisted in calling "his own" people, but it was likewise true that the war material for this outrage had been supplied by the Reagan administration.

I have to admit, also, and with shame, that my own personal animosity against Bush was a factor in itself. I had simply detested the way in which he had lied his way as vice president through the Iran-*contra* scandal, cringe-makingly claiming to have been "out of the loop" while the White House ran an off-the-books private government based on illegal profits from the Ayatollah and some Central American mobsters. And I had coldly hated the way in which he won the 1988 election, allowing his less fastidious operators to smear the wretched Michael Dukakis with racist innuendo about Willie Horton. During the day in Aspen I hung out with my press colleagues and attended the increasingly bellicose high-level briefings at which Mrs. Thatcher shed all her earlier gloom and began to puff out like the ruff of some great cat in her enthusiasm for a fight. Here was an area of the world where the British had bases and traditions and expertise: What price fatboy

Helmut Kohl now? One felt one could actually see her inserting the lead into the presidential pencil. In the evenings, I would go to the unfashionable edge of Aspen and hang out at Owl Farm in Woody Creek, home of the storied Hunter Thompson. In these booze-fueled and crepuscular surroundings, in the intervals of our own midnight gunplay with rows of empty bottles ranged against high-velocity rifles, the talk was all of the war-machine and its revival: of the United States finding a new fear-object after the fall of Communism, and speculations of a similar tone.

I have never been able to rid myself of the view that Bush was not really surprised to read the first reports from Kuwait—I watched him receive them very calmly—and only became upset when he learned that Saddam Hussein had taken the entire country. The whole thing stank of a pre-arranged carve-up gone wrong. It was almost impossible to read the transcript of his envoy's last meeting with Saddam and to form any other opinion. Ambassador April Glaspie, whom I had known briefly in London, explicitly told the Iraqi dictator that the United States took no position on his quarrel with the Kuwaitis. Had Saddam taken only the Rumaila oil field and the Bubiyan and Warba islands, there would have been no *casus belli*. I printed the Glaspie memorandum in *Harper's* magazine, along with some highly critical commentary, and made several speeches and media appearances saying that any war would be fought, in effect, on false pretenses. (It had not occurred to me at the time, or not with full awareness, that if Saddam Hussein could have been so crazy as to go for broke, and to steal all of Kuwait when he could have had a lucrative chunk of it for the asking, why then he might be such a deranged megalomaniac that he could no longer discern even his own interests.)

The official rhetoric of the Bush administration made me suspicious as well. Saddam Hussein was suddenly compared to Hitler by people who had never noticed the resemblance before. Alarmist official propaganda—about Iraqi armored divisions poised on the Saudi border, and about Kuwaiti babies being thrown out of incubators to die on the cold floor—proved to be exaggeration or fabrication. The Saudi tyranny appeared to be the chief beneficiary of the dispatch of Coalition forces, while Saddam's mad blustering against Israel—and Arafat's wicked and stupid decision to embrace Saddam—seemed to mean yet another excuse for relegating the question of Palestinian statehood to the end of the queue. So with a fairly good conscience

I continued to write and speak against the impending war, and to point out all the contradictions in the Bush position. After all, if Saddam was really Hitler, then surely we were committed not just to rescuing Kuwait but to invading Iraq and finding it a new government? And what gave us the right to do that, we the pals of the Saudis, betrayers of the Kurds, and horsetraders with the Iranian mullahs?

Every now and then, however, I found myself repressing a misgiving or two. Kuwait may not have been a model state, but it had a certain openness and, as Edward Said pointed out publicly, had made room on its small territory at least for a limited parliament, as well as for many Palestinian refugees. All reports from Iraqi dissidents seemed to suggest that the reign of terror inside the country was actually even worse than Washington was alleging. And it seemed that Saddam Hussein was absolutely incapable of realizing that he had made a calamitous mistake. I flew with Bush's party on Air Force One to Saudi Arabia, asking annoying questions at every opportunity and further irritating the Saudis by asking if I could have an interview with their honored Muslim guest, Field Marshall Idi Amin of Uganda. Then I went up to Dhahran, to the gigantic base where the Coalition was assembling its armada. It was at once clear that Iraq had no chance of holding off, let alone defeating, such a vast and sophisticated force. Any Iraqi conscripts put in the way of this juggernaut would simply be vaporized. Had the Ba'athists learned nothing from their previous military adventures?

When the war did come, not only were those luckless soldiers vaporized but so too were many civilians. Power stations, water supplies, bridges, and other crucial facilities in major cities were likewise hit with so-called smart bombs. And yet, it became clear, the Iraqi leadership was not going to be made to suffer alongside "its" people. Saddam's Republican Guard units between Kuwait City and Baghdad were left unscathed, while a column of scruffy stragglers and camp followers, trudging away from Kuwait after the surrender, was hit from the sky again and again and smeared all over the road of the Mutla Pass: the press gave this the unimaginative name of the "Highway of Death" but I thought, and wrote, and still think, that it was a grotesque carnival of turkey-shooting sadism. Before the war, my old Marxist comrade Fred Halliday had broken ranks to some extent and told the Left: "You can avoid war, but only by leaving Kuwait in the hands of Saddam Hussein. You can be anti-imperialist, but you will have to decide if imperialism is worse than fascism." I had been briefly swayed by this but was later to write with scorn that Comrade Halliday had been proved wrong. With Bush, you could have both imperialism *and* fascism: American and Saudi power restored and the Kuwaiti monarchy returned to power, with a chastened Saddam Hussein allowed to keep his own throne and bluntly admonished to remember from now on who was the boss. This was the very worst of both worlds. When General Norman Schwarzkopf gave his personal permission for Iraq to use its helicopter gunships to restore order in the Iraqi Shi'a south, I thought I had seen the absolute limits of political cynicism.

It was only on revisiting the region in the immediate aftermath that I slowly came to realize that my own logic could be turned, or rather could turn itself, against me. What if the war *had* led to the downfall of Saddam Hussein, instead of his confirmation in power? Would I not have been morally obliged to say that this was justifiable? The curse-word "fascism" is easily enough thrown around, including by me on occasion, but I give you my oath that it makes a difference to you when you see the real thing at work. Again, it was the element of the sadistic and the irrational — the *Götterdämmerung* aspect — that caught and held my attention. On his way *out* of Kuwait, with nothing left to fight for, Saddam Hussein had given the order to set fire to the oilfields and also to smash the wellheads, and thus allow the crude black stuff to run directly into the waters of the Gulf, and there thickly to coagulate. This deliberate eco-catastrophe was almost the equal of his draining of the southern marshes and subsequent incineration of the deliberately aridified environment: the smoke plume from that nightmare had been seen with the naked eye from the space shuttle. Yet with the birds and marine animals of the Gulf choked to death *en masse*, and the sky itself full of fumes and specks that sometimes blotted out the sun, the predominantly "Green" Left and anti-war movements could still not find a voice in which to call this by its right name. On my way through Europe I went to an anti-war "service" in a beautiful Renaissance church in Rome. The slogan was *L'Italia repudia la guerra*. "Italy repudiates war" — noble words taken from the country's anti-fascist postwar constitution. As I sat amid this highly civilized and polished congregation, all of its members really quite put out by American vulgarity and militarism, I found myself abruptly and chronically bored and repelled by the prevailing smugness. To repudiate war in this morally neuter way was to allow fascism a clear run.

Once I had crossed Turkey and made an illegal entry into northern Iraq at the Habur checkpoint, I entered on a scene that did a bit more than merely change my outlook. The Kurdish provinces of Saddam Hussein's dominion had been turned into a howling wilderness. In company with a clever, witty, tough-minded Iraqi-Jewish photographer who had seized this moment to "trickle" back to his ancestral country, and with two Kurdish militants as guides, I worked my way down the Zab River and through the mountains toward the once thickly populated towns and cities of the lower-lying areas. Nothing prepares you for how lush and green the uplands are.* Nor could anything have prepared me for the chain of wrecked and gutted and poisoned cities that showed Saddam's unquenchable thirst for destruction. This is perhaps how the Scottish Highlands or the Irish farmlands might have felt after the "clearances": village after village and township after township voided of population and then dynamited or bulldozed, while on charred and desolate bits of the landscape ugly blockhouse encampments had been built to "concentrate" those thereby dispossessed. This was grim enough but then, along a road dotted with the hulks of T-34 Russian-built tanks, came something more reminiscent of eastern Poland in the early 1940s.

The Kurdish city of Halabja had been hit by Iraqi chemical weapons in March of 1988, losing over five thousand of its citizens in just one afternoon. Three years later, it was still possible to interview and to photograph people whose wounds were still burning and suppurating, or whose lungs had been corroded. It was also possible to do a little work to counter the "denial" campaign that some "experts" had already begun, claiming that it had been the Iranians who bombed the town. There were several unexploded chemical bombs still wedged in the basements of ruined buildings, with Iraqi Air Force markings on their casings, and I had myself photographed by Ed Kashi while crouching next to one of these.

It was, in fact, only after the ghastly war with Iran was *over* that the truly horrific work in Iraqi Kurdistan had begun. Employing a Koranic

---

* I used to make a point, later on in Washington, of arguing that no operations in Iraq should ever again be given the stupid code-name prefix of "Desert." Mesopotamia is *not* a desert.

verse — the one concerning the so-called *Anfal*, or "spoils," specifying what may be exacted from a defeated foe — the Iraqi army and police destroyed more than 4,000 centers of population and killed at least 180,000 Kurds.* The remainder were packed into the concentration centers mentioned above, or else loaded onto trucks and deported to the southern regions, where their mass graves are being dug up to this day. In the town of Shaqlawa, where the Kurdish guerrillas had taken advantage of Saddam's defeat in Kuwait to set up a provisional headquarters, I heard some gut-twisting but half-credible rumors. It was said that thousands of men and boys of the Barzan clan had been taken away — this much could be proved — but taken away to be used as guinea pigs in tests of biological and chemical weaponry, and of fragmentation weapons. I have since learned that it's very incautious to doubt any atrocity story, however lurid, if it is laid to the charge of Saddam Hussein.

From Shaqlawa it wasn't too terribly far to the still-disputed cities of Suleimanya and Kirkuk, to which the temporarily demoralized Iraqi army had withdrawn. Our crappy Turkish rental car had died on us without a whimper. Jalal Talabani, the bearlike socialist who was the leader of the Patriotic Union of Kurdistan, lent us a jeep and two stalwarts so that we could proceed farther and faster. The two *Pesh Merga* soldiers, Hoshyar Samsam and Ali, had taped a photograph of President George Bush — wearing a jogging suit, of all things — to the windshield of the jeep. After a while, I was moved to ask if they felt they had to do this. (I think I may have wondered what I would say if we ran into any smart-ass reporter I knew.) The straightness of their answer shamed the deviousness of my question. "Without your Mr. Bush," they said, "we think we and our families would all be dead." I didn't have to look very closely at my surroundings to see, and to appreciate, the blunt truth of this. It was one of those common-sense moments that make one doubt the value of one's superior education. I decided that it would be merely flippant to say that he was not "my" Mr. Bush.

The Western soldiers up in this part of Iraq were mainly British, as were many of the planes and helicopters, but the vast airdrops of food and clothing and medicine were largely American-organized and the emplacement of

---

* Today, in an echo of the Latin American vernacular about those who were, rather than had, "disappeared," Kurdish people describe certain towns or groups as having been "Anfalled."

a "no-fly zone" over the region, preventing the renewal of any coordinated assault by Saddam, depended very considerably on United States Air Force bases in neighboring Turkey. Though Bush and Thatcher had had no desire whatever to become drawn into the internal dynamics of Iraq after the retrieval of Kuwait, domestic public opinion had rebelled at the sight of hundreds of thousands of Iraqi Kurds in flight, starving on the hillsides and machine-gunned along the roads. Was this any way to end a war for "liberation"? For me the immediate question became, Was I to be a part of this public opinion or not? I felt that I had no choice. Well then, what had become, or what was left, of my formerly proud "anti-war" stance? Was it anything much more than an affectation, or a residue?

All those who have had similar or comparable experiences will recognize the problem at once: it is not possible for long to be just a little bit heretical. To see American and British forces greeted by the people as liberators; to see the people's evident disappointment that this liberation was only to be partial; to see a nearly exterminated population regain its pulse and begin returning and rebuilding: this took a bit of assimilating. And my old Left training wasn't entirely useless to me, either. With the exception of the Mahabad Republic, briefly proclaimed with Communist support in Iranian Kurdistan after the Second World War and swiftly put down by the Shah, this was the closest that the Kurds, the largest population in the world without a state of its own, had come to controlling a piece of the earth that was distinctively theirs. Nor could I help noticing how many red flags were on display, how few mullahs there seemed to be, and how many invocations of old internationalist slogans were to be heard. It was chaotic and improvised; the men had a tendency to give the women back seats and to feel themselves naked unless festooned with weapons; the atmosphere was somewhat tribal for my taste but, as Orwell said when analyzing his own mixed feelings about republican and anarchist Catalonia, "I recognized it at once as a state of affairs worth fighting for." The idea of "Reds for Bush" might seem incongruous, but it was a very great deal more wholesome than "pacifists for Saddam."

With Ed Kashi I produced a short book about the Kurdish struggle, and I kept in touch with Barham Salih, the Kurdish representative in Washington, who had gone home to start reconstructing his country. (He is today the elected prime minister of the autonomous northern region.) The rest of

Iraq meanwhile was retaken by Saddam Hussein as the private property of himself and his horrifying sons. Limitations to the reach of this crime family took the form of UN-mandated international sanctions, and of "no-fly" zones in the airspace of the country's northern and southern provinces, which at least prevented a renewal of air-supported mass murder against the Kurdish and Shi'a populations. Almost every single day, Saddam's forces fired on the British and American planes that patrolled and enforced those zones. As well as being in a state of unstable ceasefire, then, Iraq was also in a condition of being "half-slave and half-free": a volatile situation that clearly could not continue indefinitely.

Other things—Bosnia, Rwanda—emerged to trouble the sleep of those who cared about human rights. But what I had learned in Iraq was working somewhere in my mind. I got hold of a copy of the video that showed how Saddam Hussein had actually confirmed himself in power. This snuff-movie opens with a plenary session of the Ba'ath Party central committee: perhaps a hundred men. Suddenly the doors are locked and Saddam, in the chair, announces a special session. Into the room is dragged an obviously broken man, who begins to emit a robotic confession of treason and subversion, that he sobs has been instigated by Syrian and other agents. As the (literally) extorted confession unfolds, names begin to be named. Once a fellow-conspirator is identified, guards come to his seat and haul him from the room. The reclining Saddam, meanwhile, lights a large cigar and contentedly scans his dossiers. The sickness of fear in the room is such that men begin to crack up and weep, rising to their feet to shout hysterical praise, even love, for the leader. Inexorably, though, the cull continues, and faces and bodies go slack as their owners are pinioned and led away. When it is over, about half the committee members are left, moaning with relief and heaving with ardent love for the boss. (In an accompanying sequel, which I have not seen, they were apparently required to go into the yard outside and shoot the other half, thus sealing the pact with Saddam. I am not sure that even Beria or Himmler would have had the nerve and ingenuity and cruelty to come up with that.)

So, whenever the subject of Iraq came up, as it did keep on doing through the Clinton years, I had no excuse for not knowing the following things: I knew that its one-party, one-leader state machine was modeled on the precedents of both National Socialism and Stalinism, to say nothing of Al

Capone. I knew that its police force was searching for psychopathic killers and sadistic serial murderers, not in order to arrest them but to *employ* them. I knew that its vast patrimony of oil wealth, far from being "nationalized," had been privatized for the use of one family, and was being squandered on hideous ostentation at home and militarism abroad. (Post-Kuwait inspections by the United Nations had uncovered a huge nuclear-reactor site that had not even been known about by the international community.) I had seen with my own eyes the evidence of a serious breach of the Genocide Convention on Iraqi soil, and I had also seen with my own eyes the evidence that it had been carried out in part with the use of weapons of mass destruction. I was, if you like, the prisoner of this knowledge. I certainly did not have the option of un-knowing it.

From time to time I would be asked to sign a petition against the sanctions, which were said to be killing tens of thousands of young and old Iraqis by the denial of medical supplies and food. I couldn't bring myself to be persuaded by this pseudo-humanitarianism. In the same period, Saddam had built himself a new palace in each of Iraq's eighteen provinces, while products like infant formula—actually provided to Iraq under the oil-for-food program—were turning up on the black market being sold by Iraqi government agents. More and more, it seemed to me, anyone who really cared for the well-being and survival of Iraqis should be arguing for the removal of the insane despotism that had necessitated the sanctions and that was eating the country alive.

The verdict of insanity was important all by itself. It seemed increasingly obvious to me that Saddam Hussein was *not* a rational actor, did *not* understand the elementary business of deterrence and self-preservation, and for this reason remained a danger, as psychiatrists phrase it, both to himself and to others. One of the manifestations of his megalomania was an ever-increasing piety. He had himself photographed, and painted on huge murals, in the robes of a mullah. He ordered that the *jihadi* slogan *Allahuh Akbar* ("God Is Great") be added to the national flag of Iraq. He began an immense mosque-building program, including the largest mosque in the Middle East, named for "the Mother of All Battles." He had a whole Koran written in his own blood: this macabre totem was to have been the centerpiece of that mosque. His party and state rhetoric became increasingly frenzied and jihadist in tone, and he stopped supporting secular forces among the Palestinians and instead began financing theocratic ones, such as Hamas and Islamic Jihad. An Iraqi bounty was officially and openly paid to the family of any Palestinian suicide bomber. Yet none of this—none of it, including the naming of the slaughterhouse-campaign against the Kurds after a *sura* of the Koran— would unconvince the utterly smug Western "experts" who kept on insisting that his Caligula regime was a "secular" one. To the contrary, it was precisely the genuine secular forces in the country—the Kurds, the Communist and Socialist movements, and the independent trade unions—that Ba'athism had set out deliberately to destroy. And it then filled the resulting vacuum with toxic religious propaganda of the crudest kind. Anyone who heard an Iraqi radio or television broadcast in the last decade of the regime can readily confirm that the insistent themes were those of "martyrdom" and holy war.

I slowly began to make friends with the Iraqi exiles—authentic secularists for the most part—who were advocating "regime change." Quite where this rather awkward, euphemistic formulation originated I cannot be certain. It seems to have crept into currency at about the time, during the Clinton administration, when Congress passed the Iraqi Liberation Act, making it long-term American policy to replace Saddam Hussein and short-term policy to set up a budget for his Iraqi opponents. This half-way house gave a temporary home to the idea that, while Iraqis were not strong enough to do the job themselves, the USA was not exactly undertaking to do it for them, either. Out of such sheepish, shame-faced half-acknowledgments, the "regime change" discourse began to chug into a sort of life.

Spike Milligan once wrote a book about being a shambolic conscript in some forgotten cookhouse in the wartime British Army and titled it *Adolf Hitler: My Part in His Downfall.* The attempt to change political Washington's mind about Saddam Hussein has since been the subject of so much lurid invention and paranoid disinformation that I really think it is time that I named myself, along with the other conspirators involved, and gave an account of what we did and why we did it.

The first of our faction was Kanan Makiya. In his books *The Republic of Fear* and *Cruelty and Silence,* about the Saddam tyranny and the wars and famines and plagues it had sponsored, he had shown remarkable forensic skill combined with a nicely astringent polemical style. I knew that he had in an earlier career been a Trotskyist, of a faction different from my own, and so when I read his critique of my own previous stand in his *Cruelty and Silence*, I was most of all impressed by how accurately he quoted me and by how gently he delivered his reproofs. (I had become too accustomed to the pseudo-Left new style, whereby if your opponent thought he had identified your lowest possible motive, he was quite certain that he had isolated the only real one. This vulgar method, which is now the norm and the standard in much non-Left journalism as well, is designed to have the effect of making any noisy moron into a master analyst.)

Makiya is an Iraqi of partly English parentage whose family calling was that of architecture. Possibly the most penetrating of his many books about Saddam and Saddamism is called *The Monument*. It is an intense, illustrated study of the vast parade ground and double arch in central Baghdad, constructed by Saddam Hussein to immortalize his "triumph" in the wars against Iran. I enclose the word "triumph" in quotation marks here not to ironize it, but to draw attention to its root in Roman barbaric and sadistic display: if modern public relations had allowed such a thing, then Saddam would certainly have dragged Persian captives at his chariot wheels before having them butchered as gladiator-fodder or fed to the feral. I have visited this obscene place several times now. The matching "arches" are each of two crossed swords or sabers or scimitars held by beefy forearms that were modeled, by trembling sculptors, from the dictator's own limbs. The big blades meet, and intersect. From the wrist of each arm are slung great steel nets, filled to overflowing with the empty helmets of Iranian soldiers, holed with bullets and shrapnel, and gloatingly heaped up. They purposely evoke a pyramid of skulls. Iraqi schoolchildren were paraded to see this foulness. I think of it whenever I hear some fool say, "All right, we agree that Saddam was a bad guy." Nobody capable of uttering that commonplace has any conception of radical evil.

My first instinct might have been to dynamite such a Golgotha but Kanan was always collected and cool. "No, Christopher, we shall ask to have it rededicated as a place of memorial for *all* the victims of Ba'athism, Arab and Kurdish and Persian. I don't even want it bombed if the bombing ever comes. There will be an Iraq Memory Foundation, and this will be where

we put it."* We were talking on the campus of Brandeis University, where
he taught then, and I had finished explaining to his class how I had begun
to change my mind about the first Gulf War. It seemed to me that in Kanan
I had found someone who preserved in himself everything that was worth
keeping about the tradition of the "Left Opposition" that had so encouraged
us when we were younger.

At a certain moment at the end of that first Gulf War, the Kurdish guerrilla forces had briefly occupied the centers of two or three northern Iraqi cities and captured a huge trove of documents belonging to the Saddam regime.
These massive steel file cabinets contained the sort of self-incriminating
evidence that would make future "denial" impossible: here were the still-
reeking records of the killing fields, the mass graves, the torture sessions, and
the illegal weapons. The Kurdish leadership had about one satellite phone to
go around in those days, but it knew enough to call Peter Galbraith, whom I
briefly introduce as our next co-conspirator.

I had known Galbraith, son of the author of *The Affluent Society*, since
my first year in Washington in 1982. With a handful of others, he shored up
or otherwise constituted the human-rights "Left" on the staff of the Senate
Foreign Relations Committee. Whether it was helping Benazir Bhutto run
in a reasonably free election in Pakistan in 1988, where I joined them both
in Karachi, or getting a hearing on the Hill for Chilean or Czech or South
African dissidents, Peter was one of those who would always be available
for a late-night phone call pleading for a break for just one more victim. He
not only arranged to get this massive file of Iraqi documents picked up, and
personally saw to its being transported across the Euphrates River under fire,
but then made sure that it was adopted as an official public resource by the
Library of Congress. One by one, the building blocks for a legal and international arraignment of the Saddam Hussein regime were being assembled.

A tremendous comrade in precisely this aspect of the work was Ann
Clwyd, who had been the Wales correspondent of the *New Statesman* when
both of us were young. As a fiery leftist MP on Tony Blair's backbenches, she

---

* Kanan got his museum, and the Memory Foundation is now an archive for victims and
survivors whose narrative would otherwise never have been set down. This remarkable
achievement remains a continual cause of spite and resentment.

sponsored an initiative-group called *"Indict,"* which called on Britain's attorney general, and the law officers of equivalent nations, to prepare to bring Saddam Hussein to trial for international offenses that ranged from the taking of British hostages in Kuwait to the gassing of Kurdish civilians. (That this never quite happened is probably the fault of the bad conscience of those Western governments who had colluded with Saddam Hussein when he was a profitable business partner, but that doesn't in the least affect the case that we regime-changers were making: indeed, it rather reinforces it.)

Again, if one were trying to assemble an informal international for the overthrow of fascism in Iraq, one could not dispense with Rolf Ekeus. He was and is the quintessential Swedish Social Democrat, personally and politically dedicated to every conceivable good cause from multilateral disarmament to the abolition of apartheid. (His brilliant wife, Kim, had been Sweden's liaison with Nelson Mandela and the ANC since the 1960s.) Rolf had represented his country as ambassador in Washington and at the UN, and had after the Gulf War been placed in charge of the United Nations inspections in Iraq. It was said of him, correctly, that he had found and destroyed more Iraqi WMDs than the Coalition forces had managed to identify, let alone to neutralize, in the entire course of the war. And it had been, for him, a highly educational experience. Invited to a private meeting with Tariq Aziz, Saddam's Catholic Christian crony and then–foreign minister, he had been offered a straight-out bribe of $2.5 million on condition that his inspection reports become more lenient. In that eventuality, he was calmly assured, this little trifle would be considered a mere first installment. (Ambassador Ekeus had a long and deserved reputation for incorruptibility, and the chances of his acceptance must have been reckoned as extremely close to nil, so if you conclude from this that the Iraqis were trying the same strategy on all United Nations personnel, you are probably using your head.) After the bribery was refused, an attempt was made to poison Rolf. And after that failed, his crucial defector-informants, the Kamel brothers, who were Saddam Hussein's in-laws and who had exposed the special "ministry of concealment" set up to deceive the inspectors, were lured back from Jordan to Iraq and murdered under a flag of truce. But those who make the presumption of innocence in the case of homicidal dictators take a lot of persuading. When it was decided to resume UN "inspections" once more, as a weak alternative to the Bush-Blair call for the existing resolutions

to be enforced, Kofi Annan did at least call for Rolf Ekeus to be reappointed
to the task he had already shown that he could do. The French and Russian
and Chinese delegations made certain that another quite different Swede got
the post instead: a bureaucrat under whose supervision both Iraq and North
Korea had made the word "inspections" look risible.

The other great influences in our little conspiracy were Barham Salih, the
aforementioned Kurdish envoy to Washington, and Kenneth Pollack, a liberal member of the Clinton administration's National Security Council. In
1990 he had vainly tried to warn a sunken and complacent CIA that Saddam
Hussein was mobilizing for an invasion of Kuwait and had been met with
stupid condescension from the sort of "intelligence" bureaucrat who believed
that Iraq was run by a cynical but rational calculator. (And also, needless to
add, by a modernizing "secularist.") Ken's book, regrettably and sensation-
ally titled *The Threatening Storm*, was in fact one of the best pieces of closely
marshaled evidence and reasoning ever to emerge from the wonk-world, and
made a lucid, devastating case that Saddam Hussein and his system should
be treated, on all the past and then-existing evidence, as staggeringly guilty
until proven innocent. And such innocence could only really be established
by having a government in Baghdad that was not a genocidal and paranoid
and megalomaniacal version of the Sopranos. To call for real inspections was
actually to demand regime change. People choose to forget it now, but the
Pollack book did more than any presidential speech ever did to win over the
"policy community" in Washington, just as it was Barham Salih who did
more than anyone else to persuade the Congress, one vote at a time.

There came a day when my friend Jim Hoagland, an extremely knowl-
edgeable and careful correspondent and columnist for the *Washington Post*
who had been visiting and studying Iraq for several decades, asked if I would
like to meet Ahmad Chalaby, the founder of the "Iraqi National Congress."
I naturally said yes: every other Iraqi I knew who had stood up to Saddam
Hussein had lost at the very least a family member, or at the very most a whole
villageful of relatives and friends, so a man who hoisted a public standard
against the regime and made a full-time job of it commanded my axiomatic
respect. He presented himself at my apartment in Washington, wearing a
leather jacket that didn't especially suit him, and greeted the friends I'd hastily assembled to meet the person who maintained that he could bring down

the despot. Chalaby has since become so well hosed with bile and spittle that I feel obliged to say several things in his defense. The first is that he made no grandiose claims. The case against Saddam Hussein was already complete, and whatever their reservations might be, in their hearts everybody knew this. How could one bring an end to the misery of the Iraqis, and the ongoing insult to international law and comity, with the minimum of violence? Chalaby's preferred strategy at that stage was to get American support for the indigenous Iraqi and Kurdish opposition forces, so that Saddam's clique—a Sunni tribal minority of the Sunni minority—could be isolated and brought down. Much of the Iraqi Army was on or near the verge of mutiny and desertion (this later proved to be true). The Shi'a were ready to rise in revolt if they could be persuaded that they would not again be abandoned as they had been in 1991. (This also proved to be the case.) In quasi-autonomous Kurdistan there were bases, and battle-tested fighting forces, which could lend serious back-up to any coordinated initiative. (Such had already been demonstrated, as I knew without having to be told.) Truth to tell, though, I was more impressed by the "civil society" element in Ahmad's conversation. If I mentioned or inquired about any Arab or Kurdish or Iranian intellectual, he seemed to have read their most recent book the day before. When it came to Marxism, he knew all the Iraqi Communists I had ever met, and even when it came to Trotskyism, he actually knew the meaning of the phrase "permanent revolution"—this is an acid test by the way—and furthermore knew that it was an expression originated by Parvus and not by Trotsky. On the next occasion when we met, he spent a good deal of time discussing the Bloomsbury Group and the shadings of difference between Lytton Strachey and John Maynard Keynes. Perhaps I seem too impressionable: at the time it seemed exciting and interesting that someone with a genius for politics was not just another monomaniac, but could discuss culture and literature as if these things, too, were at stake in the battle against the mirthless, ruthless totalitarians.*

---

* I had of course heard that Ahmad had once been indicted—by a military court in Jordan when it was Saddam's ally—for being a shady businessman. I have also read persuasive evidence that this was a frame-up, as were many other charges—"puppet of the CIA," for one absurd example—that were made against him. My main difference with him is, and remains, his alignment with a confessional bloc in the Iraqi parliament. But without him, there might well not be an Iraqi parliament.

An Anglo-Arab Trotskyist; a son of a Canada-born socialist economist; a passionate Welshwoman of the Labour movement; a Swedish Social Democrat and internationalist; a Kurdish socialist who had spent many years as a political prisoner; a mild and almost wonk-like think-tanker (if I do beg his pardon for saying so); and an exile member of the old Baghdad financier class, whose first training was that of mathematician. What a multifariously sinister crew! But this was the original combination of influences by which political Washington was eventually persuaded that Iraq should be helped into a post-Saddam era, if necessary by force. I specify the *dramatis personae* because of the near-unbelievable deluge of abusive and calumnious *dreck* that has since descended, and become encrusted and hardened. Those who tried to rid Iraq and the world of Saddam Hussein have been represented as part of a "neoconservative cabal," agents of a "Jewish lobby," and accused of forging evidence and fabricating pretexts for war. Chalaby's organization alone, with its negligible budget and minuscule staff, has been credited with single-handedly poisoning the informational well of the intelligence services of the United States, Britain, France, and Germany, all of which at different times had independently certified that Saddam Hussein had possession of, or was in measurable reach of, weapons of mass destruction. In reality, this amateur coordination of small battalions and discrepant individuals was the most open conspiracy in which I have ever taken part.

After I had written a few polemics about Iraq, and taken part in several television debates on the subject, I received a call one day from the Pentagon. It was from Paul Wolfowitz, Donald Rumsfeld's deputy, asking if I would like to come and see him. This would make my second visit to the Defense Department, since during the run-up to the previous Gulf War I had been invited to speak to the Policy Planning Staff *against* the intervention. So I thought, sure, if only for the sake of irony and symmetry. Wolfowitz I only knew by reputation, and by reputation he actually *was* a member of the neoconservative cabal: one of that influential group of former liberals, strongly pro-Zionist, some with connections to the Leo Strauss school of intellectuals at the University of Chicago, who had moved into the study of strategy during the Reagan years and made their peace with the hawkish wing of the Republican Party.

The thing that struck me most, once I had presented myself at his office, was the extent to which Wolfowitz wanted to live down precisely this image. The first thing he showed me was a photograph of the "Situation Room" in the mid-1980s, where, around the table I could see President Reagan and most of his foreign-policy team, from Weinberger to Shultz to Donald Regan, slumped in attitudes of mild exhaustion. Off to the side was a more youthful Wolfowitz. He told me that this picture, which had pride of place in his office, was of exactly the moment when the Reaganites had narrowly voted to dump the Ferdinand Marcos dictatorship in the Philippines in 1986 and to recognize the election victory of his opponent Cory Aquino.* "It was the first argument I won," said Wolfowitz proudly. "I said that if we supported a dictator to keep hold of a base, we would end up losing the base and also deserving to do so. Whereas," he went on, "by joining the side of 'people power' in Manila that year, we helped democracy movements spread through Taiwan and South Korea and even I think into Tiananmen Square in 1989." He gave me a friendly smile: "It was the opposite of a Kissinger policy."

All right, I admit I was intrigued. Wolfowitz took the view that, great as the risks of "democratization" might be, they were as nothing to the risks of dictatorship: the most unstable and volatile system of all. The only area of the globe after 1989 where this had not been tried was the Arab sphere. It was time to confront the Bush/Powell/Kissinger consensus that had left Saddam Hussein in possession of Iraq after 1991. I suspect that, if the Democrats had won the election of 2000, and if Wolfowitz had remained a Democrat and been given the self-same job, many liberals and leftists in Washington would have been praising him for tackling the racist assumption that Arabs preferred, or even needed, to be ruled by despots.

That night I was going with Kanan Makiya to a private dinner in the Cleveland Park section of the city, to help set up the Committee for the Liberation of Iraq. It turned out that Wolfowitz was to be the after-dinner speaker. He made a very forceful and lucid presentation, without notes, so that in a way I could have skipped the meeting we'd had at one of America's three "Ground Zeros" that afternoon. But I still would not have missed seeing that Reagan-era photograph. When the dinner was over—we had heard the news that Vaclav Havel and Lech Walesa would adorn the letterhead of the Committee—Kanan and I walked slowly back through a drenching

---

* See, for the best account of this upheaval in real time, James Fenton's book *The Snap Revolution*.

rain that neither of us really noticed. It had been a whole quarter of a century since Saddam Hussein had taken control of Iraq: Hitler had ruled for twelve years and Stalin for about twenty-five. "I think, comrade," I told him as the water started to run down my back and we bid *au revoir*, "that this time you are really going home." We closed with "next time in Baghdad": a promise that we kept the following summer.

It is *here* that I ought to make my most painful self-criticisms. I saw Wolfowitz a few more times between then and the ultimate decision to intervene, which was made about six months later. I also got to know a bit about the near-incredible incompetence and disloyalty of the CIA and the State Department. I was able to satisfy myself that those within the administration who were making the case for "regime change" were sincere in what they believed and were not knowingly exaggerating anything for effect. And I was able to ask for assurances. For example, it was widely alleged on the anti-war Left that General Ariel Sharon would seize the pretext offered by the fog of war in Iraq and expel all the Palestinians from the West Bank. The then-head of the Middle East Studies Association actually came to my house to try and persuade me on this point. When I asked Wolfowitz if the Pentagon had thought of this contingency, he said that he had had one of the Israeli commanders into his office only the previous day, and told him that American sympathy for Israel did not extend to expansion or colonization and that once one of the Arab "rejectionist" strongholds had been removed from Saddam's control, the United States would be in a position to ask for the dismantlement of settlements to begin. (At a rally not long before this, called by American Jewry to protest the suicide-bombing campaign that Saddam Hussein was helping to bankroll, Wolfowitz had been aggressively booed for reminding the crowd that the Palestinian people were suffering, too.)

On another occasion, when the Turkish government was being more than usually obnoxious, and refusing the use of American bases on Turkish soil for the deployment of a "northern front," unless Turkish troops were also to be allowed into Iraqi Kurdistan, I asked Wolfowitz whether the United States would permit such a sell-out. Again he was without ambivalence: Turkish boots on Iraqi soil would not be allowed. If the Turks insisted on exacting that price, the liberation of Iraq would go ahead without them (which it did).

Wait a moment, did I not just promise to be "self-critical"? Of course, what I *should* have been asking Wolfowitz, instead of bending his ear about these enterprises of such moral pith and geostrategic moment, was: "Does the Army Corps of Engineers have a generator big enough to turn the lights of Baghdad back on?" or perhaps "Has a detachment of Marines been ordered to guard the Iraq National Museum?" But, not being a professional soldier or quartermaster, nor feeling myself able to advise those who were, I rather tended to assume that things of this practical sort were being taken care of. It would have been like asking if we'd remembered to pack enough rations and ammunition. I feel stupid and ashamed to this day that I didn't ask the sort of question that Commander Hitchens would have insisted upon before even taking a ship into convoy. As Peter Galbraith was later to say so ruefully to me, surveying the terrifying damage done by unchecked looting, and the misery that this in turn inflicted on Iraqi society: "You never get a second chance to make a good first impression." This was to say the least of it: I probably now know more about the impeachable incompetence of the Bush administration than do many of those who would have left Iraq in the hands of Saddam. Some of it was almost quixotically American — the huge gleaming generator brought by truck across Jordan to Baghdad proved to be too digital and streamlined to be plugged into the Iraqi "grid," and we might have done better to buy some clapped-out equipment from Belarus or Ukraine. But some of the failures were infinitely more culpable than that and, even though they don't alter the case against Ba'athism, have permanently disfigured the record of those of us who made that case.

As the Iraq debate became more intense, it became suddenly obvious to me that I couldn't any longer remain where I was on the political "spectrum." Huge "anti-war" demonstrations were being organized by forces that actually exemplified what the CIA and others had naïvely maintained was impossible: a declared alliance between Ba'athist sympathizers and Islamic fundamentalists. The partisans of the failed One Party/One Leader state were now linking arms with the adorers of the One God. Some saw, or thought they saw, something "ironic" in this. My old friend Nick Cohen wrote scornfully that on a certain date, "about a million liberal-minded people marched through London to oppose the overthrow of a fascist regime." But what is "liberal-minded" about the Muslim Brotherhood and its clone-groups, or about the rump of British Stalinism, or about the purulent sect into which

my former comrades of the International Socialists had mutated? To them—
to the organizers and moving spirits of the march in other words—the very
word "liberal" was a term of contempt.*

I did a few things in swift succession. I resigned my position as columnist
for *The Nation* after an unbroken stint of twenty years man and boy as a bi-
weekly contributor. There was no further point in working for a magazine
that sympathized with the sort of "anti-war" culture I have just mentioned.
I then booked a ticket for Quatar, the small but relatively open monarchic
state which now housed both Al-Jazeera (then a new idea in the media) and
the American Central Command or "Centcom." I could see that the end-
game was approaching and I wanted to make my plans in advance. Changing
planes on the way through England to the Gulf, I consciously made my last
appearance as a man of the Left. I had said "yes" to the invitation—a very
flattering one—to be a speaker at the annual *Tribune* rally at the Labour
Party conference in Blackpool. This by tradition was the climactic event for
the radical rank-and-file. And *Tribune*, often all over the map politically and
journalistically, and frequently looking as if it had been designed and printed
at the last moment and in the pitch dark, had at least been the only paper in
England to furnish George Orwell with a weekly column. May I be forgiven
for quoting *My Life in the Bear Pit*, the taped diaries of David Blunkett, the
blind Yorkshire socialist and proletarian who at the time was Tony Blair's
home secretary:

> Odd little snippet from conference: I don't think I recorded the
> weird little paradox about the *Tribune* meeting and the fact that
> they'd made a terrible blunder by inviting Christopher Hitchens,
> who they believed to be a left-wing journalist—which he has been,
> but he is vehemently anti–Saddam Hussein and gave the most bril-
> liant lecture about the background and the detail of the individuals
> and why taking on Saddam Hussein was so important. Everybody
> sat there in absolute silence...

---

* To be fair, Ian McEwan's highly acute novel *Saturday*, which is easily the best evocation of
this street-theater event, does capture the anguish of many "liberals" who did turn out. His
work was also the first to isolate the unstinting self-regard that underlies the terribly OK-
seeming mantra of "Not In Our Name."

I don't remember the silence being quite absolute, because I had mentioned some courageous socialists like Barham Salih and Rolf Ekeus of whom some of the audience had at least heard. Attending the rally was Chris Mullin, one of the best and bravest and wittiest *Tribune* socialists ever elected to the House of Commons. May I quote his published diaries, too (*A View from the Foothills: The Diaries of Chris Mullin*), concerning the same evening?

> The speeches were lacklustre with one notable exception: Christopher Hitchens, who argued the case for military intervention in Iraq. He appealed to those present "as internationalists, as people who can think for yourselves." It was not a war on Iraq that was proposed, he argued, but a war on Saddam. He urged the left to be a bit self-critical.... "If the left had had its way, General Galtieri would still be the President of Argentina; Milosevic would still be in power in Belgrade; Kosovo would be an empty wilderness; Mullah Omar would still be in Kabul."

I step over some further kind things that Chris had to say, and come to his "counterarguments," put to me over a subsequent cocktail: "chaos, civilian casualties, *the danger that Saddam Hussein if cornered will resort to chemical weapons.* Christopher dismissed them all. He reckons the regime is crumbling and that the odds are it will implode without the need for an invasion. Fingers crossed that he is right."

The "WMD" question, as everybody hopes now to forget, was very often a rhetorical tool in the hands of those who wanted to leave Saddam Hussein in power. Attack him, and he would unleash the weapons of horror that he had wielded so promiscuously before. This resembled one of those "prisoners' dilemma" games, where each forced choice tightens the noose and reduces the number of options. Meanwhile, every concession that Saddam *did* make was the direct consequence of the believable threat of force. Do any of the anti-war types ever ask themselves what would have happened if the Coalition forces had sailed home without firing a shot?

I had been closer to the scenery of WMD-use than most people, but I thought, and wrote, that Saddam's command over such weaponry in 2002–2003 was more latent than blatant. He certainly had some resources, some scientists, some elements and ingredients, and a long criminal record of both use and concealment. If I could have had it proved to me beyond doubt that he did NOT have any serious stockpiles on hand, I would have argued—did in fact argue—that this made it the perfect time to hit him ruthlessly and conclusively. It would both punish the previous use and prevent any repetition of it. It would also bring Iraq into verifiable compliance with the ever-flourished and ever-cited UN and its important resolutions, thus allowing the lifting of economic sanctions and—according to the most vocal critics of such sanctions—saving hundreds of thousands of Iraqis from being or becoming civilian casualties.

In all my discussions with Wolfowitz and his people at the Pentagon, I never heard anything alarmist on the WMD issue. It was presumed that at some level Iraq remained a potential WMD state, and it was assumed that Saddam Hussein would never agree to come into compliance even with Hans Blix's very feeble "inspections" (which indeed he never did). This in itself was yet another proof of the inherent lunacy of the regime, and of the naïveté of those who thought that it, or its deranged leader, could ever be treated as a rational actor. It was this that I had meant when talking to Chris Mullin about the approach of an "implosion" point. By holding a referendum and claiming the first-ever 100 percent turnout (and 100 percent proportion of the turnout as a "yes" vote, at that) and by opening the wings of the horrible Abu Ghraib prison that contained the murderers and rapists and thieves who were part of the surplus value of his system, Saddam had given warning of the approach of his Ceausescu moment: a crazy meltdown of authority. Given the already-existing "chaos" in Iraq, and the divide-and-rule means by which the regime exploited religious and tribal hatreds, a meltdown was more likely to lead to a Rwanda on the Gulf than to a Romania. Absent a Coalition force, it would also lead to invasions from Iran, Turkey, and Saudi Arabia. Everything therefore pointed to the need for the international community to intervene at last, and on the right side for once, in maimed and traumatized Iraq, and to help it make the transition to some version of its right mind.

The WMD could be taken as emblematic of everything foul and wasteful about the Ba'athist system. I can remember only one instance where I was in any way "briefed" by anyone at the Defense Department. Underneath a Sunni mosque in central Baghdad, the parts and some of the ingredients of a chemical weapon had been located and identified with the help of local informers. I was told this off the record, and told also that I was not to make any use of the information. It was thought that, when the use of a holy place to hide such weaponry was disclosed by the intervention, it would help to change Muslim opinion. I still have the photographs that were taken in that mosque after the liberation, showing the cache of weaponry just where I had been told it would be. But if I was ever naïve about anything having to do with Iraqi WMD, it was in believing that the production of evidence like that, or indeed any other kind of evidence, would make even the most limited impression on the heavily armored certainties of the faithful.

# Coda: Amateur Archaeology in Iraq

During all this I never quite lost the surreal sense that I had become in some way a pro-government dissident and that of all the paradoxes of my little life this might have to register as the most acute one. But it was the demonstrators in the streets—I was teaching at Berkeley for much of the first spring of the Iraq war—who struck me as the real conformists of the scenario. Accused of becoming a sell-out by working for the interwar Yugoslav republic, Rebecca West's guide (and covert lover) Constantine, in *Black Lamb and Grey Falcon*, confesses that, yes: "For the sake of my country, and perhaps a little for the sake of my soul, I have given up the deep peace of being in opposition." I, too, began to find that I could see things from the point of view of the governors and that I was on the side of those now striving to build up a new state in Afghanistan and Iraq. In any case, the opponents of the war were themselves aligned with the views of other governors and states, many of them much more smelly than George W. Bush.

I still cannot bear to imagine the idea of a victory for Putin and Chirac and Annan and Schroeder, let alone the Chinese or the Saudis, but in the event the glad moment came when Saddam Hussein outdid himself and refused to save his evil system even by making the small concession of admitting and proving to the UN that he didn't currently possess any workable WMDs. I crossed the Kuwaiti border into Iraq not long after the first wave had gone racing up toward Baghdad and saw a little of the barbaric state to which southern Iraqi society had been reduced by a combination of Saddamism and the sanctions that it had necessitated. In Kuwait City I had watched Saddam Hussein's Scud missiles being shot out of the sky as they were fired randomly toward his now-liberated former colony, and smiled as I saw all the members of the press corps donning gas masks and running to the shelters to avoid the shower of chemical weapons, gases, and nerve-agents which never turned up—and in which they later claimed never to have believed. I can say for myself that I didn't bring, or wear, or own, a gas mask, or believe that any element of Saddam's armed forces—except the imported and *jihad*-minded "Fedayeen Saddam" (a suggestive name in its own right)—would do any real fighting. As I left Kuwait, the European press was awash in ridiculous babbling about a last-ditch defense of Baghdad that would be the equivalent of "Stalingrad."

And that was just the hacks. A few days later came a more considered piece by the cultivated Jonathan Raban, deploying almost faultlessly the wrinkled lip across which he and his fellow members of the Anglo-American *bien-pensant* classes viewed the deplorable crudity of the U.S. of A.:

> Passionate ideologues are incurious by nature and have no time for obstructive details. It's impossible to think of Paul Wolfowitz curling up for the evening with Edward Said's *Orientalism*, or the novels of Naguib Mahfouz, or *The Seven Pillars of Wisdom*, or the letters of Gertrude Bell, or the recently published, knotty, opaque but useful book by Lawrence Rosen, *The Culture of Islam*, based on Rosen's anthropological work...

Made perhaps unintentionally absurd by that use of the expression "curled up" to depict the act of reading ("You'll usually find me," says Bertie Wooster to Florence Craye in *Thank You, Jeeves*, "curled up with Spinoza's latest"), Raban's *Guardian* effusion became ever more vulnerable to ridicule as he began to discourse knowingly on the "body" of the Islamic *ummah* or "community" as if it were a passive female form capable of violation, for all the world as if Saddam Hussein had never invaded and tried to amputate and subjugate the two Muslim states of Iran and Kuwait, besides repeatedly raping and torturing and disfiguring his "own" captive nation.

In point of fact, Paul Wolfowitz wrote his doctoral dissertation on water and salinity in the Arab world, has lived for many years with an Arab woman scholar with close connections to Palestinian reformers, speaks more Arabic than Jonathan Raban, was married previously to an anthropologist with a special interest in the Muslim societies of Malaysia and Indonesia, was himself a diplomat in Jakarta and speaks some of the Bahasa language, too, and once telephoned me to disagree with a detail in something I had written about the Indonesian novelist Pramoedya Ananta Toer. Wolfowitz was for many years the dean of a major school of Johns Hopkins University and is thanked by name in the acknowledgments of Azar Nafisi's brave, beautiful book *Reading Lolita in Tehran*: a study of the relations between literature, sexuality, and power under Muslim theocracy that can stand comparison to anything written by Edward Said or even Naguib Mahfouz. If anyone was being colonial or "orientalist" here it was Jonathan Raban, a most refined Englishman who didn't believe that a mere Yank could know anything about the exotic latitudes where only travel writers like himself were authorized to tread. But his tone of infuriated condescension was vastly preferable to the way in which the BBC's on-air bookers and interviewers, telephoning me as if to make sure they couldn't be accused of undue bias, would flatly and simply decline to pronounce Paul Wolfowitz's name correctly. "Volfervitz," they would say, putting a sinister top-spin on it. I remember a time in the 1970s when a certain Colonel X of the old le Carré school would sit in a discreet office at the BBC, occasionally asking program producers if they intended to make regular use of "this chap Hitchens, fascinating as he no doubt can be." But at least in those days of nudge-and-wink political invigilation, it was considered minimal good manners to get someone's name right. How hard could it be, I would inquire icily (and sometimes after the BBC caller had begun by addressing me as "Chris") to pronounce the name phonetically or as it was spelled? "Oh all right," one of them said grudgingly: "this fellow Wolfervitz who seems to be the power behind the scenes, with his neo-con cabal..." I made the man stop and begin all over again.

I prefer to think that I am not unusually thin-skinned when it comes to clumsy innuendos on the Jewish question. But this sort of stuff was a complete give-away, and I do think that one must never just sit there when it is being vented. As an undergraduate at Oxford I was once asked by a friendly don at All Souls if I would help him arrange a gentle punting trip for Sir Max Mallowan—also a fellow of the college, by then rather elderly—and Lady Mallowan. I agreed readily, and not just because Lady Mallowan was better

known as Agatha Christie. Sir Max had been the *doyen* of the British archaeological expedition in Mesopotamia between the wars, and could be mentioned
in the same breath as Gertrude Bell when it came to the treasure-house that
was the Iraq National Museum. The afternoon drifted by agreeably enough
and I must have passed muster in some way because I was then invited to dine
at the Mallowan home in nearby Wallingford. Around their table, in a house
festooned with Middle Eastern miniatures and statuettes, I very suddenly felt
myself congealing with unease. The anti-Jewish flavor of the talk was not to
be ignored or overlooked, or put down to heavy humor or generational prejudice. It was vividly unpleasant and it was bottom-numbingly boring. (I had
the excuse, if I can call it that, of not having read any of the "Agatha Christie"
effusion. I have checked it since, and been surprised by many things about
it, most of all its popularity. How right Raymond Chandler was to scorn
her trudgery. There must be some connection between the general nullity
of Christie's prose and the tendency of her detectives to take Jewishness as
a symptom of crime. After 1945 she learned to hold down the bigotry a bit
but one of the 1950s efforts, titled *They Came to Baghdad*, is all about a well-
funded and Iraq-based plot for a New World Order, featuring clammy Jewish
employers and a deeply sinister scheme called "the Wolfensohn merger.")

When I went back to Iraq again, after the liberation was complete, I was
myself engaged on a sort of "dig," and I decided to travel with Paul Wolfowitz.
It was in its own way an archaeological and anthropological expedition.
Here are some of the things we unearthed or observed. Unnoticed by almost
everybody, and unreported by most newspapers, Saddam Hussein's former
chief physicist Dr. Mahdi Obeidi had waited until a few weeks after the fall
of Baghdad to accost some American soldiers and invite them to excavate his
back garden. There he showed them the components of a gas centrifuge—
the crown jewels of uranium enrichment—along with a two-foot stack of
blueprints. This burial had originally been ordered by Saddam's younger son
Qusay, who had himself been in charge of the Ministry of Concealment, and
had outlasted many visits by "inspectors." I myself rather doubt that Hans
Blix would ever have found the trove on his own.

Not long after that, a sandstorm near Baghdad uncovered a bizarre
row of shimmering airplane tailfins. These proved to be the gravemarkers
of a squadron of expensive Russian-built MIG-25 jet fighters. The point of

the burial was and still remains unclear: one might as well set a jet engine on fire as immerse it in a dune. But the instinct for "hugger-mugger interment" among the eerie upper echelons of the Ba'ath Party seems to have been strongly ingrained. Iraq is almost the size of California. I dare say that they buried other military secrets that we will never know about.

Near the northern town of Kirkuk, in the June that followed the invasion, a total of eight million dollars in cash was dug out of the garden of Saddam Hussein's personal secretary. Along with this came a further few million dollars' worth of jewelry, "belonging" to Saddam Hussein's wife. In the end, Saddam Hussein himself was pulled in an undignified manner from an underground hole where he had taken ignominious refuge.

But the worst of all the unearthings and diggings and disinterments took place not far from the ruins of Babylon, in the town of Al-Hilla. On 13 May 2003, not long after the liberation, frenzied local people had begged American forces to come and help, and also to bear witness. Ever since 1991 and the massive repression of the Shi'a uprising, the site had had an evil and disgusting reputation. It was said by witnesses that three truckloads of people, three times a day, for a month, had been driven here. Forced into pre-dug mass graves, they were then either shot or buried alive. Seizing the chance to identify their missing loved ones, local people had swarmed to the place as soon as Saddam's regime disintegrated, and uncovered three thousand bodies with their bare hands before calling for help from the Coalition. By the time I got there, the excavation process was becoming more dignified and orderly but nothing could render it less obscene.

Lines of plastic body bags were laid out on the ground, sometimes "tagged" with personal items and identifying documents. Where digging was complete, the ground had been consecrated as a resting place. Elsewhere, the ghastly spadework continued. The two men in charge of the scene were a Major Schmidt from New Jersey and Dr. Rafed Fakher Husain, a strikingly composed Iraqi physician. "We lived without rights," he told me with a gesture of his hand toward this area of darkness. "And without ideas." The second sentence seemed to hang in the noisome air for longer than the first, and to express the desolation more completely. There were sixty-two more such sites, I was to learn, in this province of southern Iraq alone.

It was mid-July, when the Mesopotamian heat can without effort bring off the achievement of 120 degrees. This means a constant smearing of oneself with sunscreen and the exuding of drenching perspiration. The hair becomes matted and damp. The clothes cling. And then the wind gets up...I suddenly realized that a paste was forming all over me, made up of various greases and slimes, natural and artificial, and thickly overlaid by a crust from the clinging filth of a mass grave. I hope never again to feel so utterly befouled. It was in the nostrils, in the eyes...on the tongue and in the *mouth*. And the chance of a wash, let alone of a cleansing shower, was a good way off. I was eventually able to have that shower, almost weeping with mingled disgust and relief, in the al-Rashid hotel in Baghdad, but the rest of Iraqi society was still digging itself out of a shallow grave and those who fetishized the ideal of death and the grave—Ba'athist and Islamist—were getting ready to blast further hecatombs all across the landscape. "Scum of the earth," I wrote in my notebook, meaning by this cliché the Saddamist–Al Quaeda alliance and not the gritty residue that had been my nauseating carapace. After that, not even the abattoir stench from the execution sheds in newly liberated Abu Ghraib could shake me as much. I do remember thinking that attempts to clean out and restart that horror-prison were doomed, and that it should simply have been demolished, with salt strewn over the ruins. I wish that I had made that point more forcibly, too.*

Also unearthed, but this time in paper form and in the state archives, were documents showing that a surprising number of "anti-war" politicians in several countries were the beneficiaries of "Oil for Food" kickbacks—in other words of money stolen directly from the suffering Iraqi people about whom they orated. There was also a letter from my old friend Naji Sabry al-Hadithi, who had ended up as Saddam Hussein's last foreign minister. It was addressed to Saddam himself, in the closing moments of the regime, and it expressed concern, of a sort that I believe is worth recording.

---

* It impressed me very much to see my Kurdish friends, including Iraq's first-ever democratically chosen president, Jalal Talabani, publicly voice their opposition to the death penalty for Saddam Hussein and the other convicted war criminals. This appeal to clemency arose partly from their adherence to the Socialist International and also from their wish to begin Iraq again without a blood reckoning. After what they had endured, their forebearance was something extraordinary. In Kurdistan itself, where tribal retributionism was not so much in evidence, Barham Salih personally declined to sign death-warrants for the Islamist gangsters who had murdered his guards and very nearly slain him on his own doorstep.

It was distressing, wrote Naji, to see the reports of Iraqi civilians rushing forward to greet advancing American and British soldiers. Such deplorable events were discrediting the heroic Saddamist struggle in the wider world. Might it not be advisable, he suggested to his leader, to send some of the suicide-martyrs of the *Fedayeen Saddam*, disguised as civilians, to detonate themselves as soon as they drew close enough to the new arrivals? That would soon enough teach the British and Americans to suspect all Iraqis as "terrorists," and to keep their distance.* There was something horribly simple about this idea, and I wondered for a while why a foreign minister should even be suggesting such a vile thing. Later reports, to the effect that Naji had been shopping on the other side of the street and providing secret information to the Coalition via "back channels," at least supplied a likely motive. In Saddam's Iraq, if you wanted to cover yourself, the best thing was to propose the most exorbitantly cruel and extreme measures. Poor old Naji, then, to be reduced to this wicked expedient.

Anyway, Naji's scheme was indeed adopted, as were some other "measures." A woman in the town of Nasiriyah was publicly hanged for welcoming the liberators. We have video footage of other Iraqis having their tongues cut out or their extremities lopped off for the same offense, by the sort of black-cowled holy warriors who have become so drearily familiar to us since. It matters to me to remember this Saturnalia of butchery, because of third-hand observers who like to mock the idea that Iraqis ever saluted their liberators with "sweets and flowers" or whatever the sneer happens to be.

I cannot exactly vouch for the kinds of sweets or the sorts of flowers, but in Iraq I saw some quite extraordinary things and I will not be made to deny the evidence of my own eyes. Along the road from Basra one day in the summer of 2003, traveling all the way to the holy Shi'ite cities of Najaf and Karbala, I sat in a very lightly armed American convoy of civilian cars and saw people run to the roadside, with no advance notice of our arrival—I know this because I know we hadn't planned in advance to take that road—and simply wave and smile and show signs of happiness. It was completely unlike anything stage-managed, which in the Iraq of Saddam had involved great orchestrated ululations and contortions and mad avowals of the willingness for blood-sacrifice.

---

* This document was originally published by my old friend Patrick Cockburn, perhaps the best chronicler of the war and certainly its most fervent and intelligent critic.

It was normal and proportional, and in its way rather beautiful, and I give the lie to those who say I did not see those crowds or clasp those hands.

Landing by chopper on another occasion in the Marshes, I did see a less-spontaneous (they knew we were coming) and more hysterical greeting. But the Marsh Arabs were hardly likely to react any other way, having had their ancient riparian habitat once destroyed by Saddam and now reflooded by the Americans. In those amazing reed palaces that could by a stretch have dated back to the mythical Abraham, the enthusiasm and hospitality might have been prepared but could not possibly have been feigned.

As for Kurdistan, I had already seen this land when it was Saddam's people who had the mastery of it. Here one met an even more respectful joy, in a territory which did not any longer require—or ask for—a single Western soldier. Here, we were the guests in a different sense because the people of northern Iraq already had secure stewardship of their own affairs and were firmly but politely outgrowing their former protectors. To witness this was wholly, profoundly satisfactory: I am sorry for those who have never had the experience of seeing the victory of a national liberation movement, and I feel cold contempt for those who jeer at it.

Naji Sabry's horrible suggestion that such enthusiasm be quelled in such a way—he had the grace to look abashed when I next saw him in exile in Quatar—of course makes the additional implicit point that the Ba'athist leadership knew, and took for granted, that it had suicide squads at its disposal. This in turn suggests a long and official collusion between the Saddam regime and the religious zealots. Abu Nidal had become by this time quite old hat (he was actually murdered by Saddam's police just as the Allies were surrounding Baghdad Airport, lest he disclose anything inconvenient). Captured by the Coalition while still under Iraqi protection was Abbu Abbas, leader of the gang that had rolled Leon Klinghoffer in his wheelchair from the deck of the *Achille Lauro* cruise ship. He had had to be released after his arrest in that episode because he was traveling on a diplomatic passport. An Iraqi diplomatic passport. Now, belatedly, he was under lock and key. Still not yet apprehended is Mr. Mehmet Yassin, the man who mixed the chemicals for the bomb that hit the World Trade Center in 1993, and then flew straight to Iraq after the FBI so incautiously granted him bail. Iraq was then a country that was as difficult to enter as it was hard to leave...

This thieves' kitchen dimension, of a country run by criminals and sadists, was not confined to the drugs-and-thugs corruption and terrorism side. And once again, I was to pick up the spoor of an old connection. Rolf Ekeus came round to my apartment one day and showed me the name of the Iraqi diplomat who had visited the little West African country of Niger: a statelet famous only for its production of yellowcake uranium. The name was Wissam Zahawi. He was the brother of my louche gay part-Kurdish friend, the by-now late Mazen. He was also, or had been at the time of his trip to Niger, Saddam Hussein's ambassador to the Vatican. I expressed incomprehension. What was an envoy to the Holy See doing in Niger? Obviously he was not taking a vacation. Rolf then explained two things to me. The first was that Wissam Zahawi had, when Rolf was at the United Nations, been one of Saddam Hussein's chief envoys for discussions on nuclear matters (this at a time when the Iraqis had functioning reactors). The second was that, during the period of sanctions that followed the Kuwait war, no Western European country had full diplomatic relations with Baghdad. The Vatican was the sole exception, so it was sent a very senior Iraqi envoy to act as a listening post. And this man, a specialist in nuclear matters, had made a discreet side trip to Niger. This was to suggest exactly what most right-thinking people were convinced was *not* the case: namely that British intelligence was on to something when it said that Saddam had not ceased seeking nuclear materials in Africa.*

I published a few columns on this, drawing at one point an angry email from Ambassador Zahawi that very satisfyingly blustered and bluffed on what he'd really been up to. I also received—this is what sometimes makes journalism worthwhile—a letter from a BBC correspondent named Gordon Correa who had been writing a book about A.Q. Khan. This was the Pakistani proprietor of the nuclear black market that had supplied fissile material to Libya, North Korea, very probably to Syria, and was open for business with any member of the "rogue states" club. (Saddam's people, we already knew for sure, had been meeting North Korean missile salesmen in Damascus

---

* This verifiable account is often confused with a bungled attempt to sell some forged documents from the embassy of Niger in Rome: a false trail that, whether out of cupidity or design, wasted the time of several already time-wasting "inquiries."

until just before the invasion, when Kim Jong Il's mercenary bargainers took fright and went home.) It turned out, said the highly interested Mr. Correa, that his man Khan had *also* been in Niger, and at about the same time that Zahawi had. The likelihood of the senior Iraqi diplomat in Europe and the senior Pakistani nuclear black-marketeer both choosing an off-season holiday in *chic* little uranium-rich Niger...well, you have to admit that it makes an affecting picture. But you must be ready to credit something as ridiculous as that if your touching belief is that Saddam Hussein was already "contained," and that Mr. Bush and Mr. Blair were acting on panic reports, fabricated in turn by self-interested provocateurs. So I am proud of what our little international of volunteers was able to manage in this element of the crisis, too. It can be just as useful to expose the laughable as it is important to unmask the hateful: as I had slowly discovered in those riverside Thames-to-Tigris moments, covering as they did the waterfront from Adolf Hitler through Agatha Christie to Oscar Wilde.

# Postscript

I was having an oppressively normal morning at the dawn of 2007, flicking through the banality of quotidian email traffic, when I idly clicked on a message from a friend headed "Seen This?" The attached item turned out to be a very well-written story by Teresa Watanabe of the *Los Angeles Times*. It described the death, in Mosul, Iraq, of a young soldier from Irvine, California, named Mark Jennings Daily, and the unusual degree of emotion that his community was undergoing as a consequence. The emotion derived from a very moving statement that the boy had left behind, stating his reasons for having become a volunteer and bravely facing the prospect that his words might have to be read posthumously. In a way, the story was almost too perfect: this handsome lad had been born on the Fourth of July, was a registered Democrat and self-described agnostic, a UCLA honors graduate, and during his college days had had fairly decided reservations about the war in Iraq. I read on, and actually printed the story out, and was turning a page when I saw the following:

"Somewhere along the way, he changed his mind. His family says there was no epiphany. Writings by author and columnist Christopher Hitchens on the moral case for war deeply influenced him..."

I don't exaggerate by much when I say that I froze. I certainly felt a very deep pang of cold dismay. I had just returned from a visit to Iraq with my own son (who was then twenty-three, as was young Mr. Daily) and had found myself in a deeply pessimistic frame of mind about the war. Was it possible that I had helped persuade someone I had never met to place himself in the path of an IED? Over-dramatizing myself a bit in the angst of the moment, I found I was thinking of William Butler Yeats, who was chilled to discover that the Irish rebels of 1916 had gone to their deaths quoting his play *Cathleen ni Houlihan.* He tried to cope with the disturbing idea in his poem "Man and the Echo":

> Did that play of mine send out
> Certain men the English shot?...
> Could my spoken words have checked
> That whereby a house lay wrecked?

Abruptly dismissing any comparison between myself and one of the greatest poets of the twentieth century, I feverishly clicked on all the links from the article and found myself on Lieutenant Daily's MySpace site, where his statement "Why I Joined" was posted. The site also immediately kicked into a skirling noise of Irish revolutionary pugnacity: a song from the Dropkick Murphys album *Warrior's Code.* And there, at the top of the page, was a link to a passage from one of my articles, in which I poured scorn on those who were neutral about the battle for Iraq...I don't remember ever feeling, in every allowable sense of the word, quite so hollow.

I writhed around in my chair for a bit and decided that I ought to call Ms. Watanabe, who could not have been nicer. She anticipated the question I was too tongue-tied to ask: Would the Daily family—those whose "house lay wrecked"—be contactable? "They'd actually like to hear from you." She kindly gave me the email address and the home number.

I don't intend to make a parade of my own feelings here, but I expect you will believe me when I tell you that I emailed first. For one thing, I didn't want to choose a bad time to ring. For another, and as I wrote to his parents, I was quite prepared for them to resent me. So let me introduce you to one of the most generous and decent families in the United States, and allow me to tell you something of their experience.

In the midst of their own grief, to begin with, they took the trouble to try to make me feel better. I wasn't to worry about any "guilt or responsibility": their son had signed up with his eyes wide open and had "assured us that if he knew the possible outcome might be this, he would still go rather than have the option of living to age fifty and never having served his country. Trust us when we tell you that he was quite convincing and persuasive on this point, so that by the end of the conversation we were practically packing his bags and waving him off." This made me relax fractionally, but then they went on to write: "Prior to his deployment he told us he was going to try to contact you from Iraq. He had the idea of being a correspondent from the front-lines through you, and wanted to get your opinion about his journalistic potential. He told us that he had tried to contact you from either Kuwait or Iraq. He thought maybe his email had not reached you..." That was a gash in my hide all right: I think of all the junk email I read every day, and then reflect that his precious one never got to me.

Lieutenant Daily crossed from Kuwait to Iraq in November 2006, where he would be deployed with the "C," or "Comanche," Company of the Second Battalion of the Seventh Cavalry Regiment—rather unpromisingly General Custer's old outfit—in Mosul. On the 15th of January 2007, he was on patrol and noticed that the Humvee in front of him was not properly "up-armored" against IEDs. He insisted on changing places and taking a lead position in his own Humvee, and was shortly afterward hit by an enormous buried mine that packed a charge of some 1,500 pounds of high explosive. Yes, that's right. He, and the three other American soldiers and Iraqi interpreter who perished with him, "went to war with the army we had," as Donald Rumsfeld so carefully put it. It's some consolation to John and Linda Daily, and to Mark's brother and two sisters, and to his widow (who had been married to him for just eighteen months) to know that he couldn't have felt anything.

Yet what, and how, should *we* feel? People are not on their oath when speaking of the dead, but I have now talked to a good number of those who knew Mark Daily or were related to him, and it's clear that the country lost an exceptional young citizen, whom I shall always wish I had had the chance to meet. He seems to have passed every test of young manhood, and to have been admired and loved and respected by old and young, male and female, family and friends. He could have had any career path he liked (and had won a George C. Marshall Award that led to an offer to teach at West Point). Why are we robbed of his contribution? As we got to know one another better, I sent the Daily family a moving statement made by the mother of Michael Kelly, my good friend and the editor-at-large of *The Atlantic Monthly*, who was killed near the Baghdad airport while embedded during the invasion of 2003. Marguerite Kelly was highly stoic about her son's death, but I now think I committed an error of taste in showing this to the Dailys, who very gently responded that Michael had lived long enough to write books, have a career, become a father, and in general make his mark, while their son didn't live long enough to enjoy any of these opportunities. If you have tears, prepare to shed them now...

In his brilliant book *What Is History?*, Professor E.H. Carr asked about ultimate causation. Take the case of a man who drinks a bit too much, gets behind the wheel of a car with defective brakes, drives it round a blind corner, and hits another man, who is crossing the road to buy cigarettes. Who is the one responsible? The man who had one drink too many, the lax inspector of brakes, the local authorities who didn't straighten out a dangerous bend, or the smoker who chose to dash across the road to satisfy his bad habit? So, was Mark Daily killed by the Ba'athist and bin Ladenist riffraff who place bombs where they will do the most harm? Or by the Rumsfeld doctrine, which sent American soldiers to Iraq in insufficient numbers and with inadequate equipment? Or by the Bush administration, which thought Iraq would be easily pacified? Or by the previous Bush administration, which left Saddam Hussein in power in 1991 and fatally postponed the time of reckoning?

These grand, overarching questions cannot obscure, at least for me, the plain fact that Mark Daily felt himself to be morally committed. I discovered this in his life story and in his surviving writings. Again, not to romanticize him overmuch, but this is the boy who would not let others be bullied in school, who stuck up for his younger siblings, who was briefly a vegetarian and Green Party member because he couldn't stand cruelty to animals or to the environment, a student who loudly defended Native American rights and who challenged a MySpace neo-Nazi in an online debate in which the swastika-displaying antagonist finally admitted that he needed to rethink things. If I give the impression of a slight nerd here I do an injustice. Everything that Mark wrote was imbued with a great spirit of humor and tough-mindedness. Here's an excerpt from his "Why I Joined" statement:

> Anyone who knew me before I joined knows that I am quite aware and at times sympathetic to the arguments against the war in Iraq. If you think the only way a person could bring themselves to volunteer for this war is through sheer desperation or blind obedience then consider me the exception (though there are countless like me).... Consider that there are 19 year old soldiers from the Midwest who have never touched a college campus or a protest who have done more to uphold the universal legitimacy of representative government and individual rights by placing themselves between Iraqi voting lines and homicidal religious fanatics.

And here's something from one of his last letters home:

> I was having a conversation with a Kurdish man in the city of Dahok (by myself and completely safe) discussing whether or not the insurgents could be viewed as "freedom fighters" or "misguided anti-capitalists." Shaking his head as I attempted to articulate what can only be described as pathetic apologetics, he cut me off and said "the difference between insurgents and American soldiers is that they get paid to take life—to murder, and you get paid to save lives." He looked at me in such a way that made me feel like he was looking through me, into all the moral insecurity that living in a free nation will instill in you. He "oversimplified" the issue, or at least that is what college professors would accuse him of doing.

In his other emails and letters home, which the Daily family very kindly showed me, he asked for extra "care packages" to share with local

Iraqis, and said, "I'm not sure if Irvine has a sister-city, but I am going to personally contact the mayor and ask him to extend his hand to Dahok, which has been more than hospitable to this native-son." (I was wrenched yet again to discover that he had got this touching idea from an old article of mine, which had made a proposal for city-twinning that went nowhere.) In the last analysis, it was quite clear, Mark had made up his mind that the United States was a force for good in the world, and that it had a duty to the freedom of others. A video clip of which he was very proud has him being "crowned" by a circle of smiling Iraqi officers. I have a photograph of him, standing bareheaded and contentedly smoking a cigar, on a rooftop in Mosul. He doesn't look like an occupier at all. He looks like a staunch friend and defender. On the photograph is written "We carry a new world in our hearts."

In his last handwritten letter home, posted on the last day of 2006, Mark modestly told his father that he'd been chosen to lead a combat platoon after a grenade attack had killed one of its soldiers and left its leader too shaken to carry on. He had apparently sounded steady enough on the radio on earlier missions for him to be given a leadership position after only a short time "in country." As he put it: "I am now happily doing what I was trained to do, and am fulfilling an obligation that has swelled inside me for years. I am deep in my element...and I am euphoric." He had no doubts at all about the value of his mission, and was the sort of natural soldier who makes the difference in any war.

At the first chance I got, I invited his family for lunch in California. We ended up spending the entire day together. As soon as they arrived, I knew I had been wrong to be so nervous. They looked too good to be true: like a poster for the American way. John Daily is an aerospace project manager, and his wife, Linda, is an audiologist. Their older daughter, Christine, eagerly awaiting her wedding, is a high-school biology teacher, and the younger sister, Nicole, is in high school. Their son Eric is a bright junior at Berkeley with a very winning and ironic grin. And there was Mark's widow, an agonizingly beautiful girl named Snejana ("Janet") Hristova, the daughter of political refugees from Bulgaria. Her first name can mean "snowflake," and this was his name for her in the letters of fierce tenderness that he sent her from Iraq. These, with your permission, I will not share, except this:

One thing I have learned about myself since I've been out here is that everything I professed to you about what I want for the world and what I am willing to do to achieve it was true....

My desire to "save the world" is really just an extension of trying to make a world fit for you.

If that is all she has left, I hope you will agree that it isn't nothing.

I had already guessed that this was no gung-ho Orange County Republican clan. It was pretty clear that they could have done without the war, and would have been happier if their son had not gone anywhere near Iraq. (Mr. Daily told me that as a young man he had wondered about going to Canada if the Vietnam draft ever caught up with him.) But they had been amazed by the warmth of their neighbors' response, and by the solidarity of his former brothers-in-arms—1,600 people had turned out for Mark's memorial service in Irvine. A sergeant's wife had written a letter to Linda and posted it on Janet's MySpace site on Mother's Day, to tell her that her husband had been in the vehicle with which Mark had insisted on changing places. She had seven children who would have lost their father if it had gone the other way, and she felt both awfully guilty and humbly grateful that her husband had been spared by Mark's heroism. Imagine yourself in that position, if you can, and you will perhaps get a hint of the world in which the Dailys now live: a world that alternates very sharply and steeply between grief and pride.

On a drive to Fort Knox, Kentucky, and again shortly before shipping out from Fort Bliss, Texas, Mark had told his father that he had three wishes in the event of his death. He wanted bagpipes played at the service, and an Irish wake to follow it. And he wanted to be cremated, with the ashes strewn on the beach at Neskowin, Oregon, the setting for his happiest memories of boyhood vacations. The first two of these conditions had already been fulfilled. The Dailys rather overwhelmed me by asking if I would join them for the third one. So it was that in August I found myself on the dunes by an especially lovely and remote stretch of the Oregon coastline. The extended family was there, including both sets of grandparents, plus some college friends of Mark's and his best comrade from the army, an impressive South Dakotan named Matt Gross. As the sun began to sink on a day that had been devoted to reminiscence and moderate drinking, we took up the tattered Stars and Stripes that had flown outside the family home since Mark's deployment and walked to his favorite spot to plant it. Everyone was supposed to say something, but when John Daily took the first scoop from the urn and spread the ashes on the breeze, there was something so unutterably final in the gesture that tears seemed as natural as breathing and I wasn't at all sure that I could go through with it. My idea had been to quote from the last scene of *Macbeth*, which is the only passage I know that can hope to rise to such an occasion. The tyrant and usurper has been killed, but Ross has to tell old Siward that his boy has perished in the struggle:

> Your son, my lord, has paid a soldier's debt;
> He only lived but till he was a man;
> The which no sooner had his prowess confirm'd
> In the unshrinking station where he fought,
> But like a man he died.

This being Shakespeare, the truly emotional and understated moment follows a beat or two later, when Ross adds:

> Your cause of sorrow
> Must not be measured by his worth, for then
> It hath no end.

I became a trifle choked up after that, but everybody else also managed to speak, often reading poems of their own composition, and as the day ebbed in a blaze of glory over the ocean, I thought, Well, here we are to perform the last honors for a warrior and hero, and there are no hysterical ululations, no shrieks for revenge, no insults hurled at the enemy, no firing into the air or bogus hysterics. Instead, an honest, brave, modest family is doing its private best. I hope no fanatical fool could ever mistake this for weakness. It is, instead, a very particular kind of strength. If America can spontaneously produce young men like Mark, and occasions like this, it has a real homeland security instead of a bureaucratic one.

But Mark Daily wasn't yet finished with sending me messages from beyond the grave. He took a bag of books with him to Iraq, which included

Thomas Paine's *The Crisis, War and Peace,* Ayn Rand's *Atlas Shrugged* (so, nobody's perfect), Stephen Hawking's *A Brief History of Time,* John McCain's *Why Courage Matters,* and George Orwell's *Animal Farm* and *Nineteen Eighty-four.* And a family friend of the Dailys, noticing my own book on Orwell on their shelf, had told them that his father, the Trotskyist militant Harry David Milton, had been "the American" who rushed to Orwell's side after he had been shot in the throat by a fascist sniper. This seemed to verge on the eerie. Orwell thought that the Spanish Civil War was a just war, but he also came to understand that it was a dirty war, where a decent cause was hijacked by goons and thugs, and where betrayal and squalor negated the courage and sacrifice of those who fought on principle. As one who had argued strongly for the liberation of Iraq—perhaps more strongly than I knew in this particular case—I had grown coarsened and sickened by the degeneration of the struggle, and the sordid news of corruption and brutality (Mark Daily told his father how dismayed he was by the appalling scenes at Abu Ghraib) and by the paltry politicians who squabble for precedence while lifeblood is spilled by young people whose boots they are not fit to clean.

It upsets and angers me more than I can safely say, when I re-read Mark's letters and poems and see that—as of course he would—he was magically able to locate the noble element in all this, and to take more comfort and inspiration from a few plain sentences uttered by a Kurdish man than from all the vapid speeches ever given. Orwell had a rather similar experience when encountering a young volunteer fighter in Barcelona, and realizing with a mixture of sadness and shock that for this boy all the tired old slogans of liberty and justice were still authentic. He cursed his own cynicism and disillusionment when he wrote:

> For the fly-blown words that make me spew
> Still in his ears were holy,
> And he was born knowing what I had learned
> Out of books and slowly.

However, after a few more verses about the lying and cruelty and stupidity that accompany war, he was still able to do a kind of justice to the brave young man:

> But the thing I saw in your face
> No power can disinherit:
> No bomb that ever burst
> Shatters the crystal spirit.

May it be so, then, and may death be not proud to have taken Mark Daily, whom I never knew but whom you now know a little, and—I hope—miss.

# Something of Myself

Ah wad some power the giftie gie us
To see ourselves as others see us.

— Robert Burns

Many men would take the death-sentence without a whimper, to escape the life-sentence which fate carries in her other hand.

— T.E. Lawrence

Plato says that the unexamined life is not worth living. But what if the examined life turns out to be a clunker as well?

— Kurt Vonnegut: *Wampeters, Foma and Granfalloons*

————◄O►————

A BOUT ONCE OR TWICE every month I engage in public debates with those whose pressing need it is to woo and to win the approval of supernatural beings. Very often, when I give my view that there is no supernatural dimension, and certainly not one that is only or especially available to the faithful, and that the natural world is wonderful enough — and even miraculous enough if you insist — I attract pitying looks and anxious questions. How, in that case, I am asked, do I find meaning and purpose in life? How does a mere and gross materialist, with no expectation of a life to come, decide what, if anything, is worth caring about?

Depending on my mood, I sometimes but not always refrain from pointing out what a breathtakingly insulting and patronizing question this is. (It is on a par with the equally subtle inquiry: Since you don't believe in our god, what stops you from stealing and lying and raping and killing to your heart's content?) Just as the answer to the latter question is: self-respect and the desire for the respect of others—while in the meantime it is precisely those who think they have divine permission who are truly capable of any atrocity—so the answer to the first question falls into two parts. A life that partakes even a little of friendship, love, irony, humor, parenthood, literature, and music, and the chance to take part in battles for the liberation of others cannot be called "meaningless" except if the person living it is also an existentialist and elects to call it so. It could be that all existence is a pointless joke, but it is not in fact possible to live one's everyday life as if this were so. Whereas if one sought to define meaninglessness and futility, the idea that a human life should be expended in the guilty, fearful, self-obsessed propitiation of supernatural nonentities...but there, there. Enough.

The clear awareness of having been born into a losing struggle need not lead one into despair. I do not especially *like* the idea that one day I shall be tapped on the shoulder and informed, not that the party is over but that it is most assuredly going on—only henceforth in my absence. (It's the second of those thoughts: the edition of the newspaper that will come out on the day after I have gone, that is the more distressing.) Much more horrible, though, would be the announcement that the party was continuing forever, and that I was forbidden to leave. Whether it was a hellishly bad party or a party that was perfectly heavenly in every respect, the moment that it became eternal and compulsory would be the precise moment that it began to pall.

A memoir of the New School for Social Research, where I have the honor to be an occasional visiting teacher, describes how in the immediate post-1945 period Erich Fromm gave a lecture on "The Struggle Against Pointlessness." I have never been able to trace even one paragraph of this talk, though I hunger to know what it said. Attending the lecture would have been many young men just out of uniform, coming to the school on the GI Bill and having just inflicted a defeat on the fascist Axis. They can hardly have considered that struggle to have been "pointless" but then what of the millions who died so horribly in Europe and Asia and who died having barely lived? What was the "point" of them, except perhaps as ghastly illustrations of a wider point?

Attempts to locate oneself within history are as natural, and as absurd, as attempts to locate oneself within astronomy. On the day that I was born, 13 April 1949, nineteen senior Nazi officials were convicted at Nuremberg, including Hitler's former envoy to the Vatican, Baron Ernst von Weizsacker, who was found guilty of planning aggression against Czechoslovakia and committing atrocities against the Jewish people. On the same day, the State of Israel celebrated its first Passover seder and the United Nations, still meeting in those days at Flushing Meadow in Queens, voted to consider the Jewish state's application for membership. In Damascus, eleven newspapers were closed by the regime of General Hosni Zayim. In America, the National Committee on Alcoholism announced an upcoming "A-Day" under the non-uplifting slogan: "You can drink — help the alcoholic who can't." (*"Can't"*?) The International Court of Justice at The Hague ruled in favor of Britain in the Corfu Channel dispute with Albania. At the UN, Soviet Foreign Minister Andrei Gromyko denounced the newly formed NATO alliance as a tool for aggression against the USSR. The rising Chinese Communists, under a man then known to Western readership as Mao Tze-Tung, announced a limited willingness to bargain with the still-existing Chinese government in a city then known to the outside world as "Peiping."

All this was unknown to me as I nuzzled my mother's breast for the first time, and would certainly have happened in just the same way if I had not been born at all, or even conceived. One of the newspaper astrologers for that day addressed those whose birthday it was:

> There are powerful rays from the planet Mars, the war god, in your horoscope for your coming year, and this always means a chance to battle if you want to take it up. Try to avoid such disturbances where women relatives or friends are concerned, because the outlook for victory upon your part in such circumstances is rather dark. If you must fight, pick a man!

Sage counsel no doubt, which I wish I had imbibed with that same maternal lactation, but impartially offered also to the many people born on that day who were also destined to die on it.

I suppose that one reason I have always detested religion is its sly tendency to insinuate the idea that the universe is designed with "you" in mind or, even worse, that there is a divine plan into which one fits whether one knows it or not. This kind of modesty is too arrogant for me. However, I have been unblushing enough to write a book that is largely about myself, and I thought it might be of interest if I said a few words about what I am actually "like." (In this, I am going by what I often feel, as a reviewer, is missing in standard works of memoir and autobiography.)

Here's one way to start. Every month, my lustrous colleagues at *Vanity Fair* select a personality and subject him or her to what is known as "The Proust Questionnaire." The great Marcel did not actually devise this form of self-interrogation, but on two occasions in his life he was seduced into answering one. I have here amalgamated the two sets of questions.

> ***What do you regard as the lowest depth of misery?*** (Just to give you an idea, Proust's reply was "To be separated from Mama.") I think that the lowest depth of misery ought to be distinguished from the highest pitch of anguish. In the lower depths come enforced idleness, sexual boredom, and/or impotence. At the highest pitch, the death of a friend or even the fear of the death of a child.
>
> ***Where would you like to live?*** In a state of conflict or a conflicted state.
>
> ***What is your idea of earthly happiness?*** To be vindicated in my own lifetime.
>
> ***To what faults do you feel most indulgent?*** To the ones that arise from urgent material needs.
>
> ***Who are your favorite heroes of fiction?*** Dennis Barlow, Humbert Humbert, Horatio Hornblower, Jeeves, Nicholas Salmanovitch Rubashov, Funes the Memorious, Lucifer.
>
> ***Who are your favorite characters in history?*** Socrates, Spinoza, Thomas Paine, Rosa Luxemburg, Leon Trotsky.
>
> ***Who are your favorite heroines in real life?*** The women of Afghanistan, Iraq, and Iran who risk their lives and their beauty to defy the foulness of theocracy. Ayaan Hirsi Ali and Azar Nafisi as their ideal feminine model.
>
> ***Who are your favorite heroines of fiction?*** Maggie Tulliver, Dorothea, Becky Sharp, Candy, O, Bertie's Aunt Dahlia.
>
> ***Your favorite painter?*** Goya, Otto Dix.
>
> ***Your favorite musician?*** J.S. Bach, Bob Dylan.

*The quality you most admire in a man?* Courage moral and physical: "anima"—the ability to think like a woman. Also a sense of the absurd.

*The quality you most admire in a woman?* Courage moral and physical: "anima"—the ability to visualize the mind and need of a man. Also a sense of the absurd.

*Your favorite virtue?* An appreciation for irony.

*Your least favorite virtue, or nominee for the most overrated one?* Faith. Closely followed—in view of the overall shortage of time—by patience.

*Your proudest achievement?* Since I can't claim the children as solely "mine," being the dedicatee of books by Salman Rushdie and Martin Amis, and poems by James Fenton and Robert Conquest.

*Your favorite occupation?* Travel in contested territory. Hard-working writing and reading when safely home, in the knowledge that an amusing friend is later coming to dinner.

*Who would you have liked to be?* Prometheus, Oscar Wilde, Emile Zola.

*Your most marked characteristic?* Insecurity.

*What do you most value in your friends?* Their continued existence.

*What is your principal defect?* Becoming bored too easily.

*What to your mind would be the greatest of misfortunes?* Loss of memory.

*What would you like to be?* One who understood music and chess and mathematics, or one who had had the courage to bear arms.

*What is your favorite color?* Blue. Sometimes red.

*What is your favorite flower?* Garlic.

*What is your favorite bird?* The owl.

*What word or expression do you most overuse?* Re-reading a collection of my stuff, I was rather startled to find that it was "perhaps."

*Who are your favorite poets?* Philip Larkin, Robert Conquest, W.H. Auden, James Fenton, W.B. Yeats, Chidiock Tichbourne, G.K. Chesterton, Wendy Cope.

*What are your favorite names?* Alexander, Sophia, Antonia, Celeste, Liam, Hannah, Elizabeth, Wolfgang.

*What is it you most dislike?* Stupidity, especially in its nastiest forms of racism and superstition.

***Which historical figures do you most despise?*** Stanley Baldwin, the Ayatollah Khomeini.

***Which contemporary figures do you most despise?*** Henry Kissinger, Osama bin Laden, Josef Ratzinger.

***Which events in military history do you most admire?*** Thermopylae, Lepanto, the defense of Little Round Top at Gettysburg, the mutinies in the German Army in 1918 and the German General Staff in 1944, the Royal Navy's Arctic convoys.

***Which natural gift would you most like to possess?*** The ability to master other languages (which would have hugely enhanced the scope of these answers).

***How would you like to die?*** Fully conscious, and either fighting or reciting (or fooling around).

***What do you most dislike about your appearance?*** The way in which it makes former admirers search for neutral words.

***What is your motto?*** *"Allons travailler!"* (This more imperative version of "Get on with it!" is annexed from Emile Zola, though E.M. Forster somewhat overextended it by enjoining us to "get on with your own work, and behave as if you were immortal.")

Though this is only a party game (which is the form in which Proust was twice persuaded to play it), it can be revealing. Reviewing my own answers, I, at any rate, can see where I give away more of myself than might be obvious. Take the answer to the question about the "principal defect." I used also to play the game of "If you were an animal, what animal would you be?" When others chose for me, I was quite frequently a fox. Lately, however, there have been quite a few nominations of "badger." This is not merely a question of my becoming stouter and more grizzled. It is the "down" side of what I consider one of my happier skills, as well. In other words, I would often rather have an argument or a quarrel than be bored, and because I hate to lose an argument, I am often willing to protract one for its own sake rather than concede even a small point.

Plainly, this unwillingness to give ground even on unimportant disagreements is the symptom of some deepseated insecurity, as was my one-time fondness for making teasing remarks (which I amended when I read Anthony Powell's matter-of-fact observation that teasing is an unfailing sign of misery within) and as is my very pronounced impatience. The struggle, therefore, is to try and cultivate the virtuous side of these shortcomings: to be a genial host while only slightly whiffled, for example, or to be witty at the expense of one's own weaknesses instead of those of other people.

I am often described to my irritation as a "contrarian" and even had the title inflicted on me by the publisher of one of my early books. (At least on that occasion I lived up to the title by ridiculing the word in my introduction to the book's first chapter.) It is actually a pity that our culture doesn't have a good vernacular word for an oppositionist or even for someone who tries to do his own thinking: the word "dissident" can't be self-conferred because it is really a title of honor that has to be won or earned, while terms like "gadfly" or "maverick" are somehow trivial and condescending as well as over-full of self-regard. And I've lost count of the number of memoirs by old comrades or ex-comrades that have titles like "Against the Stream," "Against the Current," "Minority of One," "Breaking Ranks" and so forth—all of them lending point to Harold Rosenberg's withering remark about "the herd of independent minds." Even when I was quite young I disliked being called a "rebel": it seemed to make the patronizing suggestion that "questioning authority" was part of a "phase" through which I would naturally go. On the contrary, I was a relatively well-behaved and well-mannered boy, and chose my battles with some deliberation rather than just thinking with my hormones.

I am fairly proud, therefore, that my better and longer-meditated quarrels have won me at least some respect: respect that I could have forfeited if I had missed—as the French so quenchingly say—a perfectly good opportunity for keeping my mouth shut. After years of pursuing Henry Kissinger with allegations—liar, murderer, war criminal, pseudo-academic, bore—that made many observers say in print that if he had any balls at all he'd have to sue me, he instead lost his composure and made some hysterically slanderous counterallegations, which ended up with his lawyers withdrawing rather than mine. That was well worth the time it took me.

During the 1992 election I concluded as early as my first visit to New Hampshire that Bill Clinton was hateful in his behavior to women, pathological as a liar, and deeply suspect when it came to money in politics. I have never had to take any of that back, whereas if you look up what most of my profession was then writing about the beefy, unscrupulous "New Democrat," you will be astonished at the quantity of sheer saccharine and drool. Anyway, I kept on about it even after most Republicans had consulted the opinion polls and decided it was a losing proposition, and if you look up the transcript of the eventual Senate trial of the president—only the second impeachment hearing in American history—you will see that the last order of business is a request (voted down) by the Senate majority leader to call Carol and me as witnesses. So I can dare to say that at least I saw it through.

When the late Pope John Paul II decided to place the woman so strangely known as "Mother" Teresa on the fast track for beatification, and thus to qualify her for eventual sainthood, the Vatican felt obliged to solicit my testimony and I thus spent several hours in a closed hearing room with a priest, a deacon, and a monsignor, no doubt making their day as I told off, as from a rosary, the frightful faults and crimes of the departed fanatic. In the course of this, I discovered that the pope during his tenure had surreptitiously abolished the famous office of "Devil's Advocate," in order to fast-track still more of his many candidates for canonization. I can thus claim to be the only living person to have represented the Devil *pro bono*.

Very often the test of one's allegiance to a cause or to a people is precisely the willingness to stay the course when things are boring, to run the risk of repeating an old argument just one more time, or of going one more round with a hostile or (much worse) indifferent audience. I first became involved with the Czech opposition in 1968 when it was an intoxicating and celebrated cause. Then, during the depressing 1970s and 1980s I was a member of a routine committee that tried with limited success to help the reduced forces of Czech dissent to stay nourished (and published). The most pregnant moment of that commitment was one that I managed to miss at the time: I passed an afternoon with Zdenek Mlynar, exiled former secretary of the Czech Communist Party, who in the bleak early 1950s in Moscow had formed a friendship with a young Russian militant with an evident sense of irony named Mikhail Sergeyevitch Gorbachev. In 1988 I was arrested in Prague for attending a meeting of one of Vaclav Havel's "Charter 77" committees. That outwardly exciting experience was interesting precisely because of its almost Zen-like tedium. I had gone to Prague determined to be the first visiting writer not to make use of the name Franz Kafka, but the numbing bureaucracy got the better of me. When I asked why I was being detained,

I was told that I had no need to know the reason! Totalitarianism is itself a cliché (as well as a *tundra* of pulverizing boredom) and it forced the cliché upon me in turn. I did have to mention Kafka in my eventual story. The regime fell not very much later, as I had slightly foreseen in that same piece that it would. (I had happened to notice that the young Czechs arrested with us were not at all frightened by the police, as their older mentors had been and still were, and also that the police themselves were almost fatigued by their job. This was totalitarianism practically yawning itself to death.)* A couple of years after that I was overcome to be invited to an official reception in Prague, to thank those who had been consistent friends through the stultifying years of what "The Party" had so perfectly termed "normalization." As with my tiny moment with Nelson Mandela, a whole historic stretch of nothingness and depression, combined with the long and deep insult of having to be pushed around by boring and mediocre people, could be at least partially canceled and annealed by one flash of humor and charm and generosity. That's what I meant by my "vindication" answer a few paragraphs further back.

I therefore am glad that I waited as long as I did before ingesting and digesting Marcel Proust, because one has to have endured a few decades before wanting, let alone needing, to embark on the project of recovering lost life. And I think it may be possible to review "the chronicles of wasted time." William Morris wrote in *The Dream of John Ball* that men fight for things and then lose the battle, only to win it again in a shape and form that they had not expected, and then be compelled again to defend it under another name. We are all of us very good at self-persuasion and I strive to be alert to its traps, but a version of what Hegel called "the cunning of history" is a parallel commentary that I fight to keep alive in my mind.

My deep vice of lack of patience had its worst outcome, I feel sure, in the raising of my children.

---

* In the report of our arrest in the Prague Communist paper *Rude Pravo*, another production that if read aloud could cause flying creatures to fall stunned from the sky, it was rightly reported that some of the suspicious foreigners detained were thought to be sympathizers with Leon Trotsky. As a sort of editorial nudge to keep the prejudices of the readers awake, as well as the readers themselves, there followed a parenthesis explaining that Trotsky was a pseudonym for "Bronstein." Every little bit helps, or so the crack editorial team must have thought.

Many men feel somewhat useless during the early childhood of their offspring (as well as paralyzed with admiration for the way that women seem somehow to know what to do when the babies arrive). I don't think I can take refuge in the general weakness of my sex. Confronted with infancy, I was exceptionally no good. (Anything I don't say here is only intended to spare others, not myself.) Like not a few men, I set myself to overcompensate by working ever harder, which I think has its own justification in the biologically essential task of feeding and clothing and educating one's young, but I was really marking time until they were old enough to be able to hold a conversation. And I have to face the fact that the children of both my marriages learned much, much more about manhood and nurturing from their grandparents—my magnificent in-laws—than they did from me. That is one lapse, and not just a lapse in time, that I know I shall not make up for. One cannot invent memories for other people, and the father figure for my children must be indistinct at best until quite late in their lives. There are days when this gives me inexpressible pain, and I know that such days of remorse also lie in my future. (I distinguish remorse from regret in that remorse is sorrow for what one *did* do whereas regret is misery for what one did *not* do. Both seem to be involved in this case.)

The only recourse—my own promise and vow—was and is to get a bit better as they get older. Hence this example, which I hope I'll be able to improve upon before they come and screw down the lid (or whatever it is). As he grew older, which was mostly in my absence, my firstborn son, Alexander, became ever more humorous and courageous. There came a time, as the confrontation with the enemies of our civilization became more acute, when he sent off various applications to enlist in the armed forces. I didn't want to be involved in this decision either way, especially since I was being regularly taunted for not having "sent" any of my children to fight in the wars of resistance that I supported. (As if I could "send" anybody, let alone a grown-up and tough and smart young man: what moral imbeciles the "anti-war" people have become.) Anyway, sometime late in 2007 I felt it was time that I myself went back to Iraq, and asked Alexander if he would like to come along. The plan was to limit the visit to the Kurdish north, which—as I told his mother—was reasonably safe. When we disembarked on free soil at Erbil Airport, there was a group of Kurds waiting to greet me as a friend and ally and I felt at that moment as if my boy might feel that his old father had not been entirely a jerk.*

To be the father of growing daughters is to understand something of what Yeats evokes with his imperishable phrase "terrible beauty." Nothing can make one so happily exhilarated or so frightened: it's a solid lesson in the limitations of self to realize that your heart is running around inside someone else's body. It also makes me quite astonishingly calm at the thought of death: I know whom I would die to protect and I also understand that nobody but a lugubrious serf can possibly wish for a father who never goes away.** Incidentally, I have also learned a bit about the importance of avoiding feminine embarrassment ("Daddy," wrote Sophia when she enrolled at the New School where I teach, "people will ask 'why is old Christopher Hitchens kissing that girl?'") and shall now cease and desist.

In his *Minima Moralia*, Theodor Adorno made a beautiful corkscrew or double-helix-shaped aphorism about the Hays Office, which was then the headquarters of moralistic and ideological invigilation of the movie industry. Under its unsmiling rules, no double beds could be shown, no "race-mixing," no untoward conduct or *risqué* speech. Nonetheless, ventured Adorno, an intellectually and aesthetically satisfying film could be made, observing all the limitations prescribed by the Hays Office, on the sole condition *that there was no Hays Office.*

When I first came across this morsel of condensed reflection, I realized

---

* The sequel, which I cannot *not* tell, was this. We received an invitation to come down to Baghdad, which was in those awful days considered to be lethally unsafe even in the "Green Zone." I told Alexander that it was his decision to make, and that nobody would think any the less of him for declining. He very coolly replied "But let's go," and so we did. I tried not to show how proud I was, which I now think was a mistake.

** Many writers, especially male ones, have told us that it is the decease of the father which opens the prospect of one's own end, and affords an unobstructed view of the undug but awaiting grave that says "you're next." Unfilial as this may seem, that was not at all so in my own case. It was only when I watched Alexander being born that I knew at once that my own funeral director had very suddenly, but quite unmistakably, stepped onto the stage. I was surprised by how calmly I took this, but also by how reluctant I was to mention it to my male contemporaries. That changed only when one of these, my friend Chaim Tannenbaum, invited me home to view his own first son, Moses. "You haven't met the *kaddish*," was his unforgettable way of phrasing the invitation. This was also when I appreciated the entire implication of the poem that Jorge Luis Borges had given me—see page 199.

In Paris with James Fenton and Martin Amis, 1979. *(Angela Gorgas, © Angela Gorgas)*

With Angela Gorgas, shot by Martin, Paris, 1979. *(Martin Amis and Angela Gorgas, © Angela Gorgas)*

With James
Fenton and
"The Skip."

With Martin at the
Soames house in Hamp-
shire, taking a break
from croquet, 1977.

Reviewing the situa-
tion with Martin in
Cape Cod, 1985.

Passing on our genes: with Louis Amis and Alexander Hitchens, Cape Cod, 1985.

In Cyprus with Alexander.

Shoulder to shoulder with Salman during his time in hiding: *(standing)* Andrew Wylie, SR, David Rieff, Your Humble Servant, Ian McEwan, Elizabeth West; *(foreground)* Erica Wylie, Carol Blue, and Martin Amis. *(© Elizabeth West)*

On the beach with Salman, at an undisclosed location (somewhere near West Egg, c. 1992). (© *Elizabeth West*)

With Ian and Martin in Uruguay near Charles Darwin's landfall. This is where I started writing *god Is Not Great*.

*"I begged you not to buy that book by Christopher Hitchens."*

Famous at last: the *New Yorker* knows who I am. *(© David Sipress/CondéNast Publications/ www.cartoonbank.com)*

Advising George Bush to leave Nicaragua alone and stop trading arms for hostages in Iran, at Christopher Buckley's wedding in 1984. Lucy Buckley and Camilla Horne appear to be enthusing with this advice-not-taken.

With Nelson Mandela at the British Embassy in Washington, D.C.

On *Firing Line* with William F. Buckley, Harrison Salisbury, and Robert Conquest.

Taking the oath of citizenship from Michael Chertoff on Thomas Jefferson's birthday, 2007. I am holding a copy of the Virginia Statute on Religious Freedom.

With Susan Sontag, Victor Navasky, and Carol. *(Annie Leibovitz)*

With the First Lady at Sidney Blumenthal's birthday in 1994. This was before he disgraced my other family name, and well before he became Mrs. Clinton's muck-spreader against Barack Obama in the 2008 election.

Speaking up for the *intifadah* with Edward Said at Columbia University.

Making a documentary in Scotland.

At last, a party of positive non-belief to which I can be fully committed. With Professors Daniel Dennett and Richard Dawkins and Dr. Sam Harris, at the inaugural meeting of the "Four Horsemen" faction at my home in Washington. I look and feel flattered by the implied parity. *(Photo by Josh Timonen)*

what a large role it had already played in my own life. "Let's just go in and enjoy ourselves," Yvonne had said after a long moment when the Hitchens family had silently reviewed the menu — actually of the prices not the courses — outside a restaurant on our first and only visit to Paris. I knew at once that the odds against enjoyment had shortened (or is it lengthened? I never remember). "You should be nicer to him," a schoolmate had once said to me of some awfully ill-favored boy. "He has no friends." This, I realized with a pang of pity that I can still remember, was only true as long as everybody agreed to it. There are more robust versions of the same contradiction: a plug-ugly labor union/*Cosa Nostra* figure, asked at a Senate hearing if he thought his outfit was too powerful, looked around a couple of times and leaned into the mike before saying: "Senator: being powerful's a bit like being ladylike. If you have to *say* you are, then you prolly *ain't*." British diplomats and Anglo-American types in Washington have a near-superstitious prohibition on uttering the words "Special Relationship" to describe relations between Britain and America, lest the specialness itself vanish like a phantom at cock-crow. Never ask while you are doing it if what you are doing is fun. Don't introduce even your most reliably witty acquaintance as someone who will set the table on a roar. "Martin is your best friend, isn't he?" a sweet and well-intentioned girl once said when both of us were present: it was the only time I ever felt awkward about this precious idea, which seemed somehow to risk diminishment if it were uttered aloud.

The fragility of love is what is most at stake here — humanity's most crucial three-word avowal is often uttered only to find itself suddenly embarrassing or orphaned or isolated or ill-timed — but strangely enough it can work better as a literal or reassuring statement than a transcendent or numinous or ecstatic one. Ian McEwan wrote a morally faultless essay just after the atrocities of 11 September 2001, noting that almost all voicemail messages from those on the doomed aircraft had ended with this very common trinity of words, and adding (in an almost but not quite supererogatory fashion) that by this means the murder victims had outdone and outlived their butchers.

But for me this Hays Office problem complicates the ancient question that Bertrand Russell answered (to my immense surprise) in the affirmative. If you were offered the chance to live your own life again, would you seize the opportunity? The only real philosophical answer is automatically self-contradictory: "Only if I did not know that I was doing so." To go through the entire experience once more would be banal and Sisyphean—even if it did build muscle—whereas to wish to be young again and to have the benefit of one's learned and acquired existence is not at all to wish for a repeat performance, or a Groundhog Day. And the mind ought to, but cannot, set some limits to wish-thinking. All right, same *me* but with more money, an even sturdier penis, slightly different parents, a briefer latency period...the thing is absurd. I seriously would like to know what it was to be a woman, but like blind Tiresias would also want the option of re-metamorphosing if I wished. How terrible it is that we have so many more desires than opportunities.

So I wouldn't be Hitch again, whatever the inducement. Nor would I have carried my green card in my wallet, as I loyally did every day for more than two decades (because I respected the law that said I should) if my adopted country had in fact subjected me to random stops and searches for it. Even if it were possible to cast my horoscope in this one life, and to make an accurate prediction about my future, it would not be possible to "show" it to me because as soon as I saw it my future would change by definition. This is why Werner Heisenberg's adaptation of the Hays Office—the so-called principle of uncertainty whereby the act of measuring something has the effect of altering the measurement—is of such importance. In my case the difference is often made by publicity. For example, and to boast of one of my few virtues, I used to derive pleasure from giving my time to bright young people who showed promise as writers and who asked for my help. Then some profile of me quoted someone who disclosed that I liked to do this. Then it became something widely said of me, whereupon it became almost impossible for me to go on doing it, because I started to receive far more requests than I could respond to, let alone satisfy. Perception modifies reality: when I abandoned the smoking habit of more than three decades I was given a supposedly helpful pill called Wellbutrin. But as soon as I discovered that this was the brand name for an antidepressant, I tossed the bottle away. There may be successful methods for overcoming the blues but for me they cannot include a capsule that says: "Fool yourself into happiness, while pretending not to do so." I should actually *want* my mind to be strong enough to circumvent such a trick. I try to deny myself any illusions or delusions, and I think that this perhaps entitles me to try and deny the same to others, at least as long as they refuse to keep their fantasies to themselves. Karl Marx phrased this most perfectly by saying that critics should "pluck the flowers from the chain, not so that men may wear the chain without consolation, but so that they may break the chain, and cull the living flower." So I was "a touch appalled" (as I once did hear Ronald Dworkin drawlingly say) when I read the following, in the memoir of my beloved friend Christopher Buckley. It's drawn from a speech that was delivered at his father's funeral:

> We must do what we can to bring hammer blows against the bell jar that protects the dreamers from reality. The ideal scenario is that pounding from without we can effect resonances, which will one day crack through to the latent impulses of those who dream within, bringing to life a circuit that will spare the republic.

There's a bit of metaphor mixture there—and an odd recurrence of that same "bell jar" that has shadowed me for so long—but I was beginning to swell with admiration for it until I noticed that it was a Buckleyism being cited by Henry Kissinger (during whose speech at the memorial I had stepped out into the rainswept street rather than be counted as "among" his audience). Hardest of all, as one becomes older, is to accept that sapient remarks can be drawn from the most unwelcome or seemingly improbable sources, and that the apparently more trustworthy sources can lead one astray.

Gore Vidal, for instance, once languidly told me that one should never miss a chance either to have sex or to appear on television. My efforts to live up to this maxim have mainly resulted in my passing many unglamorous hours on off-peak cable TV. It was actually Vidal's great foe William F. Buckley who launched my part-time television career, by inviting me on to *Firing Line* when I was still quite young, and giving me one of the American Right's less towering intellects as my foil. The response to the show made my day, and then my week. Yet almost every time I go to a TV studio, I feel faintly guilty. This is pre-eminently the "soft" world of dream and illusion and "perception": it has only a surrogate relationship to the "hard" world of printed words and written-down concepts to which I've tried to dedicate my life, and that surrogate relationship, while it, too, may be "verbal," consists of being glib rather than fluent, fast rather than quick, sharp rather than pointed. It means reveling in the fact that I have a meretricious, want-it-both-ways side. My only excuse is to say that at least I do not pretend that this is not so.

Another question one is frequently asked about one's life—and probably has to ask oneself—is: Under what conditions would you lose, or "give" it? I start with a slight bias against the question, which itself has some Hays Office and Heisenberg difficulties. Every November of my boyhood, we put on red poppies and attended highly patriotic services in remembrance of those who had "given" their lives. But on what assurance did we know that these gifts had really been made? Only the survivors—the living—could attest to it. In order to know that a person had truly laid down his life for his friends, or comrades, one would have to hear it from his own lips, or at least have heard it promised in advance. And that presented another difficulty. Many brave and now dead soldiers had nonetheless been conscripts. The known martyrs—those who actually, voluntarily sought death and rejoiced in the fact—had been the kamikaze pilots, immolating themselves to propitiate a "divine" emperor who looked (as Orwell once phrased it) like a monkey on a stick. Their Christian predecessors had endured torture and death (as well as inflicted it) in order to set up a theocracy. Their modern equivalents would be the suicide murderers, who mostly have the same aim in mind. About people who set out to lose their lives, then, there seems to hang an air of fanaticism: a gigantic sense of self-importance unattractively fused with a masochistic tendency to self-abnegation. Not wholesome.

The better and more realistic test would therefore seem to be: In what cause, or on what principle, would you *risk* your life? I reflect on the times when I nearly lost mine. One occasion—in Northern Ireland—I have already described on pages 147–148. If I had had a moment to think then, as my life ebbed away, my last thought would have been that I was dying while feeling, and doubtless looking, a bloody fool.* It also wouldn't even have been in a "good cause," which is how many people, including my father the Commander, most desire to picture their deaths. In my case it would have been journalistic ambition and youthful foolishness and also—since I had

---

* Our Friday lunch vernacular, that used to distinguish between "plain fools" and "damn fools," upgrading or downgrading as necessary to "bloody fool" and "fucking fool," might have classified me as the latter, also.

blundered my way into an ambush—what the British soldiers of the time rather unfeelingly called an "own goal."

In Sarajevo in 1992, while being shown around the starved, bombarded city by the incomparable John Burns, I experienced four near misses in all, three of them in the course of one day. I certainly thought that the Bosnian cause was worth fighting for and worth defending, but I could not take myself seriously enough to imagine that my own demise would have forwarded the cause. (I also discovered that a famous jaunty Churchillism had its limits: the old war-lover wrote in one of his more youthful reminiscences that there is nothing so exhilarating as being shot at without result. In my case, the experience of a whirring, whizzing horror just missing my ear was indeed briefly exciting, but on reflection made me want above all to get to the airport. Catching the plane out with a whole skin is the best part *by far*.) Or suppose I had been hit by that mortar that burst with an awful shriek so near to me, and turned into a Catherine wheel of body-parts and (even worse) body-ingredients? Once again, I was moved above all not by the thought that my death would "count," but that it would not count in the least.

I have sometimes discovered this sense, of my own relative unimportance, to be somewhat consoling. In Afghanistan a few years ago, I was stupid enough to get myself cut off and caught, in the outwardly lovely western city of Herat, hard by the Persian border, in a goons' rodeo duel between two local homicidal potentates (the journalistic euphemism for this type is "warlord"; the image of the "goons' rodeo" I have annexed from Saul Bellow). On me was not enough money, not enough food, not enough documentation, not enough *medication*, not enough bottled water to withstand even a two-day siege. I did not have a cellphone. Nobody in the world, I abruptly realized, knew where I was. I knew nobody in the town and nobody in the town knew (perhaps a good thing) who I was, either. And the local airport had been closed, so that the excrement-colored capital city of Kabul, so far away, seemed suddenly like Parnassus. As all this started to register with me, the square began to fill with those least alluring of all types: strident but illiterate young men with religious headgear, high-velocity weapons, and modern jeeps. I had the chance for one phone call, on a quavering line from the lobby of a terrible hotel. It went through, and an American Special Forces guy told me to wait just where I was. He told me later that when he first pulled up with his team, and saw me standing in the mob with a shopping bag of books and papers and a nervous grin, he thought I had "balls of brass." He soon lost that impression, and came to appreciate what a danger and nuisance I was, to myself and others. But we still see each other, and correspond (and, heroic as he is, he once soberingly told me, concerning the American presence in Afghanistan: "We're blondes out there, man. Dumb and innocent as the day is long").

After a stay in the military post, where among other things I met an officer with the surname of Marx who told me he was a Michael Moore fan, and where not one of the narcotics "enforcement" team believed in the starkly deranged "war on drugs," I got myself onto an evacuation plane that was at least pointed at the capital city. Gazing out the window at the deforested and browned-over hills that had once been vineyards, and exhaling with relief at my deliverance, I began to feel a really shocking agony in my upper jaw. Had I been clenching my teeth with anxiety over the past few days? The question soon became immaterial as I understood that something was really, deeply wrong with at least one of my fangs and tusks. I could either "do" Afghan dentistry or take the long and penitential flight home to Washington. I remember almost every second of it, mainly because I don't cry all that easily and by the time I was in Dupont Circle, I was white with misery. Of the later pain I was forced to think: Is this the sort of pang that women speak about with childbirth, where the memory simply and mercifully obliterates the recollection of what one's peeled nerves can inflict? (In those days I had the same dentist as Vice President Dick Cheney, so was able to imagine my physician's deft fingers inside those massive shark-like jaws, so ready to slam shut on any sentence to do with torture.) Finally weaned from analgesics and helpless puking, I was able to imagine—actually I obviously mean was quite *un*able to imagine—what my death would have been like if I had remained stranded in western Afghanistan and, like most people in the history of our primate species, been killed by my own teeth.

On the most recent occasions when I have faced either torture or death, the circumstances were either dubious or avoidable. My career as a writer was transfigured in 1992, when Graydon Carter succeeded Tina Brown as editor of *Vanity Fair* and asked me to become a regular columnist. In those days the magazine was commonly and misleadingly referred to as "glossy" or even "glitzy," and I privately suspected that there would be a trade-off for the many extra readers and extra dollars which I was being offered. Sooner or later would come pressure to write "down" a bit, or to simplify things for the customers, or to make certain concessions to overliteral fact-checking. (On the contrary, every copy editor and researcher on the magazine does their unstinting best to encourage you to do the same.) My bet with Graydon was essentially a simple one. In exchange for all this salary and all this freedom and all this exposure, he was to be able to ask me to write about, or to undergo, anything. A friend of mine named John Rickatson-Hatt used to say that he would try anything once "except incest and Scottish dancing." With Graydon this has translated into my saying yes to undergoing a Brazilian bikini wax, and to writing an essay on why women weren't funny as well as one on the origins of the term *blowjob*. It's led to much else besides, including volunteering to have myself waterboarded (very much more frightening though less painful than the bikini wax) and to attending a series of rallies in Beirut in the spring of 2009. One of these was nasty enough—a huge Hezbollah event in the south of the city where great phalanxes of segregated men and women gathered under a banner showing a triumphant nuclear mushroom crowd—and the other was positively inspiring in that it was a colossal, informal, unsegregated, unregimented open-air gathering of Christians, Druze, Sunni Muslims, and secularists in coalition against the Syrian bullies and assassins and their Iranian proxies. I was exalted and exuberant enough, shortly after departing the latter, to make a mistake that still sometimes causes me to whistle and twitch, and even to jerk awake.

Walking along Hamra Street, the still-fashionable boulevard of the city, I suddenly saw a swastika poster. This, I needed no telling, was the symbol of the Syrian Social Nationalist Party. (As a sort of insurance, the Asad regime in Damascus maintains not one but *two* totalitarian surrogate parties in Lebanon: the Shi'a-run Hezbollah, and the SSNP, which has historically Greek Orthodox Christian roots. This two-track sectarian policy has no effect on those who are determined to define Ba'athism as "secular.") Turning to my friends Michael Totten and Jonathan Foreman, who were my company on the stroll, I made some biting comment or other and took out my pen to deface the offending display. Not unlike the young man of Calcutta, who tried to write "fuck" on a shutter (and had got to FU, when a pious Hindu knocked him ass over tip in the gutter), I managed a four-letter word or so before being grabbed very hard from behind. A weaselly but wiry little tough guy kept hold of my jacket while speed-dialing for back-up with his other hand. How true it is that on occasions of true fear things seem to slow down and speed up: there were suddenly gaunt-looking creeps everywhere, with wolfish expressions on their faces. I had, without knowing it, disfigured a poster that commemorated one of their "martyrs."

I suppose I could see that I had a kicking of some sort in my immediate future, and I am still wet with gratitude at the way that Michael and Jonathan stuck by me when they could easily have edged away, but what scared me the most was the way the first man wouldn't let go of me. I could see the trunk of the car opening up, and one of those private-prison cellars that all Beiruti gangs so much enjoy maintaining. It was about three o'clock on a brilliantly sunny afternoon.

I got a kicking and a smacking when the gang found its courage, and suffered torn and bloody clothes and broken sunglasses (and was just very slightly mortified when Jonathan wrote later how awful it had been to see this happening to a sixty-year-old man), but in the end there were enough bystanders around to make further horror difficult for the SSNP to bring off. They did terrify one cab driver into refusing us, but a second cabbie was bolder and we contrived to speed away. As we did so, one of the pro-Asad Nazis lunged through the window and caught me a poke high on my cheekbone, aiming for my eye. The pain and damage were negligible, but the look on his face is with me still: it was like meeting the enraptured gaze of one's torturer, or staring down the gunbarrel of a twitching psychopath. I later learned that the last man in trouble on this block—a Sunni Arab journalist who had only tried to photograph the swastika flags—was still in hospital after three months' intensive care.

Attempting to salvage a rag of pride from my having fled the scene, I did my stuff as best I could. With a group of tough Druze members of the Socialist Party I went back to the same corner an hour later to find it unpatrolled. And I kept my date to speak at the American University of Beirut, a night or so after that, even though the SSNP had by then produced a nasty poster with my name and face on it. (The tough Druze Socialist posse, you can be very sure, were invited along to that event, also.) But the plain fact is that I was rattled, and that I knew perfectly well that—had I really understood what I was doing on my little anti-swastika excursion—I would not have done it.

I still make sure to go, at least once every year, to a country where things cannot be taken for granted and where there is either too much law and order or too little. (Worst of all, I have found, are those post-Hobbesian places—such as the Congo—where tyranny and anarchy manage a fearful symmetry, and occur simultaneously.) One of the articles for Graydon Carter that won me the most praise was an essay titled "Visit to a Small Planet," in which I described acquiring another identity and bribing my way into North Korea. Every time I got a tribute to the success of this piece I felt a slight access of shame, because only I could appreciate what a failure it was. I had exerted all my slack literary muscles to evoke the eerie wretchedness and interstellar frigidity of the place, which is an absolutist despotism where the slaves are no longer even fed regularly (and is thus its own version of the worst of all possible worlds), but I knew with a sick certainty that I had absolutely not managed to convey to my readers anything of how it might feel to be a North Korean even for a day. Erich Fromm might perhaps have managed it: in a place with absolutely no private or personal life, with the incessant worship of a mediocre career-sadist as the only culture, where all citizens are the permanent property of the state, the highest form of pointlessness has been achieved. When my friend Tom Driberg had come home from the British Parliament's delegation to the opening-up of the Nazi camps, he had felt himself inadequate to the task of describing them, at a dinner table which included Dylan Thomas. (It occurs to me now that perhaps a dinner table wasn't the ideal setting to begin with.) "They should send poets there," remarked Thomas. And one wishes that they had, or that some poets had gone of their own volition, if only to contest Theodor Adorno's later and highly dubious statement that after Auschwitz there could be no poetry.

My own efforts have certainly schooled me in my shortcomings as a writer, as well as proved to me what I suspected: that I lack the courage to be a real soldier or a real dissident. I have seen just enough warfare and political violence to know that, while I was pleased not to "crack" at first coming under fire, I could never be a full-time uniformed combatant or freedom fighter, or even war correspondent. And I have been arrested and locked up frequently enough—for short enough periods of time—to know that my faculties of resistance in that crucial department are slight as well. On the sole occasion when I came close to being tortured, by professional waterboarders who were nonetheless under my orders, I was so ashamed of how quickly I had been "broken" that I asked them to do it again, and lasted perhaps a few seconds longer for the sake of appearances.

# A Short Footnote on the Grape and the Grain

In the continuing effort to gain some idea of how one appears to other people, nothing is more useful than exposing oneself to an audience of strangers in a bookstore or a lecture hall. Very often, for example, sitting anxiously in the front row are motherly-looking ladies who, when they later come to have their books inscribed, will say such reassuring things as: "It's so nice to meet you in person: I had the impression that you were so angry and maybe unhappy." I hadn't been at all aware of creating this effect. (One of them, asking me to sign her copy of my *Letters to a Young Contrarian*, said to me wistfully: "I bought a copy of this to give to my son, hoping he'd become a contrarian, but he refused." Adorno would have appreciated the paradox.)

More affecting still is the anxious, considerate way that my hosts greet me, sometimes even at the airport, with a large bottle of Johnnie Walker Black Label. It's almost as if they feel that they must propitiate the demon that I bring along with me. Interviewers arriving at my apartment frequently do the same, as if appeasing the insatiable. I don't want to say anything that will put even a small dent into this happy practice, but I do feel that I owe a few words. There was a time when I could reckon to outperform all but the most hardened imbibers, but I now drink relatively carefully. This ought to be obvious by induction: on average I produce at least a thousand words of printable copy every day, and sometimes more. I have never missed a deadline. I give a class or a lecture or a seminar perhaps four times a month and have never been late for an engagement or shown up the worse for wear. My boyish visage and my mellifluous tones are fairly regularly to be seen and heard on TV and radio, and nothing will amplify the slightest slur more than the studio microphone. (I think I did once appear on the BBC when fractionally whiffled, but those who asked me about it later were not sure whether I was not, a few days after September 11, a bit angry as well as a bit tired.) Anyway, it should be obvious that I couldn't do all of this if I was what the English so bluntly call a "piss-artist."

It's the professional deformation of many writers, and has ruined not a few. (I remember Kingsley Amis, himself no slouch, saying that he could tell on what page of the novel Paul Scott had reached for the bottle and thrown caution to the winds.) I work at home, where there is indeed a bar-room, and can suit myself. But I don't. At about half past midday, a decent slug of Mr. Walker's amber restorative, cut with Perrier water (an ideal delivery system) and *no ice*. At luncheon, perhaps half a bottle of red wine: not always more but never less. Then back to the desk, and ready to repeat the treatment at the evening meal. No "after dinner drinks" — most especially nothing sweet and never, ever any brandy. "Nightcaps" depend on how well the day went, but always the mixture as before. *No mixing*: no messing around with a gin here and a vodka there.

Alcohol makes other people less tedious, and food less bland, and can help provide what the Greeks called *entheos*, or the slight buzz of inspiration when reading or writing. The only worthwhile miracle in the New Testament — the transmutation of water into wine during the wedding at Cana — is a tribute to the persistence of Hellenism in an otherwise austere Judaea. The same applies to the seder at Passover, which is obviously modeled on the Platonic symposium: questions are asked (especially of the young) while wine is circulated. No better form of sodality has ever been devised: at Oxford one was positively expected to take wine during tutorials. The tongue must be untied. It's not a coincidence that Omar Khayyam, rebuking and ridiculing the stone-faced Iranian mullahs of his time, pointed to the value of the grape as a mockery of their joyless and sterile regime. Visiting today's Iran, I was delighted to find that citizens made a point of defying the clerical ban on booze, keeping it in their homes for visitors even if they didn't particularly take to it themselves, and bootlegging it with great *brio* and ingenuity. These small revolutions affirm the human.

At the wild Saturnalia that climaxes John Steinbeck's *Tortilla Flat*, the charismatic Danny manages to lay so many women that, afterward, even the females who didn't receive his attentions prefer to claim, rather than appear to have been overlooked, that they were included, too. I can't make any comparable boast but quite often I get second-hand reports about people who claim to have spent evenings in my company that belong to song, story, and legend when it comes to the Dionysian. I once paid a visit to the grotesque holding-pen that the United States government maintains at Guantánamo Bay in Cuba. There wasn't an unsupervised moment on the whole trip, and the main meal we ate—a heavily calorific affair that was supposed to demonstrate how well-nourished the detainees were—was made even more inedible by the way that water (with the option of a can of Sprite) flowed like wine. Yet a few days later I ran into a friend at the White House who told me half-admiringly: "Way to go at Guantánamo: they say you managed to get your own bottle and open it down on the beach and have a party." This would have been utterly unfeasible in that bizarre Cuban enclave, half-*madrassa* and half-stockade, but it was still completely and willingly believed. Publicity means that actions are judged by reputations and not the other way about: I never wonder how it happens that mythical figures in religious history come to have fantastic rumors credited to their names.

"Hitch: making rules about drinking can be the sign of an alcoholic," as Martin Amis once teasingly said to me. (Adorno would have savored that, as well.) Of course, watching the clock for the start-time is probably a bad sign, but here are some simple pieces of advice for the young. Don't drink on an empty stomach: the main point of the refreshment is the enhancement of food. Don't drink if you have the blues: it's a junk cure. Drink when you are in a good mood. Cheap booze is a false economy. It's not true that you shouldn't drink alone: these can be the happiest glasses you ever drain. Hangovers are another bad sign, and you should not expect to be believed if you take refuge in saying you can't properly remember last night. (If you *really* don't remember, that's an even worse sign.) Avoid all narcotics: these make you more boring rather than less and are not designed—as are the grape and the grain—to enliven company. Be careful about up-grading too far to single malt Scotch: when you are voyaging in rough countries it won't be easily available. Never even think about driving a car if you have taken a drop. It's much worse to see a woman drunk than a man: I don't know quite why this is true but it just is. Don't ever be responsible for it.

# Thinking Thrice about the Jewish Question...

> The Jewish people and their fate are the living witness for the absence of redemption. This, one could say, is the meaning of the chosen people; the Jews are chosen to prove the absence of redemption.
>
> —Leo Strauss: "Why We Remain Jews" [1962]

> I think I may well be a Jew.
>
> —Sylvia Plath: "Daddy" [1962]

In the early days of the December that my father was to die, my younger brother brought me the news that I was a Jew. I was then a transplanted Englishman in America, married, with one son, and, though unconsoled by any religion, a nonbelieving member of two Christian churches. On hearing the tidings, I was pleased to find that I was pleased.

Immediately above is the opening paragraph of my essay for Ben Sonnenberg's quarterly *Grand Street* in the summer of 1988. It was reprinted quite a bit, and gave the eponymous title to my first collection of essays, *Prepared for the Worst*. It was my earliest and until now my only excursion into memoir, was largely positive and even upbeat if only because my semi-Semitism was on my mother's side rather than, as with Sylvia Plath, a distraught paternal bequest, and it closed with the easily uttered words "To be continued..."

For the first forty-odd years of my life I had thought of myself as English, latterly with ambitions to become an Anglo-American. This national self-definition underwent an interesting change as a consequence of my maternal grandmother's outliving both of my parents. Yvonne took her own life at a distressingly young age. My father's robust health began to fail him in his late seventies and he died in late 1987. My brother, Peter, in the meantime, had become engaged to a Jewish girl and had taken her to meet "Dodo"—old Mrs. Dorothy Hickman—our only surviving grandparent. Later, and after she'd congratulated him on his choice, she rather disconcerted Peter by saying: "She's Jewish, isn't she?" He had agreed that this was the case and then she'd disconcerted him even further by saying, "Well, I've got something to tell you. So are you."

How had this taken so long to emerge, and why was it still to be counted as a family secret? My mother had not wanted anyone to know, and indeed my father had been all his life unaware of the fact, and was to remain so to the end. I have now been back through all the possible recollections and am fairly sure that I can guess the reason, but here's the trail I followed.

In what was once German Prussia, in the district of Posen and very near the border of Poland, there was a town called Kempen which had, for much of its existence, a Jewish majority. (It is now called Kempno and is about an hour's drive from the Polish city of Wrocław, formerly Breslau.) A certain Mr. Nathaniel Blumenthal, born in Kempen in 1844, decided to leave or was possibly taken by his parents, but at all events arrived in the English Midlands and, though he married "out," became the father of thirteen Orthodox children. It appears that he had disembarked at Liverpool (the joke among English Jews is that some of the duller emigrants did that, imagining that they had already reached New York) and settled in Leicester by 1871. On later census forms he gives his occupation as "tailor." In 1893, one of old Nate's daughters married a certain Lionel Levin, of Liverpool (the Levins also hailing originally from the Posen/Poznan area), and the British bureaucracy's marriage certificates certify them as having been wed "according to the rites of the German and Polish Jews." My mother's mother, whose birth name was Dorothy Levin, was born three years later, in 1896.

It doesn't seem to have taken them long to decide on assimilation, in that by the time of the First World War the Blumenthal family name had become

"Dale" and the Levins were called "Lynn." This might have had something
to do with the general revulsion against German names at that epoch, when
even the British Royal Family scrapped its Saxe-Coburg-Gotha titles and
became the House of Windsor, conveniently metamorphosing other names
like "Battenberg" into "Mountbatten." But nominal assimilation didn't quite
extend to the religious kind. Dodo could recall drawing the curtains on Friday night and bringing out the menorah, and also fasting on Yom Kippur
("even if only for my figure, dear"), but she also remembered being discreet
about this because in Oxford, where my great-grandparents had by then
moved, there was a bit of low-level prejudice.

My father had died very soon after Peter brought me the Jewish news,
and I had flown over to England for the funeral (which Dodo was too frail
to attend) and then gone at once to see her. What I wanted to understand
was this: How had I been so incurious, and so easily deceived? She seemed
determined to act the part of a soap-opera Jewish granny ("I could always see
it in you and your brother: you both had the Jewish brains..."), and she certainly and rather abruptly *looked* Jewish to me, which she hadn't while I was
growing up. Or perhaps better to say, when I was a boy I wasn't in any sense
Jew-conscious: Dodo had dark ringletted hair and a complexion to match,
and when I registered this at all, it was with the stray thought that she looked
like a gypsy. But when you are young you take your relatives for granted,
and even if you do ask childishly awkward questions you tend to accept the
answer. "Hickman" wasn't an especially exotic name—my mother used to
laugh that she couldn't wait to get rid of it and then wound up marrying a
Hitchens—and when Peter and I asked what had happened to Dodo's husband, we were hushed with the information that he had "died in the war."
Since all family stories of all kinds were always about "the war" we accepted
this without question, as being overwhelmingly probable. It was years later
when Peter discovered that Dodo had been married to a drunken and adul-
terous wife-beater, Lionel Hickman by name, who had continued our *mischling* tradition by converting to Judaism in order to marry her, given her an
all-around vile time, and then been run over by a tram during the blackout
that accompanied the Nazi blitzkrieg. Killed in the war, to be sure.

As I sat with the old lady in her little suburban parlor in the south London
suburbs, I kept asking myself if I had any memories that might amount to

premonitions of, or other awarenesses of, this heritage. Once one starts looking for such things, I know, the chance of "discovering" them has a tendency
to increase. There on the mantelpiece was a photograph of Yvonne, looking
young and blonde and venturesome and obviously quite well equipped to
"pass" as a Gentile. "She didn't much want to be a Jew," said Dodo, "and I
didn't think your father's family would have liked the idea, either. So we just
decided to keep it to ourselves." This was becoming dispiriting. My father
had been a reactionary and a pessimist—the *Private Eye* caricatures of Denis
Thatcher had always reminded me of his insistently Eeyore-ish tone, sometimes taken up by my brother—but not at all a bigot. If anything about
Yvonne's ethnic background might have given him check or pause, it would
have been the discovery that her ancestors had identified themselves as German. The Commander's view, echoing that of the Morgenthau Plan, was
that post-1945 Germany would have been better if totally depopulated...
But this he would not have thought of as a prejudice.

I was suddenly visited by a long-ago memory of my father's father, breaking into a harangue when it became generally known in family circles that
his elder grandson had declared for the Labour Party and for socialism. This
must therefore have been about 1964 or perhaps, given the glacial pace at
which news was delivered on his side of the family, as late as 1965 or '66. He
favored me, I remember, in his rather grinding and harsh Portsmouth tones,
with a sort of bestiary of sinister surnames, all tending to show the unsound-
ness of Labour's then-parliamentary Left. I can remember it now: "Look at
them: Sidney *Silverman*, John *Mendelson*, Tom *Driberg*, Ian *Mikardo*" (this
last a Portsmouth lad into whom, along with the fat-headed future Labour
Prime Minister James Callaghan, my schoolmaster grandpa had attempted
to wallop the rudiments of an education). At the time I hadn't any idea what
he meant to convey by all this, unless it was to identify unpatriotically German names—my later pal Tom Driberg had suffered cognomen-persecution
all his life without being in the least Jewish—but I was later able to guess
by a sort of reverse-engineering.* The old man was very forbidding in manner at the best of times: I can't imagine what it would have been like for my

---

* I should say in fairness that my brother, Peter, firmly believes that the latter explanation—
ordinary xenophobia rather than Jew-hatred in other words—is the likelier explanation.

mother, let alone her mother, to be introduced to the patriarch in 1945, when her marriage to the Commander was first mooted. One of the Commander's very few surviving letters makes my point for me: it's to his brother Ray and is dated 28 March 1945, from HMS *Jamaica*, which means that the warship must have been lying at anchor in the nearby Portsmouth harbor:

> Dear Ray,
>
> Many thanks for your letter of felicitation. Yes I quite agree that it *does* need a sense of proportion to enter the homestead and emerge unscathed and I thought it as well to put Yvonne through this acid test before enquiring whether she was further interested...

I don't think it would or could have taken Yvonne very long to decide against embarking upon some easy chat with her prospective father-in-law, about the long line of milliners, tailors, kosher butchers, and (to be fair) dentists from which I now know she had sprung. Looking back, I can't see my grandpa ever having had much use for any of the above professions. What he liked, or what I remember him liking, was lavishly illustrated histories of Protestant missionaries in Africa. On this topic, she could have been of little comfort or joy to him.

Sitting now with Dodo and recalling all this, I had to ask myself what Jewishness had meant to me, if anything, when I was a boy. I was completely sure that it meant nothing at all until I was thirteen, except as a sort of subtext to the Christian Bible stories with which I had been regaled at prep school. In some odd fashion the Nazarene Jesus had been a sort of rabbi, and horribly executed under the mocking title of "King of the Jews," but it had also been the Jews who most thirsted for his torture and death. Very, very occasionally some boy would make a mean or meaning or even demeaning remark about this, but in my early life there were no actual Jewish targets at which to direct such stuff. Moreover, the Nuremberg trials were a recent memory and, though most of our TV and movie fare still made it seem as if the Second World War had been a personal matter between Hitler and the better sort of English or British person, there were moments of documentary footage which showed the barely conceivable human detritus of the Final Solution, being bulldozed into mass graves. My mother in my hearing, when I was very small, had once used the expression "anti-Semitism" and I remember feeling with a sort of qualm that without having it fully explained, I somehow knew what it meant.

In Cambridge later on, there were Jewish boys at the school, and I suppose I noticed that they tended to have curlier hair and fleshier noses, rather as I had been led to expect. They also had names which were different—Perutz, the son of the Nobel Prize winner; Kissin, the clever boy who recommended that everyone read the *New Statesman*; Wertheimer, who wore a big lapel-button saying that "Hanging Is Murder." They were among the few support-ers of my failed Labour campaign of 1964 and I suppose that, subliminally, they confirmed my grandfather's view that there was something almost axi-omatically subversive about Jewishness. In history classes I read about the Dreyfus case and in English class wrote a defense of Shylock against his Venetian tormentors. There was mild, occasional anti-Jewish vulgarity to be heard among some of the more dense boys—always a version of the same cliché about the Jews being over-sharp in business—but one almost never saw or heard it directed at an actual Jew.

In the summer of 1967, between my leaving my boarding school and going to Oxford, and while I was undergoing my long-distance postal mentorship with Peter Sedgwick, the various Arab "republics" and feudal monarchies made common cause, it seemed, in a war to extinguish the State of Israel. It seemed to me obvious that here was a tiny state, clinging to the seaboard of the Eastern Mediterranean, and faced not with defeat but with existential oblitera-tion. Like many leftists of the time, I sympathized by instinct with the Jewish state. I didn't do so completely without misgivings: I had heard so many foam-flecked Tories raving on about the hated "Nasser" ever since the Suez war of 1956 that I was on my guard at hearing the same rhetoric again. And I sent off in the mail for a pamphlet that was co-produced by the "Israeli Socialist Orga-nization" and the "Palestine Democratic Front," a screed which purported to offer a nonsectarian solution but also proved to be written in a jargon that was based on no known language. Events anyway outpaced the pamphlet. Israel's paratroopers were soon at the Wailing Wall and at Sharm el-Sheikh, and all the braggadocio of Nasserism rhetoric was shown as both rather empty and rather hateful. In those days I still thought, as most people did, of the struggle between Israel and "the Arabs" and not Israel and the Palestinians.

"But just look how the press treats the Israelites [*sic*]," said Dodo with indignation, abolishing my reverie and recalling me to the unchanging present in this respect. "We've never been liked, you know. I suppose I shouldn't say it, but I think it's because they're jealous." By this stage of my life I knew slightly too much to accept this ancient self-pity as the explanation of everything, but I didn't want to have an argument with my sweet and sad old grandma so I took my leave and, turning at her little garden gate, somewhat awkwardly uttered the salute "Shalom!" She responded, "Shalom, shalom" as easily as if we'd always greeted and parted this way and, as I wrote it down at the time, I turned and trudged off to the station in the light, continuous English rain that was also my birthright.

# Landscapes of Memory

"The deep, deep sleep of England," wrote Orwell half-admiringly and half-despairingly about the eternal and unchanging charm of the southern English countryside as seen from the train between the English Channel and London itself. Being newly returned from the ever-freshening hells of the Spanish Civil War, he remembered enough to add rather severely that England might not jerk out of this slumber until it was abruptly roused by the roar and crash of bombs. (Not far from the peaceful, rural Anglican churchyard in which he lies buried are the Cotswold villages of Upper and Lower Slaughter. Upper Slaughter is almost the only village in England that does *not* have a war memorial to commemorate the fallen of 1914–1918. These few hamlets are known in the war-memorial literature as "blessed," if you can imagine such a designation. What does that make the dead of the other hamlets?)

Even though I grew up in south coast naval towns where whole sleeves of streetscape had been stripped to show the scars of Nazi bombardment, I never failed to be struck by how swiftly one could slip from the city, into the woods or along the back roads and onto the downs, and be transported*

---

* All right, even the word "transported" has its nasty modern ring of deportation. Indeed, the early martyrs of the British Labour movement were peasants from the Dorset village so bewitchingly named Tolpuddle who were transported to Australia for the offense of forming a union.

into a landscape that was almost contemplative in its quietude. The off-beat names of the Hampshire and Sussex villages—Warblington was one of my favorites, with its flinted Saxon church, but East and indeed West Wittering ran it pretty close—seemed to convey a near Wodehousian and Blandings-like beatitude and serenity. There were two especially favorite places within an easy drive, one of them the renowned Selbourne, where Gilbert White had observed the ecology of just one little place in order to produce a micro-masterpiece of natural history, and then Chawton, near Alton. Some readers may already have caught their breath, I hope enviously.

It was as easy as breathing to go and have tea near the place where Jane Austen had so wittily scribbled and so painfully died. One of the things that causes some critics to marvel at Miss Austen is the laconic way in which, as a daughter of the epoch that saw the Napoleonic Wars, she contrives like a Greek dramatist to keep it off the stage while she concentrates on the human factor. I think this comes close to affectation on the part of some of her admirers. Captain Frederick Wentworth in *Persuasion*, for example, is partly of interest to the female sex because of the "prize" loot he has extracted from his encounters with Bonaparte's navy. Still, as one born after Hiroshima I can testify that a small Hampshire township, however large the number of names of the fallen on its village-green war memorial, is more than a world away from any unpleasantness on the European mainland or the high or narrow seas that lie between. (I used to love the detail that Hampshire's "New Forest" is so called because it was only planted for the hunt in the late eleventh century.) I remember watching with my father and brother through the fence of Stanstead House, the Sussex mansion of the Earl of Bessborough, one evening in the early 1960s, and seeing an immense golden meadow carpeted entirely by grazing rabbits. I'll never keep that quiet, or be that still, again.

This was around the time of countrywide protest against the introduction of a horrible laboratory-confected disease, named "myxomatosis," into the warrens of old England to keep down the number of nibbling rodents. Richard Adams's lapine masterpiece *Watership Down* is the remarkable work that it is, not merely because it evokes the world of hedgerows and chalk-downs and streams and spinneys better than anything since *The Wind in the Willows*, but because it is only really possible to imagine gassing and massacre and organized cruelty on this ancient and green and gently rounded landscape if it is organized and carried out against herbivores.

In the German tongue, in the Polish town
Scraped flat by the roller
Of wars, wars, wars...

—Sylvia Plath: "Daddy" (1962)

"If this is Upper Silesia," observed P.G. Wodehouse after being interned in Poland by the Nazis in 1940, "what on earth must Lower Silesia be like?" He was being flippant, but with the excuse that he could have had no idea of what was about to make this region famous.

When it came time for me to make my "roots" visit, in search of my mother's Polish and German ancestors, it was actually for the lower-lying latitudes of Silesia that I set off. The city of Wrocław, which until 1945 had been called Breslau, was the big historic melting-pot town that set the tone even for places across the Prussian border like Kempen/Kempno. When Dodo and others spoke of the place of their forebears, it was "Breslau" that they rather proudly if sadly named. And it was easy to see why. There was nothing provincial about it. In his book *Microcosm*, co-written with Roger Moorhouse, Norman Davies illustrates its eminence as a hub of Bohemian and Prussian life as well as the epicenter of the Silesian question, itself the trigger of the Seven Years' War. "Wars, wars, wars": reading up on the region I came across one moment when quintessential Englishness had in fact intersected with this darkling plain. In 1906 Winston Churchill, then the minister responsible for British colonies, had been honored by an invitation from Kaiser Wilhelm II to attend the annual maneuvers of the Imperial German Army, held at Breslau. The Kaiser was "resplendent in the uniform of the White Silesian Cuirassiers" and his massed and regimented infantry...

reminded one more of great Atlantic rollers than human formations. Clouds of cavalry, avalanches of field-guns and — at that time a novelty — squadrons of motor-cars (private and military) completed the

array. For five hours the immense defilade continued. Yet this was
only a twentieth of the armed strength of the regular German Army
before mobilization.

Strange to find Winston Churchill and Sylvia Plath both choosing the word
"roller," in both its juggernaut and wavelike declensions, for that scene.

I had a ghost or two at my elbow the entire time I was on (what is now)
Polish soil. These revenants were of two kinds. The first, which was the nicest, had been gently summoned by my relatives known and unknown. Every
article and review and book that I have ever published has constituted an
appeal to the person or persons to whom I should have talked before I dared
to write it. I never launch any little essay without the hope—and the fear,
because the encounter may also be embarrassing—that I shall draw a letter
that begins, "Dear Mr. Hitchens, it seems that you are unaware that..." It is
in this sense that authorship is collaborative with "the reader." And there's no
help for it: you only find out what you ought to have known by pretending
to know at least some of it already.

It doesn't matter how obscure or arcane or esoteric your place of publication may be: some sweet law ensures that the person who should be scrutinizing your work eventually does do so. Thus I came into contact with a woman
who was, or would have been if they had known of each other, and thus was
anyway, my mother's first cousin. She now lived on the coast of Norfolk. One
of her Blumenthal/Dale relatives had seen one of the reprints of my original
article for Ben Sonnenberg, to which I had given the additional title: "On
Not Knowing the Half of It." Cast your bread on the waters...I'll condense
the time that all this took but simply say that by the time I arrived in Poland
I had a goodish oil-painting portrait of Nathan Blumenthal, a fair piece of
his genealogy, and two chief questions remaining. Why had he left when he
did, and were there any of his relations still around?

Jane Austen died two years after the Battle of Waterloo, where the combined forces of the Duke of Wellington and (as some British historians
remember to mention) the Prussians under Marshal Blucher put an end to
the Napoleonic era. On the territories of the Prussian/Silesian frontier, the
echoes of this and later events are very far from being "noises off." In particular was this true for the Jews of Kempen/Kempno. In 1812 Napoleon

had issued his emancipation decree, liberating the Jews from ancient church-mandated legal disabilities. In 1814/1815 the Kempen Jews had begun the construction of a rather magnificent synagogue in a sort of neo-Palladian style. At the time, they constituted perhaps eighty percent of the town. I found it unsettling yet confirming to think of this side of my mitochondrial DNA being replicated in this context: I have had my mother's wing of my genetic ancestry analyzed by the *National Geographic* tracing service and there it all is: the arrow moving northward from the African savannah, skirting the Mediterranean by way of the Levant, and passing through Eastern and Central Europe before crossing to the British Isles. And all of this knowable by an analysis of the cells on the inside of my mouth.

I almost prefer the more rambling and indirect and journalistic investigation, which seems somehow less...deterministic. In Breslau/Wrocław, where I arrived on the day that Professor Leszek Kolakowski died, a national hero, and was honored to be invited to speak at a meeting in his memory, I was lucky to be introduced to Mr. Jerzy Kichler, the head of the local Jewish community and a veteran of the Polish-Jewish diaspora. He also helps curate the city's Jewish cemetery, around which he guided me. It's like a memorial to Atlantis or Lyonesse: these are the stone buoys that mark a drowned world. From this city came the parents of Edith Stein, later martyred as a convert to Catholicism (and as a nun) in Auschwitz. Max Born, the Nobel laureate in physics in 1954—and the man to whom Einstein wrote that celebrated 1926 letter about god's refusal to play dice with the universe—was born here, to a father who hailed from Kempen. (Max's daughter Irene moved to Cambridge and married a leader of the Enigma/Ultra disencryption team: their daughter became famous under the name Olivia Newton-John.) Born's conversion to Lutheranism did him no more good than Edith Stein's when the Nazis applied their own laws about who was a Jew. Dietrich Bonhoeffer, another son of this place, had a twin sister who married a converted Jew. He was hanged in Flossenburg concentration camp—his murder commemorated in one of W.H. Auden's weaker poems—on almost the last day of the war in April 1945.

One must beware of the temptation to invest everything with significance in retrospect, yet it chills the soul a bit to learn that from this great city-center of humane science and medicine, which produced the good doctor Alois

Alzheimer as well as the physicist Max Born, Professor Fritz Haber moved his operations to Berlin in 1914 in order to place his chemistry skills at the service of a military government in search of weapons of mass destruction. (He oversaw the German chlorine-gas attack at Ypres and after 1918 concerned himself with the development of Zyklon-B, thus radically attenuating his own posterity.)

Mr. Kichler was an excellent guide through all this, offering information when it was requested and leaving me alone when I seemed to need that. Together we made a point of visiting the tomb of Ernst Geiger, one of the originators of Reform Judaism, and of Ferdinand Lassalle, founder of the first German Social Democratic party (who in a private letter from Karl Marx to Friedrich Engels had been rather regrettably described as a "Jewish nigger"). He had been born on 13 April, the birthday that I share with Thomas Jefferson, Seamus Heaney, Alan Clark, Eudora Welty, and Orlando Letelier. The dates and the territory could also be made to "fit" with my own historical obsessions: when Nathan Blumenthal was born in 1844, Marx was just beginning to publish his *Economic and Philosophical Manuscripts* in the Rhineland to the west and, by the time he first turned up in English paperwork in 1871, Rosa Luxemburg was being born, in the Russian-Polish town of Zamość far to the east.

Between these two points lay a sort of burned-over district, charred and trampled and desecrated in every direction and in every fashion. Trotsky had referred to the Hitler-Stalin pact as "the midnight of the century," and it was across this terrain that the midnight had fallen. Wrocław/Breslau lies along the River Oder and boasts more than a hundred bridges. One of the best ways to see it is like Venice, from the various "arms" and "shoulders," as the natives say, of the waterways. Between it and Kempen/Kempno are many rolling fields and green copses and forests, both coniferous and deciduous. But even the greenery can seem bleak at best or menacing at worst, when one recalls what was done in the shadow of those trees.

At least in Wrocław/Breslau the old "White Stork" synagogue had been restored, for a community of a few hundred, and the Jewish cemetery's stones when possible repaired or re-lapidated. But in Kempen/Kempno there was only desolation. Trying to translate back to English landscape, one would need to be evoking Oliver Goldsmith or Thomas Gray, or John Clare, on the abandonment and emptiness. But even that would be relative, and as much to do with the loss of sheep as the loss of people. Old Mr. Kichler and I could easily have missed—and nearly did miss—the turnoff for the town. An obscure crossroads, some railway tracks intersecting, a large and illuminated McDonald's hamburger sign: this could have been a nondescript Nowheres-ville in mid-prairie America. The local nickname for the eastern or Yiddish part of Kempen/Kempno was, it turned out, "Kamchatka"—the most extreme part of Siberia. Nobody quite seemed to know how such an irretrievably bare title came to be conferred, but it seemed apt enough. And the place seemed bizarrely unpeopled: when I later looked at the photographs I had taken, there wasn't a soul to be seen. My late friend Amos Elon has written the best history of the German-Jewish relationship: it's called *The Pity of It All*. I was very stirred to find, when I opened it, that he had placed on his epigraph page the opening lines of James Fenton's poem "A German Requiem":

> It is not what they built. It is what they knocked down.
> It is not the houses. It is the spaces between the houses.
> It is not the streets that exist. It is the streets that no longer exist.

The lines recurred to me as I heard the echo of my footsteps. The noble old synagogue had been profaned and turned into a stable by the Nazis, and left open to the elements by the Communists, at least after they had briefly employed it as a "furniture facility." It had then been vandalized and perhaps accidentally set aflame by incurious and callous local "youths." Only the well-crafted walls really stood, though a recent grant from the European Union had allowed a makeshift roof and some wooden scaffolding to hold up and enclose the shell until further notice. Adjacent were the remains of a *mikvah* bath for the ritual purification of women, and a kosher abattoir for the ritual slaughter of beasts: I had to feel that it was grotesque that these obscurantist relics were the only ones to have survived. In a corner of the yard lay a pile of smashed stones on which appeared inscriptions in Hebrew and sometimes Yiddish. These were all that remained of the gravestones. There wasn't a Jew left in the town, and there hadn't been one, said Mr. Kichler, since 1945.

As we paged through the surviving municipal records, it actually became fairly easy to see how a once-flourishing community might have decided to start emigrating well before that, and at about the time that Nathan had. Subsequent to the 1812 Napoleonic edict abolishing anti-Jewish laws, the indigenous religious prejudices had reasserted themselves. Starting in 1833 there had been a series of Prussian measures, often associated with the name of a statesman named Wagner, increasing taxes for Jews and making them pay for the upkeep of Christian schools and institutions, as well as adding to their burden of military service. After the aspirations of 1848 had been crushed, it got worse yet: the leader of the ultraright authoritarians in the Prussian state parliament became Professor Friedrich Julius Stahl. (He'd been born Joel Golson, and it wasn't enough for him to have converted to that bastardization of primitive Judaism known as Christianity: no, like Stalin after him he also wanted a surname of steel.) Amos Elon takes up the story:

> In the largest German state, where two-thirds of the Jewish population lived, he enunciated the "philosophical" basis for continuing discrimination against his former co-religionists. He was not a great thinker but an able propagandist, persuasively articulating the conservative demand for "authority" and the sacred union of church and throne.

1848 had been a year of revolution and liberation for much of Europe, but other people's ardent nationalism isn't always, as they say, "good for the Jews." It seemed probable that the brighter members of the Blumenthal clan would have seen and felt the atmosphere thickening. In this period, also, according to the records, there had been quite a severe epidemic of cholera. Outbreaks like that aren't always good for the Jews either: they sometimes even manage to get themselves blamed for the plague, or for the poisoning of the wells.

But had the family left anyone behind? It's a common enough name so I wasn't sure how I would be able to distinguish between cadet and collateral branches, but the necessity for making such a discrimination was soon enough removed from me. The editor of the local newspaper, Mr. Miroslaw Lapa, had produced an illustrated history of the Jews of Kempen/Kempno, titled in Polish *Kepinscy Zydzi*. Its photographs showed some of the major splendors, including the imposing temple in its high old times and the family groups gathered contentedly in front of thriving shops. There were few pictures of the later miseries, but there were some lists of names...Every Blumenthal I could find in the index had wound up on the transports to Auschwitz. So that was that.

I once spoke to someone who had survived the genocide in Rwanda, and she said to me that there was now nobody left on the face of the earth, either friend or relative, *who knew who she was.* No one who remembered her girl-hood and her early mischief and family lore; no sibling or boon companion who could tease her about that first romance; no lover or pal with whom to reminisce. All her birthdays, exam results, illnesses, friendships, kinships — gone. She went on living, but with a *tabula rasa* as her diary and calendar and notebook. I think of this every time I hear of the callow ambition to "make a new start" or to be "born again": Do those who talk this way truly wish for the slate to be wiped? Genocide means not just mass killing, to the level of extermination, but mass obliteration to the verge of extinction. You wish to have one more reflection on what it is to have been made the object of a "clean" sweep? Try Vladimir Nabokov's microcosmic miniature story "Signs and Symbols," which is about angst and misery in general but also succeeds in placing it in what might be termed a starkly individual perspective. The album of the distraught family contains a faded study of

> Aunt Rosa, a fussy, angular, wild-eyed old lady, who had lived in a tremulous world of bad news, bankruptcies, train accidents, cancerous growths — until the Germans put her to death, together with all the people she had worried about.

We live only a few conscious decades, and we fret ourselves enough for several lifetimes. The various eggs and zygotes and other ingredients necessary for the subsequent conception and generation of the non–Anglo-Saxon half of the present author thus continued migrating, rather like the lucky and clever rabbits who left for Watership Down in good time, before the nozzles of poison had been callously shoved into the inlets of the ecology. Lonely and uncertain and angst-burdened as my grandmother's and mother's lives were in some ways to be, they took place in refulgent sunshine compared to what they had missed by their forebears having gotten the hell out of Kempno.

I still wasn't completely done with my investigations of this enthrallingly upsetting region of the past. In the case of another relative—my ancestor-in-law David Szmulevski, a sort of great-uncle—the trail also went as far as Auschwitz but just for once did not end there. Born in the town of Kolo in the Poznan district in 1912, this man had a crepuscular existence on the edge of my family's awareness. He had, it was said, been a leading anti-Nazi resister. He owns a chapter to himself in the anthology *They Fought Back*, a book which combats the wretched image of European Jews as fatalistic and passive. He had smuggled photographs out of Auschwitz—the *anus mundi* or heart of darkness—that showed the transmutation of human beings into refuse and garbage.* He had been some kind of figure in the postwar Polish government (and then there were some whispers of a scandal involving art theft) before being expelled to France in 1968, after the infamous anti-Semitic and "anti-Zionist" purge of the Communist Party.

I had been on his track, in a small and amateur way, for a decade. I had arrived in Paris to try and find him, only to learn that he had recently died. There was no forwarding address. I went to see Daniel Singer, the late disciple of Isaac Deutscher, who from his apartment near the Matignon was himself a single-cell headquarters for anything to do with the Polish-Jewish-Marxist diaspora. He sent me to a man in downtown New York who lent me the only book in Yiddish that I possess—the memoirs of David Szmulevski—and also a very hastily typed English translation. The title of the volume is *Resistance in the Auschwitz-Birkenau Death Camp*. But the back-story was also of considerable interest and the lack of a post-story was perhaps more absorbing still.

Szmulevski had quite early in his life developed a hunger to leave the isolated village of Kolo (which means "wheel") and had volunteered to become a young Zionist pioneer. Leaving from a Romanian port and landing in Palestine under the British mandate, he had worked on a very tough kibbutz and also on the waterfront in Tel Aviv. From his pages one could count off the swift evolutions of an interwar political consciousness: he observed that Arab workers were paid less and treated more rudely, and he began to run into free-thinking people—one young girl in particular—who gave him horizons

---

* The intention had been to arouse the world's conscience by initially showing these to the Vatican. This appeal did not work.

much wider and more thrilling than the *shtetl* or the *shul*. (You think it's a stretch to connect Professor Max Born to Olivia Newton-John? Szmulevski's was almost the same Poland-to-Palestine route that was followed by Simon Pirsky, later Shimon Peres, the president of Israel, whose first cousin is Betty Pirsky or Lauren Bacall.)

I have quite recently found Szmulevski's Polish Communist-era file, which states unambiguously that in the 1930s he had joined the Communist Party of Palestine. His own memoirs, written post-1968, make no mention of this and give the impression—without exactly making the claim—that he had really preferred the Jewish-Socialist *Bund*. However that may be, he attended a militant Jewish workers' meeting one day in 1936 and volunteered to leave Palestine in order to fight the rising menace of Hitlerism—in Spain. He became a member of the Polish battalion of the International Brigade that was named for the great national poet Adam Mickiewicz. He was wounded, and was succored in hospital by the better-off American-emigrated branch of his family—the family of my wonderful late mother-in-law—which also sent a son to that war.*

Escaping to France after the victory of Spanish fascism, Szmulevski soon found that Europe's pain had hardly begun. He was arrested by the German invaders of Paris and shipped back home, to Auschwitz, where he was employed as a "roofer" in the actual building of the labor-camp section of the place. People a few years older than me who did their National Service in the British Army say that you never, ever forget your "number": the digits that become "you" for the duration. Szmulevski's number in Auschwitz, I have learned, was 27849 (a relatively low one). He wore it for the rest of his life. Able to make contact in the newly drafted slave-labor force with veterans of Spain and other hardened comrades, he had at least the chance of keeping up morale and of surviving.

---

* I pause to mention that, with my sister-in-law's uncle Ernest Halperin, this makes three widely dispersed ancestral relations of mine who fought for the Spanish Republic: something to tell my own descendants, some of whom carry their blood, if they will only hold still and listen to my tales. This is also probably the largest difference between the two sides of my family: apart from the traditional stories of British daring, the only example of heroism and gallantry ever related to me by the Commander was that of the Francoist General Jose Moscardo who refused to surrender the besieged Alcazar even when the Red forces threatened to execute his son Luis.

His memoir is strangely artless and appealing, at times almost naïve. Here is his account of helping to organize a clandestine Yom Kippur service, at which the *Kol Nidre* prayer could be decently sung by the slaves and the condemned, in Auschwitz in the winter of 1943. To his own boyhood *shtetl*, he recalls:

> ...unable to form a *minyan*, Jews from surrounding villages and settlements would come with their families. Even if they had a *minyan* [the quorum of ten (male) Jews that is needful for a service to be held] they would still have needed a cantor or a prayer-leader with the proper amount of feeling. The melody of that particular prayer is dear to the heart of every Jew, even if he is not observant.
>
> I did not take the way along which my father would have led me. My life journey distanced me from religious tradition and moved me closer to those who fight for justice on this earth, like those who took up arms against fascism—on the battlefields of Spain, in the French partisan groups and also in the death camp known as Auschwitz-Birkenau...
>
> To me, the facilitation in the camps of any action forbidden by the Germans was part of the struggle against the Hitlerite enemy. Ever since then, when I pass a synagogue on Yom Kippur Eve there comes before my eyes the picture of the barracks in Auschwitz where a small number of worshippers was able to experience the atmosphere of the High Holy Days.

These are noble, even exalted, sentiments, which would provide some evidence for those who maintain that religion is at least a supplier of consolation. But they are somehow boringly expressed: they have a tinge of the "Popular Front" to them, with their "facilitations" and other rather wooden expressions. They don't possess the defiant excitement of Primo Levi, who once wrote so bitingly that if he was god, he would have wanted to spit on anyone who prayed in Auschwitz. In a way Szmulevski survived precisely because he was a good Party man. He lived to help arrange the postwar trials of the Auschwitz criminals, including one historic session that was organized by Germans and not by the Allies. He was able to testify and also to bring important photographic evidence. In 1960 he was garlanded with a high Resistance decoration by Josef Cyrankiewicz, the Socialist-turned-

Communist prime minister of Poland who had been a fellow inmate of the same camp.

And this is where my real problem with him begins to take on shape. I sit in Poland, reading again his bureaucratic prose, and find that he claims to have taken up a job "within the national administration" after 1945. What does it mean, this post "within the national administration"? It means, as I eventually discover from the Polish "Ministry of Interior" archives in the Hoover Institution at Stanford, that Szmulevski was a full colonel responsible for Department Seven of the *Milicja Obywatelska* or "Citizen's Militia," headquartered in an old Warsaw palace that had been a seat of secret police authority since tsarist days. He never once alludes to this in his account of being forced out of Poland in 1967, preferring to blame historic anti-Jewish prejudice for the whole business.

Since the fall of the Berlin Wall in 1989, historians have become both more accurate and more honest—fractionally more brave, one might say—about that "other" cleansing of the regions and peoples that were ground to atoms between the upper and nether millstones of Hitlerism and Stalinism. One of the most objective chroniclers is Professor Timothy Snyder of Yale University. In his view, it is still "Operation Reinhardt," or the planned destruction of Polish Jewry, that is to be considered as the centerpiece of what we commonly call the Holocaust, in which of the estimated 5.7 million Jewish dead, "roughly three million were prewar Polish citizens." We should not at all allow ourselves to forget the millions of non-Jewish citizens of Belarus, Russia, Ukraine, and other Slav territories who were also massacred. But for me the salient fact remains that anti-Semitism was the regnant, essential, organizing principle of all the other National Socialist race theories. It is thus not to be thought of as just one prejudice among many.

You can't visit the area, though, without noticing the marks of what became a second erasure. The city of Wrocław/Breslau had been almost schematically rebuilt by the Communists along the lines of its prewar layout and architecture, and right down to its main square and Grass Market it looked like a storybook German town. But in that case, where *was* everybody? (And where had they gone? You can find one—restored—Jewish cemetery but try finding another one where any of the tombstones are incised in German.) I went to call on the mayor, a sturdy, thoughtful man named

Rafal Dutkiewicz, who ruefully said that the problem with citizenship in his rather large bailiwick was that "nobody is really 'from' here." Again I consult the rugged statistics offered by Professor Snyder: almost eight million German civilians were expelled or fled (or fled and returned and were then expelled) from Poland at the end of the Second World War. The eastern German lands from which they had fled or been pushed were then annexed by Poland. To make up the shortfall of population, Poles were moved into these Silesian provinces. And as if to encourage *that* process, the eastern half of prewar Poland was in turn annexed by the big brother Soviet Union, and a million expelled Poles became settlers in the areas from which Germans had been evicted. A huge zone of silence and complicity was created by this double negation.

There's no exact moral equivalence between these crimes against humanity. It's true that perhaps 600,000 Germans were killed in the whole business, which also involved the cleansing of Germans from the Czech lands, but many of these died in the fighting which the Nazis had so insanely prolonged. (Breslau/Wrocław was declared a "Fortress" or "*Festung*" city by the Third Reich and actually surrendered *after* the fall of Berlin itself, by which time it had been so much reduced to shards that there was nothing left to fight over.) So you could say, as some people defensively say about the leveling of such cities as Dresden and Würzburg, that the Nazis started it, and the Germans were punished for it.

What people still do not like to admit is that there were two crimes in the form of one. Just as the destruction of Jewry was the necessary condition for the rise and expansion of Nazism, so *the ethnic cleansing of Germans was a precondition for the Stalinization of Poland*. I first noticed this point when reading an essay by the late Ernest Gellner, who at the end of the war had warned Eastern Europeans that collective punishment of Germans would put them under Stalin's tutelage indefinitely. They would always feel the guilty need for an ally against potential German revenge. It is exactly the fear of revenge that motivates the deepest crimes, from the killing of the enemy's children lest they grow up to play their own part, to the erasure of the enemy's graveyards and holy places so that his hated name can be forgotten.

And thus to my final and most melancholy point: a great number of Stalin's enforcers and henchmen in Eastern Europe were Jews. And not just a great number, but a great proportion. The proportion was especially high in the secret police and "security" departments, where no doubt revenge played its own part, as did the ideological attachment to Communism that was so strong among internationally minded Jews at that period: Jews like David Szmulevski. There were reasonably strong indigenous Communist forces in Czechoslovakia and East Germany, but in Hungary and Poland the Communists were a small minority and knew it, were dependent on the Red Army and aware of the fact, and were disproportionately Jewish and widely detested for that reason.* Many of the penal labor camps constructed by the Nazis were later used as holding pens for German deportees by the Communists, and some of those who ran these grim places were Jewish. Nobody from Israel or the diaspora who goes to the East of Europe on a family-history fishing-trip should be unaware of the chance that they will find out both much less and much more than the package-tour had promised them. It's easy to say, with Albert Camus, "neither victims nor executioners." But real history is more pitiless even than you had been told it was.

> He could be as scathing as the Russian Hebrew writers in his denun-
> ciations of Jews and Israel—more precisely the Israeli government.
> He followed Mendele when he compared Jews to hunchbacks ("Jew-
> ish Slavery and Emancipation," 1951) though he also echoed Kafka's
> allegory of Jewish deformity, "A Report To An Academy." Berlin
> believed that emancipation had turned the Jews into homeless,
> psychologically deformed strangers trying to gain acceptance in the
> Gentile world.
> —David Aberbach on the centennial of Isaiah Berlin, June 2009

"*Die Judenfrage*," it used to be called, even by Jews. "The Jewish Question." I find I quite like this interrogative formulation, since the question—as Gertrude Stein once famously if terminally put it—may be more absorbing than the answer. Of course one is flirting with calamity in phrasing things this

---

* My brave friend Anne Applebaum is about to confront this neglected aspect of the hidden history of the region in her study of the imposition of Communism after 1945. Of course it goes without saying that once Stalin had consolidated his power, he began to eliminate local rivals, many of whom like Artur London and Lazslo Rajk were also Jews. Interestingly, there was never such a show trial in Poland.

way, as I learned in school when the Irish question was discussed by some masters as the Irish "problem." Again, the word "solution" can be as neutral as the words "question" or "problem," but once one has defined a people or a nation as such, the search for a resolution can become a yearning for the conclusive. *Endlösung*: the final solution.

But it could be that any search for any "solution" is in itself potentially lethal or absurd. The Jewish quest for some ultimate answer to the "question" has taken intensely religious and nationalist forms as well as, in more recent times, the identification of huge numbers of Jews with Marxism. My mother's family was not involved in any of the grandeur or tragedy of this: they sought to get by and to assimilate and to survive, while making a few observant gestures in the direction of their ancient faith and a few protective gestures in defense of the State of Israel.

In my mother's case I have become convinced that she was willing to give up even the smallest adherence to the synagogue if it would smooth the accession of her two sons into polite English society, and that she only began to feel passionate about the Jewish state in the Middle East as she began to experience her own desperate need for a new start somewhere else: it was either that fresh beginning or an end to every hope. Our very last telephone conversation, when she expressed a desire to immigrate to Israel after the Yom Kippur War of 1973, was bewildering to me at the time and has sent me down many pathways since. And I always keep open the possibility that I could be mistaken and that she might have had her own reasons for being reticent. This is from a letter sent to me recently by one of her oldest friends:

> She told me that she went to live with an aunt and uncle in Liverpool in a very Jewish community—perhaps went to school there or secretarial college and her first boyfriends were medical students up there. I have no idea how long she was there but it sounded as though she was happy and from there I presume she went into the WRENS [Women's Royal Navy Service]. At what time she decided to conceal her Jewishness I have no idea, possibly on going into the WRENS.

This seems probable enough when I think about it: the Royal Navy was a fairly big tent and broad church but even in a wartime battle against Hitler a

Jew (or "Jewess") might have been conspicuous. On HMS *Jamaica* my father had had a literary shipmate named Warren Tute, who became a minor novelist in the postwar years and wrote one rather successful book, *The Cruiser*, in which my father appears under the name (no first or "Christian" name) of Lieutenant Hale. At one point in the story the master-at-arms of the vessel, which is called HMS *Antigone*, is mentally reviewing the ship's crew:

> He knew that Stoker First Class Danny Evans would be likely to celebrate his draft by going on the beer for a week in Tonypandy and then spending the next three months in the Second Class for Leave. He knew that Blacksmith First Class Rogers would try and smuggle Service provisions ashore for his mother and that Telegraphist Jacobs was a sea-lawyer who kept a copy of Karl Marx in his kitbag.

Martin Amis often points out that you can tell a lot about a novelist by the trouble he takes over the names of his characters, and Tute clearly didn't break much of a sweat inventing a Welshman named Evans or a blacksmith named Rogers. By the same token, he didn't mean us to think that the name "Jacobs" was anything more than a synonym for the vaguely suspect and unsound. I don't think he was misrepresenting the atmosphere of the Navy by much: Jacobs would not have been persecuted (my father would never have countenanced anything remotely like that), but I don't exactly see him rising through the ranks, either. "You catch it on the edge of a remark," as Harold Abrahams observes of discreet English non–philo-Semitism in *Chariots of Fire*, and that's how I caught it, deciding to subtitle my first essay on the subject "Homage to Telegraphist Jacobs." How much more lazy a phrase could there be than "a copy of Karl Marx," and yet wasn't there still something in this age-old identification of the Jew with the subversive? If so, good. Remember that it is "free-thinking Jews," not Jews as such, who are defined as the undesirables by T.S. Eliot in *After Strange Gods*.

If my mother's intention in whole or in part was to ensure that I never had to suffer any indignity or embarrassment for being a Jew, then she succeeded well enough. And in any case there were enough intermarriages and "conversions" on both sides of her line to make me one of those many *mischling* hybrids who are to be found distributed all over the known world. And, as someone who doesn't really believe that the human species is subdivided by "race," let alone that a nation or nationality can be defined by its religion, why should I not let the whole question slide away from me? Why—and then I'll stop asking rhetorical questions—did I at some point resolve that, in whatever tone of voice I was asked "Are you a Jew?" I would never hear myself deny it?

As a convinced atheist, I ought to agree with Voltaire that Judaism is not just one more religion, but in its way the root of religious evil. Without the stern, joyless rabbis and their 613 dour prohibitions, we might have avoided the whole nightmare of the Old Testament, and the brutal, crude wrenching of that into prophecy-derived Christianity, and the later plagiarism and mutation of Judaism and Christianity into the various rival forms of Islam. Much of the time, I do concur with Voltaire, but not without acknowledging that Judaism is dialectical. There is, after all, a specifically Jewish version of the eighteenth-century Enlightenment, with a specifically Jewish name—the *Haskalah*—for itself. The term derives from the word for "mind" or "intellect," and it is naturally associated with ethics rather than rituals, life rather than prohibitions, and assimilation over "exile" or "return." It's everlastingly linked to the name of the great German teacher Moses Mendelssohn, one of those conspicuous Jewish hunchbacks who so upset and embarrassed Isaiah Berlin. (The other way to upset or embarrass Berlin, I found, was to mention that he himself was a cousin of Menachem Schneerson, the "messianic" Lubavitcher *rebbe*.) However, even pre-enlightenment Judaism forces its adherents to study and think, it reluctantly teaches them what others think, and it may even teach them *how* to think also.

In her preface to his collection of essays *The Non-Jewish Jew* Tamara Deutscher, widow of the great Isaac, relates the story of how her husband, future biographer of Leon Trotsky, studied for his *bar mitzvah*.* Considered the brightest boy in any *yeshivah* for years gone by or for miles around, he was set to speak to the following question: somewhere in the looped intestines of Jewish lore there is mention of a miraculous bird which visits the world only at intervals of several decades and then only very briefly. On its periodic landings it delivers and leaves behind a beakful of bird-spit. This avian drool,

---

* Born in the extremely depressed hamlet of Chrzanow, a few miles north of Auschwitz, he was later to be expelled from the Polish Communist Party for "exaggerating the dangers of Nazism." The year was 1932.

if you can seize hold of even a drop of it, has wonder-working properties. Now comes the crucial question (surely you saw it coming?): Is the bird-spit to be reckoned as *kosher* or as *treyfe*? The boy Isaac spoke for several hours on the rival theories of this dispute, and on the competing commentaries on those rival theories, and of course on the commentaries on those commentaries. He used to say later that such onerous mental and textual labor did not serve to train the mind at all but rather — like the rote memorization of the Koran — stultified it. I am not sure that I agree. Much of my Marxist and post-Marxist life has been spent in apparent hair-splitting and logic-chopping, and I still feel that the sheer exercise can command respect. It may even build muscle...

Should I, too, prefer the title of "non-Jewish Jew"? For some time, I would have identified myself strongly with the attitude expressed by Rosa Luxemburg, writing from prison in 1917 to her anguished friend Mathilde Wurm:

> What do you want with these special Jewish pains? I feel as close to the wretched victims of the rubber plantations in Putamayo and the blacks of Africa with whose bodies the Europeans play ball...I have no special corner in my heart for the ghetto: I am at home in the entire world, where there are clouds and birds and human tears.

An inordinate proportion of the Marxists I have known would probably have formulated their own views in much the same way. It was almost a point of honor not to engage in "thinking with the blood," to borrow a notable phrase from D.H. Lawrence, and to immerse Jewishness in other and wider struggles. Indeed, the old canard about "rootless cosmopolitanism" finds a perverse sort of endorsement in Jewish internationalism: the more emphatically somebody stresses that sort of rhetoric about the suffering of others, the more likely I would be to assume that the speaker was a Jew. Does this mean that I think there are Jewish "characteristics"? Yes, I think it must mean that.

During the Bosnian war in the late 1990s, I spent several days traveling around the country with Susan Sontag and her son, my dear friend David Rieff. On one occasion, we made a special detour to the town of Zenica, where there was reported to be a serious infiltration of outside Muslim extremists: a charge that was often used to slander the Bosnian government of the time. We found very little evidence of that, but the community itself was much riven as between Muslim, Croat, and Serb. No faction was strong enough to predominate, each was strong enough to veto the other's candidate for the chairmanship of the city council. Eventually, and in a way that was characteristically Bosnian, all three parties called on one of the town's few Jews and asked him to assume the job. We called on him, and found that he was also the resident intellectual, with a natural gift for synthesizing matters. After we left him, Susan began to chortle in the car. "What do you think?" she asked. "Do you think that the only dentist and the only shrink in Zenica are Jewish also?" It would be dense to have pretended not to see her joke.

The Jewish Orthodox word for a heretic—which a heretic may also use for himself or herself—is *apikoros*. It derives from "Epicurean" and perfectly captures the division between Athens and Jerusalem. One notorious *apikoros* named Hiwa al-Balkhi, writing in ninth-century Persia, offered two hundred awkward questions to the faithful. He drew upon himself the usual thunderous curses—"may his name be forgotten, may his bones be worn to nothing"—along with detailed refutations and denunciations by Abraham ibn Ezra and others. These exciting anathemas, of course, ensured that his worrying "questions" would remain current for as long as the Orthodox commentaries would be read. In this way, rather as when Maimonides says that the Messiah will come but that "he may tarry," Jewishness contrives irony at its own expense. If there is one characteristic of Jews that I admire, it is that irony is seldom if ever wasted on them.

One of the questions asked by al-Balkhi, and often repeated to this day, is this: Why do the children of Israel continue to suffer? My grandmother Dodo thought it was because the *goyim* were jealous. The seder for Passover (which is a shame-faced simulacrum of a Hellenic question-and-answer session, even including the wine) tells the children that it's one of those things that happens to every Jewish generation. After the *Shoah* or *Endlösung* or Holocaust, many rabbis tried to tell the survivors that the immolation had been a punishment for "exile," or for insufficient attention to the Covenant. This explanation was something of a flop with those whose parents or children had been the raw material for the "proof," so for a time the professional interpreters of god's will went decently quiet. This interval of ambivalence lasted until the war of 1967, when it was announced that the divine purpose could be discerned after all. How wrong, how foolish, to have announced its discovery prematurely! The exile and the *Shoah* could now *both* be understood, as part of a heavenly if somewhat roundabout scheme to recover the Western Wall in Jerusalem and other pieces of biblically mandated real estate.

I regard it as a matter of self-respect to spit in public on rationalizations of this kind. (They are almost as repellent, in their combination of arrogance, masochism, and affected false modesty, as Edith Stein's "offer" of her life to expiate the regrettable unbelief in Jesus of her former fellow Jews.) The sage Jews are those who have put religion behind them and become in so many societies the leaven of the secular and the atheist. I think I have a very good idea why it is that anti-Semitism is so tenacious and so protean and so enduring. Christianity and Islam, theistic though they may claim to be, are both based on the fetishizing of human primates: Jesus in one case and Mohammed in the other. Neither of these figures can be called exactly historical but both have one thing in common even in their quasi-mythical dimension. Both of them were first encountered by the Jews. And the Jews, ravenous as they were for any sign of the long-sought Messiah, were not taken in by either of these two pretenders, or not in large numbers or not for long.

If you meet a devout Christian or a believing Muslim, you are meeting someone who would give everything he owned for a personal, face-to-face meeting with the blessed founder or prophet. But in the visage of the Jew, such ardent believers encounter the very figure who *did* have such a precious moment, and who spurned the opportunity and turned shrugging aside. Do you imagine for a microsecond that such a vile, churlish transgression will ever be *forgiven*? I myself certainly hope that it will not. The Jews have seen through Jesus and Mohammed. In retrospect, many of them have also seen through the mythical, primitive, and cruel figures of Abraham and Moses. Nearer to our own time, in the bitter combats over the work of Marx and Freud and Einstein, Jewish participants and protagonists have not been the least noticeable. May this always be the case, whenever any human primate sets up, or is set up by others, as a Messiah.

The most recent instance of Jewish belief in a rescue from the agonies of doubt and insecurity is Zionism. The very idea begins as a Utopia: Theodor Herzl's novel *Altneuland*, about "the return," is the only Utopian fiction ever written that has come true (if it has). But I have learned to distrust

Utopias and to prefer satires. Marcel Proust was laughing at Herzl when he advocated a new "Gomorrah" where same-sex people could have their own Levantine state (he actually might have liked some areas of today's Tel Aviv). Arthur Koestler, drifting over the Arctic in a Zeppelin in 1932, dropped a Star of David flag onto the tundra of Novaya Zemlya and claimed it for a Hebrew national home. Stalin himself set aside a special province for Jews in the faraway territory of Birobidjan... By the time my mother told me that she wanted to move to Israel in 1973, the Utopian element was still being emphasized but with perhaps a fraction less enthusiasm. It was more because I thought she might be risking herself by moving to a zone of conflict that I uttered discouraging noises. But I was also becoming aware that she might be taking part in the perpetuation of an injustice. I didn't myself visit the Holy Land until a couple of years later but when I did, I was very much dismayed.

Long before it was known to me as a place where my ancestry was even remotely involved, the idea of a state for Jews (or a Jewish state; not quite the same thing, as I failed at first to see) had been "sold" to me as an essentially secular and democratic one. The idea was a haven for the persecuted and the survivors, a democracy in a region where the idea was poorly understood, and a place where—as Philip Roth had put it in a one-handed novel that I read when I was about nineteen—even the traffic cops and soldiers were Jews. This, like the other emphases of that novel, I could grasp. Indeed, my first visit was sponsored by a group in London called the Friends of Israel. They offered to pay my expenses, that is, if on my return I would come and speak to one of their meetings.

I still haven't submitted that expenses claim. The misgivings I had were of two types, both of them ineradicable. The first and the simplest was the encounter with everyday injustice: by all means the traffic cops were Jews but so, it turned out, were the colonists and ethnic cleansers and even the torturers. It was Jewish leftist friends who insisted that I go and see towns and villages under occupation, and sit down with Palestinian Arabs who were living under house arrest—if they were lucky—or who were squatting in the ruins of their demolished homes if they were less fortunate. In Ramallah I spent the day with the beguiling Raimonda Tawil, confined to her home for committing no known crime save that of expressing her opinions. (For some reason, what I most remember is a sudden exclamation from her very restrained and respectable husband, a manager of the local bank: "I would prefer living under a Bedouin *muktar* to another day of Israeli rule!" He had obviously spent some time thinking about the most revolting possible Arab alternative.) In Jerusalem I visited the Tutungi family, who could produce title deeds going back generations but who were being evicted from their apartment in the old city to make way for an expansion of the Jewish quarter. Jerusalem: that place of blood since remote antiquity. Jerusalem, over which the British and French and Russians had fought a foul war in the Crimea, *and in the mid-nineteenth century*, on the matter of which Christian Church could command the keys to some "holy sepulcher." Jerusalem, where the anti-Semite Balfour had tried to bribe the Jews with the territory of another people in order to seduce them from Bolshevism and continue the diplomacy of the Great War. Jerusalem: that pest-house in whose environs all zealots hope that an even greater and final war can be provoked. It certainly made a warped appeal to my sense of history. In the less heroic and shorter term, what of justice and its Jewish resonance?

Suppose that a man leaps out of a burning building—as my dear friend and colleague Jeff Goldberg sat and said to my face over a table at La Tomate in Washington not two years ago—and lands on a bystander in the street below. Now, make the burning building be Europe, and the luckless man underneath be the Palestinian Arabs. Is this a historical injustice? Has the man below been made a victim, with infinite cause of complaint and indefinite justification for violent retaliation? My own reply would be a provisional "no," but only on these conditions. The man leaping from the burning building must still make such restitution as he can to the man who broke his fall, and must not pretend that he never even landed on him. And he must base his case on the singularity and uniqueness of the original leap. It can't, in other words, be "leap, leap, leap" for four generations and more. The people underneath cannot be expected to tolerate leaping on this scale and of this duration, if you catch my drift. In Palestine, tread softly, for you tread on their dreams. And do *not* tell the Palestinians that they were never fallen upon and bruised in the first place. Do not shame yourself with the cheap lie that they were told by their leaders to run away. Also, stop saying that nobody knew how to cultivate oranges in Jaffa until the Jews showed them how. "Making

the desert bloom"—one of Yvonne's stock phrases—makes desert dwellers
out of people who were the agricultural superiors of the Crusaders.

In the mid-1970s, Jewish settlers from New York were already establish-
ing second homes for themselves on occupied territory. From what burning house were *they* leaping? I went to interview some of these early Jewish
colonial zealots—written off in those days as mere "fringe" elements—and
found that they called themselves *Gush Emunim* or—it sounded just as bad
in English—"The Bloc of the Faithful." Why not just say "Party of God"
and have done with it? At least they didn't have the nerve to say that they
stole other people's land because their own home in Poland or Belarus had
been taken from them. They said they took the land because god had given
it to them from time immemorial. In the noisome town of Hebron, where all
of life is focused on a supposedly sacred boneyard in a dank local cave, one
of the world's less pretty sights is that of supposed *yeshivah* students toting
submachine guns and humbling the Arab inhabitants. When I asked one of
these charmers where he got his legal authority to be a squatter, he flung his
hand, index finger outstretched, toward the sky.

Actually—and this was where I began to feel seriously uncomfortable—
some such divine claim underlay not just "the occupation" but the whole
idea of a separate state for Jews in Palestine. Take away the divine warrant for
the Holy Land and where were you, and what were you? Just another land-
thief like the Turks or the British, except that in this case you wanted the
land without the people. And the original Zionist slogan—"a land without a
people for a people without a land"—disclosed its own negation when I saw
the densely populated Arab towns dwelling sullenly under Jewish tutelage.
You want irony? How about Jews becoming colonizers at just the moment
when other Europeans had given up on the idea?

The great Jewish historian Jacob Talmon once wrote an open letter to
Prime Minister Menachem Begin in which he specified that he didn't particularly care about the Arabs and their so-called rights and complaints. What
disturbed him was the Messianic tone of the Israeli regime, which seemed to
assume that destiny and prophecy would act as a solvent to all the apparently
insoluble questions. Thus to my second worry, which even in the relatively
palmy days of the mid-1970s was this. All questions of right to one side, I
have never been able to banish the queasy inner suspicion that Israel just did

not look, or feel, either permanent or sustainable. I felt this when sitting in the old Ottoman courtyards of Jerusalem, and I felt it even more when I saw the hideous "Fort Condo" settlements that had been thrown up around the city in order to give the opposite impression. If the statelet was only based on a narrow strip of the Mediterranean littoral (god having apparently ordered Moses to lead the Jews to one of the very few parts of the region with absolutely no oil at all), that would be bad enough. But in addition, it involved roosting on top of an ever-growing population that did not welcome the newcomers.

I regard anti-Semitism as ineradicable and as one element of the toxin with which religion has infected us. Perhaps partly for this reason, I have never been able to see Zionism as a cure for it. American and British and French Jews have told me with perfect sincerity that they are always prepared for the day when "it happens again" and the Jew-baiters take over. (And I don't pretend not to know what they are talking about: I have actually seen the rabid phenomenon at work in modern and sunny Argentina and am unable to forget it.) So then, they seem to think, they will take refuge in the Law of Return, and in Haifa, or for all I know in Hebron. Never mind for now that if all of world Jewry *did* settle in Palestine, this would actually necessitate further Israeli expansion, expulsion, and colonization, and that their departure under these apocalyptic conditions would leave the new brownshirts and blackshirts in possession of the French and British and American nuclear arsenals. This is ghetto thinking, hardly even fractionally updated to take into account what has changed. The important but delayed realization will have to come: Israeli Jews are *a part of* the diaspora, not a group that has escaped from it. Why else does Israel daily beseech the often-flourishing Jews of other lands, urging them to help the most endangered Jews of all: the ones who rule Palestine by force of arms? Why else, having supposedly escaped from the need to rely on Gentile goodwill, has Israel come to depend more and more upon it? On this reckoning, Zionism must constitute one of the greatest potential non sequiturs in human history.

One of my first reservations about Zionism was and is that, semiconsciously at least, it grants the anti-Semite's first premise about the abnormality of the Jew. I once heard Avishai Margalit, one of Isaiah Berlin's most brilliant disciples, phrase this very memorably during a lecture he gave at the

New School. The Zionist idea, he said, was supposed to take the deracinated European Jew—the so-called *luftmensch* or person made of thin air—and make a man of him. How to achieve this? By taking him from his watchmaker's shop in Budapest or his clinic in Vienna and putting a hoe in one hand and a gun in the other. In Palestine. The resulting sturdy farmer-soldier would then redeem the shuffling, cringing round-shouldered shopkeeper or usurer. This was the Leon Uris movie version of events, the theme music of which—I suddenly remember—my mother had at one point possessed on a long-playing record. Margalit pointed out that this "project" absolutely *mandated* a conflict with the Arab population, because it necessarily involved not just the occupation of their land but the *confiscation* of it. "Some say that this is the Israelis' original sin," he said deadpan. "With this I do not agree but I think we can call it Israel's immaculate misconception."

For myself, I don't feel like an apologetic *luftmensch*; I positively prefer the watchmaker and the bookseller and the doctor to the hearty farmer and colonist, and I pause to note that Arabs are retained on this forcibly Judaized land mainly in order that someone be available to do the hoeing and digging and heavy lifting that most Israelis are now too refined to do for themselves. There's a certain amount of ambiguity in my background, what with intermarriages and conversions, but under various readings of three codes which I don't much respect (Mosaic Law, the Nuremberg Laws, and the Israeli Law of Return) I do qualify as a member of the tribe, and any denial of that in my family has ceased with me. But I would not remove myself to Israel if it meant the continuing expropriation of another people, and if anti-Jewish fascism comes again to the Christian world—or more probably comes at us via the Muslim world—I already consider it an obligation to resist it wherever I live. I would detest myself if I fled from it in any direction. Leo Strauss was right. The Jews will not be "saved" or "redeemed." (Cheer up: neither will anyone else.) They/we will always be in exile whether they are in the greater Jerusalem area or not, and this in some ways is as it should be. They are, or we are, as a friend of Victor Klemperer's once put it to him in a very dark time, condemned and privileged to be "a seismic people." A critical register of the general health of civilization is the status of "the Jewish question." No insurance policy has ever been devised that can or will cover this risk.

# Edward Said in Light
# and Shade (and Saul)

———◄○►———

I N THE COURSE of a long engagement with this whole tortured
*Frage*, I made a friendship that taught me a very great deal. It was at
a conference in Cyprus in 1976, where the theme was the rights of small
nations, that I first met Edward Said. It was impossible not to be captivated
by him: of his many immediately seductive qualities I will start by mentioning a very important one. When he laughed, it was as if he was surrendering
unconditionally to some guilty pleasure. At first the very picture of profes-
sorial rectitude, with faultless tweeds, cravats, and other accoutrements (the
pipe also being to the fore), he would react to a risqué remark, or a disclosure
of something vaguely scandalous, as if a whole Trojan horse of mirth had
been smuggled into his interior and suddenly disgorged its contents. The
build-up, in other words, was worth one's effort. And very few allusions were
wasted on him: he appeared to have memorized most of *Beyond the Fringe*
and *Monty Python* and to be an excellent mimic of anything that smacked of
the absurd. He could "do," I remember, a very vivid George Steiner…

I had not particularly liked the way in which he wrote about literature in
*Beginnings*, and I was always on my guard if not outright hostile when any
tincture of "deconstruction" or "postmodernism" was applied to my beloved
canon of English writing, but when Edward talked about English literature
and quoted from it, he passed the test that I always privately apply: Do you

truly *love* this subject and could you bear to live for one moment if it was obliterated?

I was on my way to Israel from Cyprus and he gave me some Palestinian contacts to look up, mainly at Birzeit University near Ramallah. Everybody he suggested I meet proved to be welcoming, sane, secular, and realistic. Over the years, whenever I went to Beirut or Syria or elsewhere in the region, he always seemed to have access to people of that stripe. Though he never actually joined it, he was close to some civilian elements of the Democratic Front for the Liberation of Palestine, which was the most Communist (and in the rather orthodox sense) of the Palestinian formations. I remember Edward once surprising me by saying, and apropos of nothing: "Do you know something I have never done in my political career? I have never publicly criticized the Soviet Union. It's not that I terribly sympathize with them or anything—it's just that the Soviets have never done anything to harm me, or us." At the time I thought this a rather naïve statement, even perhaps a slightly contemptible one, but by then I had been in parts of the Middle East where it could come as a blessed relief to meet a consecrated Moscow-line atheist-dogmatist, if only for the comparatively rational humanism that he evinced amid so much religious barking and mania. It was only later to occur to me that Edward's pronounced dislike of George Orwell was something to which I ought to have paid more attention.*

After Cyprus, the next time I saw Edward was in New York. And, when I went to call on him up in Morningside Heights, I discovered the sidewalk around his building was alive with cops and "security" types. It was the era of the Jimmy Carter–Anwar Sadat–Menachem Begin "Camp David" deal, where the three leaders had attempted to square the circle by confecting an agreement in the absence of any representative of the Palestinians. Perhaps a bit sensitive to this rather conspicuous lacuna, Sadat had had one of his public fits of improvisation and caprice and declared—without asking any permission or giving any notice—that the good Professor Edward Said of Columbia University might perhaps make the necessary interlocutor for his

---

* The last time I heard an orthodox Marxist statement that was music to my ears was from a member of the Rwanda Patriotic Front, during the mass slaughter in the country. "The terms *Hutu* and *Tutsi*," he said severely, "are merely ideological constructs, describing different relationships to the means and mode of production." But of course!

dispossessed (and in this case excluded) people. It was the first time I had seen the media cliché in full action but yes, within hours the world had beaten a path to Edward's door and I in turn had to beat my way through to his apartment for dinner.

He was dismayed at Sadat's presumption and embarrassed — as was his lovely Lebanese wife, Mariam — at the unsolicited attention it had earned him. I learned a lot that evening, including a crucial thing about Edward that so many people failed ever to understand about him. This was that he did NOT consider himself a direct victim of 1947/48 and the Israeli triumph. His family had in the long run lost a lot of property in Jerusalem and suffered a distinct loss of pride, but he firmly declined to call himself a refugee. He had left Jerusalem for Egypt in good time, completed his studies at a parodic English-style boarding school in Cairo (with Omar Sharif wielding the puni-tive gym shoe as the sadistic "head boy" of Kitchener House) and gone on — with his original American passport — to qualify many times over at various universities in the United States. He owed his current eminence at Columbia to the special encouragement of Lionel Trilling.

However, it was precisely because he wasn't a penniless or stateless refugee (even if the family had lost the lovely old house in Jerusalem where Martin Buber later lived) that he felt such a strong responsibility for those who were. I was to grow used to hearing, around New York, the annoying way in which people would say: "Edward Said, such a suave and articulate and witty man," with the unspoken suffix "for a Palestinian." It irritated him, too, naturally enough, but in my private opinion it strengthened him in his determination to *be* an ambassador or spokesman for those who lived in camps or under occupation (or both). He almost overdid the ambassadorial aspect if you ask me, being always just too faultlessly dressed and spiffily turned out. Fools often contrasted this attention to his *tenue* with his membership of the Pal-estine National Council, the then-parliament-in-exile of the people without a land. In fact, his taking part in this rather shambolic assembly was a kind of *noblesse oblige*: an assurance to his *landsmen* (and also to himself) that he had not allowed and never would allow himself to forget their plight. The downside of this *noblesse* was only to strike me much later on. I continued to observe how tightly and crisply he was buttoned and tied, as well as to notice that the well-wrapped contents were under pressure. I once walked

Martin Amis up through the Morningside Heights area to go and call upon Edward—whose reviews and essays I had been urging Martin to print in his literary pages at the *New Statesman*—and on our arrival the good professor was perhaps slightly over-solicitous at the idea that we'd come on foot. His 'hood, at that time of the late New York seventies, could be described as a bit hairy. (After dinner, he had once sweetly insisted on walking me to the subway.) "If you mean," said Martin, "that the guys round here seem to style their hair by shoving their dicks into the light-socket..." I didn't think this was one of his absolute best, but I turned to see the Parr Professor of English and Comparative Literature fighting down a great eruption of anarchic mirth in which he almost certainly disapproved of having indulged.

Reading his autobiography many years later, I was astonished to find that Edward since boyhood had—not unlike Isaiah Berlin—often felt himself ungainly and ill-favored and awkward in bearing. He had always seemed to me quite the reverse: a touch dandyish perhaps but—as the saying goes—perfectly secure in his masculinity. On one occasion, after lunch in Georgetown, he took me with him to a renowned local tobacconist and asked to do something I had never witnessed before: "try on" a pipe. In case you ever wish to do this, here is the form: a solemn assistant produces a plastic envelope and fits it over the amber or ivory mouthpiece. You then clamp your teeth down to feel if the "fit" and weight are easy to your jaw. If not, then repeat with various stems until your browsing is complete. In those days I could have inhaled ten cigarettes and drunk three Tanqueray martinis in the time spent on such *flaneur* flippancy, but I admired the commitment to smoking nonetheless. Taking coffee with him once in a shopping mall in Stanford, I saw him suddenly register something over my shoulder. It was a ladies' dress shop. He excused himself and dashed in, to emerge soon after with some fashionable and costly looking bags. "Mariam," he said as if by way of explanation, "has never worn anything that I have not bought for her." On another occasion in Manhattan, after acting as a magnificent, encyclopedic guide around the gorgeous Andalusia (*Al-Andalus*) exhibition at the Museum of Modern Art, he was giving lunch to Carol and to me when she noticed that her purse had been lost or stolen. At once, he was at her service, not only suggesting shops in the vicinity where a replacement might be found, but also offering to be her guide and advisor until she had selected a suitable new *sac à main*. I could no more have proposed myself for such an expedition than suggested myself as a cosmonaut, so what this says about my own heterosexual confidence I leave to others.

His insecurity, in other words, didn't show at all where he feared it did, in his carriage or his turnout. Nor did he let it show when he was lecturing, or otherwise performing in public. I wish I knew anything about music, but to watch him sit down at the piano was to see someone instantly becoming less self-conscious rather than more (a thing I have sometimes noticed with other artists, as with Annie Leibovitz instantly acquiring confidence by picking up a camera). No, what made Edward uneasy was the question of Islam.

He was so much the picture of different kinds of assimilation that it was almost a case of multiple personalities. He could at one moment be almost a cosmopolitan Jew of the Upper West Side, music-loving, bibliophilic, well-traveled, multilingual. When I asked him for a one-on-one tutorial about George Eliot and *Daniel Deronda*, for a lecture I planned to give after my own discovery of the occulted Judaism in my own family, he invited me to his apartment—he had by then moved to the Claremont area—and gave me one of the best sessions I have ever had with a teacher: drawing out all the ambivalences of commentary on Anglo-Judaism from Sir Leslie Stephen to Virginia Woolf, from F.R. Leavis to Lord David Cecil, and making an *excursus* or two to take in Proust, Sainte-Beuve, and Steven Marcus. Considering that the novel was among other things a romanticization of Zionism that almost completely failed to mention the non-Jewish inhabitants of the territory, I thought that this was exemplary on Edward's part. But this was the other personality at work also: the donnish Englishman with pipe and tweeds, saying, "You might take a look at Frank Leavis on this point, even if it is a bit stodgy." Edward had attended St. George's Church of England school in Jerusalem—I assert this with knowledge and confidence in spite of the scurrilous campaign of lies on the subject that was later published in *Commentary* magazine—and felt himself to be a member of the small and somewhat derided Palestinian-Anglican communion in the city. He once invited me to lunch with the then-Anglican-Arab bishop of Jerusalem (a man later and rather too stereotypically arrested in a gentleman's lavatory during an interval in the Lambeth Conference of the Church of England) and demonstrated great interest in the liturgy and the rituals of the old place.

Arab nationalism in its traditional form was the way in which secular Arab Christians like Edward had found and kept a place for themselves, while simultaneously avoiding the charge of being too "Western." It was very noticeable among the Palestinians that the most demonstrably "extreme" nationalists—and Marxists—were often from Christian backgrounds. George Habash and Nayef Hawatmeh used to be celebrated examples of this phenomenon, long before anyone had heard of the cadres of Hamas, or Islamic Jihad. There was an element of overcompensation involved, or so I came to suspect.

It took a while for this disagreement between us to crystallize. I at first thought Edward's *Orientalism* was a very just and necessary book in that it forced Westerners to confront their own assumptions about the Levant and indeed the whole of the Orient. (My favorite example here was provided by the art critic Robert Hughes, whose Australian family referred contentedly to Indonesia as "the Far East," when if you could separate their colonial cosmology from their actual geography it was in fact their "Near North.") In time I came to see that Edward underrated Turkish imperialism, say, when compared to French or British conquests, and was rather grudging about the relative importance of German scholarship, but *Orientalism* was a book that made one think.* It was with his much lesser effort, *Covering Islam*, that I began to realize that there was an apparently narrow but very deep difference between us.

As he defended the book one evening in the early 1980s at the Carnegie Endowment in New York, I knew that some of what he said was true enough, just as some of it was arguably less so. (Edward incautiously dismissed "speculations about the latest conspiracy to blow up buildings or sabotage commercial airliners" as the feverish product of "highly exaggerated stereotypes.") *Covering Islam* took as its point of departure the Iranian revolution, which by then had been fully counter-revolutionized by the forces of the Ayatollah. Yes, it was true that the Western press—which was one half of the pun about "covering"—had been naïve if not worse about the Pahlavi regime. Yes, it was true that few Middle East "analysts" had had any concept of the latent power of Shi'ism to create mass mobilization. Yes, it was true that almost every stage of the Iranian drama had come as a complete surprise to the media. But wasn't it also the case that Iranian society was now disappearing into a void

---

* The best critique of it is Ibn Warraq's *Defending the West*.

of retrogressive piety that had levied war against Iranian Kurdistan and used medieval weaponry such as stoning and amputation against its internal critics, or even against those like unveiled women whose very existence constituted an offense? ("Living in the Islamic Republic," Azar Nafisi was later to say in her *Reading Lolita in Tehran*, one of the many books that demonstrate the superiority of literature over religion as a source of morality and ethics, "is like having sex with someone you loathe." As the many male victims of rape in the regime's disgusting jails can testify, this state-run pathology of sexual repression and sexual sadism is not content to degrade women only.)*

Edward genially enough did not *dis*agree with what I said, but he didn't seem to admit my point, either. I wanted to press him harder so I veered close enough to the *ad hominem* to point out that his life—the life of the mind, the life of the book collector and music lover and indeed of the gallery-goer, appreciator of the feminine and occasional *boulevardier*—would become simply unlivable and unthinkable in an Islamic republic. Again, he could accede politely to my point but carry on somehow as if nothing had been conceded. I came slowly to realize that with Edward, too, I was keeping two sets of books. We agreed on things like the first Palestinian *intifadah*, another event that took the Western press completely off guard, and we collaborated on a book of essays that asserted and defended Palestinian rights. This was in the now hard-to-remember time when all official recognition was withheld from the PLO. Together we debated Professor Bernard Lewis and Leon Wieseltier at a once-celebrated conference of the Middle East Studies Association in Cambridge in 1986, tossing and goring them somewhat in a duel over academic "objectivity" in the wider discipline. But even then I was indistinctly aware that Edward didn't feel himself quite at liberty to say certain things, while at the same time feeling rather too much obliged to say certain other things. A low point was an almost uncritical profile of Yasser Arafat that he contributed to *Interview* magazine in the late 1980s.

In those days, though, an adherence to Arafat was at least compatible with the Algiers declaration of the PLO, which Edward had striven to bring

---

* I am absurdly proud that James Fenton's poem "The Ballad of the Imam and the Shah," which first appeared in his collection *Manila Envelope* and which foreshadows some of these pregnant admonitions, is dedicated to me.

about. To remember this agreement now is to recall an almost-vanished moment: the PLO was to renounce the clauses in its charter which either called for the demolition of the Israeli state or suggested that Jews had no place in Palestine to begin with. At Algiers, Edward's reasoning prevailed and the "Left-rejectionist" alliance, of George Habash and Nayef Hawatmeh, after stormy and emotional debate, lost. Morally, I felt that this deserved more praise than it received: Edward and those others who had left the land of pre-1947 Israel now in effect gave up their ancestral claim to it, in order that the generations dispossessed or expelled or occupied after 1967 could have a chance to build a state of their own in at least a portion of "the land." This self-denying renunciation had a quality of nobility to it.

But in those days the Palestinian "rejectionists" were secularists and left-ists. Here was another moment, then, when one was witnessing the death of a movement rather than the birth of one (also, the birth of a movement based on death). There came a day I can't forget when I was in Jerusalem with my old comrade Professor Israel Shahak. This honest and learned old man, a survivor of the ghettos of Poland and the camp at Bergen-Belsen, had immi-grated to Israel after the war and later become the loudest individual voice for Palestinian rights and the most deadly critic of the Torah-based land-thieves and vigilantes. Shahak it was who had introduced me to the life-giving work of Benedict (formerly Baruch, until he was excommunicated and anathema-tized) Spinoza. One of the great unacknowledged moral critics of our time, Shahak did not save his withering reproaches only for the Zionists. I wish I could replicate his warm *Mitteleuropa* gutturals on the page:

> Christopher, you have maybe followed this new debate in Gaza between forces of the Hamas and of Islamic Jihad? You have not? Then I must tell you: it will much repay your interest.

Here was the ominously emergent great subject (we are speaking of the late 1980s and early 1990s). The "Islamic Jihad" forces in Gaza were saying in their propaganda that *the whole of Spain*, and not just Andalusia, was land stolen from Islam and that its immediate return should be demanded. The Hamas strategists were responding that, full as the Palestinian plate cur-rently was, this might not be the moment to call for the Islamization of the entire Iberian peninsula. Perhaps for now, just the return of Andalusia would do. However, and almost as if not to be outdone, the Hamas website did feature the *Protocols of the Elders of Zion*, an anti-Semitic fabrication originally perpetrated by the Christian-Orthodox right wing in Russia which (because a forgery after all is at least a false copy of a true bill) it is wrong to describe even as a forgery. At around the same time, my friend Musa Budeiri, a professor at Birzeit University on the West Bank, told me that religious Muslim students were coming to him and announcing that they would no longer be studying for the humanities course that he taught because it required that they take instruction in Darwin...

As I later found on revisiting Gaza, I was being given by Shahak and Budeiri a premonitory glimpse of the new form that paranoid militant Islam was beginning to adopt. Hitherto, the Palestinians had been relatively immune to this *Allahu Akhbar* style. I thought this was a hugely retrograde development. I said as much to Edward. To reprint Nazi propaganda and to make a theocratic claim to Spanish soil was to be a protofascist and a supporter of "Caliphate" imperialism: it had nothing at all to do with the mistreatment of the Palestinians. Once again, he did not exactly disagree. But he was anxious to emphasize that the Israelis had often encouraged Hamas as a foil against Fatah and the PLO. This I had known since seeing the burning out of leftist Palestinians by Muslim mobs in Gaza as early as 1981. Yet once again, it seemed Edward could only condemn Islamism if it could somehow be blamed on either Israel or the United States or the West, and not as a thing in itself. He sometimes employed the same sort of knight's move when discussing other Arabist movements, excoriating Saddam Hussein's Ba'ath Party, for example, mainly because it had once enjoyed the support of the CIA. But when Saddam was really being attacked, as in the case of his use of chemical weapons on noncombatants at Halabja, Edward gave second-hand currency to the falsified story that it had "really" been the Iranians who had done it. If that didn't work, well, hadn't the United States sold Saddam the weaponry in the first place? Finally, and always—and this question wasn't automatically discredited by being a change of subject—what about Israel's unwanted and ugly rule over more and more millions of non-Jews?

I evolved a test for this mentality, which I applied to more people than Edward. What would, or did, the relevant person say when the United States intervened to stop the massacres and dispossessions in Bosnia-Herzegovina and Kosovo? Here were two majority-Muslim territories and populations being vilely mistreated by Orthodox and Catholic Christians. There was no oil in the region. The state interests of Israel were not involved (indeed, Ariel Sharon publicly opposed the return of the Kosovar refugees to their homes on the grounds that it set an alarming—I want to say "unsettling"—precedent). The usual national-security "hawks," like Henry Kissinger, were also strongly opposed to the mission. One evening at Edward's apartment, with the other guest being the mercurial, courageous Azmi Bishara, then one of the more distinguished Arab members of the Israeli parliament, I was finally able to leave the arguing to someone else. Bishara (who incidentally told me that Israel Shahak had been the best and the kindest professor at the Hebrew University of Jerusalem, where he had studied) was quite shocked that Edward would not lend public support to Clinton for finally doing the right thing in the Balkans. Why was he being so stubborn? I had begun by then—belatedly you may say—to guess. Rather like our then-friend Noam Chomsky, Edward in the final instance believed that if the United States was doing something, then that thing could not *by definition* be a moral or ethical action.

There came an awful day when I picked up the phone and knew at once, as one does with some old friends even before they speak, that it was Edward. He sounded as if he were calling from the bottom of a well. I still thank my stars that I didn't say what I nearly said, because the good professor's phone pals were used to cheering or teasing him out of bouts of pessimism and insecurity when he would sometimes say ridiculous things like: "I hope you don't mind being disturbed by some mere wog and upstart." The remedy for this was not to indulge it but to reply with bracing and satirical stuff which would soon get the gurgling laugh back into his throat. But I'm glad I didn't say, "What, Edward, splashing about again in the waters of self-pity?" because this time he was calling to tell me that he had contracted a rare strain of leukemia. Not at all untypically, he used the occasion to remind me that it was very important always to make and keep regular appointments with one's physician.

The rather striking thing was that, from then on, he actually became much *less* sorry for himself. He would often tell quite stoically of soul-devouring doses of "chemo"—he eventually put himself in the hands of some very advanced physicians at Long Island Jewish Hospital—and there were days when it was upsetting to see him so thin, as well as times when it seemed unnatural to see such an elegant man become so bloated. One evening he asked me if it might be a good scheme to talk to Susan Sontag about the metaphors of illness on which she had herself become so toughened an expert. I thought definitely yes, if only because they would have so much else to discuss. I know they did have the dinner but the only "metaphor" that I ever distilled or derived from Edward's eventually lethal sickness was this. Very soon after he found that he was ill, he resigned his position on the Palestine National Council, and telephoned me quite happily to tell me so. It was almost as if the intimation of mortality had emancipated him from the everyday requirements of party-mindedness and tribal loyalty. (I have sometimes noticed in other people that a clear-eyed sense of impending extinction can have a paradoxically liberating effect, as in: at least I don't have to do *that* anymore.)

Inevitably came the time when he angrily repudiated his former paladin Yasser Arafat. In fact, he described him to me as "the Palestinian blend of Marshal Petaín and Papa Doc." But the main problem, alas, remained the same. In Edward's moral universe, Arafat could at last be named as a thug and a practitioner of corruption and extortion. But he could only be identified as such to the extent that he was now and at last aligned with an American design. Thus the only truly unpardonable thing about "The Chairman" was his readiness to appear on the White House lawn with Yitzhak Rabin and Bill Clinton in 1993. I have real knowledge and memory of this, because George Stephanopoulos—whose father's Orthodox church in Ohio and New York had kept him in touch with what was still a predominantly Christian Arab-American opinion—called me more than once from the White House to help beseech Edward to show up at the event. "The feedback we get from Arab-American voters is this: If it's such a great idea, why isn't Said signing off on it?" When I called him, Edward was grudging and crabby. "The old man [Arafat] has no right to sign away land." Really? Then what had the Algiers deal been all about? How could two states come into being without mutual concessions on territory?

I did my best even so to get a hearing for Edward's reservations, and at his request I even wrote an uninspired introduction to his little anti-Oslo book *Peace and Its Discontents*, but my heart was not quite in it. The second so-called Palestinian *intifadah,* organized or incited in response to one of Ariel Sharon's staged provocations at the Al Aqsa mosque, reeked to me of racist and religious demagogy and of that dull, sinister "sacrificial" incantation that has since become so nauseating on a world scale.

Worse than that, in retrospect it cheapened and degraded the previous Palestinian appeals for solidarity. If the Palestinian people really wish to decide that they will battle to the very end to prevent partition or annexation of even an inch of their ancestral soil, then I have to concede that that is their right. I even think that a sixty-year rather botched experiment in marginal quasi-statehood is something that the Jewish people could consider abandoning. It represents barely an instant in our drawn-out and arduous history, and it's already been agreed even by the heirs of Ze'ev Jabotinsky that the whole scheme is unrealizable in "Judaea and Samaria," let alone in Gaza or Sinai. But it's flat-out intolerable to be solicited to endorse a side-by-side Palestinian homeland and then to discover that there are sinuous two-faced apologists explaining away the suicide-murder of Jewish civilians in Tel Aviv, a city which would be part of a Jewish state or community under any conceivable "solution." There's that word again . . . *

If a difference of principle goes undiscussed for any length of time, it will start to compromise and undermine the integrity of a friendship. I was aware by 2001 that some of our conversations had become just very slightly reserved, and that we were sticking to "safe" topics. The political distance between us had widened much faster than our personal relations would yet have shown: I had urged *The Nation* to publish Kanan Makiya's work on the Saddam Hussein regime, and when Edward rang the editors to complain, he was at first quite unaware that it had been my idea. His immediate riposte was vulgar in the extreme, containing the innuendo that Kanan was a paid agent, even a traitor.** Then all at once our personal and political

---

* Edward had a personal horror of violence and never endorsed or excused it, though in a documentary he made about the conflict he said that actions like the bombing of pilgrims at Tel Aviv airport "did more harm than good," which I remember thinking was (a) euphemistic and (b) a slipshod expression unworthy of a professor of English.

** In his attacks on fellow Arabs — Fouad Ajami being another recipient of his ire — Edward often became distressingly thuggish and *ad hominem.* Perhaps I was right to notice that softness on the USSR, which had been the special practitioner of such defamatory tactics.

quarrels were made very abruptly to converge. In the special edition of the *London Review of Books* published to mark the events of September 11, 2001, Edward painted a picture of an almost fascist America where Arab and Muslim citizens were being daily terrorized by pogroms, these being instigated by men like Paul Wolfowitz who had talked of "ending" the regimes that sheltered Al Quaeda. Again, I could hardly credit that these sentences were being produced by a cultured person, let alone printed by a civilized publication.

I resolutely refuse to believe that the state of Edward's health had anything to do with this, and I don't say this only because I was once later accused of attacking him "on his deathbed." He was entirely lucid to the end, and the positions he took were easily recognizable by me as extensions or outgrowths of views he had expressed (and also declined to express) in the past. Alas, it is true that he was closer to the end than anybody knew when the thirtieth anniversary reissue of his *Orientalism* was published, but his long-precarious condition would hardly argue for giving him a lenient review, let alone denying him one altogether, which would have been the only alternatives. In the introduction he wrote for the new edition, he generally declined the opportunity to answer his scholarly critics, and instead gave the recent American arrival in Baghdad as a grand example of "Orientalism" in action. The looting and destruction of the exhibits in the Iraq National Museum had, he wrote, been a deliberate piece of United States vandalism, perpetrated in order to shear the Iraqi people of their cultural patrimony and demonstrate to them their new servitude. Even at a time when anything at all could be said and believed so long as it was sufficiently and hysterically anti-Bush, this could be described as exceptionally mendacious. So when the *Atlantic* invited me to review Edward's revised edition, I decided I'd suspect myself more if I declined than if I agreed, and I wrote what I felt I had to.

Not long afterward, an Iraqi comrade sent me without comment an article Edward had contributed to a magazine in London that was published by a princeling of the Saudi royal family. In it, Edward quoted some sentences about the Iraq war that he off-handedly described as "racist." The sentences in question had been written by me. I felt myself assailed by a reaction that was at once hot-eyed and frigidly cold. He had cited the words without naming their author, and this I briefly thought could be construed as a friendly hesitance. Or as cowardice... I can never quite act the stern role of Mr. Darcy with any conviction, but privately I sometimes resolve that that's "it" as it were. I didn't say anything to Edward but then, I never said anything to him again, either. I believe that one or two charges simply must retain their face value and not become debauched or devalued. "Racist" is one such. It is an accusation that must either be made good upon, or fully retracted. I would not have as a friend somebody whom I suspected of that prejudice, and I decided to presume that Edward was honest and serious enough to feel the same way. I feel misery stealing over me again as I set this down: I wrote the best tribute I could manage when he died not long afterward (and there was no strain in that, as I was relieved to find), but I didn't go to, and wasn't invited to, his funeral.

Here is something of what I feel about friendship, and about the way in which it is a potent symbol of other things. In Martin Amis's enviably written memoir *Experience*, in the pages of which I am proud to appear several times, there is an episode about which people still interrogate me. Martin offers a slightly oblique and esoteric account of a trip on which he took me in 1989, to visit Saul Bellow in Vermont. On our buddy-movie drive up there from Cape Cod—he's almost word-perfect about this bit—he made it clear that I wasn't to drag the conversation toward anything political, let alone left-wing, let alone anything to do with Israel. ("No sinister balls," which was our colloquialism for a certain kind of too-easy leftism.) I knew I was being greatly honored by the invitation, not just because it was a huge distinction to meet Bellow but because, second only to an introduction to his father, it was the highest such gift that Martin could bestow. I needed no telling that I should seize the opportunity to do more listening than talking.

And yet it's true, as he reports, that by the end of dinner nobody could meet anyone else's eye and his own foot had become lamed and tired by its under-the-table collisions with my shins. How could this be? Now comes the chance for my own version of *Rashomon*.

Bellow had greeted us and given us drinks, and if I say so myself I had justified Martin's confidence during the predinner stage. Our host made an inquiry about Angus Wilson to which I happened to know the answer, and also a question about his own past with Whittaker Chambers to which

I could at least suggest a hypothetical solution.* Bellow in turn had read to us from some of his old writing about, and correspondence with, poor, mad, smashed John Berryman. Everything was shaping well enough. But right on the wicker table in the room where we were chatting, there lay something that was as potentially hackneyed in its menace as Anton Chekhov's gun on the mantelpiece. If it's there in the first act, in other words, the plain intention is that it will be fired before the curtain comes down. All you must do is wait. It was the only piece of printed matter in view, and it was the latest edition of *Commentary* magazine, and its bannered cover-story headline was: "Edward Said: Professor of Terror."

I hadn't completely wasted my time in dubious battle at New York and Washington and Chicago dinner parties, and I thought I knew when to raise my weary old dukes and when to keep them in my lap, but it was slightly nerve-straining to have to wonder in advance when and how this loaded barrel would be discharged. Dinner was by turns genial and sparkling, but the point came where Bellow made a sudden observation about anti-Zionism and then got up to fetch the magazine and underline his point. Indeed, I think he'd previously underlined some passages of the article as well. It was, even when tested against the depraved standard of polemic that had been set by Norman Podhoretz's editorship, a very coarse attack on Edward. I sat through Bellow's disgusted summary for a while until it calmly came to me that I couldn't say nothing. Conceivably, if Martin had not been there, I might have held my peace. But then, if he hadn't been there, neither would I have been. No, what I mean is that Bellow didn't know that I was a close friend of Edward's. But Martin did. Thus, even though I knew he wanted me to stay off anything controversial, I couldn't allow him to see me sitting there complicitly while an absent friend was being defamed. For all he knew, if the

---

* Offered a job as book critic for *Time* magazine as a young man, Bellow had been interviewed by Chambers and asked to give his opinion about William Wordsworth. Replying perhaps too quickly that Wordsworth had been a Romantic poet, he had been brusquely informed by Chambers that there was no place for him at the magazine. Bellow had often wondered, he told us, what he ought to have said. I suggested that he might have got the job if he'd replied that Wordsworth was a once-revolutionary poet who later became a conservative and was denounced by Browning and others as a turncoat. This seemed to Bellow to be probably right. More interesting was the related question: What if he'd *kept* that job?

company was sufficiently illustrious, I might even let the cock crow for him. That would surely never do. So I said what I felt I ought to say—it wasn't that much, but it was more than enough—and the carefully planned and delightfully executed evening of my very dearest friend was straightaway ruined. He suffered more agony than he needed to, because Bellow as an old former Trotskyist and Chicago streetfighter was used to much warmer work and hardly took offense at all. He later sent me a warm letter about my introduction to a new edition of *Augie March*.

I certainly didn't concur with Edward on everything, but I was damned if I would hear him abused without saying a word. And I think this may be worth setting down, because there are other allegiances that can be stress-tested in comparable ways. It used to be a slight hallmark of being English or British that one didn't make a big thing out of patriotic allegiance, and was indeed brimful of sarcastic and critical remarks about the old country, but would pull oneself together and say a word or two if it was attacked or criticized in any nasty or stupid manner by anybody else. It's family, in other words, and friends are family to me. I feel rather the same way about being an American, and also about being of partly Jewish descent. To be any one of these things is to be no better than anyone else, *but no worse*. When confronted by certain enemies, it is increasingly the "most definitely no worse" half of this unspoken agreement on which I tend to lay the emphasis. (As with Camus's famous "neither victim nor executioner," one hastens to assent but more and more to say "definitely not victim.")

On my desk is an appeal from the National Museum of American Jewish History in Philadelphia. It asks me to become a sponsor and donor of this soon-to-be-opened institution, while an accompanying leaflet has enticing photographs of Bob Dylan, Betty Friedan, Sandy Koufax, Irving Berlin, Estee Lauder, Barbra Streisand, Albert Einstein, and Isaac Bashevis Singer. There is something faintly *kitsch* about this, as there is in the habit of those Jewish papers that annually list Jewish prize-winners from the Nobel to the Oscars. (It is apparently true that the London *Jewish Chronicle* once reported the result of a footrace under the headline "Goldstein Fifteenth.") However, I think I may send a contribution. Other small "races" have come from unpromising and hazardous beginnings to achieve great things—no Roman would have believed that the brutish inhabitants of the British Isles could ever amount to much—and other small "races," too, like Gypsies and Armenians, have outlived determined attempts to eradicate and exterminate them. But there is something about the *persistence*, both of the Jews and their persecutors, that does seem to merit a museum of its own.

So I close this long reflection on what I hope is a not-too-quaveringly semi-Semitic note. When I am at home, I will only enter a synagogue for the *bar* or *bat mitzvah* of a friend's child, or in order to have a debate with the faithful. (When I was to be wed, I chose a rabbi named Robert Goldburg, an Einsteinian and a Shakespearean and a Spinozist, who had married Arthur Miller to Marilyn Monroe and had a copy of Marilyn's conversion certificate. He conducted the ceremony in Victor and Annie Navasky's front room, with David Rieff and Steve Wasserman as my best of men.) I wanted to do something to acknowledge, and to knit up, the broken continuity between me and my German-Polish forebears. When I am traveling, I will stop at the *shul* if it is in a country where Jews are under threat, or dying out, or were once persecuted. This has taken me down queer and sad little side streets in Morocco and Tunisia and Eritrea and India, and in Damascus and Budapest and Prague and Istanbul, more than once to temples that have recently been desecrated by the new breed of racist Islamic gangster. (I have also had quite serious discussions, with Iraqi Kurdish friends, about the possibility of Jews genuinely returning in friendship to the places in northern Iraq from which they were once expelled.) I hate the idea that the dispossession of one people should be held hostage to the victimhood of another, as it is in the Middle East and as it was in Eastern Europe. But I find myself somehow assuming that Jewishness and "normality" are in some profound way noncompatible. The most gracious thing said to me when I discovered my family secret was by Martin, who after a long evening of ironic reflection said quite simply: "Hitch, I find that I am a little envious of you." I choose to think that this proved, once again, his appreciation for the nuances of risk, uncertainty, ambivalence, and ambiguity. These happen to be the very things that "security" and "normality," rather like the fantasy of salvation, cannot purchase.

# Decline, Mutation, or Metamorphosis?

When the axe came into the woods, many of the trees said: "At least
the handle is one of us."

—Turkish proverb

If you desired to change the world, where would you start? With
yourself or others?

—Alexander Solzhenitsyn

TOWARD THE CLOSE of *Hearing Secret Harmonies*, which is
itself the close of his complex, majestic, rhythmical twelve-volume novel
sequence *A Dance to the Music of Time* (and also by a nice chance the volume
that happens to be dedicated to Robert Conquest), Anthony Powell's narrator
catches sight of a blue-clad person, crossing a playing field in his direction:

> Watching the approaching figure, I was reminded of a remark made
> by Moreland ages before. It related to one of those childhood memo-
> ries we sometimes found in common. This particular recollection had
> referred to an incident in *The Pilgrim's Progress* that had stuck in both
> our minds. Moreland said that, after his aunt read the book aloud to
> him as a child, he could never, even after he was grown-up, watch a
> lone figure draw nearer across a field, without thinking that this was
> Apollyon come to contend with him. From the moment of first hear-
> ing that passage read aloud—assisted by a lively portrayal of the fiend

in an illustration, realistically depicting his goat's horns, bat's wings, lion's claws, lizard's legs — the terror of that image, bursting out from an otherwise at moments prosy narrative, had embedded itself for all time in the imagination. I, too, as a child, had been riveted by the vividness of Apollyon's advance across the quiet meadow.

When I first read this passage of Powell, I put down the novel and was immediately back in the Crapstone of my Devonshire boyhood. The long-forgotten but evidently well-retained scene of my memory is as plain in my recollection as anything that happened to me yesterday. My younger brother, Peter — aged perhaps eight — has so strongly imbibed John Bunyan's Puritan classic as almost to have memorized it. (The "slough of despond," "the Giant Despair," "Doubting Castle," the fripperies of "Vanity's fair," "Oh death, where is thy sting?" Can you remember when all these used to be part of the equipment of everybody literate in English? They are as real to my brother and to me as the shaggy, wild ponies on the nearby moors.) But, coming to the very decisive page that should show Apollyon in all his horrid magnificence, Peter finds that the publishers have bowdlerized the text, and withheld this famous illustration from the version made available to the under-tens. He is not to be allowed to look The Evil One in the face.

This is one of those moments that, I choose to think, shows the Hitchens family at its best. Under an absolutely unremitting pressure from Peter, my father writes to the local library, to the bookshop, and eventually to the publishers themselves. No objection they can make is met by anything but scornful impatience; with a whim of steel my younger brother insists that if there is such an image, then he was not born to be shielded from it. I may have imagined this, but I am not certain that some harassed representative of the publisher does not actually call at our modest terrace house on the edge of Dartmoor, perhaps to confirm that this turbulent boy is really dictating such stuff to Commander Hitchens rather than acting as — say — the innocent front kid in some devil-worshipping or *Straw Dogs* coven.

I know that I mocked and teased Peter on the subject, because I was much too prone to tease him in any case, but the day came when the unabridged version arrived, and we could both solemnly turn — with parental supervision, of course, but in our own minds to protect our parents from any shock or trauma—to the color plate from hell. It was one of those pull-out pages that needs to be unfolded from the volume itself, in a three-stage concertina. And it was anticlimax defined. For one thing—Powell's summary above may have prepared you for this—it was absurdly overdone. A lizard-man or snake-man might have been represented creepily enough, but this non-artist had hugely overdone the number of possible mutations of leg, wing, and pinion and also given Apollyon a blazing furnace for a belly. The demon's wicked and gloating expression, looked at from one angle, was merely silly and bilious. I don't remember what the reaction of Yvonne and the Commander and Peter was to this long-awaited appointment with the forces of darkness, but on me it had the effect of reinforcing the growing opinion that all such images were strictly man-made, and indeed mainly designed like much of religion for the ignoble purpose of scaring children.

That's to one side. What I want to set down is the admiration I felt for Peter in taking things to their uttermost. He was already quite decided that he did not need any protection from unpleasantness, or from reality, and so it was immaterial that this particular exposure was to the unreal. "Facing it, Captain McWhirr," as Conrad puts it in his *Typhoon*. "Always facing it. That's the way to get through." To hand is a letter from Yvonne's dear friend Rosemary, in which she writes to me about the prep school Peter and I both attended and the gigantic and rather questionable chap who ran it:

> At Mount House Peter was called before Mr. Wortham for some misdemeanour and said to him: "You may be in command now but you will never quell the fires within me." (You probably know this tale.) We have all dined out on it for years...Whenever I see or hear him on TV or radio I am aware that that passionate little boy was the father of the man.

I did not in fact know "this tale," but I am certainly impressed by it because it can only have been conveyed by the mountainous Mr. Wortham himself, who must have been sufficiently disconcerted by Peter's mutinous backchat to report it to my parents. My younger brother has always since shown great steadiness under fire and in a variety of trying and testing circumstances at that, and it rather pleases me that his taunting enemies—just like the low, cheap crowd that would form around any conspicuous boy in the schoolyard—choose to mock him for being odd. He puts up with this handsomely enough, and he has lived to celebrate the total eclipse of a few politicians of the sad, ingratiating, crowd-pleasing sort, who were once nominated for certain glory by a mediocre press corps, yet had the air let out of them by Peter's questioning in public and his contempt in print. I become rather wistful when I reflect that this demonstration of Hitchensian moral courage has come at the price of a brother who isn't specially moved by our non-English ethnic heritage, and who is to outward appearances almost tragically right-wing.*

In Peter's most recent book, *The Broken Compass*, which contains several assertions and affirmations that make me desire to be wearing a necklace of the purest garlic even while reading them, there is a highly thoughtful and well-written passage on how it comes about that people do, in fact, undergo significant changes of mind. Given the absolute certainty that this process will be undergone by any serious person at least once, it is rather surprising to find how much is made out of it, and how many critics try to confect a mystery where none exists. Illustrating the same point in a different way, Peter takes the more subtle tack of showing how certain individuals will in fact alter their opinions, while often pretending to themselves and others for quite a long time that they have not "really" done so.

Analyzing the evolution of those, some of whom like myself were willing to make alliances of all kinds against Al Quaeda and its allies, he writes scornfully and—I must say—unsettlingly:

---

* My brother's case, plus the late reflection this brings on John Bunyan, convinces me again that there may have been such a thing as the Protestant or even Puritan revolution. Christopher Hill's attempt to Marxify the idea might not exactly work, but the concept of a time before kings and lords and bishops and popes is an ancient yearning. You can find it in Thomas Paine and Thomas Jefferson, and in poems like Macaulay's magnificent pastiche *Naseby*, as well as Orwell's *Nineteen Eighty-four*, where humble Smith's struggle against "Newspeak" and the Inner Party is the moral equivalent of those of Wyclif and Tyndale and Coverdale to have the Bible translated out of arcane priestly language and into plain English. Orwell's own favorite line—"By The Known Rules of Ancient Liberty"—was from John Milton. This might also go to support the satisfying idea of there being such a thing as a Protestant atheist. Much easier to imagine Peter Hitchens as an atheist than as a Muslim, let alone as a Jew or a Catholic. (When William Tyndale first went to school in medieval Oxford, I'm pleased to note, his family name was Hychyns.)

This is a very interesting halting place, as well as a comfortable one. For the habitual Leftist, it has the virtue of making him look as if he can change his mind, even when he has not really done so. It licenses him to be strongly anti-clerical and anti-religious, but in a way that Christian conservatives can tolerate.

The chapter is called "A Comfortable Stop on the Road to Damascus." The biblical cliché may seem inescapable but it actually retards understanding. There are people who attempt to demonstrate breadth of mind while only trying to have things both ways. ("Jews for Jesus" might be an example, or those "reform" Communists who tried and failed to cook a dish of "fried snowballs.") I once interviewed one of the original Stalinists-turned-dissident, the Yugoslav Milovan Djilas, who, sitting in his tiny Belgrade apartment, said that he had come to admire the work of Friedrich August von Hayek, adding hastily that he did not really agree with him about property rights: a prince-free reading of *Hamlet* if ever I struck one. However the whole point of the Damascus legend is that it refuses the very idea of the mind's evolution, replacing it with the deranged substitute of instant divine revelation.

We are forcibly made familiar, usually from febrile tenth-hand accounts of religious visionaries and other probable epileptics and schizophrenics, of those blinding and indeed Damascene moments (or moments of un-blindness when scales supposedly fall from the eyes) that constitute such revelation. Yet one suspects, as with Archimedes and his *eureka*, that Pasteur was right and that in the case of sound minds at any rate, great apparent coincidences only occur to the intellect that has rehearsed and prepared for them. It may be the same with lesser convictions and allegiances. I once spoke with a hardened senior member of the Provisional Irish Republican Army, who was in the room with his leader David O'Connell when the news came that one of their bombs had "successfully" gone off. Among the casualties was a young woman who was pregnant. But it turned out that she was also Protestant. "Well, that's two for one, then," remarked O'Connell, light-heartedly clearing the air. In that instant, his deputy says, he himself internally defected from the IRA and began the second career as an informer for the British which would wreak the most terrible revenge on his former "associates." But I believe that he had been getting ever more sickened as time went by, and that there came a "moment" that seemed dramatic and was certainly memorably disgusting, when any extra morsel would have been too much for him. (There is also such a thing as ex post facto rationalization, especially in the case of people who have repented of terrible crimes.) It could be as true to say, as some of my tutors in Oxford philosophy used to seem to argue, that it is your mind that changes *you*.

The history of the twentieth-century Left is replete with such episodes, very often and very interestingly involving moments when somebody, hearing a statement of apparent agreement, experiences a violent sense of repulsion. The brilliant Austrian Marxist Ernst Fischer, having publicly defended the Hitler-Stalin pact as a tactical imperative, had his composure destroyed not long afterward when some *dumkopf* Communist told him excitedly: "Have you heard the news? We've taken Paris!" The moron was referring to the march of the Wehrmacht up the Champs-Elysées. Fischer wanted to say that this was not at all what he had intended, but then, perhaps it had been... During the Moscow show-trials, Whittaker Chambers heard Alger Hiss say approvingly that "Old Joe Stalin certainly knows how to play for keeps," and as an old Bolshevik he found himself experiencing a similar nausea. Incidentally, what single thing did Chambers and Hiss have in common? They both believed that the victory of Soviet Communism was inevitable. As a defector from that cause, Chambers believed that he had resignedly joined the losing side. As a lifelong opportunist, Hiss thought he had placed his own bet on the winning one. So it goes.

I was once slightly friendly with Dorothy Healey, a veteran American Communist who could boast, among other things, of having recruited the nasty but pulchritudinous incendiary Angela Davis into "The Party." Dorothy had been through a lot for her beliefs, ever since becoming a working-class Red during the Depression, and for those same beliefs she had also swallowed a good deal. She had managed to explain away the Soviet repressions and invasions and, on the radio show she hosted for the Pacifica channel, would often give air time to visiting officials from Moscow. Once, not long after the expulsion of Alexander Solzhenitsyn from the USSR, she invited some Soviet cultural hack to respond to the "Cold War hysteria" that the incident had generated in the imperialist-dominated American press. The hack duly explained that Solzhenitsyn was a *provocateur* and a tool of reaction, and the author of a mendacious history of the Stalin era and ... suddenly Dorothy asked him a question she had not planned. "You say it's a terrible book full of lies?" "Yes," replied the hack. "And just how," she inquired, "do you know this?" "Because," replied the hack, "I have read it." Dorothy let a few beats go by before she said the next thing, and then she uttered — on air for all the comrades to hear — the response: "How come you have read it if it's banned for everyone else in the Soviet Union?" At that instant, she told me, she understood that without any previous intention of doing so, she had resigned from the Communist Party. Yet again, though, I feel she had been keeping the lid on a stew of misgiving for some time, and reached the point where it might bubble over at any moment.*

If all my examples of sudden or gradual change of heart or mind are taken from the Left, I think this is for two good historical reasons. One is that we don't seem to have any cases of Nazi and fascist workers and intellectuals undergoing crises of ideology and conscience and exclaiming: "Hitler has betrayed the revolution," or flagellating themselves with the thought: "How could such frightful crimes be committed in the name of Nazism?" There are good and sufficient reasons for this that I don't believe I need to explain: in his book *Koba the Dread*, which reproves me for my lenience in referring tenderly to old "comrades" on the Marxist Left, Martin Amis does say that of course one can't imagine a hypothetical "Hitch" joshing in the same manner about his former blackshirt brothers and boozing partners, because in such a case he wouldn't *be* the Hitch. No — and thanks to him for saying so — and nor by the way, in such a case, would Martin have consented for a single second to be my friend. (As the French say, if your aunt had wheels she *still* wouldn't be a bus.) For this and related reasons I always mentally cross my fingers and keep a slight mental reservation whenever "left" and "right" crimes are too glibly mentioned in the same breath. Yet now, it is those on

---

* Her story is rather preferable to the one told me by Eric Hobsbawm, who at the time of his resignation from the Communist Party was probably the only member of any academic or intellectual or scholarly repute that it still possessed. Running into him shortly after the fall of the Berlin Wall in 1989, I asked him if he'd retained his membership and was told "no." What then had finally precipitated the separation? "They forgot to send me the form asking me for the annual renewal of my membership," he said with perfect gravity, "and so I decided not to write to headquarters and remind them." Just like that, then.

the Left who have come to offend and irritate me the most, and it is also their crimes and blunders that I feel myself more qualified, as well as more motivated, to point out.

I mentioned a second historical reticence just a while ago, and here it is. Many people suspect even themselves for growing cold on a cause that once animated them. I began this book by mentioning Julian Barnes's late-life and death-anticipating memoir *Nothing to Be Frightened Of*, and its role in my own dress rehearsal with the premature pomp of finding myself briefly posthumous. In one of his early chapters, Julian describes how that "Friday lunch" from our Bloomsbury boyhood still goes on, though now it's held only once a year and takes the form of rather a stately dinner. Just to give you an idea of his tone:

> Thirty or more years ago, this Friday lunch was instituted: a shouty, argumentative, smoky, boozy gathering attended by journalists, novelists, poets and cartoonists at the end of another working week. Over the years the venue has shifted many times, and the personnel been diminished by relocation and death. Now there are seven of us left, the eldest in his mid-seventies, the youngest in his late—very late—fifties.

I guessed the name of the oldest easily enough but it was with a twinge that I suddenly appreciated that that kid at the table is still Martin. I also paused at the disclosure that Julian himself now sits down while "thumbing in" his "deaf aids": I don't remember the old lunchtimes as being at all "shouty" but perhaps this auditory distortion, too, has deep roots. Anyway, here comes a small but unignorable jab:

> The talk follows familiar tracks; gossip, bookbiz, litcrit, music, films, politics (some have done the ritual shuffle to the Right).

There is something in Julian's implicit assumption here that makes me want to object. Is it true, as I might once have said myself, that a rejection of former allegiance can simply be read off from the graph of *anni domini*—mark the senile whistle and whinny and wheeze that is compressed into that damning word "shuffle"—and thus constitutes a cliché all of its own? "When people become older they become a little more tolerant," snaps the case-hardened Komorovski to the hot young idealist Pasha Antipov in *Dr. Zhivago*. "Perhaps because they have more to 'tolerate' in themselves," replies Antipov in what for many years I considered a very cutting return serve.*

I sometimes feel that I should carry around some sort of rectal thermometer, with which to test the rate at which I am becoming an old fart. There is no point in pretending that the process doesn't occur: it happens to me when near-beardless uniformed officials or bureaucrats, one third of my age, adopt a soothing tone while telling me, "Sir, I'm going to have to ask you to..." It also happens when I hear some younger "wannabe" radicals employing hectoring arguments to which I have almost forgotten the answer. But that at least is because the arguments themselves are *so old* that they almost make me feel young again. From this kind of leathery awareness, nature itself protects the young, and a good thing, too, otherwise they would be old before their time and be taking no chances. Meanwhile, all of my children have negotiated the shoals of up-growing with a great deal more maturity than I did, and most of my moments of feeling that the world is not as bad as it might be have come from my students, especially the ones who decided in college that they wanted to join the armed forces and guard me while I sleep. (Meeting some of them later, after they have done a tour or two, has been particularly uplifting.) No, when I check the thermometer I find that it is the fucking *old* fools who get me down the worst, and the attainment of that level of idiocy can often require a lifetime.

Here is the voice of the above-mentioned Dorothy Healey on my voicemail the day after I volunteered to testify to Congress that Clinton and his aides were lying when they said they had not been slandering and defaming Monica Lewinsky. "You stinking little rat, I always knew you were no good. You are a stoolpigeon and a fink. I hope you rot in scab and blackleg hell..."

---

* Julian, for example, was much quoted for saying that the whole battle over Iraq wasn't worth the life of a single British soldier, which echoes what Otto von Bismarck said—"not worth the balls of a Pomeranian grenadier"—about the whole of the Balkans. Yet why is that sort of *realpolitik* considered to be "left" rather than conservative? Attacking me in one of the magazines of the American isolationist Right, Peter Hitchens denounced the war in Afghanistan as the sort of "stupid, left-wing war" that only people like his brother would endorse. That seemed to me nearer the mark than Julian.

There was more. I used to replay it often. Two things about it struck me. The first and most obvious was the absolutely genuine and double-distilled malice: this was from a former not-that-close friend who would happily have got up early to see me tortured. The second was exactly that whistling and senile undertone. She didn't have long to go and had been forced to admit that much if not most of her political life had been a waste of time, but here at least was something—a case of a one-time comrade turning state's evidence, so to say—that allowed her all the unalloyed energy and joy of being a young Communist again. (As it happens I was testifying *against* the most powerful man in the world and in favor of a much-derided victim: in her mind any congressional committee was still run by Joe McCarthy.)*

Alteration of mind can creep up on you: for a good many years I maintained that I was a socialist if only to distinguish myself from the weak American term "liberal," which I considered evasive. Brian Lamb, the host of C-Span cable television, bears some of the responsibility for this. Having got me to proudly announce my socialism once, on the air, he never again had me as a guest without asking me to reaffirm the statement. It became the moral equivalent of a test of masculinity: I wouldn't give him or his audience the satisfaction of a denial. Then I sat down to write my *Letters to a Young Contrarian*, and made up my mind to address the letters to real students whose faces and names and questions I had to keep in mind. What was I to say when they asked my advice about "commitment"? They all wanted to do something to better the human condition. Well, was there an authentic socialist movement for them to join, as I would once have said there was? Not really, or not anymore, or only in forms of populism and nationalism *à la* Hugo Chavez that seemed to me repellent. Could a real internationalist "Left" be expected to revive? It didn't seem probable. I abruptly realized that I had no right to bluff or to bullshit the young. (Late evenings with old comrades retelling tales of old campaigns weren't exactly dishonest, but then they didn't really count, either.) So I didn't so much repudiate a former loyalty, like some attention-grabbing defector, as feel it falling away from me.

---

* This is why Elia Kazan's *On the Waterfront*, which suggests that decent people should break the Mafia's law of *omerta*, is *still* regarded as morally dubious by many on the American Left.

On some days, this is like the phantom pain of a missing limb. On others, it's more like the sensation of having taken off a needlessly heavy overcoat.*

I can write about this now in a relaxed manner, but for a long time I felt I had to phrase any disagreement with actual or former comrades in terms that were themselves "Left." It was quite easy, for example, to argue that Bill Clinton was an acquiescent front man for all manner of corporate special interests. My book denouncing him for this, and for his disgusting crimes against women, and his "Wag-the-Dog" missile attack on Sudan, and his cruel use of the death penalty as a racist political weapon for his advancement in Arkansas, was brought out by the publishing arm of the *New Left Review*, which continued as my publisher for some time afterward. I became quite adept at the relevant dialectic. From Bosnia during the siege of Sarajevo, for instance, I could write that the old spirit of the Yugoslav socialist "partisans" was much more to be found in the anti-fascist posters and slogans of the Bosnian resistance than in the fiery yet lugubrious, defiant yet self-pitying, race-and-blood obsessed effusions of the Serbs, "socialist" though their nominal leader Slobodan Milošević might claim to be. The old slogans still sometimes strike me as the best ones, and "Death to Fascism" requires no improvement.

Sarajevo, though, was the first place where I began to realize that I had embarked upon a reconsideration that wasn't completely determined by me, or by what I already thought and knew, or thought I knew or thought. Much of it was probably dawning on me while I slept. Watching the Stalinist world succumb so pathetically, even gratefully, to its death wish in late 1989, when I happily witnessed the terminal twitches and spasms of the Hungarian and Romanian regimes, I had briefly celebrated the end of the totalitarian idea. In Hungary this had already died years previously, at least as Communism, and in Romania it had long before mutated into something grotesque and monstrous: Caligula sculpted in concrete. Milošević, too, exemplified this

---

* Some time later, I was invited by Bernard-Henri Levy to write an essay on political reconsiderations for his magazine *La Regle du Jeu*. I gave it the partly ironic title: "Can One Be a Neoconservative?" Impatient with this, some copy editor put it on the cover as "How I Became a Neoconservative." Perhaps this was an instance of the Cartesian principle as opposed to the English empiricist one: it was decided that I evidently was what I apparently only thought.

fusion of the cardboard-suited party-line populist and the hysterical nationalist demagogue. Here in grisly action was the gargoyle leader Paduk, founder
of the "Party of the Average Man" from Nabokov's 1947 *Bend Sinister*: the
common-touch, little-guy, good-fellow type with the private line in blackmail and highly enriched child abuse.

Driving around Bosnia's bombarded capital city with the bravest and
most literate reporter of my generation, John Burns, I made the slightly
invigorating discovery that must have occurred to previous Hitchenses in
deadlier war zones. Physical courage is in some part the outcome of sheer cir-
cumstance. You can't actually stay hidden forever on that corner at which the
snipers are taking aim. You will starve to death, for one thing. So make the
dash that you were going to have to make anyway, and you will have crushed
your own cowardice for a moment, which is a tremendous feeling. I was often
enough whimpering with fear but never given the chance to make fear make
me feel any safer if I cowered or did nothing. (I also discovered, as have many
others, that the stupid old propaganda line about "no atheists in foxholes" is
just that: it never crossed my mind to pray.) I merely pass this on in case it's
ever of any use. Meanwhile, though, I was kept warm and animated by my
rage at what I was seeing.

An ancient and civilized town, famous in European history as the site of a
tragic drama but also celebrated as a symbiotic meeting place of peoples and
cultures and religions (the name itself derives from the antique word *serai*, as
in "caravanserai" or place of shelter and hospitality), was being coldly reduced
to shards by drunken gunners on the surrounding hills who sniggeringly
represented the primeval hatred of the peasant for the city and the illiterate
for the educated. The first time I saw a mortar bomb burst, it did so in plain
daylight, without the possibility of a targeting error, making an evil howl as it
fell right against the wall of the beautiful and unmistakable National Library
of Bosnia-Herzegovina. I felt an answering shriek within the cave of my own
chest. When decoded, this internal yell took the form of a rather simple plea
that the United States Air Force appear in the Bosnian skies and fill with fear
and trembling the fat, red, broken-veined faces of the crack Serbian artillery-
men who had never until then lost a battle against civilians.

Again, I couldn't be entirely sure whether this was a quasi-Damascene
moment or a long-meditated one. As a young boy I had been taken by my

parents on a holiday in the Channel Islands or, as the French call them more neutrally, Les Isles Anglo-Normandes. This Anglo-Norman archipelago is anyway under British rule and has been for a long time, and I suppose I dimly knew that it was the only part of Britain that had been occupied by the Nazis. Straying away from my family to haunt a second-hand bookshop in the town of St. Helier, capital of the main island of Jersey, I found a book thrillingly titled *Jersey under the Jackboot.* Its cover photograph showed the main square where I had just eaten my lunch, with a huge red-and-black swastika flag hanging from the town-hall balcony. In front was a genial British policeman, in blue uniform and helmet, directing the traffic. Now that was a moment when I could feel everything inside me rearranging itself. It was suddenly possible to picture all my boyhood authority figures, from headmasters to clergymen and even uniform-wearing parents, as they might have looked if German authority had been superimposed on them. It had, after all, happened to the church and the state and most of the armed forces on the French side of that "Channel." The shock is with me still.

Michael Scammell's biography of Arthur Koestler says that "his intellectual nerve-endings were so finely tuned that he experienced the onset of fresh ideas like orgasms, and mourned their passing as the end of treasured love-affairs." I can lay no claim to have been half so fortunate. Brief and full of passionate intensity as it was, my moment in St. Helier wasn't quite like that. Indeed, I can't be sure that such transfiguring initial moments are even enviable. I do know what it's like, however, to mourn the passing of a love, and I remember Sarajevo for that reason. By the end of that conflict, I was being called a traitor and a warmonger by quite a lot of the Left and was both appalled and relieved to find that I no longer really cared. Again to cite the ever-eloquent Koestler, this time on the Hitler-Stalin pact from his essay in *The God That Failed.* Without admitting it to himself, I think he had been quite badly hurt by charges of "selling out" and treason from his former comrades. (Hannah Arendt remarks somewhere that the great achievement of Stalinism was to have deposed the habit of argument and dispute among intellectuals, and to have replaced it with the inquisitorial, unanswerable question of *motive.*) Anyway, here's how Koestler felt his fog of misery and doubt beginning to lift:

I remained in that state of suspended animation until the day when the swastika was hoisted on Moscow airport in honor of Ribbentrop's arrival and the Red Army band broke into the Horst Wessel Song. That was the end, from then onward I no longer cared whether Hitler's allies called me a counter-revolutionary.

Under much less arduous circumstances, I found it was taking me much longer to "let go." I had wanted the moral arithmetic to add up, while still hoping that it could somehow be made to do this on the "left" side of the column. In Bosnia, though, I was brought to the abrupt admission that, if the majority of my former friends got their way about non-intervention, there would be another genocide on European soil. A century that had opened with the Muslim Turkish slaughter of the Armenians, and climaxed in the lowest sense of that term with an attempt to erase Jewry, could well close with a Christian destruction of the continent's oldest Muslim population. This was an exceedingly clarifying reflection. It made me care much less about the amour propre of my previous loyalties. I might illustrate this better if I did so by means of two other figures who were highly important to me: Noam Chomsky and Susan Sontag.

At the time of the Milošević wars, I was still engaged in a desultory email exchange with Chomsky on another matter. He had written, as far back as 1990, that Vaclav Havel's visit to Washington after the overthrow of Czechoslovak Communism was not at all what it had seemed. For Havel to address a joint session on Capitol Hill, only months after the murders of the Jesuit leadership by death squads in El Salvador, and to make no mention of the part played by the United States in this dreadful episode, was in Noam's opinion disgraceful. (I think this "moral equivalence" canard was being resuscitated because of Havel's support for intervention in the Balkans: a policy that Chomsky detested.) Havel's speech, he intoned, was just as if an American Communist had gone to Moscow in 1938 and spoken to the Presidium as an invited guest while deliberately suppressing any mention of the purges. I tried as a friend to dissuade him from this analogy and from the conclusions that were doubtless meant to flow from it. I forget all the points I made, but I hope I kept in mind the fact that Congress was elected whereas Stalin's assembly was not, and the prevalence of censorship, torture, and murder in one case and not the other. I certainly said that Havel was the new and freely chosen representative of a small country, who had come to thank a big one which had at least rhetorically stood by it in adversity, so that the moment for a public denunciation of American war crimes was scarcely apt. I dare say that this last observation would have seemed paltry or worse to Chomsky. Anyway, at the close of one such exchange, and wearying of it a bit, I changed the subject and asked him if his co-author Edward Herman, who was then taking positions that made the names "Serbia" and "Yugoslavia" almost interchangeable, was to be regarded as his "co-thinker" on this, too. (In order to be clear: to say that the United States was bombing "Yugoslavia" seemed to me false. To say that a dictatorial and expansionist Serbia had been bombing the rest of Yugoslavia seemed to be true.) Professor Chomsky replied loftily that he did not really regard anyone as his co-thinker. This was his absolute right, but I felt that my reasonably direct question had received a rather shifty answer, and this from the man who so highly esteemed truth in language. I experienced the dismal feeling of a steep diminution of esteem on my own part, along with the premonition that this might not be the end of it.*

Susan Sontag was an admirable example of what it means, if it really means anything, to be a "public intellectual." She most certainly wasn't a private one. She was self-sustaining and self-supporting, and though she did like to follow fashion and keep herself updated, she was not a prisoner of trend. She was beautiful and dramatic, with the most astonishingly liquid eyes. She wanted to have everything at least three ways and she wanted it voraciously: an evening of theater or cinema followed by a lengthy dinner at an intriguing new restaurant, with visitors from at least one new country, to be succeeded

---

* Chomsky has since said some things to suggest that he never thought I was any good anyway: I possess several inscribed books from him that prove the contrary. As it happens I don't think it's kosher to pay him back in the same coin. In the late 1970s he wrote to me praising something I'd written about the need to try and keep *Encounter* magazine from going under: his libertarianism (and his rare-on-the-Left admiration for Orwell) has been relatively consistent. If you look back at the essays that made his name—on the incipient stages of the Vietnam War, on B.F. Skinner, on the memoirs of Kissinger, on East Timor, and on the Kahane Commission on the Sabra/Shatila massacres—you will find a polemical talent well worth mourning, and a feeling for justice that ought not to have gone rancid and resentful.

by very late-night conversation precisely so that an early start could be made in the morning. I consider myself pretty durable in these same sweepstakes but I once almost fell asleep standing up while preparing her a sofa bed in Washington after a very exhausting day of multiple meals and discussions: she had vanished to begin the next day long before I regained consciousness. She had some of the vices that attend this voracity, becoming easily impatient and sometimes making one begin all over again to try for a plateau of intimacy that one felt had already been attained. The reactionary critic Hilton Kramer once wrote, whether with deliberate or unconscious absurdity I do not know, that her beloved son (and my esteemed friend) David Rieff would not develop until he left "the Sontag circle." This seemed like rather a lot to ask. Ridiculing Kramer at the end of a dinner, she and David and I clinked glasses to my toast: "May the circle be unbroken," and later embraced on the sidewalk. Next time we met, she put me in the wrong about something where I quite possibly had been gravely wrong, but still ... *

One always had to forgive her, because whether it was the AIDS plague — the initial nightmare of which we have now chosen to forget — or politics, she could call upon both moral and physical courage. And she did not just defend AIDS victims as a "category," but generously drew upon her own struggles with carcinoma to help and advise individuals. Nobody human is ever consistent, but Susan showed herself prepared to follow where logic might compel her to go. I don't say that she did this in a straight line, but then it would be boring if it were otherwise. I now understand that my first confrontation with what was to be the rest of my political life came when I watched her address the celebrated meeting "Solidarity with *Solidarity*" in New York in early 1982. It was by then fairly easy for the "progressive" world to make the formally correct noises about a military coup in Poland, and several speakers duly did so while hurrying to add (as Susan must have guessed they would) that workers were also being repressed in El Salvador,

---

* Reflecting on this now, I think perhaps that she wanted to be sure, and also for me and others to be on notice, that she wasn't to be taken for granted and that there was always to be some demarcation between friendship and agreement. Quite probably a good thing. Many truths or useful remarks go unspoken for fear of rupturing intimacy, and after all, there never *was* a Sontag "circle," or clique. This is the point that Edmund White rather fails to apprehend about her in *City Boy*, his free-hand memoir of the higher naughtiness in New York.

not to mention the United States. I knew I was present for a real rather than a routine event when she got up and said: "I repeat; not only is Fascism (and overt military rule) the probable destiny of all Communist societies—especially when their populations are moved to revolt—but Communism is itself a variant, the most successful variant, of Fascism. Fascism with a human face." That last phrasing didn't precisely "work," or else it did work precisely because it was somewhat contradictory. Edmund White is once again wrong to say that she was "howled off the stage" in consequence: there was a sort of angry silence as the audience checked its reflexes. The comrades had already had to absorb her wounding suggestion—chosen as if on purpose to dissolve any illusions they retained—that the conservative lowbrow CIA-backed *Reader's Digest* (its very name an insult to the well-read) would have been a better Everyman guide to Communist reality than *The Nation* or the *New Statesman*.

The usual duty of the "intellectual" is to argue for complexity and to insist that phenomena in the world of ideas should not be sloganized or reduced to easily repeated formulae. But there is another responsibility, to say that some things are simple and ought not to be obfuscated, and by 1982 Communism had long passed the point where it needed anything more than the old equation of history with the garbage can. Even Susan, though, felt that she might have gone a burned bridge too far. As someone who had spent much of his life writing for *The Nation* and the *New Statesman*, I presumed on our recent friendship to call round and ask if *The Nation* could have a copy of her (clearly prepared) speech, so as to put it in print and invite a symposium of comments. She agreed, but on the startling condition that the sentence about the superiority of the *Reader's Digest* be cut out. Even then, I knew better than to pick a quarrel with her on a detail. We ran the speech as redacted by her, and I wrote an introductory passage describing the evening and therefore putting her excised sentence back in, as having been extensively reported.*

In the symposium that we eventually ran, a number of the Left

---

* You really cannot win with everybody at once: the CIA's historically more highbrow offspring *Encounter* ran a piece by Melvin Lasky accusing me of *having removed* the relevant words on purpose from her own text.

intelligentsia made the abysmal mistake of saying, in effect, that while what Susan had said might be partly true or even plain true, she would still have been much better advised not to say it. I think she herself may have feared that she was somehow "objectively" helping Ronald Reagan. But whether her mind changed her, or she changed her mind, she manifested the older truth that all riveters of the mind-forged manacles most fear, and that I here repeat: *One cannot be just a little bit heretical.*

I add for emphasis that, within a decade, official Communism had imploded beyond all hope of repair, or else mutated into overt military dictatorship as in North Korea and Cuba—the last uniformed regime in Latin America—and that in Serbia the word "fascism," or even "National Socialism," would not have been much of an exaggeration. All that remained at that point was to stop temporizing, stop clinging to consoling hand-holds and dallying in halfway houses and call for NATO and the White House to abandon an ignoble neutrality and save the name of Europe. Which Susan loudly did, and today's rescued Sarajevo has a street that bears her name.*

Hannah Arendt used to speak of "the lost treasure of revolution": a protean phenomenon that eluded the capture of those who sought it the most. Like Hegel's "cunning of history" and Marx's "old mole" that surfaced in unpredictable and ironic places, this mercurial element did quicken my own short life in the magic, tragic years that are denoted as 1968, 1989, and 2001. In the course of all of them, even if not without convolutions and contradictions, it became evident that the only historical revolution with any verve left in it, or any example to offer others, was the American one. (Marx and Engels, who wrote so warmly about the United States and who were Lincoln's strongest supporters in Europe, and who so much disliked the bloodiness and backwardness of Russia, might not have been either surprised or disconcerted to notice this outcome.)

To announce that one has painfully learned to think for oneself might seem an unexciting conclusion and anyway, I have only my own word for it

---

* In spite of the general nullity of the Left on this question, Susan was only the best known of several, including Bernard-Henri Levy, Peter Schneider, Daniel Cohn-Bendit, Adam Michnik, and others, who in their way traced a line from 1968 through 1989 to future combats with the totalitarian.

that I have in fact taught myself to do so. The ways in which the conclusion is arrived at may be interesting, though, just as it is always *how* people think that counts for much more than *what* they think. I suspect that the hardest thing for the idealist to surrender is the teleological, or the sense that there is some feasible, lovelier future that can be brought nearer by exertions in the present, and for which "sacrifices" are justified. With some part of myself, I still "feel," but no longer really think, that humanity would be the poorer without this fantastically potent illusion. "A map of the world that did not show Utopia," said Oscar Wilde, "would not be worth consulting." I used to adore that phrase, but now reflect more upon the shipwrecks and prison islands to which the quest has led.

But I hope and believe that my advancing age has not quite shamed my youth. I have actually seen more prisons broken open, more people and territory "liberated," and more taboos broken and censors flouted, since I let go of the idea, or at any rate the plan, of a radiant future. Those "simple" ordinary propositions, of the open society, especially when contrasted with the lethal simplifications of that society's sworn enemies, were all I required. This wasn't a dreary shuffle to the Right, either. It used to be that the Right made tactical excuses for friendly dictatorships, whereas now most conservatives are frantic to avoid even the appearance of doing so, and at least some on the Left can take at least some of the credit for at least some of that. It is not so much that there are ironies of history, it is that history itself is ironic. It is not that there are no certainties, it is that it is an absolute certainty that there are no certainties. It is not only true that the test of knowledge is an acute and cultivated awareness of how little one knows (as Socrates knew so well), it is true that the unbounded areas and fields of one's ignorance are now expanding in such a way, and at such a velocity, as to make the contemplation of them almost fantastically beautiful. One reason, then, that I would not relive my life is that one cannot be born knowing such things, but must find them out, even when they then seem bloody obvious, for oneself. If I had set out to put this on paper so as to spare you some or even any of the effort, I would be doing you an injustice.

I began this highly selective narrative by citing Auden on the unadvisability of being born in the first place—a view from which he quickly waltzed to Plan B: make the most of the dance (or, as Dorothy Parker elsewhere phrased it, "You might as well live"). In better moments I prefer the lyrical stoicism of my friend and ally Richard Dawkins, who never loses his sense of wonder at the sheer unlikelihood of having briefly "made it" on a planet where crude extinction has held such sway, and where the chance of being conceived, let alone safely delivered, is so infinitesimal.

When my beloved friend James Fenton came back from Indochina, having witnessed the fall of Saigon and Phnom Penh and the end, both tragic and ambiguous, of a war which so many of us had regarded as a test of sheer commitment, he was somewhat shaken. The closing words of one of his most exquisite poems from that period were: "I'm afraid that all my friends are dead." But he knew that if there were any survivors they would know how to contact him, and when some of them did, and being the conscience-determined person he was and is, he went straight back to the frontiers and the camps to see how he could be of help. The resulting poems—collected as *Children in Exile*—comprise an essential complement to their predecessors in *Memory of War*. One of the latter is titled "Prison Island." I happen to remember the genesis of this outwardly melancholy but diamond-hard poem particularly well: we had both just been verbally and aurally assailed by a braggart dogmatist who asserted of his own sect: "The possibility of defeat does not enter our calculations."

This honking, tyrannical self-regard so annoyed James, and I think so much put him in mind of the deadly certainties that had brought such havoc to his Asian friends, that he could not rest until he had caught its hubris in the net of his verses. I have a poignant memory of him reading the first draft aloud to me, in the attic room where he was then lodging. One stanza in particular caught and held me, too:

> My dear friend, do you value the counsels of dead men?
> I should say this. Fear defeat. Keep it before your mind
> As much as victory. Defeat at the hands of friends,
> Defeat in the plans of your confident generals.
> Fear the kerchiefed captain who does not think he can die.

Over the course of the last decade, I have become vividly aware of a literally lethal challenge from the sort of people who deal in absolute certainty and believe themselves to be actuated and justified by a supreme authority.

To have spent so long learning so relatively little, and then to be menaced in every aspect of my life by people who already know everything, and who have all the information they need...More depressing still, to see that in the face of this vicious assault so many of the best lack all conviction, hesitating to defend the society that makes their existence possible, while the worst are full to the brim and boiling over with murderous exaltation.

It's quite a task to combat the absolutists and the relativists at the same time: to maintain that there is no totalitarian solution while also insisting that, yes, we on our side also have unalterable convictions and are willing to fight for them. After various past allegiances, I have come to believe that Karl Marx was rightest of all when he recommended continual doubt and self-criticism. Membership in the skeptical faction or tendency is not at all a soft option. The defense of science and reason is the great imperative of our time, and I feel absurdly honored to be grouped in the public mind with great teachers and scholars such as Richard Dawkins (a true Balliol man if ever there was one), Daniel Dennett, and Sam Harris. To be an unbeliever is not to be merely "open-minded." It is, rather, a decisive admission of uncertainty that is dialectically connected to the repudiation of the totalitarian principle, in the mind as well as in politics. But that's my Hitch-22. I have already described some of the rehearsals for this war, which the relativists so plaintively call "endless"—as if it were not indeed the latest chapter of an eternal struggle—and I find that for the remainder of my days I shall be happy enough to see if I can emulate the understatement of Commander Hitchens, and to say that at least I know what I am supposed to be doing.

# Acknowledgments

I HAVE TRIED TO DEFRAY some of my debts of acknowledgment in these very pages, but I must not omit those who made it possible for me to set down the work in the first place. Much nonsense is talked in our day about the decay of publishing, and it will remain nonsense while people like Jonathan Karp, Colin Shepherd, Bob Castillo, Cary Goldstein and Toby Mundy have the ordering of things at houses like Twelve and Atlantic. I have been especially fortunate in boasting a friend and comrade, Steve Wasserman, as, at different times, my editor for reviews, my editor for books, and last and perhaps best of all my agent. I have to thank Robin Blackburn of the *New Left Review* for effecting my introduction to Steve thirty years ago, and for much else besides.

Maciej Sikierski, the unsleeping archivist for Polish affairs at the library of the Hoover Institution at Stanford University, went to uncommon trouble to assist me in tracing my families' lineages in the arduous history and geography of his indomitable country.

I sometimes like to think that I could have been one of those I praise in this book, who, like Victor Serge, had the intestinal fortitude to write "for the bottom drawer, and for history." But I know damn well that without certain editors and publishers I would have drooped like a wet sock. Undying and moist thanks, then, to Paul Barker, Anthony Howard, Harold Evans and Tina Brown, Charles Wintour, Alexander Chancellor, Charles Moore, Jeremy Treglown, Sally Emerson, Peter Stothard, Victor Navasky and Richard

Lingeman and Hamilton Fish and Betsy Pochoda, Barbara Epstein, Michael Kelly (RIP) and James Bennett and Cullen Murphy and Ben Schwarz, David Rieff, Jon Meacham and Mark Miller, Jacob Weisberg, David Plotz and June Thomas, Lewis Lapham and Gerry Marzorati, Perry Anderson and Robin Blackburn, Mary-Kay Wilmers and Inigo Thomas, Deirdre English, and Conor Hanna. All of them are heroes and heroines of the "first draft" and of the work in progress, and the readers of many other authors should not omit to thank them as warmly as I do.

Many thanks to Windsor Mann for help on archives and photographs.

To thank my adored father-in-law, Edwin Blue, and my delightful daughter for their expert assistance to a techno peasant would be to say the least of it.

Impossible, though, not to make the most special and snufflingly moist noises about Graydon Carter, Aimee Bell, Walter Owen, and David Friend. It's quite something for a writer, whose promiscuous mandate is to be interested in everything, to know that he possesses friends and backers and colleagues who are determined to give him latitude while scrutinizing every line, providing every help in the field, noticing every weakness, and enhancing every paragraph. (One short passage in this book was originally written for them.) If it were not for their intensive care and meticulous attention, I would want to call them my luck.

# Index